CHILDREN of YESTERDAY

Jan Valtin

> I have only just a minute,
>   Only sixty seconds in it,
>   Forced upon me, can't refuse it.
> Didn't seek it, didn't choose it,
>   But it's up to me to use it.
>   I must suffer if I lose it,
> Just a tiny little minute—
>   But eternity is in it.

FROM THE SERVICE PRAYER BOOK

Children of Yesterday
The 24th Infantry Division in the Philippines

Jan Valtin

with a new Foreword by Steve W. Chadde

Foreword copyright © 2014 by Steve W. Chadde
Printed in the United States of America.

AN ORCHARD INNOVATIONS BOOK
ISBN 9781951682279

Children of Yesterday, by Jan Valtin, was first published in 1946 by The Readers' Press, New York. Jan Valtin is a pseudonym of Richard Julius Herman Krebs (1904-1951).

TYPEFACE: Paperback 8.8/12.3

To
*The men of the Twenty-Fourth Infantry
Division who gave their lives at*

PEARL HARBOR

HOLLANDIA

BIAK

LEYTE

MINDORO

MARINDUQUE

VERDE

LUBANG

SIMARA

ROMBLON

LUZON

CORREGIDOR

SAMAL

MINDANAO

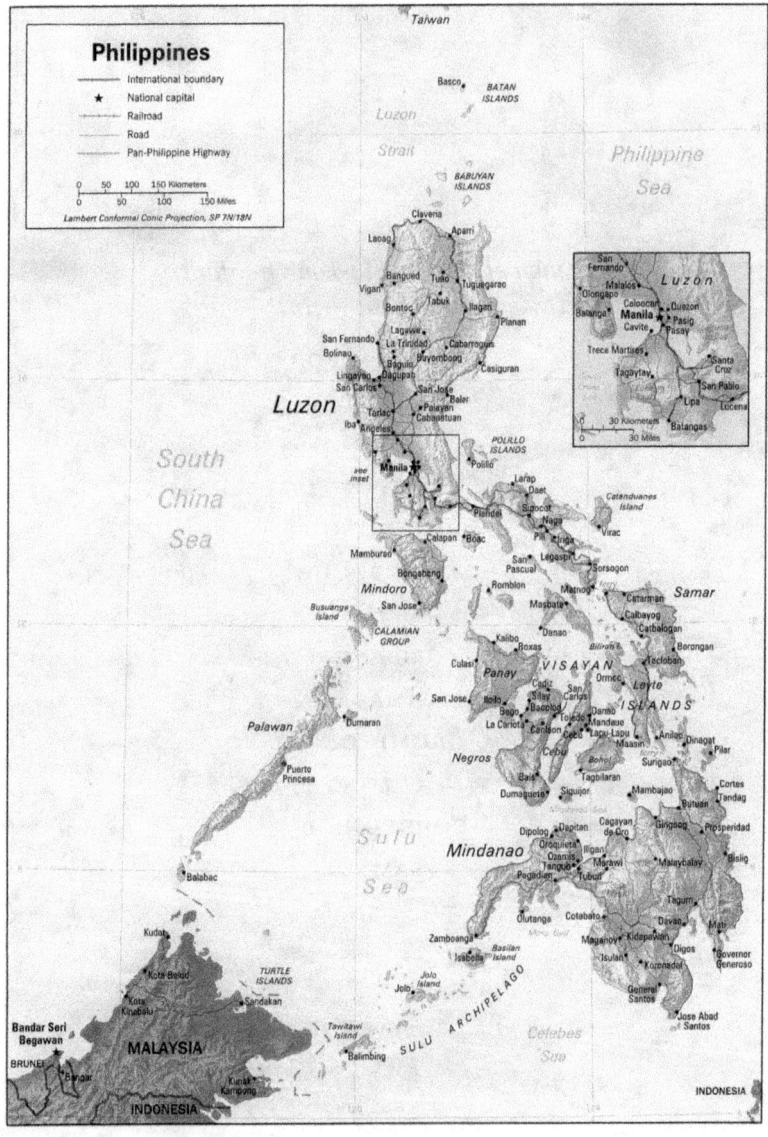

FOREWORD

CHILDREN OF YESTERDAY, authored by Jan Valtin (the pseudonym of Richard Krebs) and published in 1946, is an anecdotal history of the U.S. Army's 24th Infantry Division during its deployment to the Philippines in 1944-45. Unlike many books of the period, *Children of Yesterday* portrays the horrors of the often close-quarters fighting in graphic detail. As one who has read many such books, Valtin's work remains one of the most shocking I have yet come across while also attesting to the bravery and comraderie displayed by the American troops.

Born in Germany in 1905, as a boy, Krebs became active in the Communist movement, when his father was involved in the naval mutiny that was the start of the German Revolution of 1918-19. In 1923, he partook in the failed Communist insurgency in Hamburg.

In 1926, Krebs entered the United States illegally and settled in California. However, he spent 38 months in San Quentin State Prison following the attempted murder of a merchant navy seaman during a brawl, and was subsequently deported to Germany in 1929. He worked as a seaman until 1934, when he was again arrested and imprisoned.

Following his release, Krebs returned to the United States in 1938, and in 1940 (as Valtin) wrote his bestselling, semi-autobiographical book *Out of the Night*. The book details actions he supposedly carried out as a secret agent of the Soviet GPU, However, the truthfulness of portions of the book have since been questioned.

Valtin married American Abigail Harris in 1941. In November 1942, Krebs was indicted as a Gestapo agent. He was arrested in December 1942 but found innocent in May 1943.

In August 1943, Krebs was drafted as an infantryman in the U.S. Army, and in February 1944 was shipped overseas to the Philippines. Following the war in 1947, he was granted U.S. citizenship. Valtin passed away on January 1, 1951.

ACKNOWLEDGMENT

No soldier in combat is able to follow the course of battle beyond the ken of his own squad, section, or platoon, particularly in tropical terrain where a man often can see no farther than the front sight of his rifle. Striving to depict men in battle on a division scale, I have made use of notes generously supplied to me by my fellow combat reporters in the 24th Infantry Division.

I herewith express my appreciation to Privates Milton Haneline and Raymond Merdgan; Sergeants Luther Hendrickson, Waldo Vandeventer, Verne Mabry, and J. C. Murray; Lieutenant Alan Beaumont and Captain Lloyd Price, all of whom risked their lives to gather the factual raw material for this book.

Acknowledgment is also made to Lieutenant William D. J. Gordon for detailed first-hand data on the Division's operations in Bataan and on Corregidor.

Jan Valtin
MINDANAO, PHILIPPINES
1945

TABLE OF CONTENTS

I.	Infantry Reporter	3
II.	Invasion	15
III.	Hill 522	30
IV.	Banzai Night	36
V.	Church Bells Ring in Palo	47
VI.	Commotion in the Hills	65
VII.	The Mainit River Bridge	78
VIII.	Death-Dance in Pastrana	88
IX.	Jaro Sunday	99
X.	Silence in Carigara	114
XI.	Ghosts of Guadalcanal	129
XII.	Children of Yesterday	145
XIII.	The Breaking of Breakneck Ridge	163
XIV.	Doughboy White	174
XV.	Dragon Red	196
XVI.	Another Half Million Coconuts	217
XVII.	The Island Raiders	236
XVIII.	Return to Bataan	252
XIX.	We Storm Corregidor	268
XX.	Thunder to Davao	285
XXI.	Infantry Speaking	309
XXII.	Surrender	340

Author Jan Valtin (pseudonym of Richard Krebs) in 1950.

CHILDREN of YESTERDAY

LT. COL. THOMAS E. CLIFFORD, JR., discusses plans with his staff as Filipino guerillas look on, 1944.

CHAPTER ONE

INFANTRY REPORTER

My commanding officer in the jungles was Lloyd Price of the *Dallas News*. My section sergeant was Verne Mabry of the St. Louis *Globe-Democrat*. As I climbed from a jeep to report for duty, I found Captain Price squatting in the dust of Mindoro Island beneath a piece of sheet iron. He was desperately engaged in driving a rusty nail through the iron, using the handle of his bush knife as a hammer. His assistant, Sergeant Mabry, introduced me to our superior with a melancholy grin. Dangling above us from a scarred tent pole was a Japanese helmet full of bullet holes, spattered with dried blood, and bearing the inscription, PRO.

"Private First Class Richard Krebs," I said, "reporting for duty with the 24th Infantry Division."

Price shook the sweat from his face, cursed the rusty nail, looked me over with a smile and said, ""Welcome, don't you think you are too old for the infantry?"

"Never mind," said Mabry, his leathery face in crinkles, "we are old bastards too."

"Can I help you?" I asked politely.

"Do you know what we are doing?" demanded the captain. "No."

"We are building a table," he said.

Mabry laughed. "The fellow who was here before you went home," he explained. "He had a fighting cock named Typhoon. Typhoon was raised on vitamin pills—he won every fight. But the fellow who owned him went home, and that's why you are here. Have you ever worked in a newspaper office?"

"No," said.

"This is going to be our office," announced Captain Price.

"Its a nice place," Mabry said. "Back on Leyte we had our office dug under a pigsty. After that we had another office in a native jail. Let's give the captain a hand to straighten out that rusty nail."

This was my introduction to two of the finest men I have had the good fortune to call my comrades in tropical warfare. Without their steadfast co-operation through torrential night rains, blazing days, mud, invasion and gunfire the pages that follow would have never been written. The office we built that day on Mindoro consisted of a battered canvas roof, three sheets of iron fastened to bamboo sticks to serve as desks, three ration boxes for chairs, three decrepit typewriters with repair tools designed for six-wheel trucks, firearms, ammunition, a drainage ditch, a miniature generator, three tonettes, a bottle of atabrine pills and a filing cabinet marked, "To Accompany Troops." On one side mountains hulked purple and forbidding under an angry sun; on the other, some distance away, lay the invasion beach littered with hastily dumped supplies. There was a roar of motors in the sky and there were truck columns laden with troops rumbling inland over dusty roads. A hot wind blew volcanic sand into weapons and typewriters, and into men's ears and eyes.

I had arrived from rain-soaked Leyte that morning, after a turn along the shores of New Guinea, Biak and Windy Island. I had walked off the LCI (Landing Craft, Infantry), waded up the beach under duffel bag and Garand, pestered by bottle flies and wondering what my new assignment would be. In a field of cogon grass a sweating lieutenant had called out my name, had leered at me, and had said: "Report for duty with P-R-O."

"PRO," I had wondered, "what could that be?"

I had then asked a sergeant loafing under a *lauan* tree about the meaning of those three letters. He spat between the thick roots and said: "PRO, PRO—well, that's the 24th Division PRO-Station."

"What?"

"Prophylactic station, you dope."

I said nothing.

"It's a good deal, Mac," the sergeant had continued. "You won't be out killing Nips an' sleeping in holes full of water. You'll set up shop near the whorehouses, and all you'll do is see that the guys do a right good job of sanitation after they've had their fun."

Captain Price guffawed when I told him of my silent horror. "PRO," he said, "stands for Press Relations Office, not pro-station."

"We'd better get some paint and change our shingle," Mabry grinned. "Change PRO to P.R.O."

"Our job," the captain said to me, "is to do the combat reporting for the Division."

"We are the nursemaids of the correspondents," Mabry cut in with a sardonic grin. "We are the paragraph troopers in nowhere. Some day you'll go out to get a good story from some Joe, and then you'll find the guy with his head blown off."

We labored until darkness, and ate a meal of canned frankfurters and dehydrated potatoes, and then we went to a swift-flowing stream to wash off the day's grime. Truck drivers bathing from their vehicles in mid-river told of patrol clashes in the nearby hills. One of them had spotted a cave inhabited by Japanese soldiers. At the cave entrance three Japs sat on a case of dynamite, eating rice. The truck-driver had placed a bullet accurately into the case. The explosive blew up, killing the Japs, bringing down the cave mouth and leaving the survivors sealed in the tomb. Sergeant Mabry got the story, and after that we fled from the mosquitoes. During the night a *carabao* (water-buffalo), huge and black, disturbed our sleep, drinking water from our helmets. Mabry shooed him away with an unearthly roar. Toward morning an airplane crashed nearby and burst into flame. We ate dehydrated eggs at dawn and found Captain Price in battle dress, off to accompany a rifle battalion in the storming of Fortress Corregidor.

The Twenty-Fourth is typical of the few infantry divisions which specialized as assault spearheads in tropical terrain. In ten months of sustained fighting and incessant island raids its members have killed 25,000 Japanese warriors in the Philippines. To the participants, these ten months are like ten centuries. Packed between October 20, 1944, which was the day of the Leyte invasion, and the order to "cease firing," lay a reality which in retrospect assumes the fiber of an enormous and fantastic dream. We turn in our rifles and grenades to the supply sergeant, and we board the troopship homeward bound, looking toward home, and already the commonplace of yesterday seems to become unreal and remote in our war-sick minds. With disbelief we gaze at the immediate past, and it is as if each of us asks himself, "Was I ever a part of that?" And we brush away the memory of a tawny woman screaming in a burning hut, or of an enemy's smile in the face of violent finality, or of the stench of a friends corpse beneath the midday sun, the flies and the whining shells.

But this is not a personal history. It is the story of the men of the Twenty-Fourth Division and of the battles they fought and won without ever being sure about the necessity for their agonized giving. But give they did with choiceless and bitter extravagance. They gave with envy in their hearts for the folks at home, often worrying if a miserable allowance would buy their mothers or their children enough to eat, often angered by reports of civilian fleshpots brimming over the bleak fires of war, often hurt by wives unwilling to bear the hardships of fidelity. In their personal deeds the men took no more pride than they would in any detested job well done. They hate war more than they ever hated their enemy, but they are proud of their Division. Those who have had dealings with this Division know it as the Victory Division. It has fought many battles and lost none. Its non-secret code letter, stenciled on its trucks and guns, is "V."

My job as Division reporter, on the prowl for stories, took me at various times and places to all of the Division's units (the three infantry regiments in the 24th Infantry Division were the Nineteenth, the Twenty-First, and the Thirty-Fourth). A combat reporter's crop of notes gathered during a random days jeeping, hiking, creeping, and squatting in the Mindanao campaign yielded the following—typical—collection:

Corporal Lawrence Taylor of Wasaugal, Washington, drove a truck five miles behind American lines near Davao. After he had reached his destination, an officer remarked that the truck was riddled.

"Can't be," said Taylor. "Its new."

But there were nineteen bullet holes in the truck. The corporal then remembered that he had heard a machinegun cracking off the road but that he had paid no attention to the noise.

Colonel "Jock" Clifford, commander of the Nineteenth Infantry Regiment, offered a prize for any Japanese soldier killed by a native Mohammedan Moro. Some days later a squat Moro walked into Clifford's tent and plumped a Jap head on the Colonel's desk, demanding the prize money. Clifford, one of the finest soldiers in the Division, jumped up, roaring, "Take that damn thing off my table." An orderly seized the head and tossed it onto a nearby crossroads. The head lay there for days, kicked hither and yon by passing men and trucks, until a vulture carried it away.

Private First Class Eugene Monroe of Eugene, Oregon, and other men of his rifle platoon lay resting along a jungle trail. There was a crackling in the house-high grass. Seven Japanese soldiers mounted on water buffaloes came riding up the trail. Not one survived the fusillade. No buffalo was killed. The *carabao*s trudged on into a swamp and wallowed in the mud.

A sign posted at the entrance of a Filipino school which had been looted of all its furniture by American soldiers camping nearby read: *"Americans stand for decency and always must. If you trample on decency, you trample to death the thing that makes you Americans. Sincerely yours, Maria Padata."* The soldiers read the sign and were ashamed. They carried half of the furniture back under cover of darkness. The other half they already had used for firewood.

A patrol surrounded two Japanese in a pillbox near Bayabas. A Nisei stepped forward and yelled, "Jap soldiers—surrender!"

The Japs replied: "Come nearer so we can kill you.". . . The Nisei laughed. "It is you who face death!" he said, "unless you surrender we shall burn you." The voice in the pillbox replied calmly, "Then burn me, Americans." A rifleman tossed a phosphorous grenade. The Japanese dashed into the open and were cut down. They looked like red-headed Japs, but it was only their hair burning brightly.

On the upper Talomo River a scouting patrol found a dead enemy soldier. He had been wounded by our artillery. Then someone had stabbed him to death and stripped his rumps of flesh. Later that day, on the Kibawe Trail, the scouts found the nude bodies of fifty Japanese. The backs and legs of many had been stripped of flesh. The Japs were eating their own to retain the strength to fight

Private Byron Becker of Aberdeen, South Dakota, heard the sounds of snoring float from a bamboo hut. He found a sleeping Japanese and a club. He picked up the club and poked the Jap and said, "Hey there, wake up." But the yellow man jumped up, seized the club and aimed blows at Becker's head. The American lunged sideways, aimed his submachinegun and killed the Japanese. On that day another soldier, from Kentucky, found a sick and starving Japanese lying at the edge of a jungle trail. But the Kentuckyman, who had killed seventeen Japs in eighteen months, was tired of killing. He loaded the sick Jap on his shoulders and trudged toward bivouac. He arrived at the aid station two hours later and found that his prisoner had died on the way. He decided then that never again would he try to take a Japanese alive. Two days later, on a path leading through an *abaca* plantation, he came face to face with a ragged Japanese who hugged a package which had the size of a mine. The Jap yelled, "No shoot, I surrender." The Kentuckyman cursed and fired. The Japanese dropped dead. Searching the corpse, the American found that the other had been carrying a sleeping baby. The child, still peacefully asleep, had remained unhurt.

A little way off, Corporal William Miller of Philadelphia poked through a half-burned and abandoned village. He found a house full of pianos made in Japan. Miller liked pianos. He set aside his rifle, searched out a piano that was well tuned and beat out a few melodies. He had not played a piano since he had left home years earlier. The notes of "Beat Me, Daddy, Eight to the Bar," and "Shoot the Sherbet to Me, Herbert," had barely come to an end when a rifle shot rang out, followed by others. The corporal grasped his weapon and dived behind the piano and waited. He saw a disgusted-looking American private gaze through a window.

"Did you shoot?" yelled Miller.

The private nodded. "I shouldna disturbed you," he drawled, "but two Nips out here were gonna throw some grenades at you through the winder."

"Are they gone?" asked Miller.

"Naw," the private said, "I shot them."

Much of the Philippines war was fought in countless obscure actions most of which have never been reported in the western world. Everyone has read the dispatches on the conquest of Manila or the Battle of the Ormoc Valley on Leyte; but how many people have ever heard of Breakneck Ridge where hundreds of Americans died in typhoon-like rainstorms? or of the countless Indian-war-style raids and skirmishes on islands whose names do not appear on any globe? or of the massacres and the American graves in the unexplored foothills of Mount Apo? There are more than seven thousand islands in the Philippines, and nearly three thousand of them do not even have a name.

As combat reporters, my comrades and I specialized in recording the details of the lives of men in battle. But some of the lesser facts of war never passed the censors. Many of our combat vignettes became casualties not only for reasons of "security." Duty bound, the censors saw to it all Americans were wonderful fellows and all Japanese were blackguards; that all Filipinos were heroic allies, atrocities were committed only by the enemy, no prisoner of war was ever pressed for military information, and no American officer ever led his troops unnecessarily to death.

During an island raid in the Sibuyan Sea I saw a Japanese prisoner tied to a tree and tortured to death by guerillas. The censors refused to pass this not uncommon truth about the war in the tropics. They also stopped an account of Mindanao guerilla groups fighting on the enemy's side, and a story about an American officer who "built morale" among Moro volunteers by having them mix fresh Japanese blood with hot GI coffee; or an account of the Tacloban brothels where soldiers stood in queues two blocks long in the hot sun with military police allotting no more than five minutes to each man. The censors were sensitive, too, about the unprotested practice of robbing Jap corpses of money, watches and fountain pens; of the occasional killing of Jap wounded to save the labor of nursing and feeding them; about the mere mention of the effects of tropical diseases on our troops; about casualty figures; about the fact—long known to everyone—that enemy cadavers, if ever buried, were dumped into shallow trenches scooped out by bulldozers, or about the Army chaplain who during the burial of an American soldier was forced by snipers to jump into the grave atop the dead man and fight back. However, in a story of an infantry division's deeds, these are minor details, significant only in their accentuation of the two-sidedness of the misery and the graceless brutality of war.

One day on Mindoro I said to Captain Price, "It is a pity that all this doing and dying around us should not be recounted in some form more permanent than in hometown press 'stories'."

"I've thought about that," Lloyd Price said. "What's your idea?"

"A book," I said.

The captain looked at the gloomy sky, at the rain pouring down about us in a tepid avalanche, at the muddy road and the bleak mountains beyond.

"It's a hell of a place to write a book in," he grinned.

At times the going was rough. When we invaded Mindanao at Parang, Moro Gulf, I slogged up the invasion beach with rifle, pack, typewriter and rheumatism, and was promptly bitten by a poisonous centipede. That afternoon I tried to write in a torrential downpour in a jungled coconut plantation while rifle fire cracked in the underbrush a little way off. A hundred yards away an American colonel was shot through the back, and dogfaces were rooting out and killing Jap snipers. After a while a soldier came asking for a pair of pliers: he had found that one of the dead Japs had gold teeth and he wanted to break them out. Nobody had pliers. "Use your rifle butt," someone told him.

At another time, accompanying a reinforced guerilla battalion in the raiding of Romblon, Simara and Tablas Islands in the Sibuyan Sea, I sat writing on the town square of Romblon Town shortly after we had stormed it and killed its Japanese garrison. Not far away, in front of a building facing the square, a young rifleman sat and ate cheese. Suddenly a Japanese soldier, fully armed, dashed out of the house and across the square. The rifleman set aside his ration can, raised his rifle, fired twice. The Jap dashed into an alley. "I missed the bastard," the rifleman said. "Don't put my name in that book of yours." And with that he went back to digging cheese from his can.

Later that day I entered an abandoned dwelling where I found a water faucet still intact. I set aside my rifle and stripped to the skin and bathed. A Jap who had been hiding in the attic above me had slipped through a trap door in the ceiling. Had he waited a bit, he could have killed me with my pants off. He chose instead to double up, hold a grenade against his abdomen and commit hara-kiri. I dressed hastily, and with a feeling of nausea I waded through the mess he had made of himself, out of the house, across the street and into another building.

It was the town library. Among the bookshelves were two dead Japanese and two American infantrymen. The infantrymen were engaged in blowing a small safe they had found in the librarian's office. They cracked the safe and found it empty. In huge disgust both eased nature into the wrecked safe.

Returning to Mindoro from the Sibuyan Islands I had with me a Japanese prisoner of war. We made the trip on one of the Navy's power torpedo boats. Aboard the same craft, also bound for Mindoro, was a batch of wounded guerillas, including some women, all armed to the teeth and refusing to unload or set on "safe" their rifles even on the high seas. The guerillas, seeing the Jap, immediately wanted to kill him. Some shouted, "Use the knife," others, "Overboard with him." For six hours, lying flat on the spray-whipped deck of the speeding boat, I defended my Jap against the guerillas who could not comprehend why any Jap should be entitled to remain alive. Arriving at Mindoro, I loaded the prisoner into a truck bound for Division Headquarters, and a score of guerillas promptly piled in with him. The truck-driver, a Navy man, had never seen a live Japanese. Whenever he passed other Navy men along San Jose beach he stopped the truck, leaned out of the cab and yelled: "There's a live Jap in the truck. Want to kill him?" The sailors then would scale the truck from all sides, swinging fists, wrenches, knives, and the guerillas would yell, "Kill the Jap! Kill him!" I finally managed to get the prisoner, who was near death from fear, to Division Headquarters. An MP patrol stopped us. "Who are these characters?" the patrol leader demanded. I said, "A bunch of gorillas and one Jap prisoner." The military police sergeant roared: "Don't you know that no live Nip is allowed in Division Headquarters?" By this time I was very sick and tired of my prisoner. I had my manuscript to think of. "All right," I told the MP's, "you take this damned Jap off my hands." They did. They also gave me a receipt, scrawled on the back of a *billet-doux* from some girl in Kokomo, Indiana: "Received from Private Krebs one living Jap."

My captain, I decided, was right. The Philippines were a hell of a place in which to write a book.

Yet, some spots were not so bad for writing. I wrote through some quiet and busy weeks in Mindoro, with nothing more disturbing about me than mosquitoes, bats, dust, rain, water buffaloes. and an occasional rat hunt. And I think with pleasure of a fine office we set up in a captured enemy headquarters on Talomo Beach in Mindanao. A wall of flamboyant and impenetrable jungle loomed barely fifty yards away, artillery shells whined overhead and crashed around us for weeks on end, and the perimeter line of foxholes was only fifteen yards from my "desk," but things could have been worse. And during one period of the protracted fighting around Davao I lugged with me for professional comfort a large and rusty bed salvaged from the ruins of a shack.

But surprises never lurked far. There were a hundred blasted and burned bridges to cross during a 150-mile traverse of Mindanao wilderness. There were hundreds of 500-pound mines in the roads over which we passed, buried by diligent Japanese. There was much wreckage and the stench of death. There was a night watch in a perimeter foxhole, with intermittent firing all around, at the end of which I found that I had been on guard against night assault with an unloaded rifle in my arms; it belonged, I found later, to a mal-assigned conscientious objector who protested against his predicament in combat zones by never loading his weapon.

One day my labors were rudely interrupted by snarling overhead and a flurry of explosions; Japanese shells were bursting a stone's throw off the beach on which I had planted my bed. On another day a Jap canoe patrol blew up and sank one of our Division supply ships. A night later a crew of Nipponese knifed in among our tents with mines strapped to their chests. They passed the tents, and though they could easily have blown the Division's Press Relations staff to kingdom come, they preferred to blow up a Piper Cub and several amphibious trucks in an adjoining artillery perimeter.

But I had help from all sides. When my typewriter broke down after a two-week trek across jungle and mountains, a fellow reporter, Luther Hendrickson of Belle Fourche, North Dakota, undertook to seize one from the Japanese, "so that you can finish our book." He vanished in the direction of the enemy lines. In due time and after successive raids he returned with seven ramshackle enemy typewriters. Some of them bore Japanese characters. All the same, after days of labor with a hammer, pliers, guitar wire, rifle oil and corrugated iron, Verne Mabry and Hendrickson managed to condense the seven semi-wrecks into three workable machines by a magic system of interchanging parts.

Typical of the fellows who are the real authors of these pages was a young scout of the Division's 19th Infantry Regiment who had just returned from the battle for Fort McKinley, on the southern approaches of Manila. He came to my niche at the edge of a palm plantation and for five minutes he just stared. Then, all of a sudden, he blurted: "I want to give you a story to put in that book."

"Go ahead," I invited him.

"It's not about me." He faltered, studying a large beetle on the ground between his feet. Almost belligerently he added: "It's about my buddy. His name is Wilmer Stokes. He was a sergeant. His home? That's in Gracefield in Florida."

"Where is he now?" I asked.

"Dead," the boy said.

"Did they bury him right?"

The soldier nodded. And then the story of Wilmer Stokes' dying came out of him like a waterfall out of rock. In the fight for Fort McKinley their battalion fought over open, sun-baked country covered with grass and bushes, and criss-crossed by many shallow gullies. The Japs, naval troops from Manila, fought from many concrete tunnels and underground pillboxes. There was no shade above ground. Many Americans collapsed, overwhelmed by heat. Those still fit were parched and exhausted. Canteens were empty. Our infantry worked through mine fields which had been covered with barbed wire. Japanese machineguns were trained on the wire barricades. Japanese mortar shells had set fire to grass and bushes. There was no digging-in, no chance to halt and rest. You can't dig in under barbed wire with mines around you, the countryside afire, high explosive striking to your right and left, behind you and in front, and machinegun sprays lashing the air two feet above the earth.

In this setting Sergeant Wilmer E. Stokes was confronted with the problem of tackling a cave-and-trench fortress which defied direct fire from his tommygun. He exchanged his sub-machinegun for a flame-thrower. But he soon found that he could not tackle the holed-up Japs from open ground. The entrances to their underground strongpoint opened upon deep trenches. It was necessary to enter the trenches to reach the Japs.

Wilmer Stokes jumped into a trench and crushed a Jap's head with his boots. Then he rushed to the mouth of the cave and filled the cave with liquid fire. When his flame-thrower was exhausted, he climbed out of the trench and watched. Screams of pain came from the cave. But the Jap guns were still firing.

Sergeant Stokes grasped a second flame-thrower. Again he sprang into the trench and spurted its contents into the cave in a flaming horizontal geyser. He did the same thing a third time. Then he tossed the flame-thrower aside. He picked up his sub-machinegun and sprang back into the trench and muscled into the cave, his gun blazing.

"I waited for Wilmer to come out of that cave," the soldier said in a quiet monotone. "But he didn't come. I couldn't throw in any grenades because I figured my buddy would get hurt. So I took a chance and went inside myself. There was a lot of Japs in that cave. They were all dead. Some were burned and some were full of holes from my buddy's tommygun. Wilmer was there, too, dead; some Jap's last shot killed him."

After a long silence, during which Wilmer Stokes' comrade watched a native girl wandering to a nearby stream with a basket of laundry on her head, the soldier demanded: "Want to hear some more?"

"Sure," I said.

"Killing Wilmer did the Nips no good," he continued. "We had them with their backs against Manila Bay, and here's what happened...."

Filipino fishermen watching the battle from a canoe offshore saw a lone Japanese swim out to sea. They captured the swimmer and brought him to an American officer for questioning.

The prisoner said that there were more than a thousand Japanese in the American trap. He also said that the Japanese were willing to surrender—if given a chance.

Surrender?

A mass surrender in battle would be the most freakish event of a freakish kind of war.

The American commanders looked around for someone willing to carry a capitulation offer into the Japanese lines. A brave man volunteered. He was a middle-aged guerilla who wore a straw hat and rode astride a skinny pony. He was given a white flag and a message. The message said that the Americans would accept a surrender if the Japanese would emerge without weapons, in single file, and with their hands raised high.

Firing ceased as the messenger rode slowly across no-mans-land. Field glasses traced his progress from the American side.

The guerilla reached the enemy outposts and stopped. He was directed into a large clump of bamboo shielded by a rise of

Minutes passed. Everybody was tense.

There was a crackling of rifle fire within the Japanese positions. Men settled behind their guns. They saw the riderless pony gallop out of the bamboo. There were growls, "The goddamn, murdering..."

Then, out of the bamboo sauntered the Filipino. He waved his white flag. He retrieved his mount and rode back to the American lines. Just before he reached safety an enemy sentry fired. The shot went wild.

The messenger brought word that the Japanese commander asked for more time.

The Americans waited an hour. It was 11 A.M. and nothing happened. They waited until noon. No unarmed men filed out of the grass and bamboo trap.

At this point my informant rubbed his chin and grinned.

"What was the end of it?" I asked.

He looked at me out of a weary, yellow young face and his blue eyes shone. He showed me two Japanese officers watches on his wrists.

"We didn't want prisoners," he said. "We walked in and slaughtered the bastards." With that he turned abruptly and sauntered away.

Chapter Two

INVASION

Training for landing operations began early in October, 1944, in Humboldt Bay, New Guinea. Troops took the long, dusty ride to the beach, then were transported to their ships by small boats. The bay was choppy because of the typhoon season in the north, and many men were violently seasick.

The convoy departed Humboldt Bay, Hollandia, at 1300, Friday, 13 October.

Troops were not excited regarding the movement. The general attitude might be described as: "Were going to the Philippines—so what!"

(from the Division Record)

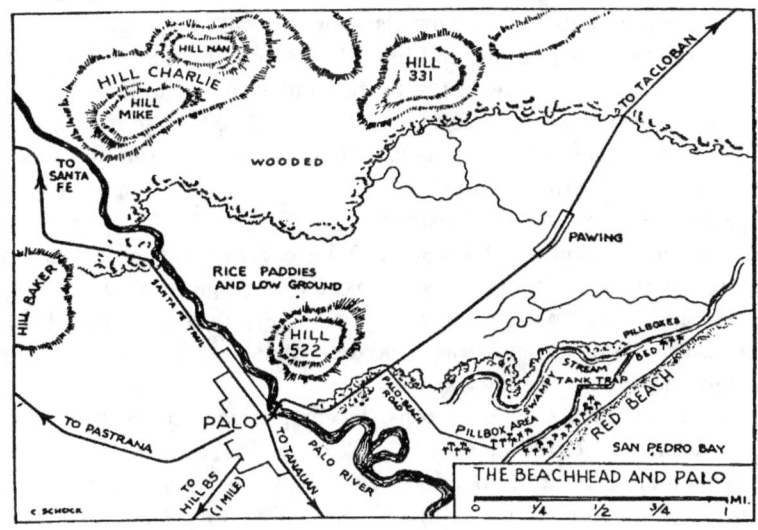

THE STORY of the American invasion of Leyte is, to me, synonymous with the story of Carmelo Giacomazzo, the woodcarver from Tunisia. It is his glory as much as General MacArthurs. He did a job, in his own quaint and peaceful way, which saved many lives and helped to make the launching of the Philippines campaign a thundering success.

The Woodcarver is squat. Black curls protrude from under his fatigue cap. He is the opposite of Hollywood's idea of a soldier. He looks like a wandering Levantine artist and to war he refers as "inglorious trouble." His hour of glory was a matter of *papier mâché*, plaster and a little paint.

The son of an Italian father and a Tunisian mother, Carmelo was born in Brooklyn, but his family moved to Casablanca, Africa, before he was three years old, where he grew up speaking Spanish, French, Italian and Arabic, but not a word of English. His early living he earned as a carpenter in North African harbor towns. He disliked the drudgery of hard labor. "I had good hands," he says. "I looked at my hands. They told me that I could make things, and more things can be shaped out of wood than fences. My hands like the feel of clay. I swore I should become a woodcarver, a sculptor!"

And a sculptor he became. He modeled in clay, then finished his work in wood. He never married. At the urging of an aunt he came to America.

He arrived in New York on March 1, 1941, an American who did not know a word of English. For five days, broke and hungry, he searched for his aunt. He could not find her. What should he do? On March 5, 1941, he joined the Army of the United States as a volunteer. He was assigned to the 24th Division and fought as a machinegunner in the leprous wilderness of New Guinea, unhappily but well. And then came the day on which the Twenty-Fourth was ordered to tighten its belt for the biggest operation in its history.

The destination was "Top Secret." A great guessing game went on along the steaming mangrove swamps and jungle paths. With the rest, Carmelo asked, "Where are we going?"—"Borneo," said the latrine attorneys. "Yap, Halmahera, Mindanao, Celebes." The Woodcarver wondered and cursed the war.

In the regiments, the battalions, the companies, in the platoons and squads men struck their tents and packed. They checked their weapons and hauled ammunition. Ended were the sweat-stained weeks of waiting, of mopping up the jungles, of digging drainage ditches and standing guard. The men shouted and were alert. They folded their cots and helped the cooks pack pots and pans, and in huge bonfires they burned the refuse that accumulates where masses of men have camped for weeks. The roadsides were lined with barracks bags; the men had stripped themselves to messkit, spoon, jungle knife, poncho, razor, rations, a shovel and their weapons. Someone chanted, "Nobody loves New Guinea..."

Day and night the trucks rumbled to the beaches. Transports hovered offshore. The roadstead was so crammed with ships that at night their anchor lights looked like the lights of some vast coastal city. And with the sound of motors rumbling in his ears, Carmelo saw officers pore over maps, heard them discuss their lack of knowledge of the terrain to be captured on "A"-Day. Difficult terrain? Map trouble? Private Giacomazzo approached a staff officer.

"Let me make you a map of the difficult terrain," he said.

"A map?"

"Sure."

"What's the idea?"

"A relief map," said Carmelo. "A map of plaster of Paris, *papier mâché*, wood—anything. A model map that shows the hills, the valleys—everything."

Could this obscure private who spoke his English with a Levantine accent be trusted with the top secret of a campaign involving many thousand men? The officers telephoned the Division. The Division said, "Impossible."

"Let me make that map," the Woodcarver persisted.

"Who is this fellow?" Headquarters inquired.

"Private Giacomazzo, a sculptor in wood."

Carmelo argued how good it would be for his buddies to see a model of the battlefield and to see just what to look for and where to go when they assaulted the beaches. More trucks rumbled down to the edge of Humboldt Bay, more jeeps and tractors and guns in an endless stream. Tools of war crammed the wide-mawed landing ships. And the colonels capitulated to the private.

There were some old maps at hand, not very accurate contour maps. And there were the aerial photographs. Could Private Giacomazzo read photomaps?

"I make you that map," he announced.

And so, after he had rendered an oath of silence, it came about that the Woodcarver from Africa was entrusted with the secret of shore points selected for the American landings in the Philippines.

From somewhere Carmelo procured a bag of plaster of Paris. He manufactured his own *papier mâché*. Paint he bagged from a team of combat engineers—blue for the streams, brown for the hilltops, green for the plantations and the swamps and the jungle-covered slopes. He fashioned a replica of now famous Red Beach. He studied the photographs the officers had given him and what he saw there he put on the map, trails and *barrios*, a coastal highway, a river, bridges, plantations and rice fields. He ate and lived and rested with his work. He worked with minute care and with pride. A mistake, he knew, might cost the lives of fellow soldiers. And then after five days and nights, he surveyed his work, checked, re-checked, and packed away his tools.

The Division's commander came and looked at the Woodcarver's work.

"Giacomazzo," the general said, "you have made a very good map. Carmelo nodded. "I guarantee it with my life," he said.

The general called his staff. They studied the relief. Then other officers came and studied it. And after that, the officers called the sergeants of the assault groups. They all studied the Woodcarver's map. They still studied it aboard ship as the Division's convoy steamed northwest.

The Japs on the beach of San Pedro Bay, Leyte, saw a lone American landing craft skirt the sands less than two hundred yards offshore. A rifle shot whipped across the water and a bullet struck the boats bow. But the lone visitor continued as if nothing was amiss, its steel ramp jutting like an insolently thrust-up lower lip.

Through a megaphone a Japanese voice roared a single word: "Lunatic!" The nutshell replied with a burst of machinegun fire that sent the Nip observers scuttling over the narrow strip of sand to the shelter of a coconut plantation. The patrolling craft continued, poking about, turning and retracing its course. At intervals a helmeted head appeared briefly over the spy-boat's bulwark, peered shoreward and slipped from sight.

That was in the early afternoon of October 19, 1944.

Japanese machineguns barked at the unwonted stranger. There followed the sullen thump of mortars firing. Soon artillery joined in punching geysers out of the sunlit sea.

With bullets striking a rapid tattoo against its rust-streaked side the patrol craft zig-zagged in almost waggish unconcern. Its machinegun spat lead into the fine gray sand. That kept the puzzled enemy away from the water's edge. But despite the near-misses of sporadic shellfire, the boat refused to leave the inshore reaches of San Pedro Bay.

Aboard the foolhardy cockleshell the helmeted man seemed satisfied. Lieutenant Edward F. Roof of Escanaba, Michigan, derived a mirthless joy from his role of target for Jap gunners. Draw fire: that was what he wanted—fire that would help him to locate the hidden gun positions of the invasion shore.

"What's the use o' worryin'. .."

His humming amid the outraged clamor of Jap weapons reassured him. As long as the craft was afloat under him it would divert the Jap gunners' attention from the water. For in the water, between the landing craft and the shore, men were swimming, probing for underwater obstacles and mines.

The bold swimmers were scouts, the stripped and silent pathfinders for the mechanized amphibious assault. The apparent suicidal impossibility of their mission made it a success. And after two hours of it the spy-boat maneuvered between the shore and the swimmers, picked them up, streaked for the offing, its rear end chugging gas in the direction of the baffled hunters.

Our naval barrage started at 0610, 20 October, 1944.

Assault waves, already loaded in LCVP's (Landing Craft Vehicle, Personnel), were swung over the side in a matter of minutes. The sea was smooth and a brilliant sun beat down. The expected air attacks failed to materialize. All assault waves crossed the Line of Departure on schedule. As they raced toward Red Beach the naval barrage lifted, and LCI's (Landing Craft Infantry) blasted the shoreline with rockets. Dive bombers delivered a final blow at the defenses just before the landing craft hit the beach.

The Division landed with two regiments abreast on a 3000 yard front. The 19th Infantry was on the south, and the 34th Infantry on the north. It soon became apparent that the naval and air bombardment had not been completely effective. . . .

(from the Division Record)

Scared? Not exactly, but scared, anyway. You go to bed early with the thought, ". . . let tomorrow take care of itself."

Reveille sounds through the ship at 0300. You stumble around in the jam-packed hold and get into your clothes. Then you head for the chow line. The sea is glassy calm and under the stars you see the silhouettes of ships and landing craft as far as the eye can see. Off to port looms an inky shoreline, still miles away.

You eat your breakfast in the heat of the blacked-out hold. Eerie red lights gleam overhead. With zero hour near, new men have little stomach for food. But the old hands are not concerned with zero hour—not yet. They are griping, "Look, the belly-robbing bastards, D-Day and no fresh eggs for breakfast."

After that there is little talking, little moving about. You brush your teeth and then shove the toilet articles into your pack. You make sure your canteens are full of water and you give your weapons a final check. You have a little trouble finding a good place in which to carry your grenades. Then you lie back and smoke and rules be damned.

Old soldiers don't think. You recognize them by their "GI-look." If they think at all they don't show it. But the battle virgins do. One is looking hard at a picture of his mother. Another is wondering if he will see the stars tomorrow night. And still another may be thinking, "When I get it, my wife'll be putting the kids to bed. She will brush her hair in front of the mirror and know nothing." Some wise guys are so nervous that they try cracking jokes. But most are quiet. "If you have to get it," you figure, "let it be a clean one—no jagged stuff in the guts." Be sure your rifle is loaded. Be sure your safety is off when the ramps go down.

Dawn is in the offing. You go on deck. The rails are crowded. You have your gear ready to wrap around you and head for shore. Not that you are in any hurry. Through the slow minutes you hear the planes roar toward the beaches. You stand and look, and there's your beachhead far off on the port bow—a crescent of sand, an expanse of palms, and beyond them the jungle-clad mountains. You see the cruisers and destroyers glide inshore and open up with rough treatment for everything that's dug in and waiting over yonder. The big battlewagons add their thunderous voices and you feel strong and elated. You see the planes bombing and strafing over the plantations and the swamps and you see the flame and the smoke. The whole beautiful morning is filled with continuous, rolling thunder.

You see the assault platoons line up on deck and you grab your rifle and go where you belong. Your sergeant is not wasting words. You clamber into your landing craft and you hit the sea. As the water buffaloes slowly circle their mother ships you suddenly find yourself saying, "What the -----'s the matter, why don't we go in?" The dangling cargo nets leer at you. The transports hovering all around you seem to look like tired beasts who've done their stint.

There is a minute's interruption. A Jap bomber has sneaked in low from the sea and is heading for the ships. Navy gunners go into action. The Jap sails out of reach of the ack-ack screen and circles the convoy.

Signals flutter and the first waves head shoreward. Soon you, too, are on the way. You crouch low between the wall-like sides of your craft. The rocket ships have moved in and the rockets scream shoreward and you wonder aloud, "How in hell can anything stay alive on that beach?" You listen to the firing and you watch the coxswain in the stern, his face composed and staring stonily ahead. You hear the invisible water foam past the bucking ramps. The assault run is long. There are still a couple of thousand yards to go.

You risk a peek at the shore. The beach is full of landing craft and men and motion. Already boats head back carrying the first casualties of the invasion. The first waves get ashore with small loss, but the succeeding waves get it hard. There is no thought that you might be the next man on the litter. It always seems to happen to somebody else.

Just then Lieutenant Art Stimson of Houston brings out a Texas flag and waves it from the stern. The coxswains eyes are narrow slits now, his sunburnt face thrust forward, his hands tight around the spokes of the wheel. Jap artillery is shelling the beach. Jap mortars and beach guns meet the incoming boats.

A large landing ship is heading out to sea, smoking from stem to stern. Several craft carrying 19th Regiment assault groups are hit and sunk. They heave like living things in pain, stern high, and there is a melee of bobbing heads in the water. "C" Company's commander is killed. A direct hit wipes out a whole squad still more than a thousand yards offshore. Cannon Company loses two section leaders, a platoon leader and some of its headquarters personnel.

Jap artillery hit four of the larger ships. A liaison officer was blown to smithereens. Three Division Headquarters officers were wounded by a shell which sank their craft under their feet. Another shell blew the Division Quartermaster and his aide dear out of their stateroom.

Sergeant Joe Babinetz of Kingston, Pennsylvania, was riding in a boat when a direct hit smashed the ramp. In a matter of seconds tons of water filled the boat Debris flew high. Wounded men screamed in the wreckage.

"Get off, get off the ship," Joe Babinetz shouted.

Men discarded their packs and helmets and dived into the sea. Babinetz, wounded by shrapnel in head and chest, remained aboard. He saw another wounded man threshing in the bottom of the waterlogged craft The man was drowning. Babinetz, bleeding fiercely, dived. He yanked the drowning comrade to the surface. A Jap mortar shell exploding in the sinking wreckage tossed a life jacket into Babinetz' face. He grasped the life jacket, secured it around the wounded man and slipped him overboard to await the rescue patrol.

The concussion of three mortar shells striking another landing boat ripped the steel and hurled its occupants through space. Lieutenant James Russell of Pawtucket, Rhode Island, felt himself thrown upward by the blast He hit the water, badly shaken, and strove to regain his bearings. He saw the sinking boat. Then he heard someone yelling for help.

"Stop your yelling," James Russell shouted.

With a few strokes he reached the sinking craft. There he saw a mangled soldier squirming under water, pinned fast by the wreckage. His lifebelt, as well as the lieutenant's, had been deflated by shrapnel. Russell slipped into the sinking boat He freed the wounded man and dragged him out into dear water. Seconds later the boat sank. Machinegun bullets snarled dose overhead. The water was a-chum with undertows and whirlpools created by the rush of shore-bound ships. Russell struggled for naked life. But he held onto the now unconscious soldier, kept him afloat, dodging the pull from whirling propellers.

Through confusion and men adrift in the sea, your boat approaches the beach. There is a noise a few inches from your head as if a gang of shipyard johnnies were belaboring the boats outside with hammers. You see the coxswains mouth wide open and you tighten your helmet. The keel scrapes sand. There is the jerk you get when a fast-going train stops suddenly. The ramp clatters down and you run out. You wade through hip-deep water. You fan out, away from the others. You dash across the narrow beach. You run as you have never run before. You run for the cover of coconut palms crippled by the bombardment. You flop down on your belly, not taking time to break your fall with your rifle. Then you see a lower spot nearby, roll into that. You rest a minute. After that you look around with your chin firmly in earth a-crawl with ants.

As LSTs cramful of tanks and artillery chum shoreward it is discovered that there are only two slots where the larger landing ships can beach. It looks as if someone bungled in the planning. But there is hope that more will get in over the shallows at high tide. This hope is false. Out of seven tank landing ships in the assault, only two make the beach and hang on there by the skin of their ramps. Two others, unable to find a fit landing place, are driven away by shellfire, and three more are cruising angrily offshore and do not make the run until much later. Battle fate would have it that the landing ships that retired took most of the tanks and artillery with them.

The smashed Jap forts and tunnels fronting the beach look like monstrous teeth smashed by some mad dentist. The tops of most palms have been shorn off. You look for dead Japs and find none. You see some of our own dead sprawled in the sand like careless sleepers. Shredded palm fronds litter the waterfront. Men are milling around the beach; a lot of supplies are piling up, and more come ashore in a violent torrent. You hear much firing but not a shot is aimed at you.

You change your mind when a rifle report that is not yours rings in your ears simultaneously with the strike of a bullet three feet away. You wish you could crawl into the earth like a worm, but what you do is turn your head to find out where that shot came from. You have a powerful urge to dig a foxhole, and that is what you do.

The sun is hot and the sniper fire is just as hot, and the machinegun fire makes your belt feel too loose around your hips. You become accustomed to the sniper fire after a while, but not to the digging. Digging a hole while hugging the ground at the same time. As long as you've been in the Army you resented digging. So you don't hurry, even though you feel that by not digging deep enough fast enough you might be helping along a bullet tagged for you. You find that there is water a foot below the surface. You mutter an obscenity and stop digging. You reach for your rifle, crawl a few feet to ground that is a little higher and start looking for a target. The malevolent crashing of mortar shells on the beach makes you wish you were a million miles away.

You see one of your own mortar squads land and you see the men rush forward to go into action. You know the fellows. They sweat under their loads and their faces are distorted as if by great pain. Halfway across the beach a Jap shell explodes. You see one man's side ripped open and a look of unbelief on his face and his hands pressing down to keep his guts from spilling. It is a beastly thing to happen in bright sunlight and under a blue sky. It takes the boy more than a minute to die. The squad leader, too, has been hit and the others are clinging to the ground, face down, their mortars useless. Then you hear a rough voice say,

"Come on."

The soldier who gets up and who makes the squad get up and pick up their weapons is Sergeant Merlin F. Martin of New London, Iowa. A pretty young wife named Bertha is waiting for him ten thousand miles away. But Sergeant Martin's chin is out and he is too busy to think of his wife just then. He rallies his men by setting an example. They dash after him into the shade of the palms. He points at a group of shell holes with overhead clearance.

"Set 'em up!" he tells his men. 'Watch me for fire orders."

With that he crawls forward for better observation. Three minutes later his mortars are lobbing high explosives onto the maze of Jap pillboxes and spider holes a couple of hundred yards away.

Or take Arthur Kmiecik whom we used to kid about his tongue-breaking name. Twenty minutes after he waded up the beach with his machinegun, his squad was pinned down on open ground by solid bands of lead pouring from a pillbox. Kmiecik is from Milwaukee; he reacted like a bull to a scarlet cloth. Together with another volunteer he picked up his gun, cradled it in his arms like a baby and went straight toward the Jap emplacement. Then he set down his gun and silenced the Nips at point blank range. Other Japs spotted him and soon mortar shells burst perilously close. Kmiecik was seething.

"Follow me," he told his squad.

Off they went, gunning for the yellow mortar men.

Elsewhere things were not going so well. The assault companies of the 34th Infantry had landed 300 yards farther north than planned. And the 19th Infantry Regiment—which had done its first fighting in the Civil War and there earned the name "Rock of Chickamauga"—was also deflected to the north and landed almost on top of the Thirty-Fourth. As a result the enemy was dangerously strong on our left—or southern—flank. He sat solidly athwart the approaches to the day's main objectives; dominating Hill 522 and the town of Palo. Both were more than a mile to the south and east.

Companies of the Thirty-Fourth lay glued to the beach, loth to budge under murderous fire. Here and there a curse, a startled cry arose as bullets shredded combat packs strapped to immobile backs. Lieutenant Barrow of "Item" Company half rose to his knees, then stood up, pistol in hand.

"Let's go, men," he urged, "we can't stay here forever."

Death stabbed through him in an instant. A clean shot through helmet and head. His fellow officers had lost control. The men clawed harder into the sand, and you could hear their bodies groan.

Landing with the fifth assault wave were bulldozers and Colonel A. S. Newman of Clemson, South Carolina. Newman commanded the Thirty-Fourth. Stocky, red-headed, deliberate, the colonel sized up the situation—the bunched-up men; the enemy's skillful crossfire; the crack of snipers' rifles from the palm tops; the mounting confusion of piled and scattered supplies and unused weapons. The Colonel rose from his crouch. Death be damned! He stood erect, a middle-aged chunk of character that mastered fear. He walked straight toward the sounds of firing. He waved his companies forward. "Get the hell off the beach," he roared above the laughter of automatic weapons. "God damn it! Get up and get moving. Follow me!"

The men responded. The officers seized the opening to rally their units forward. The specter of panic was trampled to death under "Red" Newman's combat boots.

The companies advanced. They tackled five earth-and-palm-log pillboxes along a streambed less than a hundred yards inland. Here, Captain Wai, regimental intelligence officer, was killed. A medical corpsman running to the aid of wounded in a palm grove had his midriff shot away. Three bulldozers landed and with them units of the Division's Third Combat Engineers. Their job was to build dirt ramps across a huge tanktrap which hitherto kept vehicles from leaving the beach. Rhinoceros-like, the bulldozers charged into the palms, their raised blades shielding their drivers.

Meanwhile the 19th Infantry assault waves pounded forward in their southern sector of the beachhead. After four hours of fighting one company had progressed five hundred yards inland. Another met a tank ditch, emplacements, machineguns, mortars and field artillery only fifty yards from the water's edge. The battle moved in a grim patchwork of disorder, with platoons and squads and foolhardy individualists striking out on their own. A soldier cracked and yelled that he was being chased by wolves. "King" Company became disorganized because its command boat broke down on the shoreward run. One platoon entangled in the fray did not establish contact with its mother team until the following day.

But one after another Jap snipers toppled out of palms like sacks of meal. One after another the Jap emplacements were reduced, their crews destroyed. Private First Class Frank B. Robinson of Downey, California, made himself a one-man platoon. He crawled atop a stubborn pillbox and dropped three grenades through its port. He then reached down and pulled the barrel of the Jap machinegun out of line, burning his hands in the process. A little farther he came upon a cursing flame-thrower man. The fellow had his weapon aimed at an enemy dugout, but the flamethrower refused to ignite. Robinson crept to the flank of the dug-out, picking up discarded Jap newspapers on the way. He held a match to the paper and threw the burning bundle in front of the dugout. The flame-thrower fired through the flames and the flames ignited its charge and from the dugout came a screech and the smell of burning flesh. Already Robinson was on his way to another Jap stronghold which had bothered him.

"Baker" Company of the Nineteenth charged fire-spitting emplacements with grenades. A number of its men fell under Nip lead, among them the Executive Officer, Lieutenant Buck. "Dog" Company lost men at the hands of the same Jap warriors. Sergeant Beslisle of Headquarters Company, too, met death at this spot. "Charlie" Company had landed and was immediately pinned down. "Able" Company was split by fire upon landing. The men of "Easy" Company spotted a group of 75^ blasting away at landing craft offshore; they knocked out one of the guns with bazooka rockets and captured two more. "George" Company's men killed eleven Japs of a *Teishintai* suicide platoon, but fifteen of its men were hit in the first few minutes of a subsequent encounter.

Wilford R. Stone of Watervliet, New York, saw the scout of his squad drop badly wounded thirty yards in front of a Jap fortification. Undaunted, he edged through machinegun and mortar fire and carried his wounded friend to safety.

Chester Ledford of Perry, Missouri, saw a company officer lie helpless in fire from two enemy emplacements. Together with Herman Gendron of Detroit, he dashed into the killing zone and dragged the wounded officer to cover.

And there were others who gambled their lives to save the lives of hit buddies during that merciless day; Norbut Maier of Cincinnati who rescued two wounded begging for an aid man when no aid man was near; Ted Nelson of Barnard, Missouri, who dragged three wounded out of the path of a heavy machinegun; Irwin Duane of Sacramento, California, who saved a sergeant's life by swift, accurate fire; and Leo Uzarski of Los Angeles, whose ankle had been smashed by Jap shrapnel, but who nevertheless heeded a frantic call to save three from bleeding to death.

The fighting moves inland in tortuous eddies. You note by the sun that it is early afternoon. The first self-propelled guns and the first jeeps have cleared the beach to join the pioneering bulldozer men. You watch them go and you feel the suns heat strike through your helmet in liquid hammer-blows. You feel it even in the erratic shade of the broken palms. You have become indifferent to things. You are too numb to feel fear. All you hope is that no mortar shell will tear off your leg and leave you alive. Your canteens are empty. Green coconuts knocked down by the shells are everywhere. You chop off the end of one with your machete and drink the milk. It tastes good. While you drink your eyes fall on some dead. The Japs are twisted shapes with twisted faces. Most of your own dead lie as if they were asleep. You wonder why that is so, until you see an American whose eyes have burst out of his face. The horror does not halt the little things of life. You pee and you wipe your nose. You grab to feel if that piece of soap you pocketed that morning is still there.

A small group of men is wading up from the beach. You pay no attention to them until you see some sweating, bare-torsoed GI's tear away and wriggle hastily into their shirts. You hear a sergeant bluster, "Button up, button up," and for a moment you think he is crazy.

The small group of men is moving steadily up from the water's edge. They cross the tumultuous strip of sand, and then you notice that one of the group, the leader, wears no helmet. He wears a cap and he is smoking a corncob pipe. He walks along as if the nearest Jap snipers were on Saturn instead of in the palm tops a few hundred yards away.

You stare, and you realize that you are staring at General Douglas MacArthur.

The General is trying to find the Division command post. With him is his Chief of Staff. They stop to ask a sergeant the way. The sergeant doesn't know. He is too busy to bother with gold braid. Just then Lieutenant Art Stimson—he of the Texas flag—comes running along the rim of the coconut plantation. He grins a salute and takes the generals in tow.

A few yards away you hear a begrimed soldier ask: "Who's those two guys?"

"They're the generals," somebody replies.

"What the hell are they doing up here?"

"Damfino ... they just come around, I guess."

A correspondent from the Chicago *Tribune* buttonholes you and says that he has something to show you. You figure that he wants to show you MacArthur. But his interest is in a Jap pillbox that has been knocked out twice but insists on coming back to life. It's hidden in a clump of bamboo on the beach road to Palo. It has been treated with grenades, and flame-throwers. A bulldozer completely buried it. Tough Japs inside it sing Japanese songs. They work like moles to clear the ports, and suddenly their machinegun comes back to life. From a distance you watch the bulldozer approach like the crack of doom. Riflemen cover its progress. Then your squad leader throws a handful of dirt at you to catch your attention, and when you look, he says, "Come on."

And by-and-by you kill your first Jap. You see him struggling out of a pillbox full of smoke and you see him arm a grenade by tapping it on his helmet and his eyes are on you. You fire. The Jap lets go his grenade; his face is a pinched grimace and he flops around like a caught fish. You shoot him again, point blank, seven times, and he is still, and you quickly shove a new clip into your receiver.

A driver runs by shouting to everybody that Jap bullets have disabled his truck. But some way off Corporal Irwin Duane is still at work and he says nothing. He is the gunner of a self-propelled piece of artillery, an SPM—M8. He is busy putting his shells into a pillbox, mixing earth, palm logs and Japanese flesh into one hash.

Another company commander is killed. The platoons are scattered and lose contact. Captain Louis Berdami of New Orleans stands up and takes charge. His quick thinking saves the whole right flank of the attack from bogging down. But Berdami, too, is killed in action.

Sergeant Clifford McGowan of West Concord, Minnesota, sees his company in dire trouble from enemy machinegun nests not far ahead.

He knows that staying there will cost lives. So he crawls forward inches below the trajectory of the bullets. He crawls to within seventy-five yards of the Nip gunners, determines their exact position, then directs his mortars which soon put an end to the nest.

Private Albert M. Baskin of Baltimore sees a Jap in a pillbox take pot shots at his company commander. The officer is unaware of the source of bullets slapping the ground nearby. Baskin runs up to knock out the Jap, is wounded but keeps going. He kills the Jap. The enemy, a first lieutenant, died smiling.

Another stronghold is holding up a whole platoon. Sergeant Cameron E. Hale of Port Huron, Michigan, wades through a swamp and flanks the enemy position. Fire from his automatic rifle forces the Japs to duck. This enables the platoon to rush in and finish the job, with cold steel.

One hundred yards from Red Beach a burst of shrapnel lacerates the leg of Sergeant Ignazio Amato of Brooklyn, New York. Aid men rush to evacuate him to the ships. Amato's face is ashen. He bites his lips, shakes his head, continues to lead his riflemen. The Japs have killed a guy he liked. Amato's charge is a limp. Blood is squelching from his boot. But the Japs die.

Most of us have no love for first sergeants. We all have cursed them as fat-assed tyrants. But there at the edge of San Pedro Bay, First Sergeant Russell T. Edberg, of St. Paul, Minnesota, was worth his weight in Samurai swords. A camouflaged machinegun neutralized his assault battalion and Edberg does not like it. He peers around but cannot see the gun. He stands upright and blasters forward until he sees the gun. He then shoulders back, summons a volunteer. Together they carry one of their own machineguns to the threshold of the obstinate bunker. Scores of rounds ripping through the ports fill the fort's interior with prancing ricochets. The Japs fall silent. Edberg grins a Viking grin.

As the fiery sun dipped westward, elements of the Thirty-Fourth attacked across an open swamp. Waist-deep in slime and rottenness the tired men toiled forward, paced by the thumping of their mortars. Another force of their regiment attained the highway which links Palo with Leyte's capital, Tacloban. Red Beach lay more than a thousand yards to their rear. Nearby sprawled clusters of palm and bamboo huts. A few of the huts burned down, but most seemed strangely undamaged by the hail of bullets. Pigs rummaged there among the reeking stilts, and a lean dog howled. The native inhabitants had fled to the hills. This ghost community was the village of Pawing.

On the southern sector of the beachhead the "Rock of Chickamauga" slugged toward the town of Palo and Hill 522. This fighting machine ran head-on against unyielding fortifications blocking the beach road. Assaults that day failed to crack the defense. The men were exhausted. Darkness was closing in and the night was streaming with stars. The battalions dug in. Between eruptions of explosives the still air was pregnant with the sibilant voices of mosquitoes and the chirping of myriads of cicadas. The men in their holes chewed cold rations and wondered. All battalions were there but one: the Nineteenth Infantry's First, Lieutenant Colonel Zierath, commanding. Along the perimeters men harked to the crash and thunder of an artillery barrage. Artillery had landed in force and the batteries filled the evening with the whirr and the moaning of flying steel. Along the perimeters men asked, "What are they firing at? ... What happened to the First Battalion?"

On Hill 522, hulking saturnine above the banks of the Palo River, lay the answer.

Chapter Three
HILL 522

The town of Palo was a secondary objective to Hill 522, the dominating slopes of which rose directly from the river's edge north of the town.

The enemy had intended to use this bastion as the key of his entire defense system of the Palo beaches. The height rises 522 feet directly out of the coastal flats. It has a roughly circular base approximately 1,000 yards in diameter, with precipitous sides which rise to an abrupt crest resembling a Y-shaped ridge.

The Japanese had impressed the entire male population of Palo for three months to fortify this eminence. It was pocked with bunkers. Communication trenches were seven feet deep and tunnels honeycombed the hill.

The definite extent of the Japanese tunnel system on Hill 522 may never be known. Many of the tunnel mouths were blasted in by our men. We do know that Japanese soldiers kept popping out of the hill-side for days.

(from the Division Record)

SHORTLY AFTER NOON of the invasion day Lieutenant Colonel F. R. Zierath contacted his company commanders. "Gentlemen," he said, "get ready for the mountain climbing job." The company commanders were. One of them, Lieutenant Dallas Dick of New Brighton, Pennsylvania, was wounded. Shortly after his company—"Charlie" Company—had hit the beach that morning, its commander had fallen dead at the edge of the embattled coconut grove. Dallas Dick, a quiet-spoken, slender young man with almost Indian features, had assumed command. A Jap bullet had torn through his shoulder. But despite his wound he was determined that he and no one else should lead "Charlie" Company in the assault upon Hill 522. As matters stood, Hill 522 towered nearly a mile behind the Japanese beach defenses.

The Nineteenth Regiment had been stopped by a powerful road block astride the beach road to Palo. The First Battalion could not hope to reach Hill 522 by that direct route. Scouting parties were dispatched to ferret out a back door route to that central rampart which guards the entrance into the strategic Leyte Valley.

The scouts threaded through enemy lines in broad daylight. When they returned they reported that they had found covered roundabout trails leading to Hill 522.

The battalion moved out in battle formation, "Able" Company in the lead. The guns of warships in San Pedro Bay, and field artillery freshly landed on Red Beach opened their thunderous voices in a bombardment of Hill 522. Through the stifling afternoon the cannonade continued without cessation. From the distance the flashes of bursting shells looked like fireflies exploding in a saturnalia of self-destruction. Smoke wallowed over the Y-shaped crest.

"Able" Company had not proceeded far through flat palm lands and swamp when its scouts met sudden fire. Three men were hit. All others struck the ground, sought cover.

The following companies stopped in their tracks, dispatched security patrols to guard the flanks. The fire from ahead increased in ferocity. On a front of one hundred yards there were five Japanese bunkers with walls and roofs of earth and palm logs four feet thick.

Zierath made a prompt decision. He left "Able" Company to engage the enemy. The remainder of the battalion he moved around the foe's north flank. With "Charlie" Company on the right and "Baker" Company on the left he skirted an expanse of jungle and attacked Hill 522 from the northeast

Infantrymen moved swiftly up the slope, scouts well in advance and Dallas Dick in the lead of "C" Company's panting platoons. They climbed over cliffs and pushed through thickets that stung their faces and ripped their sweat-drenched fatigues. They traveled light. Their packs had been discarded on the beach. They carried their weapons, bandoleers of ammunition, their water and a few chocolate bars, no more. On the summit above, artillery still registered with destructive fury.

Hill 522 is very steep. Trails up its sides are winding. Fatigued from a long and hectic day the men looked toward the towering crest and clenched their teeth. At times they pulled themselves up bodily by grasping lianas and overhanging roots.

'This is a job for a guy who's hung his mother," a B.A.R. gunner grumbled, shifting his twenty-one-pound weapon from his right shoulder to the left.

Dallas Dick turned around and smiled. "Let me carry that B.A.R. awhile," he said.

"No," growled the gunner, "she's my baby."

"She's your baby," grinned Dallas Dick.

Now chemical mortars hurled smoke shells and demolition charges upon the crest. And then there was a sudden, awesome silence. The barrage had lifted. The assault had reached the upper slopes of Hill 522.

"Speed it up," said Colonel Zierath.

The word was passed along the desperately toiling squads. Speed it up. It seemed an insane order. Had they not gone as fast as any able-bodied man could go across such infernal terrain? Had they not worked their lungs and hearts to the breaking point?

"Speed it up," ordered "B" Company's commander (Captain William J. Herman of South Norwalk, Conn.).

"Speed it up," yelled Dallas Dick.

Speed through these minutes meant all the difference between life and a shallow grave in alien earth.

Japs were no supermen. Too pleasant was the memory of the picture-book farms of Japan, of little women waiting to share again their wooden pillows and their mats with their long-absent men. Zierath and Herman and Dallas Dick were willing to bet ten to one that the barrage had driven the defenders out of their forts to the cover of the far slope. *But the artillery barrage had lifted.* The task force commanders were willing to bet one hundred to one that at this very moment the foe was racing up the far side of the crest to reman his temporarily abandoned guns.

Speed it up.

Dallas Dick winced under the pain of his shoulder wound. God damn it to hell! Is not the essence of leadership in combat manifest in one's ability to perform in a superior manner any task one might demand of others? Look at Lieutenant Barrow! He lived by that concept and he died for his pains. An officer and a gentleman: that meant more than the knowledge of which fork to use for shrimp and which for steak. Those who had fallen on the beach that morning were covered with flies and already stinking in the heat. Speed it up.

Dallas Dick broke into a forced march pace. He overtook the advance elements. He passed the point and came abreast of the scouts. The scouts gave him a quick, tough look and called upon their second wind and quickened their already murderous pace. No louey nor any other brass should beat *them* to the crest of that f----- hill!

A wild elation surged through Dallas Dick. He looked at the heaving backs of his scouts, at the sweat-drenched seats of their pants. "Look at those bastards," he thought. "The power and glory of America."

They passed the menacing mouths of tunnels half hidden by bamboo thickets. The tunnels were silent. They struggled over the last hundred yards, a ragged and drawn-out column rushing upward through an ominous patchwork of lengthening shadows and austere rock formations. The panorama below them was sweepingly beautiful—the beaches, the purple headlands, a great fleet at anchor, the silvery sea and the distant mountains of Samar. No one gave it a glance.

"Baker" Company attained the first crest of Hill 522 at sunset. It was welcomed with squalls of lead from two cleverly hidden pillboxes away along the ridge. The men sought the ground and waited. The tropical night swooped in and soon it was too dark for the adjustment of artillery fire. Captain Herman ordered: "Dig in. Hang on."

At this time "Charlie" Company's scouts and Dallas Dick reached the central crest of the hill. Dick signaled the scouts to halt. He leaped atop a boulder. Outlined against the evening sky he peered down the far side of Hill 522. He saw swarms of bobbing helmets, a mass of bayoneted rifles in the hands of a mob of Japanese. The Japanese were muscling rapidly toward the crest. Dick and his scouts cupped their hands and shouted to their laboring platoons.

"The Japs are coming up the other side!"

In an extravagant orgy of exertion "C" Company's men rushed to the crest. They attained the top in twos and threes. Dallas Dick dispersed them into a hasty skirmish line. Simultaneously the first rifle shots punctuated the stillness of the oncoming night. The Japs, outraced, broke into wrathful howls. While his men fired from behind rocks, from brush-fringed hollows and from the cover of the wind-twisted trunks of trees, Lieutenant Dick stood upright so that the now swiftly arriving remainder of his company could see him, assigning positions, firing all the while to help slow down the enemy advance.

A Jap came crawling uphill on hands and knees not thirty yards from Dick. Protected by a flat boulder he stopped his bear crawl and sat back on his haunches. He raised his *Arisaka* rifle and took a deliberate aim. He fired before he died under a bullet from one of "Charlie's" riflemen. His shot splintered the carbine in the lieutenant's hand. For an instant Dick stared, surprised. Then he kicked his shattered weapon aside and reached for his pistol.

The Japanese were now within grenade range. Their screaming filled the air. Rifle fire waxed to a crackling storm. Grenades were lobbed in a malevolent close range exchange. All tiredness had slipped from the men; all thought, too, of Hill 522. They fought to live—to them that was the thing that counted. The rataplan of a Jap machinegun from the left cut in with sardonic abruptness.

Dallas Dick moved to the flank to locate the gun. He found the left wing of his skirmish line in battered shape. In a shell crater lay a groaning soldier. A few paces farther lay other men whose blood oozed through their sweat-soaked clothes.

"Where is that gun?" Dick shouted.

A wounded soldier half rose and pointed to the low entrance of a cave. There was another burst: a gun-muzzle spitting fire, a savage ricocheting of bullets striking upon rock. Stragglers, still unaware of the direction of this fire, continued to move into the killing zone.

Dallas Dick shouted: "Hold it, hold it."

Then a bullet pierced his left ankle.

His teeth were bared under the sudden impact of pain.

"Get off the skyline," he warned his men.

The machinegun stopped firing for lack of further targets. The torrent of rifle shots and grenade bursts on the crest ebbed gradually. The Japanese drew back. Some fifty of their dead littered the rugged incline.

"What about that goddam pillbox?" a rough voice asked.

Over the walkie-talkie came Colonel Zierath's calm voice: "Never mind that pillbox. It's getting too dark. We'll get it tomorrow. Better dig in. Over."

"Roger," said Dallas Dick, and, "Out."

Descending night made aimed shooting impossible. Also, the muzzle blasts would betray the riflemen's positions. In the dark a man was better off without a rifle than without grenades. One could throw grenades without giving one's position away . . . provided the enemy came close enough for that.

Twice-wounded Dallas Dick refused to be evacuated to the beach. Sulfa powder on his bullet wounds, a good taut bandage around his ankle, sulfa tablets gulped with plenty of water—and water was to become bitterly scarce on Hill 522. 'That'll do," said the lieutenant. "Dig in."

"Charlie" Company's perimeter was set up in proper shape. With darkness all motion ceased. Whatever moved in the dark must be a Jap. The infantrymen had withdrawn a few paces down the slope, dug in to weather whatever the night would bring. On the other side of Hill 522, also a few yards below the crest, the Japs, too, dug in. Below them the Palo River gleamed in the dim light of stars.

While Zierath's force held the commanding bastion, another force, much smaller, trod a perilous course through Japanese lines. This group—a handful of aid men—was led by Captain Robert Munch, the surgeon of Zierath's battalion.

Captain Munch had landed with the assault waves on Red Beach. Amidst the tumultuous congestion of the water's edge he had tended the flow of wounded men, not counting the hours. During his first brief breathing spell along midafternoon he discovered that his battalion had already struck out toward Hill 522.

Would there be casualties in the fight for the Hill? Munch needed no answer. He summoned his aides and moved forward through the inferno beneath the palms. He was stopped at the edge of a swamp. Enemy snipers and machinegun bullets stopped him. He returned to the beach, his chagrin overshadowed by his determination. Staff officers advised him to spend the night on the beach. They thought it suicide to leave the perimeter at night. The swamps and plantations between the beachhead and Hill 522 teemed with Japs. Besides, the men in the foxholes were wont to blaze away at anyone who moved in the dark.

"My job is with my men," said Robert Munch.

He went to a radio. He called Hill 522. Colonel Zierath's radiomen were alert. They answered. Captain Munch requests the battalion commander to send guides down to the beachhead. He wants the guides to conduct him and his medics to Hill 522 via the secret battalion route. Riflemen on the perimeter would be instructed not to fire as the guides come through.

The guides came through: tough youths with blackened faces and eyes that could see in the dark.

When Captain Munch and his party arrived at the base of the hill they found the height surrounded by the enemy. The battalion was cut off. It was to remain cut off through forty-eight hours. For two days the men atop Hill 522 fought off swarms of pugnacious Japs. For two days they went without food. But they did not go without a surgeon. Where neither patrols nor carrying parties could penetrate, Surgeon Munch pushed through. He pushed through with litter squads and relay posts and a perseverance bigger than jagged cliffsides and Jap cunning.*

---

* Major General F. A. Irving, Division Commander, has stated that "if Hill 522 had not been occupied when it was, we might have suffered a thousand casualties in the assault. As it was, the occupation of the height cost the First Battalion, 19th Infantry Regiment, fourteen killed and ninety-five wounded, of which thirty later rejoined their units.

Chapter Four

BANZAI NIGHT

"Duty is weightier than a mountain, while Death is lighter than a feather...."
(*from a Japanese Imperial Rescript*)

SILENCE ON THE PERIMETER; a silence which is the difference between life and death. Mosquitoes roaming. A brown child meandering among machinegun muzzles, searching for its mother. Flares, white and green and red floating from paper parachutes, casting their eerie light upon the swamps and plantations of the coastal flats. The multitude of vessels of San Pedro Bay is blacked-out and still, and the tumultuous congestion on the beach has frozen into chaotic immobility.

Darkness and silence; but silence not for long. The Jap is trained to fight at night when a rifles sights cannot be seen against the black opaqueness. He is a believer in stealthy infiltration, in crawling through enemy lines to harass, disrupt and blast from the rear. He is a believer in the rapid traverse of terrain held impassable, to appear abruptly in most unexpected places. Have not these methods worked in his favor in Malaya? In Java, Cochin-China, Sumatra and Singapore? Had not western soldiers who found themselves outflanked, their lines infiltrated, invariably retreated to safeguard the continuity of their positions?

The Jap is, too, a believer in the paralyzing effect of the sudden, savage charge in the dark.

On Hill 522 grenades are lobbed to and fro across the embattled crest. The Division's artillery is pounding the roads beyond Palo to block their use to enemy reinforcements. Jap snipers still pockmark the beachhead at nightfall, but as yet the beachhead perimeter is tranquil.

Then, suddenly, there is a yell that chills the blood. The night boils with sound and motion: indistinct shapes scurrying up the notched trunks of palms like spectral baboons; shadows squirming like snakes between the lines of foxholes; insidious endeavor to make the blasted pillboxes along Red Beach come back to life at dawn; mortars thumping in the darkness; the dry crack of the Garands and the lesser bark of carbines, and the whip-crack counter barks of the long-barreled *Arisaka* rifles; the eager clatter of the automatic weapons; the howls of the recklessly rushing foe; the scraping and panting of men carrying away their dead; the moans of the wounded and the rustling of rats among the scattered corpses, and dampness falling steadily from a starlit sky.

At 0130 the enemy struck from the south along the Palo-Tacloban highway. He moved forward under the cover of a heavy mortar and machinegun barrage. Leading elements pushed rapidly toward our positions. Following forces branched into a double envelopment of our flanks. The main assault, however, bore straight down the road. It struck the perimeter at the village of Pawing.

Somewhere on the left flank of the perimeter the crews of two machineguns led by Sergeant Karl Geis, of the Bronx, could hear a mass of men approach along the Palo road. An assistant gunner inched forward to reconnoiter. He found the road empty, its surface pale in the starlight, but the sounds of men moving forward through the gloom continued. The assistant gunner wriggled to the far edge of the road. He peered along the steep embankment and he studied the blackness beyond: palms, underbrush, clumps of jungle grass taller than a man. There was a faint swishing and crackling that seemed to filter from every pore and crevice of the earth.

The enemy attacked abruptly, and in force. He attacked with mortars, automatic weapons, grenades and rifles. Both American machineguns at this point of the perimeter fired angrily. In the ensuing melee some men of their crews were wounded by grenade fragments. The "Banzai" screaming of the attackers was around them like an engulfing tide. The gunners' hands never left the triggers. Between feeding their guns the ammunition bearers of the team fired their rifles and carbines, and hurled grenades to keep the Japs from the final closing in....

Geis' gunners counted at dawn. There were one hundred and sixty Japanese dead in the path of the blackened muzzles.

Some distance forward and to the flank of the machineguns lay Corporal Jack Guttentag of New York City. He and another soldier had been separated from their platoon. They had dodged around in the dark, and once a squad of yelling Japs had rushed past them less than five feet away.

Surrounded by a battle-crazed enemy, Jack Guttentag and his companion took cover behind a toppled palm. From their haphazard shelter they could see their own machineguns spurt fire. Not far away a clump of brush was burning, and in the light of curling flames Guttentag saw a detachment of Japanese creep upon the machinegun position from the flank.

The two soldiers opened fire with their rifles. The enemy became confused. But seconds later a Japanese machinegun was firing straight at the two isolated Americans. Guttentag's companion was hit. He cried for help.

Jack fired until his rifle was shot from his hands. Then he crawled to the wounded soldier but could not find the others rifle in the dark. There was nothing to do but to clear out. He bandaged the wounded man and gave him water from his canteen when he felt a sudden stab of pain. But he was still able to stand on his feet. He put his arm around his companion's waist, and together they staggered away. Gradually Jack felt his comrade grow heavier in his arm. He continued to struggle from one palm to the next. They almost made it.

Then Guttentag fell. A burst from a machinegun had killed him.

Defending the right flank of his battalion was a machinegun section led by Sergeant Eric Erickson of Blairstown, New Jersey. The Japanese attacked like demons and Erickson's twin guns spat lead. The first onrush was thrown back. In the sweltering darkness the enemy then managed to push forward a machinegun to the cover of a nearby mound of rubble. Ericksons gunners were compelled to duck out of the path of death snarling into the flank of their emplacement. The sergeant knew that he must do something to prevent the Japs from rushing his momentarily silent position. Do it quickly.

On his belly he crawled through grass and mud. Compulsions of war are often stronger than the love of life. Rules and regulations had nothing to do with it. It was simply the urge to do what must be done.

Erickson outflanked the enemy gun. He then crept toward it until he could see the reflections of its muzzle flashes in the gunners' helmets. In quick succession he tossed three grenades.

The machinegun toppled, its gunners killed. Beatrice Erickson has reason to be proud of her man.

A lone gunner was Carl Plouvier of Howardstown, Kentucky. In the pandemonium of the "Banzai" storm his squad was broken up and pushed thirty yards to the rear. Plouvier found himself alone in a foxhole, an automatic rifle as his only companion. A band of Japs crouched scarcely fifteen yards in front.

The twenty rounds in the magazine of a B.A.R. can be expended in less than ten seconds. And Carl Plouvier was down to his last magazine. Between short bursts of fire he yelled for ammunition.

To his rear, others realized his plight. With the accuracy of big league players they tossed him bandolier after bandolier of ammunition. Plouvier burned up the rounds as fast as they came. The Japanese withdrew to reorganize before lashing out anew.

Flat behind a heavy machinegun on the perimeter lay two Clevelanders, Ernest Kolenc and Arthur Rominske. Their sector had been relatively quiet. But shortly before 5 A.M. they heard light footfalls nearing their position. In the ephemeral illumination of nearby grenade flashes they saw a group of people move toward them through no-man's land. Some figures in the group looked like women. The two men notified their sergeant.

"Hold your fire," the sergeant whispered. "Might be natives looking for lost kids and stuff."

A voice in the night said loudly: "Friends. Filipinos."

The gunners lay still and waited. The bevy of strangers was less than twenty yards away. More and more of them came on.

"Nips!" said the sergeant.

Their machinegun cut lose in a convulsion of sound. The Japanese screeched, dispersed, lunged forward. The fire fight that followed was savage and brief. Not many of the enemy escaped.

Manning a machinegun at another spot on the embattled beachhead were Samuel Jepma, a Minnesotan from Hancock, and two companions. The onset struck them at 4 A.M. This was neither a trick maneuver nor a suicide assault; it was deliberate assault executed by skilled and fanatical troops. The Japanese advanced in short rushes, bounding from concealment to cover. They did not fire until they were within forty yards of the perimeter.

Jepma could not see the attackers, but he could hear them. The sounds of their forward rushes had ceased. They were at the point of pouncing on his position. He fired several bursts into the invisible skirmish line. Cries in the dark told him that his bullets had reached their mark. But his firing had also betrayed his position.

A Japanese machinegun chattered. A slender cone of bullets sprayed inches above Sam Jepma's emplacement. Soon there was a familiar popping in the distance. A half-minute later falling mortar shells added to his troubles. Under the cover of their point barrage the enemy riflemen advanced. They fired as they came, howled, and hurled grenades.

A grenade plopped into Jepma's hole. The explosion badly wounded one of his companions. He heard his comrade thrash the earth and he knew then that death had its hand on his shoulder. One hand lifting the trigger of his gun, the other twirling the traversing mechanism, he blasted away with a hundred rounds into the darkness in front.

The Japs hugged the ground. Jepma could hear their leaders jabber instructions in the dark.

He used the breathing spell to roll his wounded comrade out of the foxhole. He turned over the gun to his remaining companion. Then he crawled out of the foxhole. On elbows and knees, without once rising to a kneeling position, he dragged the wounded soldier to the shelter of another empty hole nearby. After that he returned to his gun. He put in a fresh belt of ammunition and continued to spray the terrain to his immediate front.

But while he had tended his wounded buddy, the Japanese had worked men around to the rear of the emplacement. The two gunners now received fire from the front and from the rear. An outcry made Jepma turn. He saw that his companion had sagged into a corner of the foxhole, killed.

Jepma fired. The sequence of bursts kept the foe glued to the ground. He could hear the Japs' excited breathing, but he could not see them. "Now," he thought.

He grasped his machinegun in a bear hug and clambered out of his hole. At a crouch he carried his gun to the hole in which he had deposited his wounded comrade. Even as he was mounting the gun he could hear his assailants wriggle toward his old position. Seconds later they charged the abandoned emplacement. Sam Jepma was ready. The hammering of his machinegun became a continuous roar.

The Japanese scattered. But they were a tenacious crew. They rallied and renewed the attack. There was a metallic crack and a play of sparks. A bullet had hit the barrel of Jepma's gun. The bullet ricocheted into the night. Another bullet passed through the top of his helmet. Half stunned, Jepma continued to fire. A third bullet ripped through his shoulder. Jepma fired with dogged ferocity. All through the night he had the feeling that it was not he, Sam Jepma, who lived through this nightmare, but someone else, someone he had known, maybe, seven or eight thousand years ago. He fired until the last cartridge had passed through the burning barrel of his gun.

"Time to quit," thought Gunner Jepma.

He gave the mute machinegun a regretful kick. At his side the wounded man lay quiet.

He took the wounded man on his shoulders. He crossed the Japanese trap at a dogtrot and plunged into a swamp.

"By 0200 the Japanese had pushed to within a few feet of our positions, employing mortars and machineguns which killed or wounded all personnel in the first two three-man positions except Private Harold H. Moon...."

(from the Division Record)

In faraway Gardena, California, a mother gazes at a picture of the son she bore and cared for through workaday years. Hazel Moon found it hard to believe that never again would she hear the laughter of her boy, never again hear him tap out a surefooted rhythm to the music he loved, never again see him brush up to meet a girl, or shoulder briskly through the door, and ask, "Mom, what've we got to eat?"

Go and ask the fighting men of "George" Company of the Thirty-Fourth about Harold Moon. "He was a happy-go-lucky sort," they will say, "sloppy in garrison. He cursed the Army. He thought most officers were jerks. He didn't give a damn for anything." Moon lugged with him a phonograph whenever the Division was on the move. Between turns of fighting his hole was riotous with music. But his carelessness sheathed an indomitable courage. "A go-to-hell type of courage," they said.

At 0130 that first dark night on Leyte the foe began his most determined bid to push the invaders back into the sea. By 0200 Harold Moon knew that all of his mates in two neighboring emplacements had been wounded or killed. A squad sent forward to reinforce the threatening breach had lost its way in the tangled undergrowth beneath the palms.

Moon knew that he was the only man left to defend his point of the perimeter. He realized that if he should fail to hold out until dawn the enemy would score a breakthrough into the heart of the slender beach position.

He expended what grenades he had to repel the first onrush. His buddies in the three-man foxhole had been badly hit; one was dead, the other dying. He had their rifles and their remaining ammunition. And he had his own Thompson sub-machinegun, already smoking hot in the damp night. Fifteen feet away on one side lay the Palo-Tacloban highway; coconut palms going over into swamps on the other.

Moon heard the slurring of Japanese creeping through the darkness under the palms. He could not see the enemy and he did not want to waste his ammunition on a blind spraying of the ground. He must do something to force the enemy to show himself. He stood up in his foxhole and insulted the attackers.

"Come on, you yellow sons-of-bitches," he challenged.

The muzzle blasts of rifles stabbed through the gloom. They were firing at the sound of Moon's voice. Moon replied with quick, short bursts from his tommygun. Two of the attackers crumpled. Another burst made them quiet. Moon heard a third Jap about five yards away tap a hand-grenade against a palm log. One—two—three ... The Jap rose from his hiding place to hurl the grenade. Moon fired. The Jap gave a piercing cry. Then his own grenade exploded in his face, and the others lay low.

"Listen, Japs," Moon shouted. "Come on and fight."

Yamashita's men were trained to die. They came, this time in a rushing squad. Death clamored from the Californian's gun. The Japs changed their minds. They sank to the ground as if the earth had swallowed them. Moon's high-pitched taunts rang through the night.

A lone enemy who had succeeded in crawling to within a few yards of the one-man bastion leaped up and threw a grenade. The grenade rolled into Moon's foxhole, two seconds from bursting into forty cast-iron fragments. In these two seconds Moon killed the Japanese. He kicked the grenade into a far corner of his hole. He threw himself out over the soft earth rim of the emplacement. The grenade roared. Dirt, fire and fragments shot up high. Harold Moon was wounded in the leg. He slipped back into his foxhole, his gun at the ready.

"Come and get me, you bastards," he shouted.

That was at 0240. No one answered his challenge. There was the noise of night battle elsewhere along the perimeter, the wedge-like flashes of grenades and the lightning wake of the tracers. And there was the moaning of the wounded in adjoining holes.

"Oh, come on and fight," mocked Harold Moon.

At 0300 the nearest American machinegun was destroyed by a mortar shell. An infiltration party killed its crew. The Japs waxed bolder. Their own machineguns raked the road without opposition.

"Come and get me," Moon shouted angrily.

"Coming," a voice said from across the road.

"Who's that?" demanded Moon.

"This is a Japanese officer," the voice stated precisely.

"Thats fine," said Moon. "Come on and fight, you bastard."

The voice screamed: "Filthy American."

Moon saw a shadow dart upright on the far side of the road and vanish in an instant. The Jap had thrown a grenade.

"Missed," Moon announced. "Try again." This time he was ready. His shoes and leggings were sticky with blood from his leg wound. The officer tossed a grenade. Moon fired. Seconds of silence followed. "We both missed," said the Jap.

"So sorry," replied Moon.

"I shall try again," the officer announced.

"Try again, you crooked rat."

The duel continued for an hour. The Japanese grew wary of showing himself to that apparent maniac with the sub-machinegun. Moon shouted every insult he could think of to tease his adversary into showing himself against the blackness of palm and brush. The Jap was too seasoned to accept the bait. But he continued to accept the challenge.

Harold Moon deliberately exposed himself to get a shot at the officer. He sat on the edge of his foxhole. "Here I am," he taunted. "Now come and get me." In a flash the officer was on his knees, grenade poised. A long burst from Moons gun cut him in two.

While Moon was thus engaged, other Japs inched forward, fanning out as they came. By 0430 Moon was completely surrounded. By 0500 a Jap light machinegun had been pushed to within 20 yards of the position. Curiously, its fire ignored Harold Moon. With deadly accuracy the gun played havoc with the survivors of a platoon farther down the line.

From this point on the Californian's stand would appear a Homeric incredibility were it not a sober military fact recorded in an affidavit by Staff Sergeant Verdun C. Myers of Tecumseh, Oklahoma, at whose emplacement the sudden holocaust of fire was directed.

"Although under heavy machinegun and mortar fire himself," swore Myers, "Private Moon with extraordinary heroism exposed himself to locate this enemy machinegun, and then, remaining exposed, he directed and adjusted fire upon it, destroying the entire crew."

The night was pregnant with a weird crescendo of shrieks. There was a commotion of barely discernible shadows, of ghostly shapes darting hither and yon. The shrieks subsided into a chant of frustration, and in a clump of grass a Japanese voice jabbered. A silence followed, punctuated by the dull crashing of grenades elsewhere on the perimeter, and by the moans of the uncared-for wounded.

Through the pre-dawn blackness drifted the worried voice of Platoon Sergeant Ferguson:

"Harold, are you all right?"

No answer. The Jap voice in the *kunai* chattered on with blunt authority. There was an anxious cry, the pad-pad of feet running over palm fronds, a whimpering that seemed to filter from the brooding swamps, the croak of a bull-frog, and then there was Moons voice bellowing abuse.

"You lousy bunch of -----! Got you, didn't I." And then with coaxing derision: "Why don't you guys come over here and get my gun?"

He cut loose with a quick burst at a shadowy figure six feet away.

"Come and get it," said Moon defiantly.

Across the highway, shrieks again stabbed skyward.

"Stop your caterwauling," shouted Moon.

Somewhere off to his rear John Ferguson laughed. "Moon is all right," he said. Ferguson came from Utica, Kentucky. He was wounded and bleeding, but in this horror-filled night he had led his decimated platoon in the repulse of eight Japanese assaults, and four of these had been "Banzai" charges.

Next the enemy laid down a mortar barrage. The first shells fell short; the following exploded in the immediate rear of Ferguson's platoon. Thus bracketed, with hits creeping closer and closer, the hollow booming of the explosions signaled doom. Ferguson called for counter mortar fire. But communication wires were broken. The mortar men in the rear had only hazy knowledge of the foe's mortar positions. They fired "by God and by guess.' Their shells missed the Jap gunners.

Again Moon sprang into the breach. Sergeant Myers reports that the youth from Gardena "knowingly exposed himself to hostile mortar fire to shout range corrections to friendly mortars."

The Japanese mortars were silenced.

Minutes later there was a shout that a soldier was bleeding to death in a forward foxhole. A corpsman rushed forward. Braving the awful chance of being shot by his own friends, he slithered into the dying man's hole. A few rifle lengths distant lurked the Japanese. Unarmed, the aid man applied a tourniquet, using the wounded soldier's bayonet and belt.

Standing upright in his foxhole, Moon watched the medic work. He was unaware of the two Japanese who neared the group, sliding on their bellies. Sergeant Myers' affidavit continues:

"Hearing the Japs yell as they closed in for the kill, Private Moon turned and killed them both before they were able to harm the aid man."

And then:

"By 0545 Private Moon was running short of ammunition. His position had been the focal point of the enemy attack for over four hours. They were determined to take it. Private Moon was determined to hold it. The Japanese had worked men around on all sides of Private Moon's position.

"At dawn an entire platoon of the enemy arose and rushed the position in a desperate bayonet assault. Private Moon calmly steadied his tommygun between his knees, and calling to the Japanese to come and get him he emptied the entire magazine into them, killing eighteen (18) before they overwhelmed and killed him."

With Moon dead, the enemy pushed forward again. Dawn was on the way. From the surrounding swamps the mists rose in tormented spirals. Sergeants Myers and Ferguson realized that if any men of their platoon were to escape they would have to do so at once.

"What about our wounded?" asked Myers.

Verdun Myers, thrice wounded in three successive campaigns, was a tall, handsome man in his twenties. He was intelligent and self-taught. At home, in Oklahoma, a young wife and a child were waiting for him, hoping for him. There he was: dead weary, his hair caked with sweat and mud, his helmet creased by an enemy bullet, his uniform spotted with blood.

Earlier that night a grenade had burst in Sergeant Myers' three-man emplacement. Both of his mates had been struck down by fragments. Across the killing zone the Oklahoman had carried his disabled comrades to the center of the perimeter where medical aid was at hand. He had then returned to his hole and rejoined the fight. But now, with broad daylight in the offing and swarms of Japs surrounding the remnants of his platoon, the fit would surely die with the wounded if the fit were to attempt to lug their wounded in a dash through hostile lines.

"Hide the wounded," the two sergeants agreed.

It was the best they could do.

They probed through clumps of underbrush and grass with their last grenades. They then dragged their wounded in the undergrowth.

"Fix bayonets."

The short black steel clicked into the muzzle studs of the Garands of those who still could walk. The last of their cartridges clicked into the chambers. "What," said someone, "will the guys on the perimeter do when they see us charging up in front of their lines?" The most repugnant of all war's ironies is to be killed by one's own.

"We'll take that chance," said Myers. And then: *"On your feet—*

Follow me!"
As one man they rose and charged.
"Aaaaa-eeeeeh!"
Yelling and firing they broke through the enemy lines.

With daylight the battalions resumed the offensive. Strewn along the Palo-Tacloban road lay more than six hundred Japanese dead. No one went to the trouble of counting the corpses which littered the adjoining fields and swamps. The enemy dead were first line troops: members of the 16th Japanese Division, veterans of Manchuria and Bataan.

CHAPTER FIVE
CHURCH BELLS RING IN PALO

It was a situation in which anything could happen. . . .
(*from the Division Record*)

THE PUSH into the town of Palo was easy enough. The Nineteenth Infantry Regiment's Second Battalion left the beachhead in battle formation shortly after daylight. It entered Palo at 3 P.M. and hardly a shot was fired. Infantrymen who had fought all through the previous day and all through the night relaxed. The entrance into lush Leyte Valley, seizure of which would cut the Island in two, seemed wide open. That was on October 21.

But before dawn of October 26 all vials of wrath were poured about the vast old Spanish church of Palo. Palo River ran red with American blood. An ammunition dump burned and an American machinegun manned by Japs went berserk in the churchyard. Hostile demolition parties pierced the beachhead and forced artillerymen to close-quarter fighting. A wounded colonel made the church serve as prison and refuge for thousands; a baby was born under sniper fire; and the Division's finance office "hit the dirt" when a pay clerk counting money saw the man at the next table fall from a rifle shot (the pay clerk was Sergeant Peter F. Sullivan, of New York City, one time cashier of Sterling National Bank & Trust Company).

Intelligence Sergeant Ernest Martin of Terre Haute was hunting on a map for the village of Alangalang. There was a sudden twang and the sergeant dived for cover. When he got up to retrieve his map he found a bullet puncture alongside elusive Alangalang.

Leading a patrol on the outskirts of Palo was Sergeant Sam Needham, also of Terre Haute. He saw a smashed amphibious tank tilted on the bank of the road. "A mine did that," Needham muttered. He switched his attention to the terrain ahead. However, the disabled "Alligator" opened fire on the American patrol. Needham approached the wrecked vehicle at a cautious crawl. A bullet hit him in the leg. By now he was too angry to give up. He maneuvered his patrol until the "Alligator" was surrounded. Then he dispatched a man for a bazooka. And when the weapon was brought to him, he sent a rocket crashing into the tank. Inside it, battered and silent, lay two Japs.

At the same time, on the beachhead, Lieutenant Coleman Freeman of Baltimore, an intelligence officer, received word that an enemy suicide squad was about to charge the nearby artillery command post. He grabbed a field telephone to speed a warning. But suddenly the artillery colonel heard a gasp at the other end of the line. There was the clatter of a falling telephone and the thud of a falling body. "Out," thought the colonel. An instant later, he heard the lieutenant say evenly, "Pardon the interruption, Colonel—somebody just shot me through the ass."

While one assault force pushed into Palo, other elements of the Division fought on three separate fronts. Colonel Zierath's men on Hill 522 battled the enemy in a maze of dugouts and tunnels. Another taskforce tackled the roadblock astride the beach road to Palo. Battalions of the Thirty-Fourth fought tooth and nail for the possession of ridges flanking the coastal flats. The landscape separating these four spearheads was alive with Japanese. After the passage of the combat teams the enemy closed in again like water closing in the wake of a passing ship. A welter of clouds towered over distant summits, heralding rain.

By-passing heavy concrete fortifications, the Palo attack force moved through sporadic sniper fire and reached the junction of the Palo-Tacloban highway with the fiercely contested beach road. The latter was no more than a muddy track, earmarked to become the main artery for the flow of Division supplies from Red Beach. At this point abrupt Jap mortar fire killed and wounded several men. Among the killed was the battalion's sergeant-major. "Lets go!" The assault force crossed the area of mortar bursts at a run.

A hostile strongpoint whose fire threatened to hold up the advance was liquidated by an Army mail clerk and his friend. With nothing more than a rifle and a sub-machinegun, the two volunteers crossed a soggy field exposed to the aimed fire of the Japs. They climbed atop the noisome emplacement and silenced it with a pointblank volley through its ports. The mail clerk was Angelo F. Derago of Camden, New Jersey.

A minute later scouts spotted a Japanese column moving down the highway from the direction of the beachhead. The detachment was a remnant of the enemy force which had killed Harold Moon during the small hours of morning.

The battalion halted and crouched low. Scouts prepared a hasty ambush. Machinegun fire raked the Jap column and the survivors sprinted for the shelter of a coconut grove. By radio the battalion commander requested Division artillery to pour shells into the grove. An ammunition truck speeding along the highway suddenly slammed on its brakes. Out of his cab leaned the helmeted driver, shouting,

"Goddam, I hate running over dead Nips."

In open column to both sides of the highway, the task force resumed its march on Palo. The marchers eyed the flanking swamps and rice fields with suspicious disbelief. Makeshift mines studded the shoulders of the highway—wooden boxes filled with picric acid and armed with cocked grenades. The day was sultry and the men's fatigues were black from perspiration. Rising to their right was the massive bulk of Hill 522. Without warning artillery shells fell among the marching column. American shells, fired in error. One man was killed, another wounded.

"Let's get the hell out of here!"

The infantrymen quickened their pace. They rounded a bend in the road and ahead of them lay the bridge across the Palo River. Beyond the bridge the spire of the church stood outlined against a wall of clouds. Motionless, a man's figure stood in an aperture of the bell tower. This watcher's arms were outstretched like the arms of a man nailed to a cross. Fieldglasses showed that he was a white-haired Filipino.

The scouts peered at the bridge. They scanned the rows of nipa huts on the river's far side. There was no sound, nor any sign of movement.

Was the bridge mined? The thickets along the river bank had all the requisites of a first-class trap. Did foul play skulk in yonder church and houses? The forward scouts crossed the bridge gingerly. The point followed. Nothing happened.

"Double time!"

The battalion double-timed across the bridge. It entered Palo without encountering opposition. The lone figure in the aperture of the belltower had vanished. And then the sonorous voices of the bells rang out across the town.

The populace poured into the streets in a great welcoming surge. Ragged, dirty as they were from an almost three-year famine of clothing and soap, they danced and wept and shouted with jubilation. Even those who had lost members of their families in the fighting and bombardments of the past two days went wild with joy. Around the town square girls and women looted the hibiscus bushes of their flowers. Others came at a run, bearing palm wine in bamboo log containers. A happy crowd hoisted Lieutenant Joseph Maloy (who was later killed in action) to their shoulders and carried the grinning Yank in triumph through Palo. Children blurted what welcoming English they knew. Women screamed and laughed beneath the stone walls of the church. Riflemen, hunting for hidden Japs, took leave to measure the trimness of smiling girls. A skinny, barefooted priest clad in shorts dashed through the streets, exulting, "The bells, the bells, they are ringing again."

From a corner of the churchyard Lieutenant Colonel R. B. Spragins of Evanston, Illinois, the battalion commander, surveyed the riotous scene. He did not like it. He knew the Japs too well. What would happen to these masses of celebrating people, the colonel reasoned, if the enemy should elect to launch a Banzai charge into the streets of Palo?

Spragins sent runners to summon the mayor and the priests of the town. "Gentlemen," he told them, "there will be fighting in Palo. Your church has thick walls. I must ask you to lead your people into the church and to keep them there."

Again the bells of Palo tolled. The priests herded their flocks into the church to offer thanks for their town's liberation. All went, except the white-haired sexton and guerillas armed with captured Japanese rifles. Guards were mounted and the population of Palo pitched camp in the church.

Meanwhile the companies fanned out. At the edge of town, where a highway runs west toward Santa Fe and into the broad Leyte Valley, they struck stinging resistance. The Japanese were solidly entrenched under an agglomeration of native dwellings. Their mortars, machineguns and rifles ended any further exploration for that day. Scouts reported a massing of Jap assault troops on the spread-out battalion's left; and dusk reached over the mountains of Samar. Spragins ordered a withdrawal from the outskirts of the town. *The Division Record* tersely reports that *"A tight perimeter was set up for the night around the Palo church square, and it proved a most prescient move."*

While the tempest brewed over Palo, the Third Battalion of the Nineteenth Infantry Regiment set out to reduce the formidable roadblock at a bend of the beach road to Palo. Enemy control of this road made impossible the passage of supply convoys to the isolated forward elements of the Division.

This roadblock was a powerful and self-contained position; a series of concrete forts heavily reinforced with logs and earth. The whole was cleverly camouflaged. Connecting these strong-points was a network

CHURCH BELLS RING IN PALO

of interlacing trenches, snipers' holes and machinegun emplacements. Naval gunfire and aerial rocket shells had done their work. But advancing tanks had been stopped by a fantastic tangle of jungle brush and ditches. It was a job for infantry.

The battalion attacked in the brooding heat of early afternoon. All infantry weapons came into play, from tank-destroyers, flamethrowers, and bazookas to the silent bayonet. In bitter encounters the infantry captured a 75-millimeter gun position, anti-tank emplacements and a hornets' nest of heavy machineguns. But at the rim of a clearing, two hundred yards from the road bend, they were stopped cold. Infantry weapons were not enough to break that wall of fire. The assault teams dug in.

The riflemen cursed the day and the heat. They cursed the prospect of spending the night under the noses of Japanese bunkers. In single file a platoon of tank-destroyers ground through dense thickets. Corporal Irving Duane of Sacramento, California, was in the lead of the lumbering column. He was first to reach the rim of the clearing.

Retreat was impossible. Duane rolled his armored mount into the clearing where the field of fire was good. Through mirror sights he watched his shells pound into the enemy position. One of the guns fell silent. Other Jap guns belched flames through their disguise. Duane fixed their position in his memory. Then his periscope was shot out and he saw nothing. The blinded tank-destroyer's steel hide rang under a tattoo of bullets.

Duane maneuvered his mount into a bamboo thicket. He jumped out and borrowed a periscope from a rearward machine. Soon he was ready again for action. He led the other tank-destroyers into the clearing. His fire pointed out to them a cluster of hidden enemy nests. Before the destroyer men called it a day they had destroyed five gun emplacements and killed most of their crews. Survivors were seen fleeing through the *kunai*.

From then on the defenders of the roadblock were given no rest. Batteries of heavy mortars were packed forward at dusk. All through the night to October 22 they lobbed demolition shells onto the Jap fortifications. Ammunition carriers worked their hearts to pieces.

At sunrise the men of the Nineteenth Infantry fixed bayonets and stormed. Their assault overran the strongpoints. Two hundred and seventy-six killed enemies were counted. Sergeant Emanuel Weixelman of St. George, Kansas, led the bayonet charge.

On the heels of the infantry the Divisions Combat Engineers moved in to clear the beach road. Debris, mines, traps, log barricades and corpses were pushed out of the way. And soon the first supply convoy rolled inland in the wake of an armored bulldozer.

In the supply train was an amphibious tank manned by Rade Allen and "Andy" Sapp. Allen came from Ft. Worth, Sapp from Belleville, Illinois. As they crossed the Palo-Tacloban highway, an infantry officer jumped from a thicket and waved them to a halt. Would the "Alligator" be willing to rescue some wounded soldiers up front before they would be killed by the Japs?

"Sure," said Sapp and Allen.

The wounded men, they were told, lay in an area covered by enemy fire. To get to the spot, the amphibious tank would have to travel more than a thousand yards along the Palo highway. Enemy troops still infested marshes to both sides of the road. Rade Allen and Andy Sapp looked at each other.

Their machine clambered to the highway. The Japs did their utmost to stop it. For a thousand yards the "Alligator" lumbered down the road as fast as its tracks would move, its gun spouting fire forward and right and left, "strafing ditches, native houses and machinegun positions parallel to the highway, killing untold numbers of the enemy and demoralizing more" (quoted from a field report).

All went well until a lone Japanese leaped from a ditch and hurled a mine under the vehicle's track. The tractor stopped.

In the wrecked "Alligator's" belly the men were dazed from the explosion. Again Sapp and Allen looked at one another, and each saw that the other was wounded. They tried the engines. The tractor was dead. Through the narrow sight slots they saw the Japs close in. They tried the gun. It worked.

Three hundred yards away Lieutenant Haskel P. Miller of Wichita, Kansas, saw an amphibious tank blasted by a mine on the Palo road. He also saw a swarm of Japanese circling like wolves around an elk at bay.

Miller, leader of a machinegun platoon, acted speedily. First he directed the fire of his guns upon the Japs nearest to the crippled machine. Then he organized a party of ten men in a sortie to reach the beleaguered tractor. But sudden machinegun fire forced him to abandon the attempt.

He called for mortar fire to neutralize the Jap machinegun nest. He also called for another amphibious tank to rescue the still battling crew of its disabled brother. As the second "Alligator" clattered down the highway, the lieutenants machineguns protected its advance. The rescue became a success, and the road was cleared.

But soon another column was treading the restless highway to Palo. This time it was a ragged procession of thousands of brown men, women and children. Flanking it were silent Yanks who cleared the way by potting snipers as the caravan trod on.

On crowded Red Beach the new problem was created by the steady influx of civilian refugees. When the invasion began, the native populace had fled to the hills, away from bombs and naval cannonade. This migration was reversed as the fighting moved inland. Refuge on the still sniper-ridden beachhead seemed a smaller evil than existence among artillery barrages and mobs of exasperated Japanese.

The first civilians had begun to filter through the fighting lines onto the beachhead shortly after noon of the day of the invasion. On the morning of October 21 their number grew by leaps and bounds. They arrived in decrepit hordes, denizens of drowsing *barrios* suddenly overtaken by the juggernaut of war, led by a bare-legged patriarch. Many were ill with the afflictions of the tropics, with malaria, skin sores and wounds that had long refused to heal. Ever since the Japanese had come these people had been without medicines.

Most of the refugees carried all their possessions on their backs, or in bulging bundles atop their heads. Their expressions were a mixture of fear, fatalism and smiles. By nightfall there were thousands. A child was born on the beach in the shelter of a bulldozer blade—a husky boy.

To Colonel Alva C. Carpenter of Ft. Wayne, Indiana, the Divisions judge advocate, fell the task of caring for the charivari throng. He procured and distributed rations. He formed the men into labor gangs and set them to building an enclosure, to digging fresh water wells and latrines, and to burying the enemy dead in shallow common graves. He also set up an emergency dispensary to care for the sick. He corraled stray children and made efforts to locate their parents. He listened to countless anxious questions concerning wives, daughters, babies, and grandmothers lost in the melee of battle.

By October 22—the third day of the invasion—the crowds on the weirdly congested beach became so dense that any Japanese artillery or air attack would have resulted in hideous slaughter. Rumors were at large that Nippon's navy had come out of hiding to fight, that battleships and cruisers had been seen prowling in the Sibuyan and Sulu seas, that the Japs were steaming on in full force to blast the Americans off the Philippines. Colonel Carpenter decided to move the refugees off the beach and into Palo.

Squads of riflemen took the lead. Following them was an almost naked ten-year-old boy singing "God Bless America." Then came the silent procession of the homeless. Nearly all were bare-footed. Many of the women wore camisoles made of coconut fiber. Others wore pieces of uniform they had found on the beach. One slender young woman was decked out in flashing Spanish finery, her other valuables balanced on her head, the hem of her flowing red silk skirt trailing about small and muddy ankles. Bundles of Army rations dangled from bobbing bamboo poles. Most of the men carried bolo knives in wooden sheaths tucked in the waistbands of their shorts.

Interspersed with men from the Division's finance section, who acted as guides, the caravan trudged up the rutted beach road. As the head of the column passed the junction of this track with the Palo highway, Jap snipers opened fire. The threat of panic was quickly quelled. The refugees dispersed and huddled in the ditches. Flanking patrols destroyed the snipers.

Infantrymen had a hard time preventing natives from picking up Jap uniforms and equipment strewn along the highway. These baits had been wired, and the wires led to mines. The procession entered Palo and assembled under the statue of Christ on the town square where the mayor relayed instructions. Young Filipino volunteers were sent off to spy behind enemy lines. All others were locked into the church. The gnarled sexton ascended the tower and again the bells rang over Palo.

Around the tight churchyard perimeter the men were tense. There was continuous sniping in the streets and alleys of Palo during the early part of the night to October 22. The purpose of this harassing fire was to keep the Americans from resting; to have them drowsy with fatigue when the hour of the night surprise assault would be at hand.

On the verandah of the stone-and-tile municipal building stood Colonel Spragins. With him was Captain Bridgforth, of Yazoo City, Mississippi; short, slim, a hundredweight of human dynamite. On the wall behind them hung tattered Japanese posters announcing a "victory" dance to be held on the Palo town square that very night. It was 11 P.M. The sky was covered with clouds. The night was sultry and pitch black. Over the radio Bridgforth called the Thirteenth Field Artillery Battalion on the beach. He asked for artillery fire on all principal roads leading into town. Three hundred and fifty shells pounded the roads to Santa Fe and San Joaquin in the course of the night, blocking their use to enemy reinforcements.

Exactly at midnight the earth trembled from the blast of a major explosion. A pillar of flames mushroomed over the west section of Palo. Someone—Jap or guerilla—had set fire to a house full of Japanese ammunition. A flood of prancing glows and weaving shadows filled the outlying streets. The waiting men on the perimeter were content. The blaze cast bizarre yet helpful light into the irregular complex of buildings facing the battalions outposts. Hours passed and nothing happened.

The enemy struck at 0330. He carried machineguns in his most forward echelons. He also carried mortars, grenades, mines and fixed bayonets. His assault groups moved boldly toward the church of Palo. At a rapid pace the Japanese advanced along the streets, hugging the decrepit houses, rushing through alleys and back yards, silent, still holding their fire.

From the shelter of their shallow foxholes Louis Diaz of Amarillo, Texas, and his two companions saw them come. There was a group of five, very close, lunging out of a clump of banana trees. Diaz fired. The Japanese returned the fire as they rushed. Between shots from the hip they tossed grenades. One of Diaz' companions was killed. He died swiftly. The other was seriously wounded. Three of the attackers had fallen.

Diaz pushed aside the body of his comrade and stood upright in the foxhole. In the reddish glow of the burning ammunition dump he saw two remaining Japs pounce forward. Diaz squeezed the trigger in lightning succession. The yelling became a gurgle and a sob. The Japs tumbled. They kicked wildly at the edge of the foxhole. Diaz fired until their kicking stopped.

The whole town was in an uproar. The battalion outposts met the raiders with a murderous volume of fire. At one corner of the church square two machineguns led by Sergeant Vernon Drake of Fletcher, North Carolina, sprayed bullets down streets where Japs swarmed like harpies on a rampage. The snarling shower of lead did not deflect the attackers from their purpose. They mounted mortars on an intersection two blocks distant. Soon the high explosive "pears" plummeted out of the night. Drake's gunners were compelled to seek cover. The Japanese assault teams had vanished and Vernon Drake saw that the street ahead lay empty.

Somewhere in the row of native dwellings a dog barked. The barking turned into agonized yelps. Drake realized that the Japanese had darted into the buildings. They were making their way to the churchyard in house-to-house dashes. The clamor of a machinegun proved his guess correct. The nearest dwellings, less than thirty feet away, seethed with Japs.

Drake felt as if someone had struck him on the head with a hammer. A machinegun slug had found its mark. Dazed, and blinded by blood, he rallied his section. "Fire!" he shouted. "For Christ's sake, fire." Now his own machineguns roared, ripping into the houses across the dusty lane. Their muzzle blasts close to his head all but tore his ears away. The Japanese attempted a headlong rush across the street. Drake's crew threw them back. With morning, thirty-odd Japanese corpses lay within a radius of ten yards from Drake's position.

Forward artillery observers working from the roofs and windows of buildings drew in the curtain of fire laid by the Divisions Field Artillery to within a hundred yards of the town square perimeter. This wrought havoc among concentrations of Japanese under orders to break the American hold on Palo; but the violence of the concussions jolted the battalion's forward elements from their niches. In the vault-like gloom of the church the explosions reverberated like thunder rolling beneath the surface of the earth. Few slept, among the thousands. Bullets shattered the stained-glass windows. In the stench of cooped-up and fearful humanity children cried, a woman went insane, and another baby was born. Under the effigies of the saints couples mated, heedless of the storm. Their sighs mingled with the sounds of many mumbled prayers and the clatter of machineguns, and a priest's somber voice read mass in the tomblike darkness.

A bare hundred yards from the church, a platoon of Japanese charged a machinegun manned by Jerry Lanik. Jerry's fire drove one section of his assailants to the cover of a pile of boxes. From there they fired and flung grenades. Lanik knew that the boxes contained ammunition. Unable to reach the enemy, he poured tracer bullets into the pile until the whole thing erupted into flames. With a cloud of debris Jap heads, arms and legs were hurled into the brilliantly illuminated night. Then Lanik doubled-up under the impact of a snipers bullet.

The house under which his machinegun was mounted caught fire. The flames threatened to engulf Jerry Lanik. Scorched and wounded he fought on until a Jap sprang from a window and threw a grenade. Lanik was mortally wounded.

Nearby lay Private James B. Bagley, the assistant gunner. He, too, had been wounded by rifle fire and grenades. At home, in Kokomo, Indiana, his wife Rosalie prayed for his return. Amid devastation, fire and death he remained with his gun. About him the remnants of the Jap platoon darted like frenzied gnomes. Bagley fired until he became too weak from loss of blood to manage the machinegun's mechanism. He crawled a little way off and continued to defend his gun with his rifle.

The night fracas for Palo lasted through almost four hours. One repulse did not daunt the suicidal obsession of the attackers. Three times they rushed the town from the south and west, and one Banzai assault struck from the direction of the beachhead against the Palo River bridge. Japs popped in and out of houses fronting the church. They swirled in shouting eddies about the courthouse which served as a hospital for the many wounded. From a window Colonel Spragins directed the battle. In the glow of fires and the flashes of bursting mortar shells his unruffled presence and his close-cropped mustache remained a reassuring landmark. He disappeared from the window when shrapnel slashed his forehead. But minutes later, bandaged, he was back again on the job.

Somewhere in the square below the colonel a B.A.R. gunner emptied magazine after magazine into the Japanese onslaught. And suddenly the gunners automatic rifle jammed. The men of his squad were falling back. A burly Jap came in, lunging in the van of the attackers, howling "Banzai," a saber in one fist, a grenade in the other.

The gunner slipped his hands down the barrel of his jammed automatic rifle. He, too, was howling, for the red-hot barrel of the weapon badly seared his hands. All the same, he rushed out of the perimeter and pounded the howling Jap to death. This was the high-water mark of the attack.

This gunner's name?—Private First Class Jesse W. Martin of Dunbar, Kentucky.

The streets of Palo seemed peaceful enough during the hours of daylight, not counting occasional snipers. More refugees arrived. There were now more than five thousand crammed into the church. On street corners and in the shelter of trucks soldiers sat, digging food from ration cans, their rifles within reach and ready for instant action. Others, not on guard or on patrol, stripped in abandoned houses and doused themselves with helmets full of water. Still others slept in and under vehicles, in doorways and backyards, and in the shade of banana and hibiscus.

In the church square a dumpy guerilla counted a fistful of Japanese ears. Aid men made the rounds, distributing atabrine and tablets for the purification of water used for drinking. The wounded were evacuated to the beach. Around a broken water main Filipino women squatted, washing uniforms in exchange for soap. Gangs of native laborers were put to work, clearing away the debris of battle and burying the dead. From the streets and alleys of Palo they collected more than one hundred Japanese corpses, and there was evidence that many others had been dragged away. Thin columns of smoke rose in the distance to the west, where the Japs cremated their salvaged dead.

(Funerals are the only religious ceremonies known to Jap soldiers in the field. They dig a large hole and fill it with kindling. They place their dead on this bed of kindling and heap more wood around them and on top of them. Then a Japanese officer makes a speech. He addresses the corpses as though they were still alive. He praises their courage and promotes them to a higher rank. When he is finished he bows to the killed. Soldiers soak the pyre with gasoline and then stand at attention, bayonets fixed. The officer throws a torch onto the pile of wood, and when the flames spring up each soldier silently files by and bows.)

Artillery growled in the surrounding hills. The dull crack of grenades punctuated the afternoon. An officer walking alone through the outskirts to meet a supply convoy rolling in from Red Beach spotted two Japs prowling by the roadside. They had cut through the trunk of a large tree and they were about to stretch a wire from this tree to a point across the highway. Any truck colliding with this wire would cause the tree to fall. The officer whipped up his carbine. He shot one Jap, and the other surrendered. The American took no chances: he forced the captured Jap to strip, then marched him naked into Palo.

Night fell.

When the Division's 52nd Field Artillery Battalion moved into Palo and set up its guns, its men thought that they had come unobserved by the foe. But suddenly a shell burst to their immediate front, another to their rear. They knew then that an enemy observer could not be far away. "Bracketing" the cannoneers' positions with one short and one long round was his method of marking the spot for the benefit of Jap gunners. As a result the artillery battalion did not fire that night, but moved away under cover of darkness.

A half hour before midnight Sergeant Charles Taylor of Desha, Arkansas, in charge of a tank-destroyer, saw a squad of Japanese dart across a road into the shelter of a group of bamboo huts. Somehow this enemy team had managed to filter through the outer defenses. The sergeant waited. Soon he heard the Japs emerge from the shacks. He saw them advance in a low-crouched run. Some carried bulky bundles on their backs. Their job was demolition.

Taylor opened fire with a sub-machinegun. Two of the marauders fell, the rest scattered. But soon snipers' bullets whined past him, and other Japs who had wriggled in under cover of an adjacent first aid station lobbed grenades. The sergeant ducked the fragments. Presently a lone Jap dashed toward the self-propelled gun. This enemy carried something that looked like a heavy box.

There were three tons of ammunition and one hundred and eighty gallons of gasoline aboard the tank-destroyer. The Arkansan rushed to protect his weapon. He overtook the Jap less than three feet from his cannon and killed him. The box, he found, contained dynamite fused with a hand grenade.

A number of native huts were then burned down to open lanes of fire and to deprive the enemy of concealment. Although the Filipino populace was kept secure in the church, packed there as tight as herrings in a barrel, refugees continued to stream into town, and there was no way of stopping them. But two figures in women's clothes dodging past guards at the Palo River bridge turned out to be Japanese soldiers; both were shot to death. An enemy bombing raid set an ammunition dump ablaze. Rain fell in intermittent showers and soon became a steady torrent. Four days went by before the town and its link to Red Beach could be completely secured.

On a dark, wet night Private Charles Scott of Marengo, Iowa, on guard near the center of the beach perimeter, heard a steady tapping sound in a nearby palm grove. To the right of him was a field hospital, to his left the kitchen of the 13th Field Artillery. The strange tapping continued. The soldier investigated. He found a lone figure beating a palm trunk with a stick.

"Hey!" shouted the guard. "Crazy?"

The murky figure continued its tapping. Against an opening in the foliage the soldier saw the outline of a Japanese helmet. He raised his rifle and fired. The Jap fell.

Then all was quiet again.

Rifles cracked at 0130. An infiltration party had broken into the kitchen and hospital area. Their tree-tapping comrade's job had been to reveal the location of the guards. A cannoneer asleep in a trailer was killed. Another American groping his way through darkness and confusion met sudden death. Several wounded men in the field hospital were hit by Jap bullets. The raiders then leaped on a truck parked near the kitchen tent and ran amuck in the dark. Mounted on the truck was a heavy American machinegun. For an hour the Japs sprayed the artillery bivouac with American bullets. From all sides the surprised artillerymen returned the fire with pistols and carbines. Little could be seen in the pitch-blackness except a chaos of red muzzle flashes. Aid man Angelo Volpe, a native of Australia, crossed and re-crossed the firing zone on hands and knees, helping the wounded. Finally the machinegun jammed. The raiders dispersed and vanished in the swamps. Five dead Japanese were found at dawn, their eyes staring blind into the rain. In the artillery kitchen the cooks found every pot and pan riddled by bullets. And an officer commented drily that henceforth the cannoneers should fix bayonets on their cannon.

The finale of Nippon's farewell to Palo came in a bold and wily thrust.

Colonel Spragins' battalion had been relieved by the Third Battalion of the Nineteenth Regiment in the occupation and defense of Palo. "King" Company's riflemen had pushed southward two miles to San Joaquin.*

There they had encountered wicked resistance from concrete strongpoints, anti-tank cannon and log barricades; behind a curtain of naval gunfire they had withdrawn to Palo. Sentinels were posted at approaches and intersections. Weary soldiers curled up to sleep along the church walls, beneath verandahs and on floors of abandoned shacks. For the first time in five days these men took off their boots. The password was "Lullaby."†

Along trails winding through *kunai* grass and down brush-covered hillsides Japanese patrols lurked silently. Refugee families treading the dark trails in their endeavor to reach the security of American lines found themselves waylaid. Japs jumped from the undergrowth and halted the pilgrims. Women wailed and children whimpered.

"Keep quiet," they were told. "Come with us."

Here and there a man drew his bolo knife to defend his women. He was quickly bayoneted. Here and there a Filipino mother stepped forward intent on saving her daughter from hurt "Take me, Japanese, if you must."

The Japs laughed.

"This way!" they said. "We kill you if you make one sound." At bayonet point the natives were herded downhill. They reached a jungle-clad gully. Many more natives were there. All around them, hovering in compact groups, were Japanese soldiers. The Japs sat in the darkness, their arms clasped around their knees and hugging their long-barreled rifles. At times there was the faint scraping of a helmet rim against a rifle barrel, and then there was a hiss demanding silence. Officers moving among the huddled groups whispered instructions.

---

* Purpose of fierce Jap resistance at San Joaquin was to prevent the 24th Division from joining contact with the XXIV Corps which had invaded Leyte Island farther to the south. At that time the 24th Division had already established contact with the 1st Cavalry Division which had landed to the north, near Tacloban.

† Many Japanese are able to speak English but are unable to pronounce the Anglo-American "l."

CHURCH BELLS RING IN PALO

The sheaths of their sabers swished in the wet grass.

What did they whisper?

"We shall penetrate the town of Palo as a spear penetrates a stomach. We shall carry mines, grenades and demolition charges. We shall fire the buildings and the vehicles. We shall kill the guards and slice into the town square. We shall slice through the town until we come to the bridge. We shall blow this bridge to block the Americans' supplies. Then we shall disperse. Each squad will seek to return on its own."

Then a captain addressed the Filipinos cowering there in frightened clusters:

"We have good use for you. You shall be our advance guard and our shield. You shall lead us into Palo, a cushion against Yankee bullets."

The captain in charge of the assault team was a swarthy man with short legs and powerful shoulders. His Samurai sword had a pearl-and-ivory handle and a sheath of delicately carved leather—fishes, flowers, and a geisha with a smile and a fan. He tapped his sword. It was the signal to proceed. Kicks and bayonets prodded the civilians into the lead.

At 3 A.M. the Division's guards heard a mass of people approach them from the southwest. A flare swished toward the clouds, fleetingly illuminating the scene.

"Holy smoke," a gunner muttered, "look at that."

What he saw was a mass of unarmed people, men, women and children crowding the road, shoulder to shoulder. In the white glare of the flare their faces were like masks. Their arms hung limply and their feet lagged as if with great fatigue. Then the flare went out and it was darker than before.

Indistinct cries drifted through the night: 'The Japanese have driven us away from San Joaquin."

"Don't shoot, please . . . Filipinos."

And a hoarse bark:

"Me guerilla . . . Me guerilla."

The guards held their fire. A thin shape detached itself from the steadily advancing crowd. It sprinted frenziedly toward the American outposts. The guards sent up another flare. They saw that the runner was a native boy, his face distorted with fear and exertion. His thin voice cried piercingly, "Shoot, shoot, Japs, Japs."

Still the gunners held their fire. God damn it to hell, could they massacre a miserable lot of civilians? The native boy sprinted through the outpost line, shouting, "Shoot! Japs," until he fell in an exhausted heap. Then it was too late. Like phantoms from a nether-world the

Japanese broke through their mask. A squat, short-legged fellow in their van swung a Samurai sword. They killed all the guards except one. This lone survivor rushed through the town to alert the sleepers and the units stationed around the Palo River bridge.

Boldly the raiders broke into the town square. They overran a section of heavy machineguns in front of the courthouse. They captured an anti-tank cannon. They attached a mine to a tank-destroyer and blew it up. Two soldiers guarding a quartermaster supply dump were overpowered and killed. The raiders poured gasoline into the dump and set it ablaze. Men awaking from sleep were baffled by the absence of the familiar "Banzai" yelling.

The Japanese worked with a cold and ferocious efficiency.

They swept across the town toward the Palo River bridge, spreading havoc on the way. They mounted captured machineguns on captured trucks and sent sprays of bullets across the town square. A Jap squatting under the statue of Christ sent tracer bullets ripping into buildings from the muzzle of an American gun. An ammunition dump burst into flames, a loaded truck was burning, a jeep was blown to bits, a dozen other vehicles were mauled by flying lead. Japs surged around an emergency hospital full of wounded men. A squad of raiders armed with knives raced from truck to truck, slashing tires. Of twelve men guarding the approaches to the bridge all but three were killed or wounded. A drawn-out moan of despair arose from the crowded church. The bells of Palo rang as if in a storm of pain.

Gradually the defenders found their bearings. A platoon of engineers took charge of the far end of the bridge. Negro quartermasters, angered by their rude awakening and the burning of their trucks, reached for pistols and pitched in. Infantrymen stumbled from their resting places, half dressed and fighting mad. Lt. Col. George H. Chapman, the regimental commander, found his command post in the municipal building raked by machinegun fire. He stepped to a window and saw a bevy of Japs attacking twenty yards away. He summoned the headquarters clerks and messengers and linemen and transformed the building into a fortress. Firing from windows, the colonel and his crew accounted for twenty of the attackers.

Private Denoff, a quartermaster, awoke and smelled smoke. He soaked his blanket in a water bag, and ran to smother the fire. On the way he clubbed a Jap to death with his carbine. Wladyslaw Swarter of Wilmington, Delaware, protected Colonel Chapman who strode through the melee to investigate the situation at the bridge. A sniper made the colonel his target. Swarter saw a comrade shot at the river's edge; rushing forward he saw a Jap leap up and vanish behind a wall.

Heedless of other enemies nearby, Swarter hurdled the wall in pursuit of the sniper. The Jap suddenly stopped, faced his pursuer with a snarl. Swarter shot him through the head.

Sergeant George Nieman of Detroit, and Corporal Eugene Holdeness of Noxapater, Mississippi, were blinded with sweat while they defended their self-propelled howitzer against assaults which struck them simultaneously from several sides. Their weapon was mounted in front of a wooden building which served as an emergency hospital. Down the street some eighty Japanese attacked with grenades and fire from a captured American gun. As they approached in house-to-house dashes they hurled jugs filled with gasoline. Flames enveloped the howitzer and Sergeant Nieman was wounded. Forced to abandon their mount, the two Americans dodged into a muddy alley.

"Look!" said Holdeness.

The Japs were about to set the hospital afire.

"Let's go," said Nieman.

They climbed into an adjoining house and reached the upstairs windows. Nieman carried a carbine, Holdeness a tommy-gun. The raiders saw them and broke into a weird howl. The rat-a-tat of machinegun slugs splintered the window frames. Holdeness and Nieman did not budge. Through the rippling of the tommygun sounded the quick crack of the carbine. The Japs gave it up as a bad job. They roved on down the street toward the bridge, leaving eight of their comrades in a bloody tangle at the hospital threshold.

Home-bred initiative of individual Americans was the decisive factor in the repulse of this last foray into Palo. The monstrous intermingling of skirmishers allowed for no co-ordinated defense. You fought, and your comrade, making your own decisions, or you died. When an ammunition dump exploded fifty yards from his position, Artilleryman Charles Mott of Wichita, Kansas, rushed into the heat and carried a wounded comrade out of enemy reach. (The Japs gave wounded men the bayonet and a kick in the face, just to make sure.) Or take Corporal Nickerson of Mercer, Maine, another cannoneer. When the stores of explosives caught fire, he withdrew his section a hundred yards; but immediately after the explosion he rushed his men back into their old positions to meet the Jap onset.

Their toughest antagonist the Japs found in Frank Wisnieuski. They had scattered and pushed to the rear the riflemen assigned to protect an American machinegun emplacement. They had badly wounded the gunner, and the gunner had dragged himself to cover. There remained only Wisnieuski, the assistant gunner.

On they came, with light machineguns, rifles, grenades and

bayonets, thirty against one. They were almost on top of him. Wisnieuski said later that he did not expect to come out of it alive. He stayed there and fired. Two grenades fell directly in front of his hole. A third grenade plopped inside.

Wisnieuski jumped out of his hole as the grenade exploded. He dived back into his hole, struggled to righten his battered gun. Would the thing still fire? He did not know.

Above him, sinewy silhouettes against a gloomy sky, two enemies, bayonets down, plunged in for the kill. Wisnieuski pressed the trigger of his upset gun. It fired. His assailants tumbled like ripe fruit.

At dawn the lone gunner counted. There were twenty dead Japanese in front of his foxhole. A little way off, not far from the portals of the church, lay the body of a Jap captain. He had a swarthy face, short legs and powerful shoulders. Beneath him the ground was purplish-black. "The ugliest Nip I ever saw," a passing soldier said, and spat.

In a room of the municipal building a young man stood up, stretched, yawned, then crawled under a table and fell asleep. He was the headquarters telephone operator. While the tattoo of machinegun slugs knocked plaster from walls and ceilings, Private Bill Malzahn of Flint, Michigan, had stayed at his switchboard. During the hours of the raid he had received eight requests for artillery support from other areas of the disconnected front.

So, peace came to Palo. Throngs emerged from the church. People blinked as though they had never before set eyes on their town. Soldiers leisurely searched the pockets of enemy killed for loot and there was the smell of fresh coffee mingling with the foul smell of death. Children begged for chewing gum and grown-ups for cigarettes. Here and there an intelligence man rummaged for documents. And a tawny policeman nailed up two signs which said,

'The Chief of Police of Palo wishes all People to know that the Police Station is not a Morgue. Cadavers are NOT to be deposited There";

and,

"Ceiling Prices for GI Laundry:
Pants, 25 centavos
Shirts, 15 centavos
Socks, 5 centavos
Violators will be punished."

Chapter Six

COMMOTION IN THE HILLS

"The signal for the attack was to be the waving of a white handkerchief.... Some difficulty was experienced in finding a white handkerchief, but a search finally brought forth one still light grayish in color."

(from the Division Record)

HIS NAME IS FRED PALMER, but before we finished with the hot jumble of hills between the beachhead and the Santa Fe Trail* we had dubbed him "Waterboy." He has the neck and shoulders of a Greek god and the arms of a stevedore. His job is that of a first scout. A first scout, as everyone knows, is the man between whom and the waiting enemy lies nothing but no-man's-land and his own alertness.

The platoon lay isolated on a flat-topped hill. It was kept down by enemy machinegun fire from higher ridges in front. Only sparse grass covered the plateau, which measured some two hundred yards from edge to edge. Steep slopes matted with high jungle grass fell off into brush-choked gullies three hundred feet below. A scourge of snipers hovered on the hillsides and in the shadowy ravines. From three sides sniper fire commanded every square yard of the plateau.

All night the platoon had been there, and most of the following day. For ten hours the men had gone without water. The sun blazed on their helmets. The steel became too hot to touch. Some men tried to chew grass, but their tongues felt swollen and numb. It was as if invisible hands shoved quantities of sand down unwilling throats. There was little ammunition left, and less food. But minds kept clawing at the thought of water—of a spoonful of water, of a shady pond, of rivulets and cataracts foaming from the mountains. Peculiar how a soldier's thirst becomes as big as a house as soon as he knows that his canteen

---

* Soldiers dubbed the main highway leading through Leyte Valley the "Santa Fe Trail" because of the town of Santa Fe which is located along this road.

is empty. A man crawled fifty yards for a coconut and was killed. The nearest water was four hundred yards away.

"Hell," said Fred Palmer, "I'll go."

Across the killing zone between the foxholes he crept, thrusting his hundred and ninety pounds of bone and muscle across the open ground, face low and the rim of his helmet scraping the grass. Bullets from a neighboring ridge slapped the earth five yards to his left. Palmer crawled on.

Someone bawled: ""Get back in your damn hole, you're drawing fire."

Palmer turned sideways. His face was dripping.

"Hand me your canteens," he said.

"Christ, what a fool," the others thought.

Palmer collected the canteens. Then he moved away, dragging with him the cluster of containers. The Japs saw him go and their bullets seared the grass. The platoon replied angrily to give Palmer a chance.

He crossed the plateau in short rushes. Then he hugged the ground, rolled a few yards to dodge the snipers₁ shots, and lay still until the firing stopped. After that he jumped up again for another quick rush. The canteens rattled as he ran. Little fountains of dust danced upward inches from his feet, or so it looked. He reached the edge of the plateau and plunged down the slope and out of sight.

"Good guy—Palmer," the others said, never expecting to see him again.

An hour later Palmer returned. The crackling of rifles on the hillside signaled his return. The platoon could hear his panting a hundred yards off. He crossed the fire-raked plateau at a dog-trot. No rushes this time. The platoon sprayed the slopes to keep the snipers down. Palmer kept coming.

"Waterboy! Waterboy!"

In a flat voice an officer said, "Magnificent."

Past snipers' nests, up three hundred feet of rough hillside, across two hundred yards of death-ridden open terrain, and under a graceless sun, Palmer brought on ten gallons of water, one case of grenades and two cases of rifle ammunition.

There was another soldier who said *"I'll go,"* when the going was really tough in the hills around Palo. None of us will ever forget how he quietly gave up his life to save the life of his squad. His name was Wilber and he came from Maine. He was the type who liked to dream in the shade over a can of beer.

The squad had pushed ahead of the line and ran into trouble. There was a steep crest above them and below them was a reeking swamp. Jap machineguns jabbered from hidden dugouts and bullets whipped through the brush. And when the jabber ceased, counter-attack began. Three times in succession they tried to overrun the squad. Some came like cats. Others ran in shouting, grenade-heaving packs.

The squad lay in shallow trenches and fired. With them was Wilber. A mass migration of ants traversed the rottenness under the thickets. Ants crawled into the rifle sights, into the sleeves and over the faces of the men. One man groaned, clawing at a fragment of grenade in his neck; another died, a bullet through his mouth. After the third attack had been thrown back, the squad leader said, "Check ammunition."

Voices: "Three rounds."

"All broke."

"Two clips."

A cry: "Aid man—aid man."

Between bursts from a machinegun a Jap voice yelled, "Charlie, how are you? Oh, Charlie, you listen? By-and-by we kill you. Don't worry, Charlie."

No aid man, no grenades, and ammunition running low. The squad leader looted the belts of the corpses. He evenly distributed their meager yield. "Redistribution of ammunition." That's what the Field Manual on Infantry Tactics said. Four rounds for each man in addition to the rounds in his receiver. Wilber pulled back the bolt of his Garand. One cartridge in the chamber, one left in the clip. No more.

"I'll go," he said.

He tossed his two cartridges to the man nearest to him in the skirmish line. The other took the ammunition without thanks. The man from Maine rolled out of his slit trench and away, then darted off crabwise on hands and toes. The strike of Jap bullets marked his course along the edge of the swamp. He was on his feet now. Bent low, he ran, his face almost touching his knees. A bullet slugged his helmet, glanced. Wilber went into a somersault. Then he ran on, bareheaded, and the others waited.

Nine minutes passed. The squad was silent. Watchful, scared and glum. There was a rustling in the undergrowth up the slope, but no one fired. No one said, "Please God, let Wilber come back before they attack."

He came. Crouched low he was running along the rim of the swamp, and then he veered to scramble up the incline. He was going slower now, straddle-legged and heavy, like a woman with child. Bandoleers of ammunition dangled from his arms. More bandoleers hung round his neck.

The squad saw him. The enemy saw him, too. He hunched his shoulders for the last desperate spurt.

"Atta boy!"

Up on the crest a machinegun coughed. Wilber fell. He cried out and then he died. But someone crawled over and got the bandoleers.

The hills fringing the coastal plain of Leyte Gulf had twofold importance for the Japanese defenders of the Philippines. They were an excellent base from which to conduct forays into the beachhead and the town of Palo; and they were natural bastions flanking the highway into the Leyte Valley. Troops of the 16th Japanese Division, the onetime conquerors of Bataan, were told to hold these hills until General Yamashita could receive reinforcements from Mindanao and Luzon. Hold on they did through five bitter days.

The maps showed three hills: Hill 522, Hill "Baker" and Hill "Charlie." But the maps were wrong. "Baker" and "Charlie" turned out to be not simple hills, but massive heights topped by a jumble of ridges and knobs not discernible from the beach. Where the map showed blank spots, infantrymen found walls of jungle, thickets of head-high *kunai* grass, boulders and bushy snipers' roosts blanketing back-breaking inclines. Among the new discoveries were "Hill Baker One," "Hill Nan," "Bakers Pimple," "Hill 85," "Hill Mike," and "Hill 331" whose ridges spread like the fingers of an enormous hand. The storming of each cost agony and lives.

On Hill 522 the men of Colonel Zierath's battalion went without sleep and food for several days. The tunnels through the rock beneath their feet were full of Japs. Pillboxes silenced in the initial assault on the crest persisted in coming back to life. Japs crawled back into the wreckage during the night and resumed the fight at dawn. Captain William Herman of "Baker" Company called for artillery fire to smash the strongpoints anew. Then infantry attacked with TNT and cold steel. Fifty Japanese were killed and the remainder were driven into the Palo River.

Weary of being hungry and marooned on Hill 522, Private Angelo Mantini of Kittanning, Pennsylvania, a shoemaker in civilian life, scurried toward Red Beach in quest of food. Halfway down the hill he discovered five snipers who had ambushed a carrying party. Mantini decided that no Nip should prevent him from filling his belly. He killed all five and loaded himself with their weapons. Among the captured weapons was an American automatic rifle. Five minutes earlier, the Division commander, General Irving, had passed the scene of the encounter. The snipers, intent on wiping out the carrying detail, had let the general pass unscathed.

Another soldier set out to capture a Samurai sword. In inky darkness he blundered into an ambush and then lost his way in a swamp. Japs were all around him. For twenty-four hours the soldier played at being dead. American mortar shells plastering the enemy hideouts burst dangerously close to the man who played 'possum. A fragment hit him in the arm. He buried himself in the mire up to his face. But the mortar bursts continued to creep toward him. "It'd be hell for Aldia if she ever learned I died that way," the soldier thought. "If I have to get killed, let it be a Jap." He wept and prayed. He floundered out of the swamp and ran. Japanese machinegun slugs pierced both his legs. But his comrades found him, and as he was carried to the rear, a young soldier, grimy and taciturn, stepped up and laid a Jap saber on the wounded man's stretcher.

The enemy on Hill 522 had many automatic weapons. Eight heavy machineguns were captured there, and four mortars, but most of their weapons the Japanese had dragged into the tunnels. For days on end a grim drama was enacted at the tunnel entrances. Flame-throwers burned out many a holed-up Jap. A favorite method of tackling the tunnels was to cover up the vents and air shafts, then toss phosphorous grenades into the tunnels. The scorched and choked defenders dashed out into broad daylight. Infantrymen stationed above the tunnel mouths mowed them down.

Each night, when our infantry sat tight and silent, it was the enemy's turn to attack. The Japanese slipped out of the tunnels. Here and there an American was killed by the screaming, grenade-throwing bands. On one occasion fourteen Japs attacked two hundred riflemen; the halloo of such lunacy stopped only after the last of the Banzai-men had been killed. Later that same night thirteen Japanese charged like hooting revelers, firing machineguns and brandishing spears and clubs. They, too, were killed. Then eight other Japanese advanced in single file behind a light machinegun, swaying and chanting as they came. All eight were killed, and other Japs dragged the cadavers into the tunnels. "Dammit, when do we sleep?" asked the irate men in the platoons.

The tunnels of Hill 522 were finally silenced on the sixth day. Their entrances were blasted down with dynamite and blocked with boulders and logs. The inmates of the tunnels were left to commit suicide or to starve. Sounds of eerie ceremonies filtered from the bowels of the volcanic height. The Japanese who dies for his remote Emperor earns a place in the Yasukuni Shrine and is promoted one rank; if the battle is deemed important, he is promoted two ranks, provided he is dead.

No Japanese prisoners were taken. Jap wounded were killed.

"Now we sleep," the infantrymen growled.

They were mistaken. It is difficult to judge the size of an attack in the dark. When nerves are taut the rustling of a hog or monkey in the sword grass is enough to make every man on the perimeter blaze away, and every man is awake. This last night four Japanese penetrated the battalion defenses and suddenly charged the command post. Guards killed three of them, and the lone survivor scuttled off into the night and was never found.

The fight for the precipitous ridges of Hill 331 was a different matter. No race to the top here, but a slow, dogged ascent, first through vile jungles, then through *kunai* grass, and finally through a maze of rocks. Trails were crooked and as steep as chicken ladders. At hardly any point was the visibility more than ten feet through green confusion. When you saw a Jap you were already atop of him—or he atop of you.*

The attacking force left the beachhead shortly after noon of October 21. It crossed a swamp, then toiled uphill through a welter of underbrush. Scouts in the lead heard a clicking sound in a nearby thicket. Instantly they dropped to the ground. They signaled the company to a halt. They crawled out to the flanks, and what they saw was a Japanese machinegun ambush. The gun's muzzle pointed down a stretch of trail bordered by a palisade of bamboo so dense that it would have defied a hacking machete. The scouts fired, pumping ten bullets into the two Jap gunners. The ambush, had it not been discovered, would have cost many American lives.

A few minutes later the scouts halted again. Their rifles pointed toward a group of tumbledown nipa huts in a small clearing. The gesture meant, "Suspicious location."

Sergeant Kenneth Allen of Denver, Colorado, led a patrol to investigate. As they approached the clearing the huts spat fire and the patrol was pinned down. Alone the Coloradoan rushed past the huts with rebel yells, heaving phosphorus grenades through windows. The huts went up in smoke and flame. Japs were seen running into the jungle, their uniforms afire.

The taskforce now approached the crest of the first ridge. At this point several hundred Japanese who had lain on the reverse slope went into action. They mounted machineguns behind boulders and sprayed the trail and the forward slope. From tree-tops came the crack of

---

* The assault on the hill mass known as "Hill 331" was consummated by the First and Second Battalions of the 34th Infantry Regiment.

snipers' rifles. Other Japs diligently rolled explosives down the clifflike face of the hill. Whole squads appeared from nowhere and dropped grenades onto the skirmishers below them. Fire from Garands had no effect on the Japanese. It was like shooting at airplanes behind clouds of basalt. American grenades failed to clear the crest and rolled down upon the grenadiers as soon as they hit the ground. By 3 P.M. there were many killed and wounded. Some squads had been thrown off the upper hillsides. Whole platoons lay under murderous fire, unable to budge.

A man from the Bronx, Sergeant Louis Farber, led his squad to the top of the crest. He suddenly found himself in the path of a machinegun firing at arm's length. Four men of his squad crumpled under the blow. Farber pounced on the machinegun. The most violent moments in all the hateful violence of war are those of close combat. Farber slew four Japs in hand-to-hand combat. There followed an exchange of rapid fire across a rock not larger than a steamer trunk. Farber still fired as bullets ripped into him and through him. He died fighting.

At another spot along the ridge Joe Bartnichak, who hailed from Passaic, New Jersey, leaped among a squad of Japanese grenadiers. There was a flutter of screams. Then three Japs pounced on Joe. Bartnichak smashed the butt of his Garand into the face of one, then kicked him over a cliff. He seized the bayonet of his second assailant and killed him with little more than his bare hands. The third Jap, who had been stripped almost naked in the fray, grabbed a fallen rifle; He thrust the muzzle against Bartnichak's body and fired. Joe, too, died so that America might live.

By 3:30 P.M. the taskforce's predicament had become so untenable that a retreat was ordered under cover of a mortar barrage. It was the first repulse of an American attack in the Battle of the Philippines. But minutes after the first mortar shells fell on the ridge, the Japanese countered with mortar fire of their own. When the Americans' ammunition ran low before the withdrawal had been completed, Sergeant Howard Ritchie of Carlisle, Kentucky, risked his life to bring on more ammunition. He brought enough rounds to kill a Banzai party of thirty. But in a later phase of the battle the ping of a bullet coming from a clump of brush close by caused the sergeant to rise to his knees to locate the sniper. The snipers second bullet killed the gallant Kentuckyman.

There were some who cringed, and some who cracked, and there were others who challenged death to protect their comrades' retreat from almost certain annihilation. Their names are the names of the best that is in America: John Pergzola of Pittsburgh, Pennsylvania, who saw a heavy machinegun abandoned atop the ridge in the withdrawal and who crawled up and brought it back through snipers' nests; Anthony Lego of Durand, Illinois, who held the Japs at bay with his automatic rifle until the last man of his platoon had slipped downhill to safety; Sergeant Louis Paul of Louisville, Kentucky, whose hand was smashed by an enemy bullet but who nevertheless continued to direct his squad; Sergeant Bill Pinyon of Blue Diamond, Kentucky, who, wounded and on his way to the rear, protected the other wounded by killing snipers who waylaid the evacuation party; Sioux Private Blue Horse who refused to retreat until he had fired his last cartridge into the face of grenade-rolling Japs.

And there was that intrepid group of advanced artillery observers who calmly remained forward to spot the details of the Jap bastion for their Division's cannoneers. As the infantry disengaged, it passed the observers' party, and after withdrawing another four hundred yards the riflemen dug in for the night. The artillery spotters stayed, and the enemy was half as far away as were their own lines.

The four observers set up a radio while bullets from heavy Japanese machineguns cut the earth about them. They remained forward until they had completed the adjustment of artillery. Then, working together, they disassembled the radio, collected all their equipment, and in a cool, orderly manner, withdrew.

A day later the riflemen attacked once more, this time in a torrential rain, and paced by the rolling thunder of an artillery barrage. Everywhere men slipped and fell on the mud-bound incline. But led by Colonel "Red" Newman their assault carried the ridges of Hill 331 at the waving of a handkerchief "still light grayish in color." Aerial observers reported many Japanese working their way westward through the jungle in the direction of the Leyte Valley.

Elsewhere around the beachhead and embattled Palo, other fighting teams of the Division assaulted other hills. Colonel Spragins' battalion (Second Battalion, 34th Infantry Regiment), which had just weathered a night of Japanese charges into Palo, pulled out of town in the early afternoon of October 22 to drive to the summit of "Hill Baker." The infantrymen leaving Palo resembled a host of gaunt and disgusted ghosts, unshaven, wet and dirty after two hard nights. Hill Baker, they found, was not one hill but three or four. Each was steeper and higher than the preceding one. All were fringed by dense woods, their upper reaches covered with jungle grass, and their summits topped by naked rock.

The battalion stormed "Hill Baker One." On their way to the next hump in the hill mass they were stopped. Snipers fired from scores of foxholes dug into the slope. From treetops obscene in their bushiness machineguns fired. Some three hundred Japanese came charging around a shoulder of the height and in a pitched battle more than a hundred of them were killed. Americans, too, were killed, but never do men become accustomed to the filthy brutality of death in the jungle. Each time one falls it is horror resurrected; a gasp of fear and surprise, a cry, a rattle mingled with blood, a heaving and thrashing in the thicket, a convulsion of abysmal futility, and insects crawling toward the smell of death. Seldom is dying easy. Each soldier thinks: folks at home will never know how it is—one moment you're alive and strong, a moment later you are a goddamned mess.

A medical aid man six feet away from Colonel Spragins was hit. Japanese were near, shooting and pitching grenades. The colonel's carbine barked like a dog protecting the hurt medic. Then, again a few feet away, the battalion intelligence officer was mortally wounded. The same bullet ripped through the colonels arm. The colonel felt the pain and he felt the warm stickiness of his blood and he controlled himself and pretended that he was all right. As long as Spragins fought his men would fight as well. It was his second bullet wound in as many days. He inserted a fresh magazine into his carbine and summoned two soldiers nearby. Together the trio stood up and put shot after shot into the enemy counter-charge until the wounded aid man and the dying officer had been carried to the rear.

The battalion gave ground and spent the night atop Hill Baker One. The evening sky was a wondrous riot of colors. The ocean gleamed silver and crimson against the setting sun. The riflemen scraped out shallow holes and said "Hello and "Shit" and worse, meaning the war, the Philippines, the Filipinos, their own officers and the mosquitoes.

On the morning of October 23, the First Battalion of the Thirty-Fourth Regiment set out to capture "Hill Charlie." Guerillas had reported three hundred Japanese entrenched on the crests. The Japs had rounded up two hundred natives during the night whom they had herded to the hilltop as hostages against American shellfire and bombs.

About Hill Charlie, too, the maps were wrong. The wooded slope ended in an abrupt precipice not visible from the coastal flats, and beyond it there appeared two separate heights which were dubbed "Mike" and "Nan." The battalion began by tackling Hill Nan.

Again, as on Hill 331, Nippon's fighting men resorted to a skilful "rear slope defense." They waited in prepared positions on the far side of the crest, out of reach of direct fire. They permitted the attacking platoons to advance to within grenade range of the summit. At this stage the Japanese rushed to the crest, manned concealed machineguns and dropped a shower of grenades on the Americans below.

Three times our assault waves attained the crest; three times they were repulsed. Again the sun dipped low and the sea and the jungle glowed with hushed splendor. At 1800 that day this battalion too, was ordered to retreat so that artillery fire could be put on Hill Nan, civilian hostages or no.

Each platoon left one squad on top to cover the retreat. The enemy sensed the situation and counter-attacked immediately to turn withdrawal into rout and annihilation. With a mounting crescendo of screams the yellow men drove over the crest.

Protecting the retreat was machinegunner Therwin Schneider of Pittsburg, Kansas. When the Japs swarmed up and around, too close to be reached by the machinegun's traverse, Schneider half rose and hurled grenades. Somewhat down the slope a lieutenant and another sergeant* heard the din of the counter-attack. They quickly understood the seriousness of the situation. They grasped a sack full of grenades and back to the crest they rushed. There, they tossed grenades down the rear incline as fast as they could yank out the safety pins and pitch. Their rampage delayed the enemy thrust until their unit had safely disengaged. To boot, they dragged two wounded comrades to the rear.

Simultaneous with the struggle for Hill Nan, Hill Baker erupted again with the clangor of battle. Colonel Spragins' infantry advanced in the wake of a rolling wave of artillery fire.

This time they overran a score of snipers' nests and gained what they thought was the top of the hill. But then there appeared a "pimple" about one hundred feet higher, well fortified and manned.

Twice waves of riflemen charged the Pimple but were hurled back. They resorted to mortar fire, but mortar shells failed to make inroads on the caves and rock emplacements. Jap and American positions were too close together for artillery to pound the Pimple with success. It was tried at first. It was stopped when a shell fell into the battalion aid station and killed a soldier. After a day of sweaty and fruitless encounters the taskforce dug in for the night on the slope of Hill Baker. A Kentuckyman named James Allen saw a group of Japs draw up a heavy field piece from a valley a thousand yards away. The thought of having this cannon pound the perimeter through the night was

---

* Lieutenant Clarence E. Weigel of Hays, Kansas, and Staff Sergeant Matthew J. Ott of Camden, New Jersey.

disturbing. So Allen dragged a heavy machinegun across seventy-five yards of fire-swept terrain. He mounted it on a bald little knoll and put gunfire on the distant cannon until it was abandoned by its crew. Begrimed and dead-weary the men ate biscuits and cold hash in the dark. For a few hours that night in each three-man foxhole two men slept, oblivious of the flares, the grenades and the scattered volleys unleashed by the perimeter guards. Mosquitoes whined, men muttered in their sleep and bats sailed overhead. Artillery pounded the hills, slaughtering native women and children along with the Japs. The enemy raided the town of Palo that night, and shortly before dawn a Banzai charge swooped down from Hill Nan.

October 24 saw no decision in the commotion of the hills. Elements of Colonel Zierath's battalion stormed Hill 85. Infantry assault teams seized Hills Nan and Mike. But the Japanese on Hill Charlie held on with vigor. And on Hill Baker, Spragins' force by-passed the Pimple and fought its way to what was thought to be the true crest of the stubborn massif—but found a higher, steeper crest a few hundred yards to the west. There seemed to be no end to this much-cursed hill.

October 25 brought the decision. It also brought rain. Masses of water flooded the roads and turned jungles into quagmire. Rifles were covered with rust. Few experiences are more desolate than a breakfast of beans and pork gulped in haste in a water-filled mud-hole, with rain lashing the earth, and the day ahead a promise of misery and pain.

The battalions crossed a swamp, forded two streams, and attacked Hill Charlie shortly after dawn. The Japanese again employed their crafty "reverse slope defense." All afternoon the battle blazed in mud and torrents from the skies. At 5 P.M. two companies dug in on top of the ridge. Through the night the infantrymen sat in holes up to their necks in water.

Meanwhile, another branch of this force assaulted a height on the northeast rim of the "Charlie massif." This attack-team encountered trouble because the enemy did not do the expected.

"The hill," explains a field report, "and an open area in front of it were covered with tall kunai grass which thinned out and became shorter near the top of the hill, while the crest itself was covered with boulders and trees offering excellent concealment to the enemy.

"The men, familiar now with Japanese tactics of reverse slope defense, advanced boldly, feeling that they would have little opposition before reaching the top. When leading scouts were still a considerable distance from the crest, however, the enemy suddenly began a well-coordinated fire with rifles, machineguns and grenades.

"The company sought cover in the grass and returned the fire, but with little effect. Light machineguns were put into position on the hillside, but the slope was too steep, and they also were ineffective against the entrenched enemy. The company held on desperately until ordered to disengage at 1300."

While the infantry fell back, artillery observers pushed forward up the hillside. They crawled through the grass on hands and knees, through the withdrawing lines, and onto the edge of the expanse of boulders. A radioman from Iowa City, Bert Hughes, set up a radio behind a rock. Soon the long steel arm of Division artillery on Red Beach reached over onto the enemy bastions. Hughes heard the shells wail overhead. He noted the location of their impact and corrected the artillery's range by radio.

The Japanese spotted the observer. They sent snipers around to his right and left to wipe him out. Hughes felt quite naked now. He operated his radio in full view of the enemy. Bullets chipped his boulder. "OK," he radioed. "Fire for effect. Over. Out." With that he darted away and downhill.

The cannonade lasted two hours. Then the taskforce attacked once more through mire and downpour, and this time Charlie Hill was seized for once and all. . . .

There remained Hill Baker, the last high ground which barred the way into the Leyte Valley. All through the night artillery had pounded the jumble of ridges. Colonel Spragins' battalion slogged forward and uphill through drenching rain. It was difficult to believe that any Japanese up there could have survived the all-night barrage. Yet the Japs were there and they fought like self-confident ruffians. They gave battle from covered emplacements more than six feet deep and connected by tunnels. For observation they used a system of periscopes. From the crest of the Pimple sheets of fire slashed through the rain. It was the messiest, most brutal fighting Spragins' riflemen had experienced up to that time. The best the companies could do was to cling to their ledge of mud and blood and dripping thickets.

By then it was 5:30 P.M. The heavens darkened with twilight. The night was like a giant anus. Time to dig in. A hasty perimeter was established. The men opened ration cans in the darkness. Exhausted from six days of almost continuous exertion they ate the dreariest supper of their lives. Rain fell without abatement. Colonel Spragins decided to do the unheard of, the utterly unexpected. He decided to resume the attack and close in for a kill in the dark.

"Too hazardous," his officers protested.

Their argument was sound enough. The men were dog-tired.

Ammunition was low. Morale was low. Several battalion officers had fallen dead that day. The night was like an abyss of india ink and full of falling water. The terrain ahead was uncertain, unmapped, one great, menacing trap. In a night fight troops would become scattered. Men would lose their way in the dark and shoot at one another.

The colonel was adamant. Soaked, red-eyed, twice wounded, he stood in the rain and said:

"Alert the men. We pull out in ten minutes."

Was Spragins playing a hunch? Was it a hunch? Glumly the squads and platoons stood in the rain. Rain pattered on their helmets and squashed underfoot. The butts of their rifles were held up to prevent the barrels from filling with water. They stood in dejected silence, too tired to grumble.

"All set? Get moving."

Spragins led the way through the night. He picked a course by compass. The formations followed in single file, close so as not to lose contact with the men in front. The still column crossed a thousand yards of rough terrain and not a shot was fired. Toward midnight they reached the final crest of the hill. They stumbled upon a Japanese observation post. A network of fortifications surrounded the O.P. The stillness was ghostly. There was the breathing of many tired men and the monotonous melody of rain falling on leaves and corpses. The enemy strongpoints were unmanned. The emplacements were stocked with enemy equipment; there were kettles which contained leftovers of rice; but not a Jap was in sight. The Japanese, knowing that it was a rule of the Americans to halt all movement at dark, had gone off to spend the night in the shelter of native *barrios*. They had departed with the obvious intention of re-manning their bastions before dawn. The battalion's night march caught them sleeping—away from their defenses.

"Dig in," said Spragins.

Not many dug. The men flopped into the Jap trenches and lay still.

The rain stopped toward morning. Emerging from their beds of mud the men saw below them a broad and unobstructed valley, many towns, and a highway leading northwest: Leyte Valley and the Santa Fe Trail.

To their rear, between the captured massif and Red Beach, 1,928 killed Japs lay buried, and many more sprawled dead under the lid of jungle and swamp. The Division counted six hundred and thirty-eight wounded, missing, or dead among its own.

CHAPTER SEVEN

THE MAINIT RIVER BRIDGE

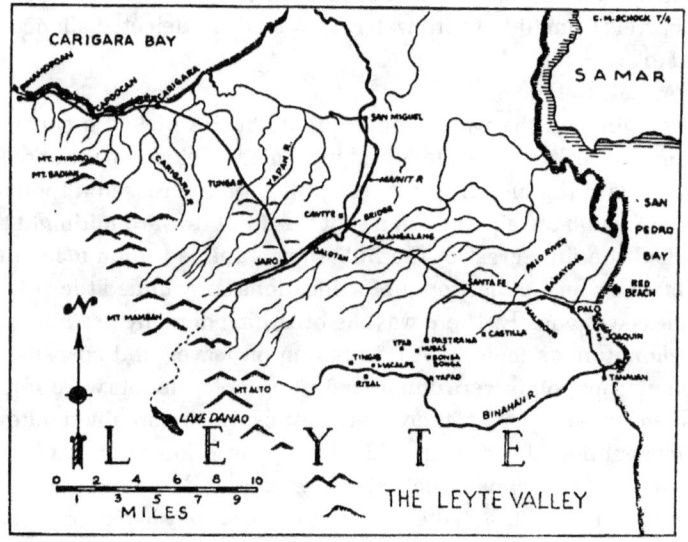

THE DIVISION DROVE across Leyte with the roar of hundreds of motors. Yamashita was given no chance to regain his balance. In the welter of churning wheels and by-passed Japanese detachments, even generals came under fire.

One sultry day at the front a sniper seemed to open fire every time the Assistant Division Commander removed his helmet to mop his brow. The sniping became so pointed that a lieutenant decided that the shots were aimed at his superior's shining bald spot. "By God, Sir," he said, "your pate is the target." Henceforth the chunky brigadier kept his helmet on. The sniper then sought other targets.*

---

* Brigadier General Kenneth F. Cramer of Wethersfield, Connecticut, one time State Senator, State Commander of the American Legion, helped to guide the 24th Division's campaigns in New Guinea, Biak and the Philippines. He was frequently cited for outstanding gallantry.

THE MAINIT RIVER BRIDGE

On another occasion the Division Commander * and a colonel stood bent over a map when a Japanese broke out of a clump of underbrush twenty yards off. He charged the two officers with a grenade, a dagger, and Banzai yells. The colonel whipped out his pistol and fired—and missed. He fired again, missed again. The Jap came on. The Division Commander braced himself to meet the Jap with a pair of dividers. The colonel kept on firing. His weapon, a .45 caliber pistol, is next to the bayonet the least efficient tool in the Army's arsenal. He fired seven times. The shots missed—or jammed—seven times. He killed his assailant with the eighth, and last, bullet.

The Leyte Valley is roughly thirty-five miles long and ten miles wide. Scores of villages dot its expanse of plantations, rice paddies and marshy fields. Forest-covered mountain ranges rise on its western flank. The valley is crossed by many meandering streams. During the dry season the country between Palo and Carigara is a tropical paradise; the skies are blue, and rice, bananas, coconuts, breadfruit and papaya grow everywhere. But in the rainy months the fields are flooded and the streams become swollen rivers, and swamps surround the stilts of native huts. Then the road to Carigara on the island's opposite coast is transformed into a ribbon of slime. The network of village paths soak into a spiderweb of knee-deep mud. The battle for the Leyte Valley was a cataract of motion along these roads and trails.

One battalion struck 8,000 yards across the Leyte Valley and stormed the town of Castilla, southwest of Palo. The last Japanese soldier alive in that community bayoneted an American in search of a drink of water. Another force struck south from San Joaquin and reached the banks of the Kabuyan River. Patrols sent into the village of Tanauan made contact with a friendly division† which had invaded Leyte farther to the south. So, an unbroken forty mile front on Leyte's east coast was established.

Mindful of enemy deviltry, the infantry teams barred all civilians from entering the captured towns. The Divisions Counter Intelligence Corps placed pro-Japanese town officials under arrest. From the beginning of the liberation, little love was lost between the soldiers and the populace. The average dogface had little respect for the stubborn courage of the average guerilla; he left the glorification of the poor "Flips" to the propagandists at home. Many an unwilling and homesick

---

* Major General F. A. Irving commanded the 24th Division until November 18, 1944. The colonel was William J. Verbeck, commander of the 21st Infantry Regiment, now teaching military science at West Point.

† The 96th Infantry Division.

liberator despaired of figuring out why men should die to liberate wretched villages and squalor set in acres of stinking mud. His own unhappiness developed in him a tendency—hardening as the messy months rolled on—to brush the *barrio* folks aside or to ignore them all except the young village women who had the hips of children and sad black eyes and long black hair with an unwashed smell.

But morale ran high when the first mail from home was distributed in the foxholes; everywhere men sat hunched over letters, some grim, some smiling, some with trembling hands, reading on at night by flashlight under ponchos, still reading after the rain had blurred the ink. Meanwhile the kitchen crews moved up their pots and pans and portable stoves, and through the sound of falling rain, the incessant rumble of trucks and the rataplan of machineguns drifted the aroma of hot biscuits.

While the rifle platoons gathered their breath for the next spring, the men of the Division's Signal Company worked around the clock. Within a week after the landing they had lost a score of men and laid a thousand miles of wires. They had installed scores of telephones, radio and radar units, toiling on with carbines slung and sweat pouring from under their helmets. One group went through five fire fights before it could lay its wire. Another group of nine was wiped out by an artillery hit. A joker planted a sign on the spot which said, *"Hard & Haggard, Electrical Installations."*

In many perilous spots artillery observers and signal men worked hand in hand. They were the eyes and ears of the cannoneers. Without forward observation and quick intelligence about targets far in front, the batteries would be blind.

An artillery reconnaissance party proceeding through brush parallel to the valley highway came face to face with a Japanese combat patrol prowling through the brush in the opposite direction. Only fifteen feet of sword grass separated the cannoneers and the Japs when they sighted one another. Muzzle to muzzle, a fusillade ensued. Sergeant John Huey of Franklin, Pennsylvania, plunged forward and killed two of the enemy. Bob Tougas of Detroit killed one Jap and stopped a Jap grenade. Corporal Bruce Gramley of DuBois Town, Pennsylvania, killed another. Sergeant Joseph Dawson of Kinden, Virginia, killed one more. And Corporal John Hutchinson of Boston, Massachusetts, was pushed over the edge of a swamp in the scramble. He tangled with three grenade-heaving enemies. A minute later he emerged. "Did they get away?" his comrades asked. Hutchinson shook his head. "They are dead," he said. This happened near Malirong on October 27.

THE MAINIT RIVER BRIDGE

Spearhead of the drive through the Leyte Valley was the Division's Thirty-Fourth Infantry Regiment. Nothing that General Yamashita threw in its way could stop it. In six days it cut Leyte in two.

Its progress was swift and sure. The battalions "leapfrogged" one another. Artillery fire paved the way. There was resistance at the Manabana River bridge, but mortars were brought into position in a matter of minutes. Mortar fire and an infantry charge drove the defenders away from the road and into the flanking hills. By late afternoon of October 26 the Second Battalion seized Santa Fe and dug in for the night. On the following day the First Battalion passed through the Second and pushed on another seven thousand yards to the outskirts of the town of Alangalang. Two thousand yards in front, broad and muddy, flowed the main water barrier of the Leyte Valley—the Mainit River.

The Japanese contested every mile of highway with tenacious rear guard actions. Each mile was paid for with agony and sweat, and each night rains fell.

Between Palo and Alangalang five bridges had been blasted by the retreating foe. Others were set afire in the face of the Division's scouts. An arch had been blown out of the center of a concrete bridge; two steel bridges were completely destroyed. But with the assault teams moved the Combat Engineers. Their bulldozers, power saws, timbers and steel trestles accompanied the advance; new bridges, or by-passes, were thrown across the streams in a matter of hours while infantry kept harassing snipers at bay. Leading elements forded the streams, their rifles held high. Or they ferried across on palm logs and rafts improvised from tarpaulins stuffed with jungle grass and brush. And always there was a fire fight.

In one of the fights for a river crossing, Bill Rigdon of Davenport, Florida, saw a friend collapse under bullets ripping from a bamboo grove. He saw his friend thresh about at the edge of the road. He saw the strike of bullets as the snipers strove to finish their job. Bill went to the rescue. He carried his friend two hundred yards through rifle fire and to the rear.

Private Walter Petrowski, an artilleryman from Lowell, Massachusetts, too, saw a comrade sag, hit by enemy bullets. The wounded man was bleeding to death. He cried for help but no medic was near. Petrowski ran forward. He tied a tourniquet around the bleeding man's thigh. Before he had finished, a burst of machinegun fire killed him at the side of the one he had tried to save.

Cannoneer R. D. Clark of Canton, North Carolina, then braved the same machinegun. He crawled forward with a field telephone and registered his battery on the enemy strongpoint. Shellfire destroyed the Jap gunners.

Driving his battalion commander in a radio jeep on a reconnaissance mission was Private Harry Meade. The jeep ran into a machinegun ambush and the party was pinned down in a roadside ditch. "Somebody's got to go back and warn the leading echelon," the battalion commander said. Meade volunteered. He jumped back into the riddled jeep. At breakneck speed he drove through sprays of automatic fire. The jeep's antenna was shot away. But Meade came through in time to warn the advancing force.

Staff Sergeant Frank Marchant of Muskogee, Oklahoma, dragged three wounded men out of the path of certain death, then guarded them until help arrived. Three scouts of the advance guard suddenly encountered a company of counter-attacking Japanese; they held their ground until their platoon could arrive and deploy. Corporal Carl F. Wolf of Whitlow, California, was wounded and the medics were at his side. "Evacuate me?" said Wolf. "Not yet." He remained with his squad until the attack was repulsed. In a drenching night rain Corporal Calvin Haren of Denton, Texas, saw a Japanese demolition team of three move stealthily toward a group of anti-tank guns well within the perimeter. The Texan blocked their way and shot two; then a machinegun opened up, killing the third.

In the sweep up Leyte Valley, tanks struck mines. There were rumbling explosions as mines burst in clouds of fire, rock and mud. There was hidden TNT in the roadbeds and under innocent appearing thresholds; and high explosives attached to telephones, stray fountain pens and ladies' slippers. There were pottery mines and wooden mines which defied mechanical detectors; the probing bayonet was then the only resort. Even coconuts were turned into traps; filled with explosive and a grenade that would burst under slight pressure upon the husk. Men of the mine disposal squads disarmed and removed more than two hundred improvised bombs along the Santa Fe Trail.

Two hours before dawn of October 28 the battalions were alerted for the attack on the Mainit River Line. Men rolled their combat packs and ate their breakfast in the dark. Early morning mists rose from the marshes. The march began.

The First Battalion took the lead. Scouts moved far in front. Strong patrols secured the flanks. The advance party followed the point, and they in turn were followed by the advance guard support, one company strong. Then came the main assault force, stretched out in open column to both sides of the highway: the riflemen, the mortar men and the machinegun crews. Cub planes ranged ahead for observation.

The taskforce approached the village of Alangalang in almost complete silence. There were no Japanese. The population had fled into the hills. Only the howling of dogs greeted the scouts.

Patrols branched off to right and left to comb the houses. Company after company traversed the ghost town and pushed on toward the river. Combat engineers made short shift of obstacles along the way. Small pieces of paper propped onto twigs were used to mark the presence of mines. Here and there Japanese corpses lay, artillery victims often without legs or arms. Already they had swollen under the dampness and the heat. Flies buzzed about the cadavers. Some of the dead had been chewed up by dogs. The scouts were more alert and the silence was more profound. Through foliage ahead loomed the large steel bridge which spanned the Mainit River between steep banks.

The collision was abrupt and violent. The crack of rifles, the urgent chatter of automatic guns and the dry thumping of mortars mingled in a tempest of noises. There were the yells of rage, the mute agony of hesitation, the cries of the wounded, the sounds made by many running men, and there were the angry answering barks of the Garands.

At first not much could be seen of the Japanese positions on the river's far side. Only lingering wisps of blue smoke. Pillboxes were covered with earth, and grass grew from this earth. The enemy gunners fired through narrow ports built into the revetments. Tunnels opening upon clumps of underbrush served as the strongpoints' exits. But after a while the continuous passage of bullets set fire to the grass in front of the pillboxes. That betrayed their location.

The leading battalion deployed: one company to the right of the road, one company to the left. Through rice fields the skirmish lines pushed toward the river. They reached the river bank on both sides of the bridge. At this point more machineguns hidden on the opposite bank erupted in a satanic concert. The whole battalion was pinned down on the river's edge. A crossing was impossible. To move on meant to die.

A withdrawal was ordered. But the men would not move. They clung to the mud. Hostile machineguns raked the fields behind them. To move rearward, too, meant certain death.

Tanks lumbered forward. They stopped at the river's bank and sprayed the Japanese defenses with machineguns. Shells from their 75 millimeter cannon transformed pillboxes into wreckage. Still, the companies were unable to move. A heavy volume of sniper fire from treetops to their rear added to their plight.

Now a Cannon Company platoon entered the turmoil. The cannoneers sent shells screaming across the river as fast as they could load their pieces. The platoon's ammunition was soon exhausted. Another platoon of Cannon Company men moved forward and continued the shelling. Under this punishment the Japanese ducked low. In rapid, intermittent dashes the companies on the river bank moved to safer positions. Another way had to be found to force the river. Scouting parties roamed the adjoining woods. At intervals they entered the river, searching for a ford.

Meanwhile, an enemy raiding party attacked a battery of field artillery almost a mile to the rear of the front. By chance, Corporal Albert Nichols of Pauls Valley, Oklahoma, was poking around for souvenirs. He saw a crouched figure running through undergrowth. At first glance he thought it was a native. But why should a native run at a crouch? Nichols looked again. This time he saw twenty Japanese about to rush his battery.

Nichols grabbed his rifle, threw himself on the ground, fired. The Japanese also fired, and they hurled grenades. The corporal heard bullets and grenade fragments strike his gun mount. He heard bullets crash into ammunition chests a little way off. He also felt a pain in his left hand. The hand was smashed. But Nichols stayed at his post. He fired. Singlehanded, he dispersed the raiders.

Not long after noon patrols reported that they had found a ford across the Mainit River. It lay some five hundred yards to the north of the embattled bridge. There was a bend, and the banks were covered with jungle. At this point the river's edge was an almost vertical twenty-foot drop.

"A ford?" Colonel Newman said quietly, "That's fine."

The regiment struck at 1400. By 1500 it had forced the Mainit River and captured the bridge. The intervening hour included that rarest of events in modern war: a bayonet charge over hundreds of yards of open ground.

"Red" Newman launched a coordinated two-battalion attack. Once more the First Battalion advanced to the river's edge. Again it was pinned down in a holocaust of fire. It kept the enemy's attention riveted to the bridge and its immediate vicinity. Meanwhile, the Second Battalion ducked low and hastened upstream to the ford.

Eight hundred infantrymen forded the Mainit River without meeting opposition. Squad after squad dropped down the steep embankment, weapons and ammunition held aloft. Many waded up to their necks in swirling water. Some lost their footing, but no weapon was lost. Ropes tied to trees on the opposite bank helped the men to hoist themselves onto the Jap side of the river. There was a wall of jungle, a belt of palm plantation, and then a stretch of open ground. The bridge and the enemy's highway defenses lay five hundred yards to the south.

"Fix bayonets!"

There was a subdued clatter as the short, black blades were slipped into the bayonet studs of the Garands.

"As skirmishers—forward!"

The skirmish lines emerged from the jungle and crossed the belt of palms at a run. "Fox" Company was in the lead and its commander, Captain Paul Austin of Burleson, Texas, well out in front. From fifty yards up the river bank, Japanese flank detachments opened fire. Machineguns hammered from a coconut grove on the left. Enemy mortars belched high explosive in a vain attempt to stem the tide. The bayonet charge swept forward. Men fired from the hip as they advanced. Others cleared the way with grenades. Automatic riflemen fired their twenty-pound weapons from the shoulder. Machinegunners kept pace and each hundred yards they halted briefly to spray the enemy lines.

A flanking attack is the most deadly form of attack. The pace was so swift that Japanese mortar shells burst in the rear of the advancing formations. The infantrymen yelled: Indian yells, their regiment's battle-cry, "Lorraine! Lorraine!", blood-curdling howls of every description, curses, hymns, obscenities, hysteric laughter. Here and there Japanese spider-holes, dug like wagon wheels to enable firing in all directions, were overrun. Grenades, rifle butts, cold steel did their work. In the dampness hung the smell of blood.

Captain Austin led the assault; between words of encouragement and quick directions he was shouting like a berserker. Three enemies armed with mortars died at his hands. His men overran mortar positions without a halt. His own mortars supported the charge by sending shells into more distant Japanese emplacements. Homer McClure of Chattanooga, Tennessee, saw a Jap machinegun cut down several men in his platoon. He loped toward the machinegun. Thirty yards from it he stumbled and fell. He raised himself to his knees and fired into the enemy nest. Machinegun bullets hit him while he fired. Not until the last round of his clip of eight had left his rifle did he fall, mortally wounded.

Sergeant James F. Schmidt of North Muskegon, Michigan, saw a soldier of his squad collapse in a spurt of machinegun fire. He rushed forward, and crawling low, he dragged the wounded man into the shelter of a tree. All this time machinegun bullets from his own company's guns as well as slugs from Jap guns whipped low above his head.

In the midst of the bayonet charge four medical aid men carrying litters ran a zig-zag race with death. They were carrying wounded out of the killing zone. Private Serafino Guinta of Brooklyn took charge of a machinegun after both the squad leader and the gunner had crumpled under hostile fire; he kept the gun spitting lead until Jap mortarmen had zeroed in on his niche. Then Guinta grabbed the gun and carried it to an alternate position. The weapon was so hot from continuous firing that the volunteer gunner badly scorched both hands. After that Guinta dashed to a nearby tank to secure an additional supply of ammunition. He carried the ammunition back to his gun. Despite his seared hands he fired until a squad of Japs threatened to close in. After his last shot was fired he again grabbed his gun and threw it onto the tank to save it from enemy hands. He babbled in a fever as aid men carried him away.

A sniper's bullet knocked away the helmet of Clinton Short of Parkersburg, West Virginia. He was leading a squad in the assault. Bareheaded he ran on, calling on his men to follow, pointing out targets right and left. Twenty yards to one side a Japanese behind a mortar threw a grenade at Short. The burst fell wide. Deafened by the concussion, Short pounced on the Jap. Both roared with rage as they collided. The yellow man brandished another grenade. The West Virginian saw the opening, ran him through with the bayonet, then fired for good measure. A minute later Short walked boldly against the next emplacement. "Follow me!" he cried. Toward the end of the long assault he fell.

Commanding the lead squad of his platoon was Sergeant Ernest ("Reckless") Reckman of Valley Stream, New York. His whooping men rushed past a camouflaged spider-hole full of Japs. Reckman's quick eyes spotted the masked position. He rallied his squad and led it in a concentric charge against the hole. At another point he discovered a cunningly hidden mortar emplacement. An instant later he rushed it, tossing a grenade as he ran. The grenade roared and Reckman jumped into the emplacement. None of the stunned enemy came out alive.

The charge now reached the Japanese machinegun positions. A fighting man named William Thomas, from Ft. Wayne, Indiana, almost fell over his squad leader who had fallen with a burst of machinegun slugs in his body. William Thomas stopped, dragged his mortally wounded noncom to a hollow in the ground, then rushed forward again and silenced the enemy machinegunner in a close-quarter duel.

Almost simultaneously a fighting man from Kentucky, also named

Thomas (Private First Class Edward R. Thomas of Trappist, Kentucky), crossed the swift-flowing Mainit River under a hail of bullets. He climbed the high bank and knocked out a machinegun nest whose crew had attempted to kill him while he was wading chest-deep in water. With fine marksmanship this second Thomas then pinned down the crews of three other hostile dugouts until reinforcements arrived to complete the job.

It was a Kentuckyman, too, Sergeant Roy Floyd of Eubank, who first reached the bridge. A third son of Kentucky(Private First Class James E. Lacefield, Louisville, Kentucky) broke through to the bridgehead almost shoulder to shoulder with Floyd; a shell wailed and there was the crash and the quick stab of flame, and fragments. The soldier fell. His back was torn open. Nonetheless, this wounded Kentuckian stood up again and dragged himself to the nearest American mortar. He told the mortarmen exactly where to fire to destroy the gun that had hurt him. Then he collapsed.

The Mainit River bridge was captured. Jap survivors scuttled through undergrowth like hares. The short, ugly noises of taking life moved on into the woods to the west.

The Japanese had left the bridge intact, but not by choice. They had mined the bridge with 200-pound bombs and with several cases of artillery ammunition. Wires attached to set off the demolition charges led to a banana grove on the west bank of the river. But the enemies stationed at the far end of the wires had met death. There had been three: one had his head bashed in; another's neck had been broken by a rifle butt; and the third had blown out his guts with a grenade.

A team of engineers under Sergeant McPeters of Bragg City, Missouri, knocked holes into the deck of the bridge. McPeters then disarmed the demolition arrangement.

Soon tanks, trucks, bulldozers and halftracks rumbled steadily across the Mainit River.

Chapter Eight

DEATH-DANCE IN PASTRANA

"This action in the Philippines is the decisive battle in which we cannot withdraw even a single step, for we have burned our bridges behind us. . . .

It is a great decisive battle on which the life of the Greater East Asia war depends, for it decides whether we lose our sea routes to southern regions."

(Radio Tokyo on the Battle of Leyte)

DAY OR NIGHT, in the tent of the Division Intelligence near Palo, work never ceased. The coding and decoding machines ticked without cessation. Enemy messages were snatched from the ether. Enemy documents found or captured, from a soldier's paybook to a colonel's diary, were subjected to thorough analysis. The stream of people summoned for questioning never ended: prisoners of war, guerillas, itinerant tradesmen, missionaries. Photographs were pieced together and translated into maps. A tight-lipped sergeant burned with care each scrap of waste paper spewed out by Intelligence. When the sorting was done, a picture resulted upon which the disposition and the missions of the combat teams were decided.

On the morning of October 26, messengers rushed from Division headquarters to the town of Castilla where the Nineteenth Regiment had established its roost. Soon other messengers were on the way to the battalions and the companies. After a relatively quiet night the "Rock of Chickamauga,, was alerted for action.

Guerillas operating in the mountains brought the news that Japanese detachments were on the march to reinforce General Shiro Makino's badly mauled Sixteenth Division in the Leyte Valley. Aerial observers reported that enemy troop barges had entered Ormoc Bay, in the west beyond the almost trackless central range. Intelligence fitted together the pieces. It was learned that the Thirtieth Japanese

Infantry Division had left its bases in Mindanao, Leyte-bound. Other reinforcements were signaled as being on the way from Cebu and Luzon.

There were but two roads by which the enemy could pump fresh forces into Leyte Valley, or escape from it. One led through Carigara in the north, the objective of the Thirty-Fourth Regiment's offensive; the other led up from the south through wild hill country by way of the town of Pastrana. The Nineteenth Regiment was given the mission to seize Pastrana and block the latter route. It was also ordered to secure the mountain passes of the central range.

The sky was leaden. Sultry heat lay heavy on the helmeted men. The leading battalion followed a trail flanked by thickets which trapped the heat. The trail led steadily uphill. For stretches the *kunai* grass had grown together above the path and then it was as if the advancing platoons were following the course of a stifling and saturnine tunnel. 'Item" Company formed the advance guard. Mortarmen, machinegunners and ammunition bearers panted under their loads. Some soldiers dropped from heat exhaustion; they were revived with water from their own canteens, helped to their feet, and pushed on with glazed eyes.

Whenever the scouts approached a bend in the trail, an air of stealthy alertness took hold of their sweat-drenched shapes. Their gait slowed. Their steps became longer, gliding. When sudden shots crackle from ambush, it is normally the leading scout who is the first to fall.

To be made a scout in jungle war is somehow akin to being selected for death. Good squad leaders select their best men to serve as scouts. Some, intent on keeping old friends alive, selected green replacements for the job. Most did not live long. But the scout shrugs, and pushes on, wary, unhappy, and aggressive. A bend in the trail: the scout grasps his rifle tighter; he probes to right and left, and forward. He knows that in the mystery of jungle growth the enemy can lie in wait and not be seen within a whisper's reach. Most often the first shot of an invisible marksman is the first herald of battle. The scout rounds the bend in the trail simply because there is nothing else to do. For a moment he pauses. He peers forward and to the flanks, and if no one shoots at him during those seconds, he regains his stride.

The first shot was fired a mile from the outskirts of the town of Pastrana. The scout fell. The shot came from an *Arasaka* rifle, from the immense crown of a breadfruit tree. The vanguard dispersed. It formed a skirmish line and flushed the thickets and treetops with fire. The sniper pitched out of the breadfruit tree. The first of many that day.

Bullets whined. They scuffed up the black earth in many spots as the advance struck the fringe of the town. The battalion pulled back, organized in assault formations, then attacked, two companies abreast, a third closely in support. The town square in sight, the charge was halted. It was thrown back by one of the most unusual fortifications encountered in the Japanese war.

The repulsing fire pounded out of what looked like a cluster of flimsy houses. But men in the forward attack waves noticed that green grass seemed to grow halfway up the sides of the huts. Men died. Many were wounded. A sergeant closest to the wall of fire said in a loud voice, "Why should grass grow up the sides of shacks?"

Twenty-four hours of savage fighting went by before the stronghold could be explored. What had resembled grass growing on the walls of huts was really a star-shaped revetment built of layers of heavy logs, reinforced with concrete and covered with mounds of earth. Grass had been made to grow over the mounds. The native houses had been built over a group of pillboxes. Other pillboxes protected the flanks of the fort. Their reinforced concrete walls were two feet thick, and they commanded clean fire lanes in all directions. Tunnels and trenches connected the various strongpoints. The whole had been built with cunning care. Part of the camouflage were foraging pigs, and womens clothing hung on lines as if put there to dry.

Mortars failed to breach the fort. The revetment sneered at machinegun bullets. Flame thrower and demolition teams were not able to advance near enough to do their part.

The assault force backed away. The fire fight continued. The men looked vicious and frustrated. Also, they were hungry. The heat was intense. Here and there were growls: "Lets get in there so we can cool off and eat."

The regimental commander called for artillery fire. The infantrymen crouched low and watched their shells engulf the star-shaped fort. Smoke billowed and there were shattering explosions. Suddenly there was silence, and a dry voice said, "Fix bayonets."

Quietly the command was passed along the skirmish lines. Then machineguns chattered and infantry jumped off to attack anew. The sun was setting.

The fort heaved and roared. It vomited thousands upon thousands of bullets. Under the somber gold and crimson of the cloud-filled sky the charge penetrated to within one hundred yards of the fort. There it was stopped. Casualties were heavy. The order was given, "Stay there, and dig in."

From among the huddles of the dead in the debris-strewn strip of no-man's-land came a faint cry for help. A wounded man raised himself to his elbow. He waved one hand feebly. The movement drew immediate machinegun fire from one of the pillboxes flanking the fort. The movement stopped. But soon the faint cry for help again came to the digging men. A sergeant said: "Somebody's got to go and drag the guy in." The sergeant was Harold Schmidt, of Ortonville, Minnesota.

In the half-concealment of battered bushes and wrecked shacks men looked at one another. Except for the cracking of rifles and the hard stutter of a machinegun, there was silence. The wounded soldier lay a scant twenty yards in front of four Japanese pillboxes. The digging men could hear his cries. Their lips were thin lines. Nothing could be done. In the night the Japs would crawl out and kill the wounded. That was one reason why so few Jap prisoners were taken. The enemy wounded? Give them a bullet, or the knife, then kick them in the face and rob them.

Again there came a cry for help; thinner now, like the plaint of a crushed child.

"Christ, we can't leave the guy," said Sergeant Schmidt. "We'll be listening to him all night."

From the fort came the sound of outlandish singing. A Japanese field gun opened up. All night it dropped scattered shells over the perimeter. In their holes the men ducked low. They listened to the crashing rumble of the bursts and to the twang of fragments among swarming fireflies. Sergeant Schmidt put aside his shovel. He sat back on his haunches and prayed. Then he tightened the chin strap of his helmet. He grabbed two grenades and he crawled out and forward into the assembly of corpses.

He found the wounded man and cut away his clothes with a bushknife. From his jungle kit he took sulfa powder and a bandage. He sprinkled the sulfa on the other's bullet wounds and after that he bandaged them and stopped the bleeding. The Japanese saw the stirring of dim shapes in murk. They fired.

"Easy now," Sergeant Schmidt said to the wounded soldier. "We are going home."

Inch after inch, foot by foot, he dragged his helpless comrade back to his own perimeter. Harold Schmidt was later killed in action.

At another sector of the Pastrana front a wounded man limped in with the message that two other soldiers lay badly mangled in front of the hostile lines. The spot was covered with wicked fire from a spiderhole. A corpsman made ready to go. But he needed help. "I'll help you," a quiet voice said. The words were spoken by an army chaplain, Harry G. Griffiths, whose home is in Clyde, Ohio. Together the aid man and the chaplain braved death to bring the wounded to cover. It was the second time in the campaign that machinegunners had aimed their bullets at the chaplain.

From dusk to dawn the Division's field artillery hammered the star-shaped fort. Huddled in muddy three-man holes, the assault force rested. The wounded of the day's collisions were evacuated to the rear. Enemy raiding parties repeatedly interrupted communications with Palo and Castilla; they cut wires and ambushed trucks and ambulances at dark road bends and near by-passes around demolished bridges. Rain squalls struck between midnight and dawn. Beneath the screaming of shells and the rolling thunder of explosions a hundred yards to the front, few managed to snatch sleep. Jap planes droned overhead. They were bombing the road, the cluttered beach, the supply ships in San Pedro Bay; and one could hear the squealing of Japanese in the darkness whenever there was a lull in the artillery concentration.

With the first tints of a pearl-shell dawn the artillery ceased firing. Batteries of heavy mortars continued the barrage. They lobbed their explosives from dose-range emplacements which the mortarmen had dug overnight. With daylight, infantry teams attacked.

They overran the fort. Surviving Jap guns unleashed a frantic final clatter. The riflemen swept through Pastrana and carried the town in house-to-house fighting. Consciously they fought for nothing more than a chance to flop down and sleep. The field piece which had shelled the American perimeter all night was captured at the northwestern edge of the town; its gunners committed hara-kiri by grenade. "King" Company pushed beyond the outskirts of Pastrana. Its soldiers set up a roadblock near a burned-out bridge astride the highway to Dagami. This severed the enemy's route of escape. Jap mortar fire fell on Pastrana in the afternoon. One shell fell into an aid station. Three American wounded were killed.

Japs died hard. Surrounded, out-gunned, out-numbered, they did not give up in battle. A Japanese soldier forced to make a decision would first seek for an attack-solution of his dilemma. He is a believer in the "spiritual power" of the bayonet. In Pastrana he fought to the last and had to be rooted out, and killed, one by one. Scattered detachments and snipers harassed the town for days.

The star-shaped fort was a shambles. Its gloomy caverns were broken and the network of trenches and bunkers was carpeted with twisted dead. Many had been torn limb from limb by the bursting shells. Many showed no visible wounds, but the force of the concussions seemed to have broken every bone in their bodies. Forty Japanese weapons trucks were destroyed in the assault. Scores of automatic weapons were captured. There were forty-one machineguns which had supported the defenses of the fort.

The storming of Pastrana by three thousand Americans was punctuated by many deeds which the sweat-encrusted men in front shrug off as incidental to a hateful job. Portly Brigadier General Cramer walked through sniper fire unscathed; not once did the proximity of death ruffle this soldier-senators bluff efficiency. "If you want to find General Cramer," the dogfaces of the Nineteenth tell you, "don't look at headquarters, look for him where the shooting is." Where Cramer walked untouched a minute before, Captain James B. Jones of Buffalo, South Carolina, an operations officer, did not. A sniper's bullet pierced his leg. The captain emitted an oath and sat down. An aid man bandaged his wound. After that, Jones limped to the nearest bush and cut himself a stick. Then he continued on his mission, which was to coordinate the actions of the battalions storming Pastrana.

Infantrymen scoured the town. No house was overlooked. The searchers worked in half-squad groups. Their first step was to surround the building; their next to scrutinize doors, windows, and thresholds for booby traps. Then two men would enter the house. They would poke from room to room, the second man covering the first. This is the "buddy system." Grenades were tossed through windows of huts suspected of harboring Japs. Flamethrowers set some ablaze. But most houses were found abandoned. Most of the furniture the enemy had chopped up as firewood for his rice kitchens. Here and there a sniper was discovered. Then a brief fight ensued, followed by the search for "souvenirs." And souvenirs ranged from battle flags to gold teeth.

That day the corpsmen were too busy to eat. One two-man team rendered first aid to more than thirty wounded. Aid Men Lawrukiewics of Kansas City, and Bill Lessard of Gary, Indiana, crawled thrice into zones swept by Japanese machinegun fire to patch up and carry wounded comrades out of the path of bullets. An emergency hospital they established in the local jail.

Stringing telephone wire from a forward observers nest to the regimental command post, two signal corps soldiers saw bullets chip the road under their feet. They dived into a ditch. The ditch was half filled with stagnant water. They heard more bullets bite into the rim of the ditch, and they heard the flat cracking of Japanese rifles in a bamboo thicket. One of the signal men was hit. The other, Pedro Echaves of San Diego, California, propped up his buddy's head so that he would not drown in the muck. Then he dashed to the aid station for help. But the jail too, was under direct fire. The medics lay nailed to the ground.

"Hey, you guys," said Echaves, "give me some morphine."

He took the morphine and raced back to his wounded comrade in the ditch. He plunged into the ditch. The snipers fired. The wounded soldier moaned. "Here I come," said Echaves. "'Everything'll be all right, Joe." He injected the morphine. As the moaning man became quiet, Echaves hoisted him over his shoulder and carried him to the aid station at a run.

The man needed blood if his life was to be saved. But the sweating medics had used up the last plasma on hand in the forward lines. They sent an emergency call to a unit fighting at the other side of the town.

Soldiers entangled in a sniper skirmish saw a bulldozer rumble into town at top speed. Hunched atop the bulldozer were two helmeted young men. One was driving. The other sprayed slugs from a sub-machinegun. The lumbering contrivance was drawing fire from all sides. Infantrymen shouted at the driver to stop. An officer sprang from an alley attempting to wave the bulldozer to a halt; seconds later he leaped for his life. The driver roared, "Get the hell out of my way."

The officer roared back, "What the hell do you think you're doing?"'

The bulldozer tore past him, past the star-shaped fort, and on into the town square. It thundered abreast of a battalion headquarters, and then the man with the sub-machinegun leaned over and dropped a neatly wrapped package.

"Here is your bloody plasma," he said.

With that, the bulldozer wheeled and clattered away and out of town. At the outskirts an enemy pillbox on the right opened fire. Bullets ricocheted from the bulldozer's raised blade. The driver whistled as the bullets struck. He changed the course of his machine. He wallowed it off the road, lowered its blade and charged the pillbox. Two swipes of the blade covered the firing ports with earth. A short withdrawal, followed by a thrust, caved in the strongpoint's side. A few more swipes of the blade buried the wreckage and its occupants. Then the bulldozer roared off as fast as it had come. Atop it the helmeted young men smoked cigarettes. (They were Technician Russel K. Herritz of Reedsburg, Wisconsin, and Private First Class Zack W. Landrum of Dumas, Texas.)

The seizure of Pastrana left the Japanese command disrupted and confused. Its main route of supply, reinforcement and escape was cut off. But there remained the twisted mountain trails which followed the cascading streams and the jungle-choked gorges east of Pastrana.

Nineteenth Infantry battle teams branched out to seize the trails and the mist-shrouded passes. The maneuver would secure the flank of the forces which then were sweeping northward in the broad valley below. Planes dropped bombs on stalled enemy columns near Bonga-Bonga, south of Pastrana. Zeroes took to the air on strafing missions, and from trails and ditches below foot troops watched the dogfights in the evening sky. The First Battalion pushed four thousand yards southwest to Macalpe to block a ford across the Binahaan River. The Second Battalion advanced upriver to Tingib Village, and there dug in for the night. And the Regiment's Third Battalion, reinforced by the first hot meal since the Red Beach landings, patrolled with vigor around Pastrana.

Many things happened that night. The Japanese did not realize the extent of the regiment's thrusts into the mountains. One Jap supply party carrying tinned fish and rice marched into an American perimeter. Enemy runners shot and killed along the trails were found to bear messages for extinct Japanese command posts. A lieutenant (Lieutenant diaries W. Dyer of Montgomery, West Virginia) leading a patrol over a twisting woodland trail saw three Japanese soldiers sound asleep in the shade of a banana grove. He decided to pounce on them and take them prisoner. The Japs screamed as they felt themselves seized roughly. Then a scout yelled, This place is lousy with Japs!" The officer was startled to see the trail ahead come to life; it had been lined with sleeping Japs, and the Japs were waking up.

The prisoners scuttled into the bushes. The patrol opened fire. Both sides were utterly surprised. Not knowing that they outnumbered their attackers ten to one, the Japanese fled. They deserted their weapons and left six dead.

Later that night an enemy convoy of horse-drawn carts loaded with artillery ammunition approached a perimeter outpost. A Jap soldier walked up to the outpost. The outpost guard did nothing. He explained later, 'The Nip looked just like a guy in my company." Then the Nip pulled out a map and asked a question in Japanese. "What?" The Jap sensed that something was wrong. He vanished in the darkness and the guard fired.

The convoy could not turn on the muddy one-lane track. Machineguns and anti-tank cannon raked the hapless column. Teamsters and convoy escort dashed madly into an adjacent swamp. Carts were splintered and overturned. The cries of dying horses filled the night Sixteen Japanese corpses were found among the carts. The trail was strewn with ammunition and with horses.

A sergeant from Connecticut could no longer endure the moaning of injured animals. He jumped out of his hole, Garand in hand. He wept as he strode along the path, shooting each horse between the eyes. "Jesus Christ," he muttered, "the horses." On his way back to the perimeter he found two Japs hiding in a smashed cart. He killed them both.

A night later—October 29—a column of Japanese approached the Pastrana perimeter openly and in single file. They were sauntering along as if they were promenading in a park in Tokyo. Outposts met them with canister fired from 37 millimeter cannon. All were killed but two. Toward morning a rummaging infantryman found the two survivors hiding under a bamboo shack. One of the two brandished a grenade. He was shot through the head before he could hurl it. The other gave himself up.

"Don't shoot me, dear Americans," was his unusual plea. "Why did you say that?" a Division interrogator asked him later. "Don't you want your divine spirit to continue to harass us?"

"No," the Jap said. "I like America."

"Why?"

"Oh, American movies."

"Have you lived in America?"

"No, sir."

"Where did you see the American movies?"

"The Japanese army shows American movies to Japanese soldiers," the prisoner explained.

"Do you know of any more Japanese soldiers who want to surrender?"

"No, sir."

"Do they believe that we will torture them?"

"Some believe so," said the Jap. "Most believe that if they surrender, they can never return to Japan. They love Nippon. The people of Nippon will kill them if they return. In Japan a soldier is dead when he is captured. Nobody writes him. His mail is lost. To be killed by Americans is better than to be killed at home."

"Will you return to Japan after the war?"

"No," the Jap said sadly. "I can never return."

More questioning brought forth that this prisoner and his killed fellows were motor mechanics sent to get a number of trucks parked in Pastrana. They did not know that Americans had captured the town two days before.

Numerous skirmishes flared up between combat patrols roaming the mountain passes and Japanese detachments attempting to traverse the watershed. Eight Japanese charged with bayonets a force of two hundred Americans bivouacked near Hubas, south of Pastrana; every man in this suicide squad was riddled with bullets. Two Banzai night attacks were repulsed in the vicinity of Ypad. A Division combat patrol of sixty pushing to the headwaters of the Binahaan River encountered a hundred Japanese not far from the village of Rizal. These Japs wore uniforms and helmets different from those worn by the Sixteenth Imperial Division, and they fought with ferocity and skill. The Americans were forced to fall back. But at dusk scouts spotted the enemy bivouac near Rizal. There were many little fires over which the Japanese cooked rice in their messkits. A sudden night artillery barrage killed most of the camped foe. They were never buried. The odor of rotting flesh lingered over the area for days.

Farthest into Leyte's mountain wilderness pushed the men of Company "A." They climbed the rugged slopes directly toward the enemy base of Ormoc. Their task was to block the old Spanish trail which links the mountain passes with Lake Danao. It was a nine-day mission.

Guerillas were enlisted as guides. The taskforce cleaved its way with machetes over nigh impassable trails. It forded many nameless streams. The nights it spent in tangled underbrush and pouring rain. Through nine days and nights no man of this team wore a stitch of clothing that was dry. Supplies of food and ammunition were limited to what each man could carry on his back.

Toward evening of the first day the company struck a Japanese outpost on the approaches to a narrow pass. The Japs fired first. A Filipino scout fell wounded. A squad of infantry then flanked the outpost and attacked. Two enemies were killed, and the survivors fled into the jungle.

On the second day a column of two hundred Japanese attempting to cross the mountains from Ormoc was stopped and dispersed. .

On the third day "Able" Company's men cut their way three miles up a deep gorge toward Lake Danao. They dug in on a bluff within the canyon. Near midnight, during a blinding rain squall, the Japanese attacked. They broke into the perimeter with bayonets and grenades, but were repulsed. At dawn twelve enemy cadavers were found between the foxholes.

By evening of the fourth day the company dug in astride the old Spanish trail. Patrols encountered more Japanese outposts to the front and rear. Three Japs were killed and the remainder chased into the lowlands.

The days that followed were a nightmare of rain, of taking life, of fatigue and hunger. The country between Mount Mamban and Mount Apo is a rugged welter of gorges and jungles. When Japs were encountered—as often as not they were less than five yards off before they could be spotted. Rations were exhausted and ammunition was soaked by the rain. For four days the riflemen lived on taro roots, wild bananas and papaya. Nights in the mountain passes were bitterly cold; fever, poisonous centipedes and chilling mists added to the suffering.

At one point, as the company toiled over a steep defile, enemy machineguns fired from the top of a ridge forty yards away. Enemy snipers moved out on bluffs overlooking the trail. Bullets cut down an aid man who hastened forward to help a wounded soldier. Grenades were pitched from treetops. The bodies of the dead could not be recovered for burial. But the use of the old Spanish trail was denied to the foe.

Near two of the blocked passes the taskforce struck booby traps at crossings. There were trip wires attached to high explosive charges, and hand-grenades hidden in bunches of bananas. The Japanese used laced jungle vines as warning devices. And there were snarls of land mines along the trails.

During a skirmish for a ridge flanking one of the passes a typhoon blew. Night was near. Trees were bent low by the storm. The bark of rifles and the rataplan of the machineguns submerged in the thunder of the heavens and the roaring wind. The jungle heaved. Rain followed in drumming cataracts.

Through inky darkness and the screeching storm a man's voice shouted: "Let's pull out of here!"

The company withdrew into a canyon on the bottom of which a "nose" jutted like some forgotten island. Here the men dug in to weather the night. Corpsmen bandaged the wounded. There was nothing to eat. The walls of the gorge reverberated with a strange and savage rumbling. Lightning was continuous. And suddenly a flash flood roared down the gorge. The soldiers huddled on the nose were on an island surrounded by a pounding surf. Through sheets of lightning they saw that the waters carried with them rocks and trees and the bodies of the dead.

At the start of its mission the company had drawn rations for 275 men. When it rejoined its regiment it had been reduced to a strength of 120.

CHAPTER NINE

JARO SUNDAY

"RESISTANCE ON LEYTE VANISHING."

(Newspaper headline, Oct. 30, 1944)

ON A SUNDAY MORNING advance patrols peered into the outskirts of Jaro. They saw forty Japanese engaged in taking a field bath in the manner approved by Nippon's Imperial Army.

The Japs had cut the tops out of two empty gasoline drums. They were filling the drums with water. Under one they then built a fire kindled with planking torn from a peasant's hut. Next to the drums they placed a wooden grating to prevent their feet from becoming muddy. When the water in the first drum was hot enough, the highest ranking officer was called. All others lined up behind him, naked, and according to rank. The senior officer took his bath first. The others followed, one by one. They soaped themselves in the first drum, and rinsed in the second. The one-star privates bathed last. After the bath they lined up, faced in the direction of the Imperial Palace in Tokyo, and bowed. The hidden watchers of this scene could not suppress their laughter. Dogs began to bark, and the patrol was forced to fade into the brush.

But these Japs, and many others like them, fought hard for Jaro. The town of Jaro, at the foot of twin-peaked Mt. Mamban and on the upper reaches of the Mainit River, is the key town of the Leyte Valley. Here the highways from Palo, Dagami and San Miguel meet and turn north to Carigara and the sea. The battle for the country around Jaro will never be forgotten by Colonel "Red" Newman, nor by any man of his command.

The thick-set, red-haired colonel folded up his map. He put away pencil and notebook. He checked his pistol and his carbine and he tightened the strap of his helmet across his chin. No one had ever seen Colonel Newman send a soldier to confront a hazard which he was not quietly willing to share. No one had ever seen "Red" Newman wavering or undecided. His movements were deliberate and sure. Aged forty-two, an infantryman to the core, the colonel was a fine combination of leader, athlete and man of letters. At West Point he had set a record by running a mile in four minutes and twenty-three seconds. In 1928 he had gone to Amsterdam with the Olympic team. He had also written and published more than a million words; but not even his friends knew his *nom de plume*. They teased him that morning when they saw him scribble in his notebook. "A man's hobby is his private affair," he smiled. "Gentlemen, prepare for the scrap."

The Third Battalion led the regiments march on Jaro. Its vanguard was "Love" Company, and the vanguard's commander, Captain Richard J. Baker of Baltimore was rated one of the coolest combat officers in the Division. The force pushed upstream along the Mainit River, past washouts and blasted bridges, and flushing snipers out of trees on the way. A soldier left to guard a bridge was rushed by a lone Japanese armed with a club; he shot his assailant fifteen times before the Jap lay still. Little happened until the battalion point approached the village of Galotan on the outskirts of Jaro. There the lead scout saw a bare-legged man scurry into a hut. He thought the other was a Filipino, and shouted for the man to come out. The answer was a bullet between the eyes. The scout's comrades raged forward. They broke down the hut and fairly tore the bare-legged enemy to shreds. Murderous fire lancing from a scattering of shacks drove the squad to cover. Another American was killed and several were wounded. The Japanese were solidly dug into the mud and excrements beneath the native houses and they intended to stay there. They had to be rooted out and killed one after another, and it was a slow and bloody task.

A young Californian, Private Lester Wyckoff, from Tehachapi, did not know that the scout was dead. He summoned a corpsman and together the two carried the fallen scout to a safer place. Only then did they see that they had rescued a dead man. Young Wyckoff, in towering anger, grabbed his Browning automatic rifle and rushed forward again, firing to avenge his comrade.

Forward with him went the squad's second scout, another Californian, Corporal Raymond Andrus from South Gate. They plunged into a short-range exchange of fire with the Japs under the shacks, and Andrus was shot through the wrist. He ran back to the aid man and said, "Hey, Mac, bind me up."

He was given first aid and Captain Baker ordered him to the rear as a walking casualty. Corporal Andrus protested. "All right," grinned Captain Baker, "get forward then, and fight." And fight he did until the last Jap under the huts of Galotan was ready to be buried in his own hole. Slowly "Love" Company's men forced an entry into Galotan. A radio operator, John Goodley of Wilmington, Delaware, lay behind a smashed well. He was waiting for messages to be transmitted to the battalion commander. But Captain Baker was too busy to think of messages just then; so Operator Goodley put his radio aside, snatched a dead man's rifle, and joined in the assault. Whenever he saw a Jap helmet appear in the murk beneath the shacks, Goodley paused, took careful aim and squeezed the trigger. He seemed oblivious of hostile bullets which kicked sprays of mud into his face. He fired until his ammunition was used up. Then, at a bear-crawl, he moved about, looking for more ammunition. Instead he came upon a wounded comrade. The wounded soldier was so badly hit that he could not be moved except on a litter. The radioman ran to the rear. He called a corpsman and guided him to the spot where the wounded man lay. On the way he picked up another clip of ammunition. While the medic worked to stop the flow of blood, Goodley stayed with him and shot away at three Japs who had made up their minds to kill the exposed group.

Captain Baker saw his aide fall wounded at his side. Another officer, Lieutenant John B. Clark of Santa Barbara, California, was wounded but continued to lead his men in the attack. But Captain Baker signaled a halt. He called for artillery fire. In not many minutes the Division's omnipresent cannoneers sent shells roaring among the shacks of Galotan. Geysers of mud, debris and enemy bodies danced under the palm fronds. The air was rent by the concussions and the earth trembled. The artillery barrage was soon stopped; infantry lay too close to the impact zone of the shells, and the dogfaces were as loath to give up their hold on Galotan as were the Japanese.

Captain Baker maneuvered platoons around both enemy flanks. "Love" Company resumed the assault. The ordeal lasted two hours. Wounded squirming in the killing zone were hit again and again. The sight of bullets slamming into the bodies of friends already down and out made the still fit go on a rampage. The Jap war left no room for mercy. You see an enemy who blinks his eyes or still kicks feebly and you bash in his skull as you run by. He may be only a poor peasants son who did not want war. But in combat he becomes a viper whose last convulsion may roll a lethal sting your way.

Private Edward Klehamer of Runnemede, New Jersey, a surgical technician, was in the front line. He was unarmed as most medics are. He saw a soldier crumple and he lunged forward to the wounded fellow's side. He began to drag him to the rear, ducking low under the zipping of lead. Then bullets struck the ground between his legs. The aid man went unscathed, but the wounded man was killed. Klehamer sat hunched over the corpse. He shook his fist at the Japanese under the huts of Galotan. The Japs fired again. Klehamer did not budge. It took an officers sharp command to make the medic abandon his attempt to drag the dead buddy out of the sights of enemy guns.

An hour later, in the same fight, the officer buckled under a crackling of Jap rifles. He fell thirty yards in front of the most advanced American squad. Klehamer dashed forward to the officers side. The firing mounted in intensity and Klehamer was unable to move. But he remained with the wounded man and tended his wounds until relief arrived. The aid man's awesome duty of facing death without the bleak privilege of dealing death had not shaken the corpsman from New Jersey. After a minute's rest and a draught of chlorinated water he said simply, "Let me go. I want to help."

The squads advancing along a river bed to flank the Japanese strongpoints were nailed down by sheets of gunfire. The riflemen sought what cover they could find. The answering fire of the Garands waxed to a staccato roar. Sergeant James McIntyre of Barlow, Kentucky, had crawled out to drag a badly hit man of his squad to a hollow in the ground. When he returned he found that his men were burning up their last clips of ammunition. The situation threatened to become a matter of rifle butts against automatic weapons.

As if by miracle, succor came. Some distance away a squad commanded by Sergeant Paul R. Willis of Dallas, North Carolina, lay in a fire fight. Firing, at this point, was sporadic. Sergeant Willis heard the tempest rage down by the river. His battle-wise ears enabled him to distinguish between the solid barks of the Garands and the whip-like cracking of Japanese weapons. He became aware that the volume of barks diminished while the flat cracking increased. "Guys over there are getting short of rounds," he said.

He acted promptly. Bent low, he raced from man to man along his skirmish line, collecting surplus ammunition. Enemy snipers in a nearby pig-pen fired at the running American. Presently Sergeant Willis was loaded heavily with bandoleers. He dashed across the highway, across a patch of rice field bordering the river. He brought the ammunition to the beleaguered squads. The men were grim, grateful.

After that, "Love" Company closed in for the kill. Under the mud-bound shacks of Galotan scores of Japanese died horribly.

While fighting raged in Galotan, Lieutenant Colonel Postlethwait, commanding the regiment's Third Battalion, dispatched several companies on a wide arc to envelope Jaro from the north. This force was halted by machineguns firing from tunnel emplacements on a wooded knoll. Postlethwait radioed for artillery fire. Soon the shells came screaming in over the heads of the pinned-down flanking force. The defenders abandoned the knoll. A patrol went forward through steep thickets. It found fifteen Japs chewed to pieces by bursting shells. The bulk of Japanese then retreated into the hills to the west. But they found the ridges occupied by Nineteenth Infantry detachments which had speared north from Pastrana. The cornered enemy sought cover in the river bed, set up machineguns and fought fiercely. He was supported by artillery pounding from yet undiscovered roosts beyond Jaro.

Out of their trap Nippon's fighting men counterattacked with fixed bayonets. On the extreme right flank of his company lay Private George Ferries of Bakersfield, California. Smoke from exploding Japanese shells obscured his vision to the front. He held his head low to the ground, his helmet turned toward the explosions and his face held sideways. What he saw off to his flank made him sit up and shout an alarm. Swarms of Japs came in a counter thrust around the shoulder of a low hill on the company's right. The riflemen met the onset, threw it back.

At this time a West Virginian, Corporal Robert L. Church, a medic, was on his way to the rear suffering from fever and battle exhaustion. He heard the noise of fighting and asked, "What's going on?" A lineman who was trying to string wire across a clump of splintered palms told him. "Plenty" the lineman said.— "Any wounded up front?"—"Quite a few," the lineman said. Shivering, barely able to stay on his feet, Church turned and gathered a litter squad. Five times he led his squad of aid men to the front to bring the wounded to safety. He did not quit until he had helped to give first aid to forty wounded soldiers in less than an hour's time. He then escorted his patients to the immediate rear where the battalion surgeon, Captain Donald B. Cameron, took over.

Men are transformed in battle. They stand alone and naked for everyone to see. The Yokohama coolie may be a docile fellow at home, but he becomes a beast of prey when he suddenly confronts you with a grenade in each hand. Someone you relied on suddenly cringes with fear. Other men whose existence you barely noticed through months and years abruptly loom before your eyes as giants of courage and of willingness to help. Private James Robinson who is married to a girl in Pauli Pike, Indiana, crawled four hundred yards through Japanese mortar and machinegun blasts to lug badly needed mortar ammunition to his outflanked squad. No one who has never carried mortar shells in tropical heat can know what that means. It means pain, crucifying pain. . . . A mortar shell made in Nippon burst and critically wounded three men. They struggled in a puddle of mud and blood and they shouted for help. Technician Clarence Temple of Sheridan, Wyoming, crawled forward and helped them while other mortar shells made in Nippon exploded far and near.... Private Howard F. Day whose wife lives in Freeport, Illinois, carried a load of mortar shells through thicket and swamp. And after delivering his shells he crawled off to the right where two enemies were sniping and killed them both.... Sergeants Andrew Koassechony of Apache, Oklahoma, and Bernard Mills of Brooklyn, risked death to save a soldier who had fallen on patrol. A Japanese machinegun hammered twenty yards away. When they reached their comrade they found that he was dead. Sergeants Mills and Koassechony brought back only the dead man's rifle and the letters and a photograph they had found in his pockets. "We thought his mother might want them," they said.

In battle men can hide nothing. There was an officer who threw himself into a ditch and wept. There was a sergeant who threw away his rifle and hid his face in his hands. A boy of nineteen went insane from fear. But there was also Sergeant James Cimmiyotti from Kimberley, Oregon, who went into a swamp and killed a sniper who had shot a man in Cimmiyotti's platoon. And there were the two "Able" Company sergeants who with their bodies protected armored self-propelled guns.

Colonel Newman had sent tank destroyers forward to deal with Japanese strongpoints at point blank range. Now, tanks and anti-tank guns were fine weapons. But on rough, overgrown ground they are vulnerable to attack by small suicide units. Tanks must move slowly along jungle-flanked roads where the terrain is treacherous and vision is bad. Japanese anti-tank assault teams were trained to strike tanks at their vulnerable points: treads, rear, observation ports and periscopes. One man uses a long pole to place a mine under a moving tread. Simultaneously another man may throw a "Molotov cocktail," a bottle filled with a mixture of oil and gasoline. This mixture set afire transforms the tank into a broiler for its occupants. At the same time other men will mount the tank and use grenades and rifles against the ports. Jap tank-hunters used smoke grenades and smoke candles to blind the crew. Or they tried to halt the tank by jamming a log between the driving wheels. Or a Jap would strap a mine to his belly and then throw himself in front of the crunching tracks. Tanks needed infantry protection to guard them against such suicidal charges. Sergeants Robert Bowman of Newburyport, Massachusetts, and Louis H. Hansel of Mount Vernon, Kentucky, were ordered to guard the steel flanks of self-propelled howitzers going into battle.

The infantry withdrew. The two noncoms led their platoon forward. As the tank-destroyers closed with the enemy nests, Bowman and Hansel drew their protecting ring of riflemen about the lumbering giants. They warded off two assaults by demolition units as the SPM's completed their mission. Then the tracked guns turned and headed rearward. Withdrawing, Sergeants Bowman and Hansel found two badly wounded soldiers. They signaled the SPM's (Self-propelled Mounts) to halt. Under aimed fire they stood upright to load the wounded aboard the tracked mounts. After that they saw them safely to cover. Sergeant Bowman was painfully wounded. Louis Hansel died in action.

At 5 P.M. October 29, the storm elements of the Thirty-Fourth entered Jaro. Carigara lay ten miles to the north. On that day thirteen Japanese transport ships carrying reinforcements to Leyte were bombed to the bottom of Camotes Sea. Seventy-six raiding Japanese planes had been shot down. The news was good. That evening an Associated Press correspondent echoing MacArthur's optimism, cabled home that "all organized Japanese resistance appears to have ceased in the strategically vital Leyte Valley." This newsman did not see the rows of cold, stiff figures on trucks rumbling to makeshift cemeteries among the swamps.

That evening Jap ammunition depots in Jaro were set ablaze by unknown hands. "Love" Company was again the vanguard of a battalion pushing north from Jaro an hour before dusk. A field report states that, "The leading platoon came under heavy fire and several men were hit. Captain Baker immediately moved forward in the face of enemy fire and supervised the withdrawal of the platoon from an untenable position, and the evacuation of the wounded. . . . Later the same day, after Company "K" had been pinned down by machinegun fire from its left flank, Company "L" was ordered to make an enveloping movement to the left. The company moved into position and attacked through a palm grove. The enemy initially held his fire and then, from well camouflaged positions on commanding ground, opened fire with five or more machineguns and thirty or more rifles. Many of our men were killed or wounded in the first minute. . .

The men of the Thirty-Fourth dug in for another night. Through the darkness artillery thundered. Captain Baker was thirsty after this day of sweat, death and filth. He reached for his canteen. The canteen was empty. A Japanese bullet had pierced it.

From midnight to dawn rifle and machinegun fire rippled. Jap infiltration parties were on the crawl. From midnight to dawn rain fell steadily upon the tired men.

In the pre-dawn darkness of October 30 Colonel Newman threw off the poncho under which he had rested. He arose, muddy, wet, but with confidence that the day would bring the decision of the battle for Leyte Valley—the break-through to the sea. His regiment's planners had worked all night in little blackout tents hidden behind jungle barricades. In the rear the engineers had toiled to make the roads fit to bear the traffic of ammunition and supplies. Between the Mainit River Bridge and Jaro two major washouts had blocked the road. The engineers had built a by-pass around one; they had brought bulldozers and they had changed the course of the river to make passable the other. The Division Command Post moved forward, hard in the wake of the fighting troops.*

The task of finding sites for the forward displacement of the Division Command post fell to Lieutenant Colonel Thomas H. Compere, a Chicago lawyer whose chief ambition it was to go back to the practice of law. On his reconnaissances far in advance of the staff he often came under hostile mortar and machinegun fire, and more than once he was a target for snipers lurking in head-high grass. A division command post in the field is a complex thing—a moving city of drab little tents, of jungle hammocks, field desks, radios, trucks and jeeps. Its numerous "sections" range from "Operations," "Artillery" and "Intelligence" through "Counter Intelligence," "Ordnance," radio, message and medical centers—to mention but a few—to the officer whose duty it is to serve the melancholy needs of the dead. The location of camp sites for the Division's brain, near enough to the front and on ground allowing for effective defense against night raids, was no easy job. On invasion day the craft carrying Compere's party was struck by shells and an aide was killed and fifteen others wounded. On Red Beach the mild-mannered lawyer had calmly gathered the fit and set out to find America's first command post in the Philippines. On another day he picked a spot so far advanced that an enemy counter-attack threatened to overrun it. Artillery fire fell among the men who laid out the camp, striking down eight. But already Tom Compere was preparing to push Headquarters into the town of Jaro.

---

* The disposition of American troops fighting on Leyte at this time was as follows: The Twenty-Fourth Infantry Division advancing on Carigara from the south after its cross-island drive; the First Cavalry Division driving toward Carigara from the east; the Seventh and the Ninety-Sixth Infantry Divisions pushing across southern Leyte toward the Japanese base of Ormoc. Japanese forces dislodged from central Leyte were streaming both toward Carigara and Ormoc, the north and south gates, respectively, of the Ormoc Valley or "Corridor."

"All right," said "Red" Newman, "we'd better slug on, then."

The road from Jaro to Carigara crosses twelve streams which flow from the gorges of the Mt. Mamban massif. Before the regiment reached Carigara, all twelve bridges had been burned or blown to wreckage. The road was blasted and mined, and the thickets and plantations along it were charred by an eighteen-hour artillery barrage. Every weapon that the Division's field artillery battalions could muster belched steel and high explosive.

The infantry attack jumped off at 8 A.M. The men who pulled northward out of Jaro that sultry morning felt they were giving their last. They cursed the existence of Carigara and they cursed the road and its vile flanking terrain. Again "Love" Company was in the vanguard. Machinegun fire flashed where the road leaves Jaro toward the village of Tunga. As on the previous day, the hurricane of bullets sprang from deep emplacements hidden under native houses. As on the previous day, men fell in bitter huddles. Again there were the groans, the blood, the wordless savagery, and corpsmen hastening to aid the fallen. Under direct fire the leading elements fell back.

Sergeant James Walker of Bowling Green, Missouri, and his section of machinegunners covered the withdrawal. They set up their guns and poured lead into the Japanese under the shacks. Four times during this duel of the machineguns Walker left cover and stood up to direct and control the fire of his gunners.

On the left flank of the stalled assault a platoon was nailed to the ground by two Japanese machineguns. Their firing came in vicious relays. Boldly three members of another American machinegun crew met the crisis. To save the platoon they sacrificed whatever shred of safety there was in lying flat. In full view of enemy gunners they mounted their weapon. Again it was machinegun against machinegun.

A mortarman who observed his comrades' plight advanced in leaps and bounds. He reached a position on a grassy bank from which he was able to get a clear view of the Japanese strongpoints. There he knelt, directing with signals of arm and hand the fire of friendly mortars emplaced in the rear. Soon mortar shells dropped on the Japs. But the enemy had spotted the observer. The guns spat and the observer died. His name was Bruno Krasowski, of Lodi, New Jersey.

Now Japanese artillery fire found the American ranks. Shells from anti-tank guns, from anti-aircraft cannon, and from heavier field pieces plowed the highway between Jaro and Tunga. Private Enos Torsch from Lachine, Michigan, located a Japanese cannon whose shells were preventing withdrawal of the forward platoons. To another soldier he called, "Come on, lets knock that baby out."

The two volunteers proceeded to a grassy knoll and brought their Garands to bear. The Jap cannoneers dived into a ditch. Pursued by the rattle of hostile automatic rifles Torsch and his buddy dodged back to cover. On the way they found a wounded comrade and took him along.

Sergeants Modester Duncan and Ralph E. Trank halted in the withdrawal because they saw that another of the wounded men had been left behind. The wounded soldier was flopping about in the road. He was trying to drag himself to shelter. Said Trank, "Can't leave that Joe there to die." Duncan agreed. Together they ran into the firing zone and carried the injured man to the rear. Duncan hails from Mooresbridge, Alabama; Tranks hometown is unknown.

Unaware of the retreat was Private Wilber Spoonhour of Chambersburg, Pennsylvania. Spoonhour was a scout. When enemy fire became thick and deadly, he was out in front of his team. He did not know that the men behind him had been ordered to withdraw. His stomach tight, he continued to advance—alone. He penetrated the Japs' line of defense. And suddenly he realized that he was isolated and surrounded by the foe. Spoonhour was scared, but he looked around. He saw exactly how and where the Japanese defenders were deployed. Then he retraced his course. On chin and toes he crept from shack to bush, from bush to ditch, from ditch to palm, from palm to mudhole, and then he suddenly stood up and shot his way back to friendly lines. The information he brought back about enemy positions saved many American lives.

Halfway in tortured no-man's-land a lone soldier lay behind a stump. The soldier was firing his Garand steadily at the slope of a brush-covered knoll which flanked the road. Japanese snipers, in turn, were firing at the man behind the stump. "'What's Andy firing at?" his comrades wondered. And then they saw. With a solid disregard for the snipers the soldier was shooting at Jap machinegunners who tried to prevent a group of corpsmen from bringing in the wounded. The lone rifleman was Andrew Zubal, Private, of Watervliet, New York.

Between Jaro and Tunga the medics were at their best. First aid stations which accompanied the advance were swamped with wounded: men ripped by bullets, men mangled by grenades, men with broken bones and biting burns, men knocked unconscious by concussions and men whose legs had been torn away by bursting shells. Captain Donald B. Cameron, Battalion Surgeon, of Calhoun, Kentucky, moved emergency stations to within thirty yards of the firing lines. He so cut short the time which would have been consumed in carrying injured soldiers farther to the rear.

Sergeant Carlton Grode of Menasha, Wisconsin, and his litter squad crawled two hundred yards through machinegun and mortar strikes to aid the critically wounded. Staff Sergeant Chester Jordon of New York Mills, New York, and his corpsmen went forward five times into no-man's-land to evacuate the fallen. Private Norval Hill from Summerfield, Ohio, advanced one hundred and fifty yards into all hell to tie a splint to a comrade's broken leg; so did Aid Man Francis T. Hall of Centralia, Illinois, and others whose names no history book will mention. Right-hand man of Captain Cameron in the job of patching smashed organisms amid the pandemonium of battle was Kenneth Seitner whose wife, Lillian, was waiting for his return in Dayton, Ohio. She waited in vain; Samaritan Seitner was killed in action.

There was a mud-splashed jeep which carried the wounded from Cameron's aid station to a field hospital behind the lines. There were little holes in this jeep, put there by snipers along the road. The jeep came forward, empty, time after time; and seconds later it pulled out loaded with men on litters. And when the jeep balked after five such expeditions, its sun-blackened driver pitched in to guide those of the wounded who still could crawl or limp. "Here, buddy, put your arm 'round my shoulder ... lean on it ... hard ... let's try and see if we can make it together. . . ." This driver's name was Elmer C. Simpson, a surgeon's aide from Denton, Texas.

The earth vibrated and the air was split. Strangling heat filled the valley. In the minds of grime-crusted men in battle there remains no trace of the often-asked and never-answered question, 'Why do we fight?" Reality was upon them and thinking stopped. They fought to stay alive—no more. There was an upsurge of a wild tenacity as old as life, teeth gnashing through abysmal weariness, a discarding of all hope and thoughts of home, a dull snarl of the protesting subconscious on the verge of shock. "Oh—oh, the bastards." "Love" Company's Captain Baker called for tanks. The tanks came. They blasted the shacks. They raked the strongpoints on the flanking ridges, then withdrew. There was little good they could do in terrain where a man could see far if he could see ten yards. Lieutenant Lewis F. Steams of Champaign, Illinois, commanding the foremost platoon, drew back his men so that artillery might be registered on the resistance.

Colonel Newman came forward then, hard, slow, quiet. He ordered a cautious resumption of the advance, without artillery. Again the tanks rumbled to the front. Lieutenant Steams deployed a squad on each side of the road to spearhead the assault. On he strode up the road, one tank in front of him, another tank to his immediate rear. The advance gained fifty yards—then Japanese fire forced the riflemen again to hug the mud. Steams crouched in the roadside ditch. He wiped the sweat out of his eyes and reloaded his carbine.

"Hang on," he encouraged his men. 'Don't give 'em an inch."

Again "Red" Newman came forward.

'What's the holdup here?" he asked.

"Better get down in the ditch, Colonel," said Steams.

Newman shook his head. "I'll get the men going okay," he said.

The colonel strode forward. Lieutenant Steams leaped out of the ditch. He shouted to his men,

"Lets go! The Colonel is here!"

The men rose from the ground. They followed their regimental commander in the assault. There was the wailing of an artillery shell, a flash and a crash, a revolt of earth and sky. The shell had hit the soldier nearest to "Red" Newman. The soldier was blown to bits. The concussion blew men across the ground as though they were leaves driven by a gust of wind. Lieutenant Steams saw the colonel clutch his belly with both hands.

"Aid man! Aid man!"

A corpsman came running, bent low, his face almost between his knees. Colonel Newman lay on the Jaro-Carigara road. Crouched over him was his orderly, Carmelo Giacomazzo, the sculptor in wood. The Woodcarver pulled a knife and cut away the colonels clothing. Blood oozed from a gaping stomach wound. Then the aid man arrived with bandages and sulfa powder and Carmelo hastened through machinegun fire to get a jeep.

Aubrey S. Newman was calm. He was in complete command of his faculties. He did not move or struggle. He looked up into the faces of the men about him and he thought of the fight that must be won.

"Keep the troops in position," he said evenly. "Send word back for mortar fire."

"That won't do," Steams shouted. "Colonel, can you hear me?"

"Yes."

"Mortars are not enough—our men are getting killed every minute."

The colonel lay still and thought. Guns jabbered and bullets whipped by. From the front came the cracking of grenades. His face was stony under the onrush of pain, but his eyes told that he was struggling to make a decision that would clear the situation. Finally he said:

"Tell Colonel Postlethwait to call for artillery fire."

Steams dispatched a runner.

"Now," growled Newman, "just leave me here and take care of those Japs."

Steams said, "I'll be damned if I'll leave you here."
They wrapped their fallen commander into a poncho and dragged him into the ditch. Soon the Woodcarver came bumping up with a jeep. They lifted "Red" Newman into the jeep and the Woodcarver drove off as gently as a mother wheeling her injured child.*

The battle of Jaro pounded on with unabated fury. Lieutenant Colonel Chester A. Dahlen, second in command, now led the Thirty-Fourth. His first order called for an artillery barrage; his second was, "Resume the attack."

The barrage was lifted shortly after noon. Infantry attacked: "Item" Company on the right of the road, "King" Company on the left, tanks in the center. Riflemen waded across rice fields through waist-deep water. They attained the next bend in the road. But two hundred yards beyond the bend they were again halted by a wall of fire. Enemy artillery, machineguns, mortars and rifles were dug in on a ridge overlooking the highway. Further on the ground was dry, fields of sword grass going over into hillsides covered with tangled vegetation. The platoons fought on to get out of the water and the slime. Then they were pinned to the ground. Again they were forced to withdraw. Again the sweating cannoneers were called upon to plow the land ahead with steel and TNT. Long Toms, the Army's biggest land guns, spoke.

Japanese shells disabled two Sherman tanks. A Jap gunner sent a 37 millimeter projectile crashing directly down the barrel of a tank's 75. The tank gunner had just opened the breach to load his cannon. The enemy shot passed through the tube and through the gunners compartment and buried itself in the tank's radio. Three men of the crew were smashed in the burst.

"Love" Company swung to the left to strike the stubborn strongholds from the flank. Five hundred yards from the road its aggressively advancing squads crossed an open field. They were struggling toward the far side of the ridge. But the enemy was on guard; his machineguns cut loose from dugouts hidden under thickets on the hillside. His bullets scythed the field. Here and there an American clawed the air, sagged, then sprawled heavily, arms and legs thrown wide as if in some macabre dance. The company was stalled in the open. No hollows or ditches were near in which to seek cover.

Captain Baker called for a radioman so that he might inform his commander of "Loves' " dilemma. A further advance was suicide, pure

---

* Months went by before Colonel Newman could rejoin the Division. But he returned in time to guide it through the difficult Mindanao campaign as its Chief of Staff.

and simple. So was retreat across the fire-raked field. To remain in position meant gradual but certain annihilation. The radioman came, a private named John Wolf. He came through soul-withering fire. Strapped to his back was a radio. On the way Wolf fell, hit by a bullet. But he staggered back to his feet. Then he fell again, and another operator came forward to take his place.

Captain Baker radioed for artillery support. Meanwhile, his company's machineguns pushed forward to throw out a curtain of lead under which his company could disengage. The machinegunners mounted their weapons on the unobstructed field. The Japanese replied by showering mortar shells on the machineguns. Sergeant Joseph E. Snipes of Eoline, Alabama, manned the first gun. Others followed; if Snipes could do it, they could, too. Snipes was wounded. Through clenched teeth he shouted insults at the Japs.

One of the machinegun crews fared badly. In rapid succession the gunner, the assistant gunner, and the ammunition bearer were hit. Only one man of that crew was left fit for action: Edward Prachazka of Downers Grove, Illinois. Prachazka did the work of four. He rolled the wounded out of the way and fired. In three minutes, more than three hundred bullets passed through the muzzle of his weapon.

"Love" Company withdrew. After that, the machinegunners withdrew. Though his gun was red hot, Prachazka picked it up together with what ammunition remained. Carrying a load designed for three he scrambled to safety across the death-ridden field.

Only one man now remained on the abandoned field. Private Thomas E. Mellinger, from Buffalo, realized the peril which threatened the machinegunners in their uncovered withdrawal. He stayed behind, firing his rifle at the Japs until the last machinegunner had slipped from sight.

But as Mellinger retreated, others again rushed forward, not to kill but to help. Private Darrel Winn of Osceola, Iowa, saw two soldiers struggling with a third whose legs had been badly hurt; he darted forward and helped. Private Jerome Bomstein of Madison, Wisconsin, crawled around the fire zone, tending the fallen. Private Morris W. Taylor, a messenger, whose home is in Coldwater, Michigan, saw a wounded buddy thrashing while a spray of bullets churned the earth around him. Taylor crept out and dragged the man into a clump of bushes. Meanwhile, not far away, a soldier named Narcisso Coronado from Center Point, Texas, had spotted a shack full of Japanese munitions; he fired tracer shells until the shack caught fire and exploded. At this point of the front the Japs jumped from their holes, milled in confusion, and disappeared.

That night the Division's field artillery hurled four hundred and eighty-six rounds of high explosive into the Japanese lines north of Jaro.

Chapter Ten

SILENCE IN CARIGARA

"Even if our earthly bodies perish on this island, our spirits will forever remain here, continuing to attack our arch enemies and defending and protecting forever our divine fatherland of Nippon."

(Hyosigi in the Japanese "Davao News")

AN OLD MAN trudged through the puddles, singing. Balanced on his head he carried a case of beer. The natives of Jaro returned from the hills. They celebrated their liberation by guzzling large stocks of beer and sake abandoned by the Japanese. Trim-bodied girls paraded their finery among the ruined buildings. "Buffaloes" and tanks, trucks, "Alligators" and jeeps rumbled through the muddy streets toward the front. Sheets of muck splashed upon the revelers. Though many of the younger women, bare-legged and laughing, were out in flashing silks, the men and children wore only rags.

Commercially the town was dead. The Japanese had killed all trade. They had fixed all prices, then bought out the merchandise with worthless money. The stores were wrecked and empty. Only here and there a rooster was swapped for a piece of American soap; then the soldier would walk off, his shoulders swinging, the cackling rooster dangling from his pack.

A Japanese found hiding in an attic was hacked to death by the crowd. Bands of guerillas descended from their mountain hideouts. Some carried old American rifles. Others bore captured Arasakas. Still others were armed with shotguns made from lengths of lead piping, with bolos, spears, and spiked clubs. They arrested every member of the pro-Japanese Bureau of Constabulary they could find, and after that they began arresting one another. Several guerilla chieftains appointed themselves to the post of Mayor of Jaro and made speeches praising freedom and insulting their rivals. American patrols endeavored to disarm the more unruly among the straw-hatted partisans, and the citizens of Jaro gloated. Patriotic banditry had become a habit during the Japanese occupation. It had often been guerilla practice to strip villagers of pigs and chickens "in the name of the fight against the Japanese." Plain thieves who had collected pigs and rice "for the liberation," then sold their loot to the Japs, had been no rarity; though when caught by bona fide guerillas the scoundrels were hanged feet up and head down in an ant-heap, and skeletons still dangled in the plantations. A Jaro lawyer made a speech, telling the people that the time was past when it was necessary to feed the irregulars a dozen pigs to make them strong enough to kill a Jap. The Americans would now kill Japs gratis. A guerilla group promptly carried off the lawyer as a "good neighbor"—i.e., collaborator. It was difficult to control the various patriotic bands. Collecting and hiding arms had long been a favorite sport of the *barrio* men in the hills. The civic disputes of Jaro were finally settled by Colonel Alva Carpenter, the Civil Affairs Officer of the Division.

While artillery thundered, the younger of the populace frolicked in outlying streets. With liberation, the rigid chaperonage system of Spanish days broke down, briefly, in Jaro as in other towns overrun in the campaign. Dancing on the flat, stinking earth between the nipa huts began at sundown and continued until dawn. Tawny maidens who had not had a piece of good soap in years, flashed their dark eyes, wriggled their bodies and laughed often. Jap rice, wine bottles, K-ration tins and struggling couples littered the slatted bamboo floors of the shacks. But the free-and-easy welcome ended quickly. (Three days later only prostitutes made dates and prices soared sky-high.) Infantry marched out of Jaro at dawn, dog-tired, silent, dirty and grim, and the morning breeze brought into town the stench of corpses decomposing on the road to Tunga.

In emergency cemeteries behind the front native labor gangs dug graves. Quartermaster trucks hauled the unpainted wooden crosses. At the edge of soggy acres lay the American dead. Their silent forms, stiffened as they had fallen, lay wrapped in blankets, or in weather-beaten tent cloth, only their muddy boots protruding. To each cross a "dog-tag" was nailed; a dead mans name, the name of his faraway home town, the name of his mother or his wife. Gently the dead were placed into their graves. Those still alive were too busy in battle to attend. There were only the laborers of the burial detail, guards armed with carbines, and there was the chaplain's voice booming beneath the hiss-wails of artillery shells speeding through the rain. At times, also, there was the crack of some sniper's weapon aimed at the lonely man before the open graves.

Near Jaro a chaplain reading the burial service saw the ground about him cut by bullets. The enemy gunner sat hidden in a fringe of brush. Bullets struck into the body of one already dead. The chaplain dived behind a pile of freshly dug earth. His escort, Captain J. J. Mason of Colonial Beach, Virginia, crept toward the fringe of the jungle to locate the Jap. Again the Jap fired. This time he was only yards away. Bullets clipped branches above Captain Mason. Attracted by the firing, a squad of riflemen infiltrated the thicket. They found the sniper in a hollow tree stump and filled him with lead. The chaplain rose. His voice rang over the graves. Artillery thundered. Overhead a Cub plane circled.

The artillery barrage laid down between Jaro and Tunga stopped at 8 A.M. At 8:20 A.M. October 31, the Thirty-Fourth Infantry resumed the attack, Carigara its goal.

"Love" Company advanced upon the rear of the ridge from which the Japanese had defied its assault the previous day. "Item" Company plowed north astride the road. "King" Company followed in reserve.

By 9:30 A.M. "Love" Company had arrived at the base of the ridge. The sky had cleared and the sun shone bright and hard. Except for solitary shots by snipers along their course, there was no evidence of the strong enemy force of the day before. But the blood-letting of the past had made the men cautious. In front of them lay a ravine. It was filled with gloom and jungle, and with the odor of stagnant water. What lurked in this draw? The company took covered positions. Private Ray Wyatt of Wilkesboro, North Carolina, volunteered to go forward and look.

"Who of you guys'll go with me?" he drawled.

Two other soldiers volunteered. They advanced toward the draw. Where the grass was short, they crawled on their bellies. They peered into the wall of thickets growing down the steep defile. There was no sound, no sign of life. "No Japs," Wyatts comrades said.

"I can smell 'em," said Wyatt.

He raised his rifle and fired into the murk of tangled vegetation. An echo rang from the hillside. The crackle of *Arisaka* rifles followed. Wyatt and his helpers dashed along the edge of the draw. They fired into the bushes as they ran. At some spots the volume of enemy bullets ebbed away, at others it swelled viciously. Then a machinegun sputtered.

"Let's get the hell out of here," said Wyatt.

They ran at a crouch. Bullets twanged past their ears. Back in "Love" Company's ranks an automatic rifle gunner named Ellis Rich, from Pineville, Kentucky, realized that Wyatt and his patrol would be mowed down before they could reach the company's line—if nothing was done. So he stood up in full view of the Japs and fired his B.A.R. toward the edge of the ravine. The enemy gunners drew in their heads. The draw was plastered with mortar shells until the jungle burned. Then "Love" Company stormed the position.

Simultaneously other companies pushed down the Jaro-Carigara highway. They came to a stream and found the bridge burned down. The infantrymen forded the stream. Before the scouts had reached the far bank, heavy fire rattled down from that side of the ridge which flanked the road. From the dark green of the slope came the taunting yells of Japs. The attack force split: two platoons pushed across the stream and on along roadside ditches to a position from where they could assault the reverse side of the ridge. Another group, supported by a tank, left the road and toiled up the forward slope. But tanks are nigh useless in tropical terrain. Soon mortar fire fell, and the tank withdrew.

Infantrymen charged the crest of the hill. They reached the top and drove out the Japanese with bullets and grenades. However, they discovered another defended hill not far away. The maps showed no trace of this second hill. From it squalls of fire nailed the platoons to the ground.

Soldiers lugged heavy machineguns to the crest of the captured ridge. A tank accompanied by an assault group circled the ridge. A short, massive artillery barrage prepared the way. In a double attack the battle teams lashed out at the second height. The charge carried the summit. The trapped defenders plunged down the rear slope and charged "Love" Company's positions. "Love" Company fell back under the impact, then held, and most Japs died in a furious three-hour fight.

On the right flank of the assault the leader of a machinegun squad, Private Stephen Mizen of River Grove, Illinois, led his team of four over rough terrain to join a company he had been ordered to reinforce. When he arrived at the designated spot on a knoll he found that the company had maneuvered to another position. His squad was alone. At this time an enemy force at the base of the knoll counter attacked. Mizen saw the Japanese darting up the slope through clumps of *kunai* and scrub palm. He knew that if the foe recaptured the knoll, there would be nothing to prevent him from breaking through to the Carigara Road. "We'll stay," Mizen decided. "Set up quick." The machinegun was mounted in less than fifteen seconds. "Give her the works," said Mizen. The machinegun hammered. Rifles cracked. The Japanese burst out in high-pitched screeching. The countercharge was repulsed.

In a gorge between the hills a crew of litter bearers was engaged in carrying away our wounded. They were harassed by snipers lurking in the underbrush. Private Hollis Hedeen, of Milwaukee, noticed their plight. He ran to a bluff on the slope.

It gave him a fair field of fire. It also exposed him to Jap eyes. There, kneeling, he engaged a bevy of snipers some fifty yards off. It was five against one. The corpsmen and their patients passed safely. Hollis Hedeen threw out his arms, pitched forward, fatally wounded.

A platoon skirting high ground stopped in its tracks under an abrupt fire from artillery pieces, from mortars, machineguns and snipers' rifles. During the first moment of stunned surprise three men were wounded. Among them was William H. Collins, the scout. The platoon retreated into a gully. Collins remained forward. Aid men dashed up. Collins pointed to the other wounded. "Get those fellows out first." He could not walk. While aid men helped the other two wounded away, the injured scout shielded their retreat with covering fire from his Garand. Only then did he follow them, half rolling, half pulling himself through the vines with his hands.

In the same test of loyalty a company commander fell. There was a threat of panic. Clarence Stubbs of Minneapolis, a lieutenant leading a platoon, quickly took charge. He scrambled about, directing his men to new positions. Stubbs was hit twice. He brushed off the corpsmen who came to carry him away until the company was safe.

A rifle squad descended the northern slope of the ridge. It was met by machinegun fire as the men emerged from the hillside thickets. Ahead of them lay an open field. In the center of this field stood a nipa hut on stilts. The hostile machinegun was firing from a hole dug under that hut. The hostile gunners were invisible. They were shooting through a slit built into a wall of earth. It was an almost perfect position: the gun's grazing bullets were able to cover every square foot of the fronting field.

"Let's knock the son-of-a-bitch out," said Sergeant William Byess of Chatsworth, Illinois, leader of the squad.

The riflemen hesitated. They knew what a machinegun could do.

"Call for mortars," someone suggested. "Set the shack afire."

Byess did not want to wait for a mortar. He detailed three men to creep around to the left, three men to creep around to the right. He put his automatic rifle gunner into a clump of bushes from where the B.A.R. man could fire at the emplacement's port. With the remaining three men of the squad he undertook the frontal attack.

"Watch my signals," he said.

Byess crawled out into the meadow. His daring inspired the others to follow his example. The Jap gun spat fire. The three miniature assault teams moved forward in alternating rushes. Approached from three sides, the machinegun could not fire on all three groups at the same time. While it pinned down one, the others advanced. Rifles barked and the B.A.R. in the clump of bushes rippled angrily. Soon the sweating men were close enough to hurl grenades.

Parallel to the skirmishing for the commanding heights, another battalion of the Thirty-Fourth Regiment drove down the road toward Tunga. "Easy" Company formed the point of the drive. In the sodden countryside far off the road, patrols protected the flanks of the advance. Lead scout for a flank patrol was Private Orville Franks of Portland, Indiana. Upon his alertness depended the life of his patrol, the security of his company, the continuity of his battalions offensive. Franks pushed through swamp, across meadows and strips of plantation, aggressive and lithe, as a good scout should be. And suddenly he stopped.

Outlined against the foliage ahead was a small, round head, an immobile face. Slowly the scout melted to the ground. He motioned his patrol to halt. Then he moved forward without making a sound.

Beyond the enemy watcher in the brush were other enemies. There were three, their shoulders hunched over a machinegun whose muzzle showed through overhanging leaves. The machinegun pointed toward the road. The slant-eyed gunners were observing "Easy" Company's progress toward Tunga. Presently the company would move into their line of fire.

Franks raised his rifle. He fired four times. The ambush was destroyed.

Later that day a Japanese artillery barrage pinned down the advance. Mortars and automatic weapons added their rough chimes. Wounded men cried for help. Orville Franks hastened hither and yon over the mushy terrain, carrying helpless comrades to the rear. For an hour he toiled, sweating across the frontiers of death, not thinking of himself. Until an artillery shell blasted the earth from under his feet. Then it was too late to think. The scout clawed the mud. To his mother the Army sent a Silver Star Medal and "regrets."

Another scout of a vanguard squad was Private Rudolph Sillato. "Be careful," his wife Bridget had written him from Rochester, New York. But this day Sillato's patrol became the target of a Jap machinegun firing from a range of about sixty yards. When a machinegun fires at you, you duck. You know that its bullets can carry death over a thousand yards and more. You hug the earth while bullets pass over you with harsh sibilance. Your urge is not to move an inch. Your urge is to sink into the ground and to stay there.

Sillato knew that the battalion was moving up the road. Something must be done to warn it. He crawled through grass and thorns while the machinegun fired. Then he crawled across the road where the Japs would surely see him. He reached a ditch, and after that he ran to carry his intelligence to the leader of the foremost platoon. The platoon maneuvered, encircling the ambush, and destroyed it.

At 11:30 A.M. "Easy" Company reached the swift-flowing Ginagan River. The bridge was wrecked. Infantry was forced to wade through gurgling water up to their armpits. At the same time entrenched Japanese on the other side unleashed machineguns and artillery. The forward echelons were forced to the ground. An anti-tank gun stood idle, its gunners clinging to flimsy cover. The company's mortar section, which had pushed forward to clear the road, was also pinned down and unable to stir. Tanks moved into the lead. Bullets clanged against their flanks. Their guns raked the Jap strongpoints on the left of the Carigara road. The Japs countered with point-blank artillery.

One tank was hit thrice in succession. The others were neutralized: giants not built to fight in the tropics. The point commander ordered a withdrawal to avoid annihilation. Withdrawal—but how? Enemy fire marked their spot like lightning hurled down by heathen gods. Even the bravest among corpsmen would not budge; one tried and was riddled on the spot. The many wounded suffered untended.

But then a boy from Ohio deliberately accepted death to give his buddies a chance to live. (He was Private Walter F. Laule, the son of Mrs. Eleanor Laule, of 2325 Selzer Avenue, Cleveland.) The anti-tank gun whose gunners were glued to cover had been towed by a jeep. A machinegun was mounted on this jeep. Walter Laule sensed that immediate offensive fire was needed to save more men from dying. He sprang into the jeep. He threw the machinegun into action. The machinegun clattered. Laule sprayed the treetops to silence the snipers. He then brought the muzzle of his gun to ground level against the enemy battery and the automatic weapons. The machinegun's clatter became an uninterrupted blast. Near and far the Japanese concentrated their fire on Laule. "E" Company seized the chance to disengage. As the last man reached cover a shell struck the jeep. The boy from Ohio was blown across the road. His death was instant.

While Walter Laule made his magnificent stand, the corpsmen worked with frantic haste. The wounded were whisked into a coconut grove at the base of the flanking ridge. Volunteers among the riflemen pitched in and helped. Private Edward Nickerson of Hingham, Massachusetts, came forward with litters and worked under fire to save the lives of more than a score of wounded comrades. Sergeant Stanley

Lewandowski of Jersey City used his poncho to improvise a stretcher on which he dragged a hurt friend out of hell. Corpsman Karl Nyren of Newton Highland, Massachusetts, sat hunched in the path of machinegun fire and saved a soldier from bleeding to death. The man's leg had been torn off. After he had bandaged him, Nyren looked for his stretcher. A mortar shell had destroyed it. So Nyren lifted his patient on his shoulder and trotted toward cover. A shell burst nearby. The violence of the concussion pitched the corpsman and his ward into a thicket. Nyren, too, was bleeding now. Nonetheless he stood up in agony. He picked up his legless comrade and staggered to cover.

The Division's field artillery thundered. For an hour the cannoneers rained explosives on the Japanese bulwarks. The battalion once more pushed forward. The advance guard came to another stream—the Yapan River—and again met embittered resistance. Those Jap fighting men were not merely the remnants of the beaten Imperial Sixteenth Division; identifications taken from enemy dead showed that the troops facing the Thirty-Fourth were from a crack regiment* of the Thirtieth Japanese Infantry Division, brought in from Mindanao.

The skirmish line moved forward, "Easy" Company on the left, "George" Company on the right, tanks in the center. A heavy machinegun put into position to clear a stretch of road was instantly smashed by a Jap shell. On the right flank enemy machinegun nests held up "George" Company's platoons. They fought through a palm grove raw with underbrush and often one could not see farther than two yards ahead. Platoon Sergeant Bowman, a well-liked leader of men, was pierced by bullets and fell dead. His men screamed with rage. They stormed the nests and slew the Jap gunners.

On the left flank, "Easy" Company's men traversed a low knoll and collided with a pillbox backed by a system of trenches. Direct cannon fire had forced the tanks to draw back. Well ahead of the company lay a squad commanded by Sergeant Edwin Wahl of Runnemede, New Jersey. That day they had pressed more than four miles through hostile countryside. But Wahl, not waiting for his company's strength, built up his squad in a skirmish line along the Carigara road and countered enemy artillery and machineguns with Garands. He pursued the unequal fight until commanded to fall back.

At a nearby spot an automatic rifle team of three had been nailed down by a skilful sniper in a breadfruit tree. The B.A.R. men lay in a shallow shell hole and the sniper waited for the first of them to show his head. Oh, they could finish off that sniper, they knew, by bringing

* The 41st Japanese Infantry Regiment, which landed on Leyte four days after the invasion to reinforce the defense of Carigara.

their automatic rifle to bear. But then the sniper would get in at least one shot. It seemed that one of the three was scheduled to die. Eventually their problem was solved by a cook, Pruitt Letson of Rogersville, Alabama.

Earlier that day Cook Letson had been hurt by shrapnel while carrying a message for his commanding officer. The blast had knocked him unconscious. He regained his senses in the battalion aid station. The aid station was a tarpaulin stretched in a small clearing. A medic was about to dig fragments of shrapnel out of Letson's flesh. But the messenger-cook felt fit enough to stand. He knew that his company had suffered heavily. He knew that manpower was needed at the front. "Let me go," he said. "I'm okay." Arriving at the front he spotted the sniper and shot him dead.

Another "Easy" Company man who refused evacuation was Sergeant Earl Prince of Cowan, Tennessee. He had been injured that morning leading an assault platoon. At the clearing station they patched him up and put him into an ambulance, hospital bound. Minutes before, he had heard an officer talk about the shortage of men in the lines. Prince climbed out of the ambulance, grinned at the corpsmen, and went on his way. He led his platoon through the remaining hours of the hot, hard day.

A tank destroyer from Cannon Company crunched to the front to deal with the strongpoint which held up "Easy" Company's advance on the left side of the road. The uncouth-looking mount pushed up the road, its stubby gun weaving like the feeler of some monstrous beetle. At this point a slim young man jumped out of the roadside ditch. Lieutenant Mario Mozzone of Seattle guided the self-propelled mount to its target. The Japanese saw the SPM and they saw that the officer standing in the road was directing its fire. From a range of less than a hundred yards they concentrated artillery fire on the tank destroyer and machinegun blasts at the man. Horizontal pillars of red flame erupted from the muzzle of the tank-destroyers cannon. The 75's shells mauled the enemy trenches. They threw the defenders into panic. They milled about from hole to hole with frenzied cries. "Easy" Company's riflemen cheered. They stood upright behind the trunks of palms and slaughtered the confused Japs with rifle fire.

Lieutenant Mozzone waved the tank-destroyer to the rear after it had expended its ammunition. Then he waved another tank-destroyer forward to continue the shelling. It rumbled up, spewing destruction. Its commander, Sergeant Joseph Klein of the Bronx, New York, saw his shells raise fans of mud, debris and Japanese. He saw Mozzone wave his arms with wild exhilaration. Then everything seemed to dissolve in sound and flame. An enemy 77 millimeter shell squarely hit the SPM. Sergeant Klein was first to recover from the shock. The steel about him was spattered with blood. Lieutenant Mozzone writhed on the road. Klein checked his gun. It was still in order. But the tank-destroyers propelling mechanism had been blown to pieces.

It was late afternoon. The Japanese doubled their fire on the wrecked SPM, the road, on the line of gray-green skirmishers. They rushed fresh troops into their battered positions. "Easy" Company was cruelly mauled. Though ordered to dig in to protect the disabled tank-destroyer, the riflemen were pressed back, yielding foot after foot of muddy soil.

Sergeant Klein feared that his machine would fall into enemy hands. He must withdraw it or destroy it. He signaled to a tank to tow it out. The tank came forward and three men leaped to the road to attach a tow rope to the SPM. At this moment another enemy shell smashed into the crippled tank-destroyer. All members of its crew were killed, except Sergeant Klein. Two of the three men at the tow rope lay dead. The sergeant from the Bronx staggered around his mount like a desolate ghost. He saw that the tracks were smashed and that the machine could not be towed. Then he went over to the tank.

"Blow her up," he said sadly.

The tank backed off and gave the tank-destroyer the coup-de-grace.

As the companies fell back under the Japanese counter barrage, the enemy seemed to sense that his time had come. He counter attacked with waves of troops who had not before been seen in the Leyte battles. The skirmish lines shuddered under the impact. But they held.

Private Emmett Ross of Mount Pleasant, Iowa, placed a mortar into action and destroyed a Jap machinegun nest. Meanwhile, Japanese machinegun detachments striking through the jungle mounted their weapons and poured murderous flanking fire into our forward lines. A lieutenant from Gallatin, Missouri, Jack Brown, took charge of the threatened left flank. He walked around, directing fire into the enveloping force and encouraging the men. In between he helped to conduct wounded soldiers to the rear.

There lay men in the killing zone who had lost an arm or a leg. They would surely have died from loss of blood and shock but for the efforts of two jeep-driving corpsmen. Alfred L. Sloan of Joplin, Missouri, and Arthur Mendenhall of Galva, Kansas, labored to the limits of human ability. Four times they loaded their jeep with badly smashed casualties and drove them through machinegun and sniper fire to the surgeons' tables. By nightfall these drivers sat in puddles of half-dried blood.

The companies retreated from open fields to dig in for the night on more protected ground. Among the last to go were a lieutenant and a private. The private, Vernon Thompson of Hopkinton, Iowa, noticed that one of the fallen who had been left as dead was moving. He crept forward to bring him back. The wounded man was heavy. The Iowan shed his equipment and managed to drag the other to cover. After that he went forward again to recover his things.

The lieutenant was Troy L. Stonebumer, a company commander. From dawn to dark he had led his team in its eleventh continuous day of battle. He had darted about under aimed bullets from enemy weapons, adjusting the fire of mortars, directing his company's actions, supervising the evacuation of the wounded. He left the battle area only after the last of his men had reached the relative safety of a new perimeter. Stonebumer was killed in action.

The night again was filled with rain. Supply trucks bogged down in the quagmire of the roads. But the tractors kept moving. Along the perimeters foxholes filled with water. By midnight the rain had driven most men from the shelters they had dug. Engineers grumbled about turning the roads into canals. Feet were like sodden sponges and full of pain. The legs of many soldiers were covered with sores from knees to toes. "Jungle rot," they called it. Resistance was low and fever rampant. The bandages of the wounded were soaked and covered with mud. Letters from home melted into pulp and bakers cursed over flour that had turned to paste.

The regiment had fared badly that day. But the enemy had fared worse.

"It was a bloody go," commented Brigadier General Cramer. "Lets pray to God that we don't have to fight like that all the way."

Under cover of darkness the Japanese retreated.

There was a general alert an hour before dawn of November 1. The men ate their breakfast cold, standing in darkness and rain. There was no smoking and no lights could be shown. Few bothered to mix their coffee powder with water from their canteens. None bothered to wash. Squad leaders distributed fresh ammunition. With daylight, as the rain became a fading drizzle, the regiment stood ready to continue the attack.

The march began at 0800. Progress was rapid.

By 1100 the advancing column traversed the terrain of the past day's battles. The roadside was littered with Japanese dead. Some lay alone and others lay in huddles. Many had no heads, no arms, no feet, victims of the Division's field artillery. Charred pits marked the places where others had been cremated. There were many hastily abandoned emplacements. There were wrecked artillery pieces, discarded rifles, machineguns, helmets, packs, range finders, sake and rice. There was a scattering of letters and photographs among the rain puddles and the blood: pictures of Japanese soldiers in strutting poses, of Japanese soldiers with their arms around smiling Filipino girls, pictures of somber-faced parents of Japanese soldiers, pornographic pictures and others of drab-looking homes in Japan.

At one point along the road under a rain shelter there was a makeshift table on which rested little boxes wrapped in white cloth. These boxes contained the ashes of cremated Japs. Usually such boxes are sent home to Nippon to the dead soldiers folks who put them into the Yasukuni Shrine. In front of the white-bound boxes stood little dishes filled with rice and water—gifts of the survivors for the dead—but the rice was quickly stolen.

By 1300 the battalions entered Tunga. Tunga was a dead town. Swarms of flies and black birds hovered over Japanese cadavers. They were the only sign of life. After a brief rest, the infantry pushed on. On to Carigara and the sea.

Only at two points there was resistance. A group of pillboxes off the highway had halted the advance guard. A tank went forward and ran into trouble. A direct hit killed the tank commander. Infantry teams closed in and finished the job.

The second nest of resistance was dealt with by Sergeant Jerome T. Palmer and his squad. Palmers home is in Milwaukee. Barricaded behind the palm logs and a mound of earth was a lone enemy machinegun. Palmer deployed his squad in a semicircle and they approached the Japanese nest in short rushes. Two Japs were killed in the final assault. Palmer pounced on the third and caught him alive.

The prisoner asked in which manner he would be killed. "Will there be torture?" His captor laughed. The Jap was happy when he learned that he would not be tortured. He gave much information of value. He had been away from Japan for five years and he was glad to be out of the war. "We Japanese hate life in the tropics," he said, adding, "Officers should be put in a cage to fight their wars while we soldiers look on."

When the regiment dug in that night its forward elements were less than two miles from Carigara. There were scattered Japanese attempts to infiltrate the perimeters during the night. About the situation on the morning of November 2, the Division Record states:

"The stage was now set for the assault on Carigara, and indications were that this would be a hotly contested point. Air reconnaissance reported extensive digging, erection of barricades and similar fortifications in Carigara, and Japanese forces in the vicinity were reported from numerous sources as strong. Guerillas brought word of continuous movement of enemy troops toward Carigara from the Ormoc Valley. A battery of 75 mm guns was reported by air observers on the western outskirts of the town. Patrols of the First Cavalry Division had probed into the area and had met resistance."

The First Cavalry Division was poised northeast of Carigara after an amphibious landing. It was determined that the attack on the coastal town should be a coordinated assault by the two divisions. With daylight the Twenty-Fourth Infantry Divisions four artillery battalions laid down a barrage which rolled from a thousand yards south of Carigara a like distance beyond it. Three thousand shells were sent on their way. The barrage stopped at 0900 and the day's advance began.

The regiment pushed down the highway in a column of battalions. Patrols ranged ahead. "George" Company swung across country to block escape routes from Carigara to the west. From the point there came a shout: "Look! The ocean!"

Eyes lit up as they caught glimpses of the sea through gaps in the expanse of undergrown plantations. There was a bay, bright and blue and wide. Jutting headlands gleamed in the morning sun. It was like a hallucination of harmony and peace floating hard at the frontiers of the shell-torn earth. The battalions crossed three streams and halted at the outskirts of Carigara.

Off on the flank a squad of riflemen had blundered into an ambush. The Japs permitted the group to advance to within twenty yards of their position before they opened fire. The squad dropped to the ground, unable further to move in any direction. The enemy settled down to a man-by-man extermination of this group. A B.A.R. man from another squad went to their aid. He stood up and shouted and so drew the Japanese fire. In this manner he also spotted the location of the hostile automatic weapons. The B.A.R. man sprayed the twenty rounds in his magazine in the direction of two enemy machineguns. Then he dodged into cover to repeat his maneuver from another spot. He saved the lives of twelve men. The ambushed squad was able to withdraw. The B.A.R. man was Sam Dodds, Private, of Bonanza, Arkansas.

From somewhere Jap mortar shells fell on a platoon advancing between a palm grove and a swamp. The shelling became a barrage which covered the route of march with a checkerboard of bursts. As the platoon withdrew and swerved to circle the zone of impact, there came a shout through the hollow crashing of explosives: "Hey, you guys, don't leave me here."

A Chinese-American from San Francisco, Corporal Leeman Chan, saw a wounded soldier lying near the center of the pattern of explosions. Chan did not wait for a corpsman. Close to the earth he crawled into the barrage. No one expected Chan to come out alive. But he reached the wounded man and grasped his belt and dragged him to the shelter of a shallow ravine.

For more than an hour the assault battalions waited at the edge of Carigara. They waited for word that the First Cavalry was ready to break into the town from the east. No word came. The brother division had been delayed by burned bridges. The battalions then moved forward without further delay. A 180-foot bridge across the Carigara River had been destroyed by the Japanese. The crossing was difficult. Strong combat patrols pushed into the town.

Not a shot was fired as troops of the Twenty-Fourth entered Carigara. The assault companies marching through the deserted streets were ready for anything that might happen. But the streets were empty and the houses were silent hulks and there was only the distant boom of the surf. Suddenly the lively chords of "Elmer's Tune" came prancing from a tumbledown shack by the roadside. Lead scouts broke into little jigs. Other leg-tired soldiers waltzed imaginary partners a few yards. Inside the shack, flushed and happy, was Corpsman Arthur Mendenhall whose jeep, two days earlier, had been flecked with the blood of comrades he had rescued. Mendenhall had discovered a piano.

The Division had crossed Leyte Island from coast to coast It had won complete control of the strategic Leyte Valley and had cut the island in two. After twelve days of "hot, dirty, sweaty and bloody battling" the Japanese were in such haste to retreat into the ramparts of the Ormoc Valley that they had fairly abandoned the town of Capoocan, west of silent, smoking Carigara. Seven Japanese ammunition dumps were discovered dug into a hillside. They were full of artillery and mortar ammunition. Of the captured store of rifle ammunition many cartridges had wooden bullets.*

---

* At this stage of the campaign, the Division's Twenty-First Infantry Regiment, which had hitherto operated on the southern end of Leyte, was on its way to Carigara to relieve the battle-weary Thirty-Fourth. The Japanese at this time were falling back along the single lane coastal road from Carigara to Pinamopoan. From Pinamopoan a winding trail led south over the mountains into the Ormoc Valley. This trail had been the route of Japanese reinforcements brought from Cebu, Mindanao and Luzon via Ormoc Bay. No good harbor lies west of Pinamopoan on the north coast of Leyte, and only trails lead to the scattered villages in that mountain-filled sector, later to be known as Breakneck Ridge.

Some three thousand Japanese cadavers were counted and buried in the Divisions drive. But victory had exacted a saturnine price: among its own the Division counted one thousand and eighty-four wounded, or missing, or dead.

Chapter Eleven
GHOSTS OF GUADALCANAL

"The bitter battle of Breakneck Ridge had begun. It was to be fought over terrain ideally suited to defense, rough, rocky hills covered with kunai grass. The Ridge itself was not a single ridge, but a series of ridges, all of which were broken into knobs. There were innumerable ground pockets which were thickly wooded natural forts and whose defensive potentialities the Japanese had thoroughly exploited. There were elaborate systems of trenches. The entire area was packed with spider-holes. The road from Pinamopoan ran steadily upward, twisting through the hills. It crossed many streams and ravines. Complicating the entire operation was a condition of almost constant rain. There were no accurate maps of the area, and difficulty was experienced in keeping our attacks from breaking into a series of un-coordinated combats. A feeling grew among staff officers that the Ormoc Corridor would become another Guadalcanal."

(from the Division Record)

OVER THE MUDDY rim of his foxhole Sergeant Lewis peered at the dark line of bushes which skirted the base of the slope. The rain had stopped. A sullen dawn invaded the black heavens over Suicide Hill. It was a hill on a ridge, one of many, and toward the south were other ridges, and beyond them lay the towns of Limon and Ormoc. There was the distant boom of artillery coming in from the shore of Carigara Bay, and the rolling thunder of explosions as the shells hit the reaches of Breakneck Ridge. Nearby nothing moved. Yet—a trained ear could sense the jabber in the undergrowth two hundred yards away.

"Hey, Matt, wake up! Gil—!"

The sergeants foot prodded the sleepers in the soggy bottom of the emplacement.

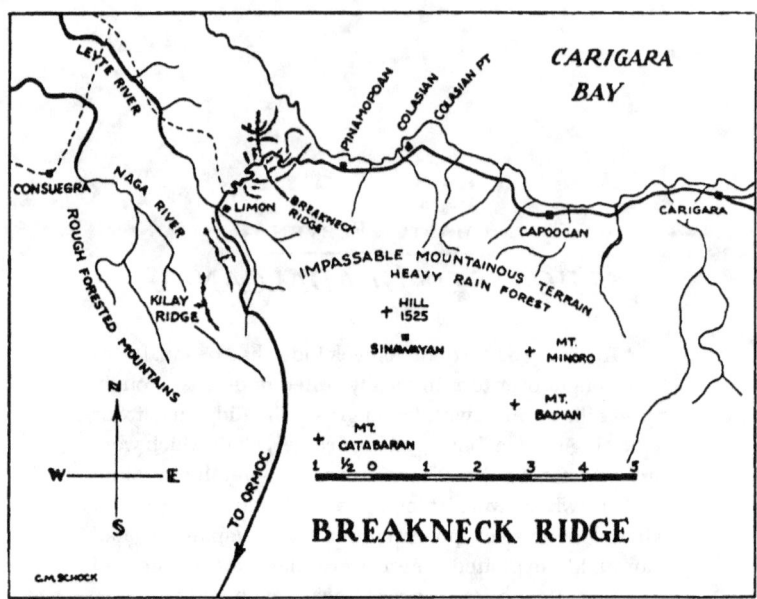

"Who's coming?"
"Dope!"
Stubby hands wiped mud from hair and eyes.
"Give 'em a bellyful."
Abruptly they were awake. Crouched over their gun, skilled fingers checking the lay, the mechanism, the belt; eyes sunken from lack of sleep searching the downward slope in front; the gunner, and the gunner's assistant. In one of the smaller holes an ammunition bearer yawned and swore softly.
"That you, Leo?" the sergeant said. "You guys had better keep awake."
"What's up, Web?"
"Nothing."
Nothing? Jap corpses littering the mushy slope were more eloquent than Web Lewis from Tennessee. In the twilight the bloated shapes of the dead sprawled like revelers frozen in weird immobility.
"So you woke us up," said the gunner.
"Take it easy."
"Wait and wait. Attack and attack and getting nowhere. Too goddam much waiting in this war. Too much shit."
"You said it."
"I'm sick of waiting."

They waited. Beyond the welter of clouds the sun was rising. It was their fifth morning on Suicide Hill.

Five days and nights in slime-ridden holes. Breakneck Ridge! "Hold that hill," the captain had said. "Don't let the bums push you off." Can't move around at night if you don't want your friends to shoot you. Piss in your hole, then sleep in it. Japs in front, Japs to both sides, Japs in the rear.

"Wonder if the Nips like war."
"They like it no more than you do."
"Then what're the bastards fighting for?"
"Damned if I know."
"What are we fightin' for?"
"So that some sons o' bitches back home can get rich."
"So that some Four F's can screw our women."
"You're crazy... Hell, my goddam lighter ran out of gas!"
"Mine works... here... If the Japs want the f-----Philippines, they can have them."

Five days of agonized exertion on hillsides that tore your heart out. Five nights in mire with muscles aching to stretch in the open. Malaria now and rheumatism later. Jungle rot. Centipedes looking for a dry place in your pants. Lice nibbling crusted sweat. Cold hash and chocolate bars in your belly and naught else. Rain water gulped from rusty helmets to slake the strangling thirst. The evil whirr of mortar fragments, and sniper bullets slapping the muck a foot away. Dysentery.

The nearness of death and the awful distance of home.

A thought, never voiced: Jesus Christ, wonder if I'll ever be walking down a lit-up street again.

"Raining again," mumbled someone in tired disgust.
"So?"
"That rain'll go on forever and the war as well/'
"And we, too," growled the sergeant.

Rain splashed sloppily on the blood-stained grass. It hissed in the bushes and rattled on the helmets. It leaked into weapons and drenched the mud-caked fatigues. The whole sky seemed an assembly of gigantic sponges. Rain swamped the holes and squalched down the boots and ran in filthy rivulets across hollow cheeks and over the unshaven chins.

Rain and the Japs.

The Emperor's men hated that machinegun on Suicide Hill. Each dawn they had attacked, and each afternoon. And each night they had moved stealthily up the wet slope, repeating their folly like robots in a continuous burlesque—tripping over wires which signaled their approach, hurling grenades and howling in the white-hot glare of counter-grenades, crumpling in the fire directed at the sounds of their advance.

It was light enough now to see the jagged backs of far mountains gray in the morning.

"Breakfast time!"

"To hell with breakfast."

Punctuating the mature dawn was a crackling of rifle fire. Single shots at first, followed by a fusillade, and then a tattoo of popping sounds came from the direction of the enemy line.

Mortars.

The men in the holes saw the projectiles come in from high-up. Mortar fire fell on Suicide Hill.

"Sit tight."

Flash and sound and quick stabbing of fragments. The shells were falling short. It was as if the morning rocked with obscene laughter. The men crouched low, their helmets turned in the direction of the bursts. No one spoke, until there was a lull in the firing. The sodden tiredness had slipped from their minds. Sweat mingled with the rain on their faces.

The gunner smiled at his assistant. "Hey, Bill," he said, "how about a nice cool glass of beer?"

"Make it a neat blonde, Matt," replied Bill dreamily.

Matt edged his face toward the rim of the emplacement. He squinted down the slope.

'There they are," he said loudly.

The border of bushes below them had come to life. There were the shapes of men running forward, dropping, springing up again and running. And there were bayonets on their rifles.

The sergeant was calm. "Fire," he said.

They breathed hard. Sweat in their eyes half blinded them. The ammunition belt writhed in somber rhythm with the rapid succession of bursts. Right and left barked the Garands of the riflemen, and other guns chattered in support from an adjoining ridge.

Here and there a Jap stopped running, floundered and died. But others came on as if driven by some fantastic obsession, bounding through rain, hugging the ground, firing wild and yelling, leaping forward again into the blaze from the machinegun's snout.

"Another belt—quick."

"Here she goes."

The attack failed, like the others. First there was hesitation, then milling confusion, then sprays of lead following the sprinting survivors to the shelter of the bushes.

"Cease fire."

"Whew!"

The gunner stared at his hands. He looked sick and exhausted. Rain hitting the barrel of the gun went up in playful wisps of steam.

Again they waited.

The hours dragged. Four of them dozed in the slime. One watched, guessing at the hour's end to wake his relief. Then noontime and half a can of hash and a chocolate bar for each man. Too weary to eat. No coffee. No cigarettes. Sniper fire in the rear kept the carriers from coming through. Coffee powder dissolved in a handful of rain, and more half-sleep populated by harassing shadows...

Transport planes hummed past above the clouds. Dropping supplies where neither truck nor carrying party could push through.

At mid-afternoon the enemy brought artillery to bear. The men on Suicide Hill watched the first shells burst a good hundred yards to their rear. The following rounds fell closer. Sixty yards. Creeping nearer. Thirty.

Against such eruption their gun became a futile toy. In their holes the men crouched low and the sergeant cursed. Cursing was no good. What was needed? Planes? Planes could see nothing but jungle. Counter battery fire? There was no telephone nor radio. Run for it? Stay and get it?

And who was then to defend this damned hill?

"Let's get out of here."

The sergeant timed the explosions. One more flash, vomiting mud.

"Now."

He grasped his rifle and led in a swift dash to a clump of undergrowth a little way off. The others followed, one by one, pitching headlong on their faces as they cleared the impact area of the shells.

Silence.

"Anybody hurt?"

"No."

"Clem—God damn you, answer. Are you all right?"

"Im all right."

"Disperse."

They moved apart, searching for low spots among the vines and roots.

"And keep our gun covered," the sergeant warned.

"All right."

They hovered in the bushes and the downpour, their rifles and carbines inches above the engulfing slush, their eyes fixed on their silent gun and on the slope ahead.

The shelling ceased. The silence was so intense that to the watchers the beat of their hearts sounded like the pounding of buried machinery. Then there was a shot down the slope, and silence again.

A lone Japanese emerged from the bushes at the base of the hill. A will to self-destruction lay in his cocky gait. Would that gun up there fire?

The gun was still.

The lone enemy shouted a few strident words. He motioned his comrades to follow. The gun up yonder had been knocked out, no doubt.

Four enemies proceeded up the slope. They came at a running crouch and in single file. Their leader kicked the mud and laughed. On him the sergeant drew a careful bead.

"Matt," he whispered, "you take the second in line. Leo—the third is your baby. Gil makes sure of the last. Bill, you watch. If one scrams, get him. Ready?"

"Let's go."

"Fire."

There was a slight disturbance in the melancholy tangle of corpses on the hillside. One of the four flopped about for a while, like a fish cast ashore. A howl arose from the thicket below.

"Now they'll wait till dark," the sergeant said.

In the rain the machinegunners lay, not moving, while the dripping hours went by. Again one watched; the others dozed. Dusk lingered an hour, and then the night towered over the hills.

At that hour two groups of men crawled toward the abandoned machinegun on Suicide Hill. They crawled with infinite caution through the blackness and the wet grass. One was that of Sergeant Web; the other was a band of Japs. And each knew that the other was not far, sliding nearer in the silence of the night.

Clem, the ammunition bearer, was first to reach the gun. There it was, untouched, like a chained dog awaiting its master.

Matt detached the barrel and vanished in the night. Gil gathered up the tripod and followed. The others lugged away what grenades and ammunition there was left. They did not go far. The sergeant selected a low spot in the ground.

"Set it up," he said.

No time to dig in. Their faces close to the ground they waited for the silhouettes of the enemy to appear over their abandoned emplacement. Minutes passed. A bullfrog croaked. A rocket flare ghosted into the rain. Now they could see the outlines of the Nip patrol, a cluster of shadowy blurs weaving low against the inky sky.

"Grenades," the sergeant said softly. "Then fire at what's left."

Breakneck Ridge—the Japs called it the "Yamashita Line."

On peacetime maps the jumble of razorback ridges and cone-shaped heights had no name of their own. They just happened to be, a desperately overgrown barrier between Carigara Gulf and Ormoc Valley, shoved there by volcanic upheavals of long ago. Map makers had shied from thorough exploration: where there were five ridges, the maps showed one; mountains of dominating height were miles removed from spots assigned to them by the maps. As the campaign progressed, the whole tormented complex was named Breakneck Ridge. Individual ridges and heights were named by the men who fought for them, a privilege paid for at an exorbitant price.

The Japanese were trapped between Breakneck Ridge and Ormoc. They were determined to hold their "corridor" not only as a fortress, but as a base for counter assault. Americans were determined to break it. The outcome of this battle was to decide the outcome of the Philippines campaign.

The Division's Twenty-First Infantry Regiment led the frontal assault on Breakneck Ridge. Opposing it in battle were elements of five Japanese divisions, veterans of Bataan, Manchuria and Singapore.*

But the battalions of the Twenty-First, on their way north to take over, were delayed by heavy rains. So, on the morning of November 3, the men of the Thirty-Fourth Regiment entered their fifteenth day of continuous battle. They left the area of Carigara at 7 A.M. in a column of battalions. Their goal was the coastal town of Pinamopoan, some seven miles to the west. Pinamopoan, at the foot of Breakneck Ridge, was the northern gateway into the Ormoc Valley.

The First Battalion, commanded by stalwart Colonel Thomas E. Clifford of Cereda, West Virginia, passed through the village of Capoocan without meeting resistance. Morale among the men, fatigued as they were, was high. They knew that relief was near, and the going that morning was good. To their right lay the beach, a crescent of black sand stretching to the headlands of Calusian Point; dark green slopes jutted skyward on their left. Between the ridges and the beach

---

* The Japanese divisions engaged in the battle for the Ormoc Corridor were the First Division, the Sixteenth, the Twenty-Sixth, the Thirtieth, and the One Hundred and Second. They were joined by other Japanese units in the later stage of fighting.

lay a belt of swampland through which the coastal road wound like a fragile ribbon.

A thousand yards west of Capoocan machinegun fire hit the vanguard. Although the road ahead seemed clear, the fire increased in intensity. The vanguard dispersed in the swamp and lay low. Scouts muscled forward to reconnoiter. They found a stream with almost perpendicular banks. There were the charred timbers of a bridge. The enemy was entrenched in the stream bed and under the bridge. He could not be reached by bullets, but he could rake the road and the adjoining swamp.

Guns of the Field Artillery pounded the area. But in the narrow defile of the stream bed the Japanese were vulnerable only to direct hits. A radio message told the artillery to cease firing. Clifford ordered the battalion mortars into action. The mortars thumped, but their shells failed to blast the Japs from their holes. A platoon of riflemen then climbed the ridge on the left to gain commanding ground. They found a Japanese ambush on a bluff overlooking the stream. "Able" Company was sent up the incline to reinforce the vanguard platoon.

The scouts groped through a fantastic tangle of thickets. The company lost its way on the hillside. It is not possible for a mass of men to move through jungle without making many noises. The underbrush crackled and there were the sounds of feet slipping on the treacherous slope. Without warning, the company came face to face with the Japs in ambush.

An immediate frontal attack was the only way out. Eleven Americans lost their lives in a wild and instant exchange of shots, and thirteen sagged wounded. The enemy counter-charged with bayonets, but was repulsed. Simultaneously, the remainder of the battalion assaulted the stream bed below.

Private Thomas Kennedy of Harrison, New Jersey, was the first man to cross the stream. Though every second soldier of his squad fell dead or wounded before he reached the bank, Kennedy jumped straight into a Jap hole, scrambled across the stream and up the far side. There he maintained a one-man bridgehead and pulled through.

From the slippery hillside "Able" Company's men hurled grenades to clear the stream bed below them. The last grenade was expended. The Japanese replied with a hoarse "Banzai!" Staff Sergeant Louis Hansel of Mount Vernon, Kentucky, half plunged, half slid down the slope. He was going to get more grenades. He got them. He lugged grenades to his comrades on the ridge, and he lugged wounded with him when he returned for more. After a squad leader was wounded, Hansel remained and led the squad in the attack.

Soon every man in "Able" Company was committed to the close range fire fight, including messengers and cooks. The company commander, Captain Jack B. Matthews of Macon, Georgia, was unaware of twelve Japanese who suddenly charged his unit from the rear. Matthews wheeled when he heard them yell as they closed in. Two runners, a radio operator, and his orderly sprang to help their captain. They warded off the thrust. The Japs vanished. But a minute later they again broke out of the jungle like a pack of wolves. They lashed out with their bayonets and screeched their high-pitched screams. In the defense group some men staggered with bayonet wounds. An automatic rifleman who rushed to their aid was wounded. A sergeant named Max Keith, of Mars Hill, North Carolina, saw the fracas. He grabbed the wounded gunners grenades and B.A.R. All twelve of the attackers were slain.

Jack Matthews then led his men in a bayonet assault. It was 6 P.M. before the last Jap defending the stream position was killed.

As resistance developed at the stream crossing west of Capoocan, another force was ordered to make an amphibious flanking attack on Pinamopoan. Their mission was to cut off the Japanese forces on the coastal road. "King" Company of the Thirty-Fourth embarked on seven amphibious tractors. They skirted the coast. Artillery bursts on the beach of Pinamopoan showed them where they should land. The "Alligators" sprayed the shore with machineguns as they came in. The riflemen then pushed ashore and up steep, grassy slopes defended by double their number of Japs.

The enemy fired from anti-tank guns, field cannon and heavy machineguns. The range was 250 yards. "King" Company replied with machineguns, rifles and mortars. The position quickly became untenable. An artillery observation plane cruising overhead reported a truck convoy of Japanese moving toward the beach. Later that afternoon the Cub plane was shot down by strafing Zeroes. A retreat was ordered. "King" Company fell back to the beach. Men carried their wounded. The "Alligators" nosed inshore to carry the taskforce to sea. The Japanese promptly counter attacked.

Two artillery observers who had accompanied the expedition saved the retreat from becoming a rout. Robert Campbell of Pipestone, Minnesota, and John W. Strasser of Maquoketa, Iowa, directed the fire of batteries emplaced five miles to the east. The howitzer shells screamed in to cover the retreat. Their bursts scattered the enemy onset. The grassy slopes caught fire. The beach shuddered under the might of the explosions. Fragments fell among "King" Company's platoons. Unflinchingly the two observers drew the barrage of their 155 millimeter batteries to within 150 yards of their own positions. Dazed and numbed, they were the last to leave the beach.

All night the Division's field artillery battalions massed their fire on Pinamopoan. On the morning of November 4, infantry slogged down the coastal road and seized the town. Two hundred Japanese dead were found in Pinamopoan. Six artillery pieces were captured. That night the spearhead of the Thirty-Fourth dug in on the foothills of Breakneck Ridge. Fresh battalions of the Twenty-First Regiment relieved them at dawn of November 5. The change of forces took place under a torrential rain. In the dim gray light the newcomers eyed the country ahead of them. Winding upward into inscrutable mountains lay the Ormoc Valley trail.

Colonel William J. Verbeck of Brooklyn and West Point, commander of the Twenty-First, led a patrol which reconnoitered the sinuous approaches to Breakneck Ridge. Upon his return he ordered the attack to proceed. Artillery observers accompanied by riflemen sliced to a height named Observation Hill. Another force advanced toward a ridge with twin peaks which later were dubbed Hot Spot Knob and Suicide Hill. Before the day ended the assault groups were split, isolated and surrounded. Snipers waylaid details carrying food and ammunition from the coast.

A scout pushing through *kunai* grass and blinding rain halted and turned. To the soldier behind him he said, "This f----- rain! I can't see a f----- thing."

"Let me go ahead for a while," the other said.

"Keep your eyes open," warned the scout.

"Okay."

Private Charles Feeback of Carlisle, Kentucky, took over the lead of the advance. Jammed under his right arm was a sub-machinegun. He used its muzzle to shove aside the head-high grass. All of a sudden he stood stock still. In a foxhole four feet away, his rifle cocked, lurked a Jap. Feeback's finger froze on the trigger of his gun. The forty slugs cut the Jap almost in two. Feeback raised his arm overhead, then pointed forward.

"All clear."

Not for long. A little further up the hillside the Kentuckyman heard a metallic tap in the grass to his right. A Jap was cocking a grenade. The grenade, tossed high, plopped down at his feet.

The volunteer scout dived sideways into the grass. The grenade roared. Feeback did not move. He waited. He waited until he saw a slant-eyed head rise cautiously in the grass. In that instant the Kentuckyman drilled it between the eyes.

That was the beginning of the bitterest fighting of the campaign. From their maze of holes and tunnels on and between the hills the Japanese had cut narrow, interlocking fire lanes through jungle and *kunai*. Machineguns spat along these lanes. Snipers fired from secret perches. Enemy mortar crews dug into the world's best hiding place covered ravines and hollows with a deadly pattern of bursts. Jap artillery grumbled from more distant ridges. The Division's assault teams seized the initial ridges and knolls. The Japanese launched counter attacks. Four Banzai charges hit the perimeters between the afternoon of November 5 and dawn of November 6. Platoons were isolated and companies were broken up. Infiltration was constant and impossible to check. Some of the Divisions units fell back. Others, cut off, held out through days of rain and foxhole death. Often it became impossible to bring out the wounded; many died in muck and rain. Companies which entered the struggle one hundred and sixty strong emerged with sixty men still on their feet before they had broken the back of the "Yamashita Line."

Japanese "Special Attacking Units" raged around the summit of Observation Hill. "King" Company was sent to reinforce the men on top. During one of their Banzai rushes the Nipponese came within grenade range of a machinegun platoon. Captain Neil Reid of Chicago, Illinois, recognized the danger. Under direct fire he moved the machinegun squads to new positions. The onslaught was repelled. The Japs streamed downhill, leaving sixty-five corpses to rot in the rain.

When ammunition ran low, volunteers from "Mike" Company set out to truck it up the road from Pinamopoan. They loaded their truck with mortar shells and machinegun ammunition and drove uphill through unspeakable mud. They met sniper bullets on the outskirts of Pinamopoan. They met machinegun bursts as their truck climbed the pass into Breakneck Ridge. Then mortar shells began to fall around them. The truck did not stop. Its engine rattled and fumed, and its double wheels churned the mire. Atop the ammunition, "Mike" Company's men lay flat. Then a mortar shell exploded hard in front. The truck stopped.

Sergeant Paul Corfield of Cato, New York, jumped from behind the shattered windshield. He wanted to check on the damage. He knelt between the front wheels and suddenly an expression of astonishment invaded his face. He sank into the mud. He moved an instant and lay still.

"Jesus Christ, they killed Paul," said Sergeant Jacob Meyer, whose home was in New Orleans.

Meyer, too, had jumped from the truck. He spotted the Jap who had killed Corfield. From the roadside he fired. Somewhere in the jungle a machinegun chattered. Sergeant Meyer fell, mortally wounded. By now Japs swarmed from the underbrush on both sides of the Ormoc Trail. Sergeant Antonio Pepe of Brooklyn, New York, yelled to his two remaining comrades: "The bastards want the ammunition. Defend that truck!"

He and Private Melvin Taylor of Alton, Illinois, lay under the truck and defended it. Behind the truck crouched Private Lester Francis of Birdsboro, Pennsylvania. The Japs swarmed closer. Pepe and Taylor fired. Francis fired. Some Japs fell, but the others came on, screaming. Bullets twanged among the tires. Grenades burst in fans of fire and mud. Taylor heard an outcry and a moan. Lester Francis was dead. Antonio Pepe was dead.

Now the boy from Illinois defended the ammunition truck alone. He defended it until a patrol, investigating the firing, drove the marauders back into the jungle.

On the neighboring hilltop an enemy thrust had cut a rifle platoon in two. The dripping sword grass blades vibrated with the din of fighting, but not much could be seen. The space between the two separated groups was occupied by Japanese. In the same space, too, American wounded lay shouting for help. Corpsman George A. Gregoric of McKees Rocks, Pennsylvania, prowled through the wedge. Thrice he came face to face with snipers and dodged into the *kunai*. He found the wounded and gave them first aid. He stayed with them until relief arrived.

The Japanese attempting to storm Observation Hill during the night were terror-stricken when their third wild charge at 5 A.M. was answered with an equally savage counter charge. Grenades and bayonets clashed at close quarters. The Japs' "Banzais" became cries of dismay; the Americans emitted howls and Yankee abuse. The man who coolly organized and led this counter thrust was Captain Tom Suber of Whitmire, South Carolina, "King" Company's commander.

Private Charles Clemmer, of Philadelphia, saw a Jap jump out of the night and shoot a squad leader through the head. Clemmer fired a burst from his automatic rifle—and missed. The Jap tossed a grenade. The grenade struck the ground between Clemmer and his assistant gunner. Clemmer grasped the grenade and tossed it back. It blasted the Japs head off his shoulders.

A mortar observer named Leon Taylor, from Fort Worth, Texas, lay under hostile artillery fire, directing the firing of his own mortars on Japanese concentrations on the hillside. When the riflemen were ordered to fall back, mortarman Taylor remained and became a sniper. He circled the hilltop, darting from niche to niche. He beat the enemy at his own game. By his marksmanship four Japanese died.

Private Edward Griggs of Comersville, Tennessee, drove a jeep three times along the fire-swept Ormoc Trail to bring five wounded soldiers to safety. Private Orville Schubert of Alice, North Dakota, covered the withdrawal despite a barrage of grenades. During a Japanese bayonet attack at 2 A.M., Technician Carmin Santangelo of the Bronx, New York, lugged four wounded men through skirmish, mud and rain. Helping him was Private Robert Miller of Saint Peter, Minnesota. Rejoining the fight, Miller carried ammunition. At dawn he spotted a trail running through a gully. He saw an enemy patrol move up the trail and stopped it with eight shots from his Garand. At his side, bent over a bleeding man, was Corpsman Willard Jenner of Sherwood, North Dakota. Jenner had tended the wounded all through that ugly night. Miller pointed at the fresh blood on the aid man's uniform: "Hey Will, you're wounded yourself," he said.

Replied Will Jenner: "I know, I know."

Commanding a platoon of heavy machineguns was Sergeant Andrew Pristas of Conneautville, Pennsylvania. In the face of enemy attacks from three sides and sniper fire from the rear, Pristas passed from machinegun to machinegun, checking on ammunition and targets. His steady words of confidence did much to keep the specter of battle-exhaustion at bay. When Japs came too close, Pristas tossed grenades. When a gunner ran out of ammunition, Pristas was at his side with another belt to help him reload quickly. When his force finally abandoned the ridge, Pristas and his gunners remained behind to prevent the Japs from breaking into the retreat. Only when friendly artillery shells began to explode in the abandoned perimeter did Pristas and his crew take to their heels.

Entrenched near a bend of the Ormoc Trail, Private Truman Simmons of Caves City, Arkansas, saw a jeep ambushed by snipers. He saw the driver slump over the wheel. Another man who was bleeding from the neck struggled to get out of the car. The Japanese now fired tracer bullets to set the gasoline in the jeep's tank afire. Simmons leaped out of his hole and raced toward the jeep. He saw that both occupants were badly wounded. He freed them from the vehicle and helped them into a clump of grass. He bandaged their wounds to stop the flow of blood and he gave them sulfa tablets and water. After that the Arkansan returned to his foxhole to fight it out with the snipers.

The jeep was later commandeered by Private Glenn Brodine of Sandpoint, Idaho, who used it to taxi wounded comrades to Pinamopoan.

Leal Marlett of Newberry, Michigan, worked in no-man's-land to treat the wounded and to mark their location for the litter squads. Then came the news that the corpsmen of an adjoining platoon had been wounded, and that the platoon needed medical help. Marlett took over the wounded aid man's job on top of his own. Like many another medic on Breakneck Ridge, Leal Marlett was killed in action.

In the pitch-blackness of the night rains a machinegun squad of four fought until all were wounded except its leader, Private Laveme E. Baker of Freeport, Illinois. Two of the men had been hit by fragments from grenades. The third had gone down under a bayonet stab in the dark. Baker manned the gun alone. He repulsed a Japanese onset. The surviving Japs hugged the ground some thirty yards away and waited. Somehow Baker managed to drag his three wounded team-mates to the rear. He himself went forward again. He salvaged his gun and mounted it in an alternate position unknown to the Japs.

Every minute of the night of November 5 to November 6 was loud with the sounds of gunfire and of men taking each other's lives. Staff Sergeant Jose Gomez of Carlsbad, New Mexico, was wounded in the leg when a Jap assault group broke into his squad's position. Gomez was carried to the aid station near the center of the hilltop. While the medics patched his leg, other wounded were brought in. "^What's up?" asked Gomez.

"They're attacking again," one of the other wounded men said.

Jose Gomez escaped the medics. He hobbled back to his decimated squad and fought until the second attack was shattered. For the second time he was then carried to the aid station. This time he did not come back.

The scout of a platoon climbing a ridge to reinforce a surrounded party of artillery observers received machinegun fire from the flank. A cunningly masked pillbox was firing down a narrow trail. The scout signaled his platoon to halt. Then, single-handedly, he engaged the strongpoint while the platoon maneuvered. The nest was destroyed with flame-thrower and grenades. The scout was Private Anthony Jasiukiewicz, American, from West Warren, Massachusetts.

Nearby another squad lay in battle. At this point the enemy tried infiltration. It was the second attack and already half of the squad was out of action. The Japanese crept on their bellies through sword grass seven feet high. Around their necks they bore canvas sacks filled with grenades. Ahead of them they pushed rifles, with bayonets fixed. The purpose of night infiltration is to cross the perimeter unobserved, then attack it from within.

Through the rushing sound of rain Sergeant Dominic Castro, of Los Angeles, heard a faint rustling. The soldier nearest him lay glassy-eyed, a victim of battle fatigue. Castro let out a piercing yell. That roused the remainder of his squad. At the same time he fired. A few feet away in the darkness Japs sprang up and threw grenades. Then they flopped to the ground to evade the fragments. An instant after the bursts they sprang forward and charged. They howled as they had been taught to howl in training camps in China and Japan. The purpose of their howling was supposed to paralyze their antagonists with fright; actually it signaled their location. On they came, their bayonets at groin-level.

The men of Castro's squad fired for their lives. Then they, too, sprang up to meet the collision. Castro was hit by a grenade. A moment later he felt a Jap bayonet go through him. He shot the bayonet wielder in the face. The force of the muzzle blast bared the Jap's skull bones. After the last round had left his magazine, Castro reversed his rifle and fought with the butt. His staying power made his squad stand fast.

A B.A.R. man named Francisco Mosteiro of Fall River, Massachusetts, had an ugly head wound caused by a grenade. But his automatic rifle clattered until the charge was repulsed; then Francisco collapsed. Another automatic rifleman spotted the muzzle flashes of a Jap machinegun which caused havoc along the perimeter; in the dripping darkness he rose to a standing position and engaged the Japanese gunners in a duel across ten yards of grass aglow from the passage of bullets.

The long night drew to an end. At 5 A.M. the enemy made his last frantic charge. It followed a barrage of machinegun, knee-mortar and artillery fire. The Japanese were within three yards of the line of foxholes and threw scores of grenades. Into one rifle man's hole plopped four grenades. He recovered three and hurled them back in a second. The fourth slipped from his hand and rolled back into the hole. The soldier crushed it into the mud with his right foot. That saved his life, but it blew off his foot. The Japs broke into the perimeter where "Mike" Company's machinegunners had their emplacements. In the gunners' ears the brutal rataplan of their guns was sweet music in the face of the Banzai men's screams. "Those little men with the long bayonets," one of the gunners said at dawn, "that's not so bad. But their howling is something that grabs your guts and twists them." There were many cries for aid men. Wounded men were wounded again, and some of the wounded were killed. The machinegunners fell back. "King"

Company counter attacked with bayonets and retook the emplacements. Dead Japs were rolled out of each recaptured hole.

Where the bayonet fails and the rifle butt misses, there is still the trench knife, the kick to the testicles, the strangling, and the gouging of the eyes. In one attack every man in a platoon commanded by Lieutenant Walter Easton of Yreka, California, was killed or wounded. Easton hurriedly moved through blackness and pouring rain and brought replacements to the line—cooks, bakers, messengers and truck drivers.

Dawn came, heavy and gray. The night rains faded into a steady drizzle. Men lay in the mud by the side of their foxholes. The foxholes were full of muddy water. The muddy water was stained with blood. Here and there a lifeless head, a hand, a knee protruded from the water-filled holes. Corpses along the edge of the perimeter resembled a congress of reptiles gazing motionless through mud-caked grass. There was no pause in the horror. All through the somber morning the Japanese pursued their counter offensive. The Division's assault teams were thrown back to the beach. At one point Lieutenant Easton, with fifteen volunteers, covered the retreat. And even after this covering force had retreated, a few remained.

Private First Class Ernest Shannon of Lamar, Kansas, went back to rescue a friend whose arm and shoulder had been mangled by machinegun fire. Sergeant John Mashek of Wyndmere, North Dakota, remained to destroy abandoned weapons to prevent their falling into enemy hands.

Of the situation on November 6, 1944, Division Record reports:

"Casualties were high. Enemy pressure had been brought heavily against our companies, and these units were pushed off their high ground positions during the morning. By 1300 they had withdrawn to the beach. "C" Company, reinforced by Filipino guides, had been sent to occupy Hill 1525, a dominating terrain feature far to the left flank, but this unit returned just before dark to report that the guides had lost their way.

"At the close of the day the Japanese had occupied Breakneck Ridge and the approaches leading to it from the north."

Chapter Twelve
CHILDREN OF YESTERDAY

> "I have been driven many times to my knees by the overwhelming conviction that I had nowhere else to go. My own wisdom, and that of all about me, seemed insufficient for that day."
>
> Abraham Lincoln

In Tunga native children cut little stops of wood with which to plug the bullet holes in the village school. The war, for them, had passed.

In Palo grown-ups and children had a liberation fiesta. On the town square the children staged a pantomime: an unwashed urchin wearing a tophat paraded on the stage; around his neck hung a sign, "President of the Philippines." A second urchin jumped to the stage. He was disguised as a Japanese and he proceeded diligently to rifle the "Presidents" pockets. Then a third little boy, garbed as "Uncle Sam," stormed upon the stage. His bare brown foot lashed to the seat of "Nippon's" pants; "Nippon" fled. Whereupon the "President" shook "Uncle Sam's" hand. In Palo, too, the war had passed.

In the town of Jaro the Division Quartermaster established a supply dump. Among his supplies there was a ton of mimeograph paper which had been damaged in a rain storm. Nevertheless, the quartermasters had carried this ton of useless paper with them from dump to dump. A little girl in Jaro saw the mass of paper. "May I have a few sheets?" asked she. They were given to her. And soon other children came and asked for paper. The children told their teachers and the teachers told the principal of their school, 'There is paper free for the asking at the Army Dump." For years the school had done without paper. Next morning three hundred children filed past the dump in silent formation. Away with them they carried a ton of paper. In Jaro the war had also become a thing of the past.

Twelve miles from Jaro General Frederick A. Irving, the Division's commander, warned higher headquarters that the road from Carigara to Pinamopoan would not support a major offensive. Higher headquarters ordered that the offensive should proceed. The road dissolved and General Irving was relieved of his command.

The offensive proceeded. Mud became as vicious a foe as the Japanese. Men huddled under ponchos wrote letters home; they wrote on the backs of ration boxes and of Japanese leaflets. Rain turned their letters into pulp before they could be censored. In the offensive men plunged ahead from clump to clump of swampy grass only to sink in morass up to their armpits; they were pulled out by ropes in the hands of their comrades. Each evening each man dug a hole in which to spend another miserable night. By midnight the holes had filled with water. There was lack of food, lack of dry clothing, and at times a shortage of ammunition. Supplies for the men on Breakneck Ridge bogged down in mud.

The road from Carigara to Pinamopoan, over which all supplies to the front must pass, was a blasted, mucky track. Five bridges along the road had been wrecked. The long bridge across the Carigara River had been set afire by saboteurs. Engineers bridged three streams with new wooden bridges. They bridged the Carigara River with pontoons. They also bridged the unruly Nauguisan River with pontoons. Bulldozers carved out bypasses for vehicles too heavy to negotiate the bridges. Bulldozers, too, filled craters caused by mines, and by enemy artillery firing from Breakneck Ridge. "All of this work," explains the Division Record, "was complicated by rains which made the entire island a sea of mud."

The Carigara-Pinamopoan road had been laid on swamp. It was no more than a rock fill which disintegrated under the pounding of heavy trucks, tanks, tractors and artillery columns. The weight of the vehicles cracked the crust of the road. Water seeped through the cracks from the swamp below. The following trucks and cannon then pressed whole patches of rock fill down into the swamp. Large holes in the road were the result. As succeeding vehicles crossed these holes, edges crumbled, and long stretches of road vanished in the swamp. Soon it became impassable even to tanks.

The Division's engineers worked twenty-four hour shifts in a stubborn bid to keep the highway open. Long stretches of corduroy were laid. Masses of native laborers were put to work with shovels. Trucks hauled rocks from distant quarries to patch the road—instead of hauling supplies. But nothing could make the road hold up. Traffic became dependent on amphibious machines which could take to the water and skirt the beach.

But the offensive proceeded.*

Americans died under bullets from American machineguns which the Japanese had captured. As "Able" Company pushed up the Ormoc Trail its scouts discovered a group of wrecked American trucks whose drivers lay killed by the roadside. They thought it the work of snipers. But as they approached they saw empty ration tins littering the road for a hundred yards. The Japs had been eating American rations taken from the ambushed trucks. The scouts turned and flashed a warning. It was too late.

It was a perfect spot for a roadblock. There was an abyss on one side, a steep *kunai*-matted slope on the other. Out of the *kunai* fired American machineguns manned by Japanese. The nearest Americans were only fifteen feet away. First man to fall was the company commander, he died in the first minute of his first dav in battle. Lieutenant Peter Babich of Morgantown, West Virginia. A platoon leader in the rear of the column, heard the shooding. He went forward to find out why the leading elements were falling back. He found machinegun fire coming from the front and the flank and he found many dead and others dying. The company withdrew. In the withdrawal Babich carried with him a wounded man, and then he retrieved his commanding officer's body. Disengaged, he ordered mortar fire to reduce the roadblock.

"Able" Company battled on Breakneck Ridge through eleven consecutive days. On one day its mortar sections threw fourteen tons of shells on a single Japanese position. The pillbox, after it was stormed, was found large enough to hold seventy-five defenders. "Bloody Knob," they called it.

A group sent out to reinforce a company which had been cut off on the slope of Suicide Hill crossed a bridge well behind the front and suddenly found itself attacked from the rear. There were Japs running and firing light machineguns as they ran. Outnumbered, surrounded, the Americans dodged under the bridge. The Japanese hacked holes into the bridge and threw grenades through the openings. The men under the bridge replied by riddling the overhead planking with bullets. The weird encounter lasted three hours before the Japs gave up. They set the bridge afire before they disappeared into the flanking *kunai*.

---

* At this time the 19th Infantry Regiment was charged with the defense the shores of Carigara Bay; the 34th Regiment guarded the Division's extended and thinly held lines of communication; while the 21st Regiment carried out the frontal attack against Breakneck Ridge.

"Baker" Company lost two-thirds of its effectives in fourteen days of fighting and steady rain. Its rations were hand-carried across two miles of sniper-infested terrain. "Dead Man's Curve" the survivors renamed their sector of the Ormoc Trail.

"Charlie," "Dog," "Easy," "Fox," "George"—every company in the Twenty-First paid its blood price for the sodden wilderness of Breakneck Ridge. . . .

November 7

On the perimeters dug-in infantry repulsed two Banzai assaults before dawn. In the gray morning the Twenty-First Regiment attacked in a column of battalions. Its objective was a ridge four hundred yards to its front. "Easy" Company seized one section of the ridge at noon. "George" Company struck a force of Japanese while crossing a ravine. Tank destroyers were hauled forward through the mud. They pounded .the ravine, without success. Then tanks joined the fight

Around the tanks the enemy swarmed in yelling packs. A tank commander was tossing grenades out of the turret As he was about to throw a grenade, a bullet pierced his hand. The grenade fell into the tank on top of a hundred rounds of 75 millimeter ammunition. The grenade was a dud. But a Jap jumped forward with a satchel full of dynamite and threw it against the rear of the turret. The tank was disabled.

Cooks and messengers, company clerks and musicians carried wounded men and fought in the front lines. A mess sergeant named James Nesbitt of Princeton, Arkansas, led a patrol which became scattered in an expanse of seven-foot-high grass. Nesbitt prowled in circles in an endeavor to gather the men of his group. He came face to face with an enemy sniper instead. The Arkansan fired first. At the same moment another sniper in the *kunai* fired at Nesbitt The cook left the hit Jap squirming in the grass and went hunting for the second sniper. He rolled through the grass to get out of the sniper's sights. A mortar shell exploded on the spot Nesbitt had just left. He lay still and rested a minute to shake off the effect of the concussion. Then he continued his hunt. He came upon the second sniper from the rear and shot him through the head.

When "Easy" Company was counter-attacked from the summit of the ridge, all members of an anti-tank gun crew were hit. There was now a breach in the company's line. Private Francis Anderson of Drake, North Dakota, crawled into the gap and defended it with nothing but his rifle. Anderson's job was that of a messenger.

The leader of a hard-pressed platoon of riflemen was killed. The platoon had become disorganized in the melee and was in danger of annihilation. The second in command, Sergeant Schomaker of Ford, Kansas, was seriously wounded. Nevertheless, Schomaker overcame his pain and led the platoon into an organized retreat.

A Japanese raiding party charged a battalion command post. Woodrow W. Haskett, of Natrona, Wyoming, a cook, was first to spot the raiders. He rushed to a light machinegun and sprayed the oncoming Japs. Haskett continued to fire until the Japanese were less than twenty feet away. They fired, emitted wild screeches, hurled grenades. Haskett's stand broke up the raid. But the soldier-cook from Wyoming lay dead at the side of his gun.

Meanwhile, "Love" Company carried out a wide flanking movement to the left. Its mission was to strike from the flank the ridge which "Easy" Company had been denied from the front. The maneuver failed. "Love" Company was thrown back by a vicious combination of mud, torrential rain, and a cliff-like mountainside manned by Japs. Night was near and the assault battalion was split in three ways: "Fox" Company grimly held on to the captured section of the ridge; "Easy" Company was embroiled at the rim of a canyon on the forward slope; "Love" Company dug its night defenses in the rear of the contested height. Masses of Japs held the intervening terrain.

Elsewhere on Breakneck Ridge things were not much better. Artillery fought thunderous duels. A group of artillery observers climbed 800-foot high Observation Hill. They found the Japanese fortifications empty. Happily they rigged up their radio and began to look for targets. Major Lemuel Blacker of Corvallis, Oregon, tested the radio.

"This is a wonderful spot," he told the regimental commander. "The Japs seem to have pulled out. We'll..."

There was a cry: "Look out!" Then there was a volley of firing and the radio went dead. Through *kunai* grass Japs were crawling to the edge of the trench system. An officer waving a sword leaped out of the grass, seven Japs at his heels. Sub-machineguns and carbines cut them down. Minutes later eight other Japs attempted to rush the trenches. All eight died. The radio came back to life. "Throw some stuff around this hill," Major Blacker told his artillery. "In a hurry... Roger... out."

At this time, too, the Nineteenth Infantry Regiment dispatched a company to find and seize a dominating height known as Hill 1525. A force had been sent there the previous day, but it had lost its way. Possession of Hill 1525 was vital because it could serve as a base from which artillery observers might direct fire on distant reaches of the

Ormoc Trail. The taskforce, with native guides, struck out on a carefully plotted compass azimuth. But strong Japanese forces descending from an intermediate ridge pushed it out of its course. Again the Filipino guides lost their way in the labyrinth of ridges and ravines. Beleaguered by Japanese, the infantrymen dug their foxholes in a hillside which they thought to be in the vicinity of Hill 1525. Actually they were far to the east of their objective. In night and rain the enemy attacked.

On one company perimeter the Japanese killed a machinegun crew and seized the weapon. The company commander, Captain Robert Kilgo, was taken aback when he heard one of his own machineguns pour fire in a "wrong" direction. Though the night was irate with the whirr of bullets, Kilgo left his command post in the center of the perimeter to investigate. He found the danger spot in the flickering light of a pile of burning equipment.

Kilgo crouched low and ran back against a stream of bullets whipping from the Garands of his own riflemen. He went to a sector of the perimeter which was not under attack. There he grabbed a heavy machinegun, and with it he raced to the gap in his company's defenses. The machinegun's crew followed hard on their captain's heels. Kilgo installed gun and crew in a matter of seconds. It saved the company from being cut to pieces in the dark.

In a simultaneous attack near the beach at Pinamopoan the Japs came silently, with machineguns, mortars, and bayonets fixed. Not far from the outposts they stood up and approached at a walk, chatting in English as they came. But following the rule that only the enemy moves in a tropical night, the outposts fired. Close combat followed. To create confusion, the Japs shouted in English. They shouted for aid men. They shouted names, "Charlie, come here quick, I'm in trouble." And they shouted false fire directions. Fifteen enemies were killed before the others abandoned the game. Toward morning a few Japanese rushed in with land-mines strapped to their bellies. Tracer bullets from Garands exploded the mines.

November 8

A typhoon raged over Breakneck Ridge. From the angry immensity of the heavens floods raced in almost horizontal sheets. Palms bent low under the storm, their fronds flattened like streamers of wet silk. Trees crashed to earth. In the expanse of *kunai* grass the howling of the wind was like a thousandfold plaint of the unburied dead. The trickle of supplies was at a standstill. On Carigara Bay the obscured headlands moaned under the onslaught of the seas. Planes were grounded and ships became hunted things looking for refuge. Massed artillery hurling barrages to the summits of Breakneck Ridge sounded dim and hollow in the tempest. Trails were obliterated by the rain. The sky was black.

Through the typhoon infantry attacked.

At 0700 twelve hundred riflemen launched an assault. They overwhelmed and flowed around enemy positions which a day earlier had refused to yield. Mortar shells drove the Japs out of their emplacements, or deeper into their spider-holes and caves. Bullets and bayonets dealt with Japanese caught in the open. Flame throwers burned those who clung to the caves. "Fox" Company pushed to the southeastern crest of Breakneck Ridge; it dug in on Suicide and Arson Hills. By nightfall it was cut off and surrounded. "Easy" Company pushed up the Ormoc road until its advance was barred by a blasted bridge. Determined Japanese detachments flanked the bridge, and the terrain was dominated by hostile machineguns, mortars and artillery firing from farther ridges. The Jap was at his best. By nightfall, "Easy" Company had been repulsed to its starting point. Over the convulsions of battle pounded the storm.

The Second Battalion (Twenty-First Infantry Regiment) struck out to find and capture mysterious Hill 1525. The battle teams left Colasion Point at dawn. All day they marched across trackless mountain country, through gale and driving rain. They met and killed a Japanese officer, and his patrol of ten. The equipment of these Japs was new and of a superior kind; documents found showed the dead to be members of the First Imperial Division. At 4 P.M. the battalion climbed the slopes of a towering height. Around them was a maze of other ridges and interlocking gullies. The jungle was dense and visibility near zero. Further exploration was halted by a force of Japs well equipped with mortars and automatic weapons. In pitch darkness and an eighty-mile wind the battalion dug in on the slopes of what its commander believed to be Hill 1525.

Another battalion under Colonel Spragins (Second Battalion, Nineteenth Infantry Regiment) toiled toward Hill 1525 to surprise the enemy from the flank. However, at dusk the colonel found that the hilltop he had seized overlooked the Leyte Valley rather than the Ormoc Trail. There lay an intervening ridge a thousand yards to the west. Hill 1525, plain and massive on the map, remained a phantom hidden in rain-filled wilderness.

A fourth battalion (Second Battalion, Thirty-Fourth Infantry Regiment) was dispatched to the Mount Badian area, flanking the Ormoc Trail to the east, and miles in the rear of the Yamashita Line on

Breakneck Ridge. This force fought over mountain paths and by mid-afternoon the column was mired by the typhoon. It did not reach its objective until the following day.

It was a hard day also for the artillery observers. Fogs, rain and jungle made visibility so bad that the observers were forced to crawl to within a hundred yards of enemy positions so that they might direct their shells into the targets. There were occasions when a whole platoon of Japanese combed an acre of jungle to hunt out and kill one hidden artillery observer.

Captain George F. Iwen of Watertown, Wisconsin, was wounded in a forward observation post and encircled by Jap patrols. The Japs did not find him. He remained among them for twenty-four hours, whispering target directions into a portable radio until he collapsed from lack of blood.

Every man in an artillery reconnaissance party on the left flank of Breakneck Ridge was killed or wounded except Sergeant Francis E. Hogg of Springfield, Ohio. Violent Japanese counter attacks were then in progress. Slowly the Americans were pressed back toward the beach. Under mortar fire and aimed snipers' bullets, Hogg remained in no-man's-land, radioing information of enemy maneuvers. With his carbine he killed a Japanese who blundered into his foxhole in the soggy *kunai*. The monstrous force of the wind blew artillery projectiles far off their intended course, and adjustment and correction became a most difficult task. The targets were not stationary. The targets were advancing concentrations of Japanese. At this time a message came to Hogg which told him that all members of an observer's team on another part of the ridge had been disabled. Their radio, keyed to another battery of field artillery, lay idle. Radioman Hogg decided to retrieve the abandoned radio. Its possession would enable him to serve two batteries at the same time. He leaped out of his foxhole and ran toward the adjoining position. Japanese gunfire killed him.

In the storm a Japanese bomber crashed near the village of Capoocan. Intelligence officers were eager to salvage the crashed bomber's sights, guns and radio equipment for a study of new wrinkles in enemy armament. But the roads between the coast and the wreck were solidly in Japanese hands. Lieutenant Frank Kennedy of Hinsdale, Illinois, an Air Corps-Infantry liaison officer, volunteered to go. Alone, cutting through jungle, he shot his way to the wreck. Fighting, he stripped the bomber of new ordnance items. A group of snipers a hundred and fifty yards away did their best to kill Frank Kennedy. When bullets failed, they brought mortars to bear. Bursting mortar shells set the wrecked bomber afire. But Kennedy hid the seized equipment in a thicket where it was later recovered. After that he shot his way out and reached a friendly amphibious tank unscathed.

On the windswept hillsides lay the wounded. About them were the torn earth, the mud, the dead, the dripping *kunai*, explosions, the stench of rottenness, and myriads of insects. Above them were the thunder and the lightning, the black sky, the whining gale and the snarl of bullets. The wounded waited for help. No wounded man was forgotten and left to die on Breakneck Ridge if there was a humanly possible way to save him.

Shortly before noon a company of riflemen working up a slope received machinegun and mortar fire from the crest. Four soldiers were wounded before they could seek cover. Private John Whitley of Iola, Texas, risked his life to crawl to the wounded and to drag them down the slope where aid men were at hand.

When a B.A.R. man crumpled in a fire fight, Private Frank Letzring of Grafton, North Dakota, ran to his aid and bandaged his wounds. A Jap bullet hit Letzring in the leg. But he took over the other's automatic rifle and helped to repel a Banzai charge. In a later action, while tackling a Japanese machinegun nest, Frank Letzring was killed.

Following the sound of moans in rain and wind, Corpsman Howard R. Cutts, of Chicago, crawled through the *kunai*. He was unarmed. One bullet creased his helmet; another slugged through his canteen. Cutts crawled on. Near a Japanese strong-point he found a soldier both of whose legs had been broken by artillery fire. Cutts used the other's rifle and bayonet as splints. "Now we are ready to move back," he told the soldier. But the man was unconscious. Cutts began to drag him gently to the rear. But then he gasped and fell sideways. A sniper's bullet had gone through Aid Man Howard Cutts. He died in an instant.

At the same time "Fox" Company of the Twenty-First lay engaged in the second day of an eleven-day fight for a knob dubbed Arson Hill. They had battled through jungle and on the upper slopes they battled through grass seven feet high. The Japanese were rarely more than ten yards off. In the tall *kunai* visibility was less than one yard. Men heard bullets zip by in the grass and they could not see a thing. They fired blind volleys to clear the *kunai*. It was like spraying bullets into a fog. Many were killed or wounded. "Fox" Company lost 35 per cent of its men. In eight days it weathered sixteen Japanese counter attacks. There was an everlasting rain, and when the typhoon blew, it blew in the enemy's favor. The Japs poured barrels of gasoline on the hillside. Then they set the *kunai* grass afire.

The tall grass blazed like all hell. A multitude of screeching birds arose to escape the flames. Wounded men cried as they burned to death. There were masses of hissing steam. Wind and rain pressed clouds of smoke close to the ground and the crackling of the burning hillside was louder than the rat-a-tat of machine guns firing from adjoining heights. "Fox" Company's men fired back through smoke and flames. Some men ran when the fire reached them. Others dug deeper into their holes and let the fire burn over and beyond their holes. All suffered hunger. The company supplies were in a nearby gully, and the jungle-filled gully was infested with snipers. But the fires cleared Arson Hill. After that the shooting was no longer blind.

Out on a flanking patrol to ferret out enemy positions was Sergeant Leroy F. Hanse and two fellow soldiers. Hanse was a farmer from Spencer, Iowa. They circled the hillside in single file, Hanse in the lead. When they found Japs, the Japs were two yards distant. Hanse whipped up his sub-machinegun and fired. He killed six. His companions killed four. The patrol moved on. There was much firing about them from *Arasaka* rifles. The Japanese were talking to one another in English to confuse and trap the patrol. But the patrol returned intact. The information it brought enabled the company commander to order artillery fire on enemy strongholds.

That night Hanse was on guard near a machinegun on the perimeter. At 10 P.M. he heard a rustling on the charred hillside below. Japs creeping through darkness. There was a slight click as the machinegunner brought his gun into the direction of the rustling. Out of the blackness a voice said in English, "Don't shoot, buddies—it's Clem."

"Clem—hell," growled Hanse. "Fire."

At dawn, almost within arm's reach of the machinegun's muzzle, they found eleven dead Japanese.

That same night, at 2 A.M., a Jap jumped into Hanse's foxhole. Hanse hit him in the face with both fists, grappled with him, threw him out. Then he dashed out after the fleeing Jap, overtook him and bashed his brains out with a shovel.

The Division Record summed up this day:

"The enemy was stubborn and resisted the advance of all elements. Enemy fire was continuous at the front, flanks and rear of all positions."

November 9

At 4 A.M. the Divisions artillery unleashed a barrage against the ridges on both sides of the Ormoc Trail. To observers it appeared that the explosions left not a square yard of jungle and *kunai* uncovered.

Heavy mortars joined the hard concert at dawn. Punctually at 7 A.M. the guns fell silent. Then fifteen hundred infantrymen arose from the morass of their foxholes to force the ramparts of Breakneck Ridge. Through quagmire, over fallen trees and up slippery hillsides men panted and fought to break the defense. It was raining hard. The clatter of heavy machineguns supported the attack. Grenades, rifles, bayonets and flame-throwers came into play. Men were running in short, rapid rushes. Men lying in the grass, behind the trunks of trees, in boggy holes, firing. Men threw grenades and on their mud-stained faces were the expressions of bitterness, of a murderous resentment, and of excruciating pain. In battle, words become as scarce as a saint's curses. Here and there a shout, a warning, a command, a snarl that goes with killing, a roar of utter fear. Some groups were halted by the spiteful chatter of enemy guns. Others pierced through enemy roosts and forged on, slower now, as if the bodies of the slain had added their weight upon the shoulders of the living. There is little a soldier in battle can see; he sees the enemy facing him, and he sees three or four comrades firing and rushing forward at his right or left. But of the outcome of the day's endeavor he knows nothing until the day is done.

"Item" Company reached the top of Breakneck Ridge at noon; it was cut off and fought for its life. "George" Company took Observation Hill, but was pressed back by a counter assault. "Easy" Company reached its objective, dug in there, and hung on. "Item" Company skirmished in support of "Love," which at dusk was forced to fall back. In the retreat the company was split

Private Francis Zines of Red Lake Falls, Minnesota, volunteered to cover the withdrawal. He lay behind a machinegun on the rain-lashed crest and fired. His fire prevented the Japanese from pressing into the rear of his company as it disengaged downhill. Zines was alone, and wounded, but he gave his last so that "Love" Company might live.

A platoon commanded by Sergeant Orian Youngblood of Roswell, New Mexico, was isolated on the central crest of Breakneck Ridge. The crest was shrouded in fog and dusk approached. From above them and from both flanks Japanese assault detachments closed in. Sergeant Youngblood remembered a cardinal rule in any good soldier's creed: "Never retreat until you receive the order to do so." But where was his company? It was nowhere in sight. Jap mortar shells came in with malevolent crashing. Jap machineguns hammered an eager tattoo. Their cross fire to the rear of the marooned platoon was designed to cut off the only route of escape. Jap riflemen approached in leaps and bounds. Youngblood heard their hoarse yells. A Jap near enough to toss grenades leaped up in the grass and swung his rifle aloft. Youngblood drilled him between the eyes. Then the sergeant from New Mexico made a decision: give way. There was no gain in letting his comrades die in this manner. He concentrated the fire of his men on the machineguns. As the hostile cross fire wavered and became intermittent, Youngblood led his platoon through the ephemeral gap. He led his platoon along wild ravines and winding stream beds, back through Japanese lines.

That same day the First Battalion of the Twenty-First Regiment slugged its way through to the slopes of mysterious Hill 1525. This force was then ordered by radio to cut through to the Ormoc Trail in the rear of the Yamashita Line. The purpose of this maneuver was to prevent the escape of Japanese troops fighting on Breakneck Ridge.

"Able" Company was left to guard Hill 1525. "Baker" and "Charlie" Companies struck out in the Japanese rear. "Dog" Company, a force of machinegunners and mortarmen, was divided to reinforce the other three. Toward noon the battalion commander radioed that he was within sight of the Ormoc Trail. But a little later came the message that the force was meeting heavy enemy fire; then that it was being attacked by superior numbers of Japanese from the front and both flanks. Two hours later came another report: the force was engaged in a fighting withdrawal in a northwesterly direction.

Meanwhile, on Hill 1525, "Able" Company was attacked from all sides.

Withdrawal is an easy word. But a withdrawal after a day of fighting means that the days wounded must be found and carried along in the retreat: helpless men with holes torn by fragments from mortar and artillery shells, men with bullet-lacerated arms and legs, men shot through the face, the belly, the lungs, men with hip-bones smashed or testicles shot away, blinded men, burned men, men with machinegun slugs in both their feet. Litter bearers scrambling over tortuous mountain trails. Machete men in front, hacking away through the thickets. On slippery hillsides, bearers fall and wounded roll into the mud; litters are then passed from hand to hand, down the cruel inclines, up along the sides of canyons, across streams and the carcasses of fallen trees. At times an enemy machinegun cuts loose and everyone lies glued to the ground until the escort of riflemen has found and killed the gunners. At times snipers' rifles crack in treetops or in the dense *kunai*. More men are wounded before the snipers can be found and killed. Then the procession moves on—wordless and competent and grim beyond words.

Let it be said to the everlasting honor of our Army that never has a wounded man been knowingly left to die in the jungle. And in that looms the towering summit of men's unwilling comradeship in war. It is greater than all monuments, greater than the highest mountains, greater than the finest speeches of generals and presidents.

An infantry private named Monroe McGee of Houston, Mississippi, went forward under machinegun fire and dragged a wounded comrade out of blood-stained mud.

An infantry sergeant named David Mumper of Joplin, Missouri, saw a wounded comrade squirming at the base of a tree stump, and he saw a sniper in a treetop fire again to take the wounded man's life. Mumper dashed forward under the sniper's sights and carried the soldier down the slope, to safety.

An infantry private named Ara Kaljian of Fowler, California, knew that three wounded soldiers sprawled on a trail would receive more wounds or be killed unless they were moved. Three times he advanced under aimed enemy fire. Each time he dragged one of the fallen men to cover.

Robert Heinig of New Haven, Connecticut, "Dog" Company's first sergeant, risked death to drag a fellow soldier out of the reach of bursting Japanese grenades.

Corpsman Wilbert Kufhal of Wausau, Wisconsin, crept through enemy lines to save the life of a soldier cut down by bullets while on reconnaissance patrol. The rescued soldier reported that two other members of the patrol lay wounded behind the Japanese lines. They lay at the edge of a dense jungle area on the far slope of the hill, and they were completely surrounded by the Japs.

There was a call for twenty-five volunteers to pierce the enemy front and to bring back the wounded. In less than a minute, twenty-five soldiers volunteered. Leading this rescue force was Lieutenant Edward S. Farmer of Berkeley, California. In a close diamond formation they pushed into the jungle; twenty-six pledging their lives to save the lives of two.

After they had wedged twenty yards through jungle, snipers' rifles cracked to their left. Bullets zipped through the tangle of vines. The riflemen swung around to challenge the snipers. "Never mind the damn snipers, let's keep going," Farmer said. They pushed on and soon there sprang up a stormy clatter to their front. Machineguns fired at the rescue party. Two soldiers sagged into the jungle, wounded. The hammering of a nearby machinegun became continuous. Lieutenant Farmer pulled the pin of a grenade. He plunged through the thickets in the direction of the firing gun. He found the emplacement and he pitched the grenade. The grenade roared and the gun fell silent. The soldiers they had come to rescue were found. Carrying four wounded, the patrol then fought its way back to its own lines.

Sergeant Reinhardt Bock of Tripoli, Iowa, found a wounded comrade from another unit in the path of a Japanese advance. The wounded man was trying to crawl to the rear on elbows and knees, and was hit again. The sergeant halted and picked up the dying man and lugged him toward a ravine. They almost reached cover. Reinhardt Bock died in a burst of Japanese machinegun fire.

In a little clearing mortars thumped in support of foot troops. A Japanese suicide squad dispatched to silence the mortars sneaked in from the flank. Staff Sergeant William Keating of Kansas City, Kansas, led his mortarmen in the repulse of the raiders. The mortars continued their thumping until observers reported that the fighting had shifted to a part of the ridge which could not be reached by the mortars from their present position. Sergeant Keating went forward to find a new position for his mortars. Mortar shells, hurled steeply into the air, need "mast clearance" not easily found in dense jungle. Keating knew that the jungle teemed with snipers—but he was determined to keep his mortars thumping.

He found another clearing, barely thirty feet wide. He ordered his section to move. Concentrated on his task, he did not see two Japanese lurking in the shade of an aranga tree. The Japs fired. Keating leveled his carbine and fired back. One of the snipers threshed the ground. The other dodged behind the tree and continued to fire. Bill Keating died, his face turned toward his men who just then were moving up their weapons to the new position.

The death of their leader did not deflect the mortarmen from their mission. The fighting team carried on. Sergeant Vernon Shipley of Moro, Oregon, sprang into the breach. He got the mortars mounted and he kept them thumping.

The Japanese counter attack on Breakneck Ridge was at its height. Behind a fallen tree on the hillside three soldiers lay in shallow holes. About them shells burst with tearing violence. Bullets struck line-like patterns into the mud. The hillside was alive with Japanese. Close to the left of the three soldiers a friendly machinegun fired in frenzied bursts. The gunner sagged, wounded. The assistant gunner took over the gun. Suddenly three Japanese jumped up six yards away and threw grenades. All three were killed by the machineguns spears. But the grenades roared. They killed the wounded gunner and they killed the assistant gunner. An ammunition bearer was hit by fragments. The wounded ammunition bearer now took over the gun. He fired four long bursts before he, too, was killed. The gun was silent.

Behind the fallen tree the three soldiers saw the silent gun. They also saw the Nips rush in, hurling grenades, shouting, shooting from under fixed bayonets. One of three yelled: "Don't let the bastards get that gun."

Private John Bresnahen of Detroit, Michigan, crawled toward the unmanned gun. With him came his two companions, Private Dewayne Nixon of Sioux Rapids, Iowa, and Private John Wingertsman of Willimantic, Connecticut. They reached the gun. The enemy understood their intention. Bullets came their way.

The three soldiers clutched the machinegun and dragged it rearward behind the tree. Nixon brought the ammunition. Wingertsman loaded the gun. Bresnahen fired until the barrel steamed in the downpour from the skies. The assault was repulsed.

Sergeant George Smith of Page, North Dakota, chose a name of his own for the height known as Suicide Hill. He called it "Pick-off Hump" because he picked off fourteen Japanese without once changing his position on the hillside.

He had his machinegun mounted at the rim of a half concealed hollow and overlooking a tree-filled canyon. Two hundred yards away and below him a dim trail wound through the undergrowth. The trail was used by enemy parties carrying ammunition to the front.

Somewhere across this trail lay a huge tree felled by the typhoon. At this spot the Japanese had to leave the hidden path to circle the fallen tree. Sergeant Smith aimed his gun at the base of the fallen tree and waited. Through thirty-six hours he did not move from his position. Every little while a Jap came ducking along the path, and when the Jap circled the tree, Smith unleashed a burst from his machinegun. He was loath to leave the spot after his ammunition had given out. About to depart, he spotted a Jap who was scrambling across the fallen tree. Smith picked up a captured rifle. He dropped the Jap with a single shot.

At nightfall Breakneck Ridge still loomed unconquered. The men who dug their foxholes on the rain-soaked slopes dug with the feeling of castaways forgotten in a cesspool. The battalion which had been sent out to cut the Ormoc Trail in the rear of the Yamashita Line was forced to fall back. A battalion sent out to rescue the surrounded force on Hill 1525 was pressed back 3,500 yards and finally dug in just short of the beach east of Pinamopoan. Another battalion whose mission it was to secure Hill 1525 was delayed by hurricane and morass. They camped in the jungle, but during the night a radio message told them that Hill 1525 had been lost to the Japanese.

November 10

At 7 A.M., through heavy rains, all battalions of the Twenty-First Infantry moved against Breakneck Ridge in a frontal assault. Battalions from the Division's other regiments fanned out to strike the enemy's flanks.

By 10 A.M. Observation Hill was captured after two hours of heavy fighting.

An Ormoc Trail bridge three hundred yards east of Observation Hill was stormed an hour later. The bridge was found wrecked beyond use.

By noon Arson and Suicide Hills were in American hands.

At 2 P.M. the battalions gathered for the attack on the remainder of Breakneck Ridge. They thrust forward under cover of gullies and ravines, but on the vile mountainsides they were pressed back to the summits they had attained at noon.

Among "George" Company's killed and wounded was the company commander. Seymour Smigrod of New York City, a platoon leader, took over. Though wounded himself, he valiantly led his battle team through the day's fighting.

"Fox" Company on Arson Hill repulsed three suicidal counter attacks. Through fog and smoke the Japanese waves penetrated to within a stone's throw of the crest. They killed the crew of a machinegun defending the company's flank. A messenger named William Phipps, of Payette, Idaho, hastened to the threatened spot. He manned the gun and fired. A Jap rose from the mud in front and hurled a grenade. Phipps sat up, shook his head and regained his balance. He crawled back to the gun and fired. Eventually the assault collapsed.

In the confusion of battle a team of automatic rifle gunners were pressed down the slope of the hill. As they fought their way back to the top, one of their number fell wounded. In the midst of heavy firing Private Jande Casde of Dirchester, Texas, crawled down the slope and saved the soldier's life.

Corpsman Merle Lemkuhl of Agar, South Dakota, rescued a wounded comrade under fire. Lemkuhl was hit by a bullet as he carried the wounded man to cover. Nevertheless, he rushed out again to give aid to another soldier who cried for help. He calmed the wounded man and then he bandaged his wounds. "All set," the corpsman shouted through the uproar of the guns. "Relax so I can drag you back." An instant later Merle Lemkuhl fell mortally wounded.

Leading an isolated platoon of riflemen was Lieutenant Benjamin Rosenblatt of Chicago. Casualties ran high and many of his men suffered from exhaustion. When Rosenblatt received an order to withdraw his group, many of those who had not been hit by bullets or grenades were unable to move. Men lay in the mud, glassy-eyed, beyond all care and all fear of death. In desperation Rosenblatt hastened along the skirmish line, urging, crying, toiling to help his men out of their holes. At the time they did not know that their lieutenant was hit and bleeding. But they rallied. With them they carried their wounded. Ben Rosenblatt was killed in action.

Rations had not reached the front at noon. Ammunition parties were stopped by swarms of snipers constantly crawling through the lines to the American rear. After a platoon leader in quest of ammunition was cut down, Sergeant John Lacy of Wilsboro, New York, assumed command. He solved the scarcity of rounds by collecting ammunition from the dead and wounded. He moved from man to man, distributing the ammunition and with it courage and cheer—"Don't give up, boys ... make 'em count... shoot only at what you can see."

Every man of a machinegun section commanded by Sergeant Louis Kepler of Deferiet, Missouri, had been killed or wounded—and the Japs pressed in. The last shot had been fired and there was no more. Kepler attempted to drag away the gun. Hostile machinegun fire pinned him down. He was determined that the enemy should not capture his weapon. He took his last grenade and pulled the pin. He placed the grenade under his machinegun and wriggled away, digging a furrow through the slime with both hands. The grenade roared. The gun was destroyed. Kepler then crept back to help the wounded members of his squad to cover.

With "Able" Company, fighting in a canyon at the base of Hill 1525, Private George Diehl of Saint Joseph, Missouri, worked his way through mortar blasts to three wounded men marooned on an exposed bluff. In relays he helped them to reach the protection of the canyon. A radio operator from "George" Company crossed the fire-swept crest of Observation Hill to aid a wounded soldier who was then vainly struggling to stop the escape of blood with a mud-encrusted bandage. The radio operator was Private Frank Shaw, of Sherman, Texas. A bullet struck him while he dragged his buddy to safety.

Toward evening tanks advanced along the Ormoc Trail to take the terrain between the captured heights and the ridges still bitterly defended by the foe. The tanks drew fire from all sides. Their progress was halted by the blasted bridge which had been captured earlier during the day. The bridge originally spanned a deep ravine. The sides of the ravine were too steep to be negotiated by the tracked giants. No by-pass was possible. Intermittent artillery and mortar fire fell on the ravine. Japanese snipers were busy in the walls of vegetation bordering the roadside. Machineguns chattered from a densely wooded ridge immediately in front. The tanks withdrew. "Item" Company's riflemen, who were dug in around the bridge, promptly found a name for the ravine. They christened it "Dead End Gulch."

The night around Dead End Gulch was filled with sound and motion. All night the Division's field artillery and mortars placed interdicting fires in front of the captured heights. Enemy night attacks in force were thus prevented. Private Mario DeMarco, of Chicago, strung a wire line under Japanese gunfire from the battalion command post to the detachments guarding the blasted bridge. Combat engineers went forward to see what could be done about Dead End Gulch.

Engineer Lieutenant Harry R. Hack of San Francisco, and Staff Sergeant Anthony DeMello of Hilo, Hawaii, took the measurements of Dead End Gulch. Hack had been a logger in civilian life. DeMello had been an ice-plant mechanic. Since the landings on Red Beach they and their company of engineers had built twelve bridges to make possible the advance of the Division's motorized strength. To them, this was just bridge job number thirteen.

Hack and DeMello jumped into their jeep. A sign on the jeep bore the legend, "Hardway Construction Co.," and the added comment, "Silence! Genius at Work." They drove to a palm plantation two miles to the rear and mobilized their men.

They cut a quantity of palm logs for trestles and stringers. Another crew of soldier-engineers went out to procure a load of heavy planking. A courier was dispatched to Pinamopoan for three boxes of long spikes. Private First Class James Johnson of Helena, Alabama, then trucked the materials through sniper fire to Dead End Gulch.

The firing there was as lively as ever. Muzzle flashes glared intermittently in the night. Rain fell. Curses were muted to whispers. The engineers hauled the logs across the gulch. They worked in knee-deep mud. They built trestles and solid supports. Then they tied palm logs together to a rugged bed of stringers. After that they lugged the heavy planks out over the gulch and nailed them one after another onto the coconut log span. At times the work was interrupted by gusts of firing from the ridge two hundred yards in front. The Japs heard the hammering and they did not like it. By 3 A.M. the bridge was completed. The engineers relaxed in the muck and slept under ponchos, oblivious of the steady thunder of artillery fire falling on Breakneck Ridge.

During the night Japanese patrols cut telephone lines from regimental headquarters to all battalions.

CHAPTER THIRTEEN

THE BREAKING OF BREAKNECK RIDGE

"The terrain is the toughest I ever saw."
MAJOR GENERAL F. A. IRVING,
*Commanding the Twenty-Fourth Infantry
Division on Breakneck Ridge*

THE JAPANESE BASTIONS on Breakneck Ridge were broken and overrun in seven days of continuous assault. The battle lines did not move forward in a solid front. They moved like the spread fingers of a thrusting hand. The frontal assault was borne by the Twenty-First Infantry Regiment. Battalions of the Nineteenth and Thirty-Fourth hacked away at the flanks and the rear of the enemy lines. The offensive was fought by battle-weary troops, over precipitous ridges, in jungle, mud and constant rain.

A single mortar platoon commanded by Lieutenant William Langford of Valdosta, Georgia, fired 7,200 rounds of mortar ammunition in support of infantry charges in seven days. And every shell fired had to be carried up Breakneck Ridge on soldiers' backs.

Sergeant John T. Kennedy of Pawtucket, Rhode Island, led his rifle squad in a charge on one of the contested ridges. Upon gaining the crest, a Jap machinegun fired from a cave. Kennedy crawled forward through clumps of grass intent on destroying the Jap gunners. He was wounded, along with other men of his squad. Japs swarmed from hidden spider-holes. John Kennedy's squad faced annihilation.

"I'll hold 'em," the wounded sergeant shouted to his men. "Get back and dig in. Get the wounded out o' here."

The squad fell back to a stretch of ground which allowed for a better defense. Half of the fit dug holes in the slush, and the other half rescued the wounded. All but Kennedy. Alone, the squad leader held a platoon of Japs at bay. He fired and fired and he threw grenades. The Japs brought on mortars. They brought down a mortar barrage on the lone

American. The men of the squad dug in and lived to fight another day. John Kennedy died in the burst of a mortar shell.

A Japanese hidden in a foxhole allowed an advancing platoon to pass. Then, after machinegun fire from the front had stopped the platoon, the Jap rose and hurled a grenade at the officer commanding the platoon. The officer fell. A rifleman, Ralph Frantz of Frackville, Pennsylvania, brought his rifle to the shoulder and fired. There was a click; the rifle failed to fire. The Jap reached for another grenade. Ralph jumped into the foxhole and slew the Jap with his hands.

A company pinned down on a hilltop by a checkerboard of machinegun nests called for artillery support. An artillery observer named Christ Frangos came forward. Almost immediately his radio was shot from his hands. Frangos crawled down the slope and laid a telephone wire to a point less than fifty yards from the Japanese positions. He maintained the wire line for forty-five minutes. In this time field artillery cleared the terrain to make possible a continuation of the advance. The mission was a success. But Christ Frangos died. His home was in Ames, Iowa.

A combat patrol probing ahead of the regimental advance received machinegun fire as it crossed a mountain stream. Sergeant Stephen Kupczyk of Chicago, the leader of the patrol, deployed his men along the stream bed in an effort to destroy the machinegun. Then rifle fire crackled from the flanks. Snipers. A scout of the patrol was badly wounded. Kupczyk saw the wounded boy flounder across the stream and collapse in the path of fire. The sergeant now rushed up the stream bed to save his scout. He reached his fallen comrade and was about to pick him up, and suddenly Kupczyk slumped forward. A sniper's bullet had killed him.

The fire fight continued. Private Claud Long of Sutton, West Virginia, had fired some sixty rounds at the Japanese machinegun roost. He now went hunting for the sniper. After some cautious prowling he found him. The sniper was dug in on higher ground between two trees. He was about twenty yards away. Long brought his automatic rifle into position. He took aim and he pressed the trigger. The automatic rifle jammed. Rain and mud do things to weapons. By this time the sniper had discovered Claud Long. The West Virginian cursed his luck. He toiled to eject a ruptured cartridge from the chamber of his B.A.R. While he worked he rolled over the ground, this way and that. The sniper fired three times at Long. The shots missed him by inches. After the third shot, Longs B.A.R. was ready again for action. He called the sniper every abusive word he could think of. Then he drilled him with twelve bullets.

Though thousands of men fought at close quarters on the slopes and in the ravines of Breakneck Ridge, the battle broke down into innumerable duels between small teams of haggard men, day and night through seven days. Take Private Herbert Jump of Covington, Kentucky. Jump was a rifleman armed with a Thompson sub-machinegun, and the leader of a rifle squad. The squad worked through tall grass toward the crest of a ridge. The lead scout discovered an enemy emplacement near the crest. There were four Japs and a machinegun in the emplacement. The Japs were waiting for Jump's squad to gain the top of the ridge where each man would be silhouetted against the sky. Then the Japs would mow down the squad at close range. Jump halted his squad. He hugged the ground and he crept toward the enemy emplacement. Three yards from it he stood up and killed the Japs with a long burst from his tommy-gun. The squad dug in for the night atop the ridge.

The Japanese counter attacked immediately. They swarmed onto a thickly overgrown knob on the ridge. From this vantage point they proceeded to bombard Jump's unit with grenades. Rifle fire against the Japs was of small avail. The enemy remained invisible, and protected by the rise in the ground, though he was no more than a stone's throw distant. The Japanese answered each volley from the Garands with shrieking laughter and with more grenades.

"I'm going to fix those birds," said Herbert Jump.

He wriggled down the slope and skirted the ridge. Then he crawled back to the crest of the ridge in the rear of the grenade throwers. He walked in on them without warning. His sub-machinegun blazed. Six of the grenadiers died. The survivors fled in panic.

The final storming of Breakneck Ridge began at 9 A.M. on November 11. It ended on November 17, when the battered assault teams fought down the southern slopes and entered the upper reaches of the Ormoc Valley near Limon. Daily progress was counted in hundreds of yards. The whole battle took place on an irregular front not more than five miles long and two miles deep. It was one of the bitterest battles of the Philippine war.

The attack was launched—two battalions abreast—from the heights captured during the previous day. One force pushed south; the other west. They gained three hundred yards in five hours of fighting. Resistance was fanatic. At noon the Japanese hurled counter attacks from commanding ground marked on the Division's maps as "Corkscrew Ridge." Among the weapons wielded in this collision were bush-knives and white phosphorus. Another stalemate threatened. Then—despite a report that the Japanese had heavily mined the Ormoc

Trail—Colonel Verbeck called tanks into action.

The engineers watched tanks and tank-destroyers rumble across the bridge they had thrown across Dead End Gulch. But once across the bridge, the tanks stopped. Verbeck came forward. Tall, wiry, blond, the irrepressible colonel strode up the Ormoc Trail with apparent unconcern. He who had fought through World War I as an infantry private, and later with the Philippine Scouts and in Alaska, understood a soldier's problems from the bottom up. "Damn good man to take along on a patrol," his men said of him, and, "Never saw anybody so thin walk so straight."

The colonel called upon the regimental Reconnaissance Platoon to protect the tanks' advance against thrusts by suicide detachments. He also called forward a mine-detector squad to clear the road ahead of the tanks. In front of them the Ormoc Trail twisted steeply toward a saddle between two ridges. On the ridges and in emplacements flanking the saddle were the Japanese. Their machineguns chattered with callous confidence.

"Get going," said Verbeck.

The going was dangerous and slow. But it was the turning point in the battle for Breakneck Ridge. On foot, leading the column with studied carelessness was Bill Verbeck. With the colonel, also on foot, was the commander of the tanks, Captain Julian van Winkle of Louisville, Kentucky. Yard after yard they guided the tanks through muddy craters, over log barricades and through heavy and continuous fire. The tanks' guns spat over the heads of the guides. Twice Captain van Winkle was wounded in the advance; but he stayed with his tanks until the summits of Breakneck Ridge had been cleared.

Meanwhile, the engineer group labored with mine detectors to dear the road for the tanks. They labored through the weirdest two days of their lives. The engineers would crawl forward on their stomachs and clear a three-foot stretch of road in front of the leading tank. Then the engineers would crawl aside, and the tank column advanced three feet—and stopped. After that the engineers crawled forward again under the bellies of the tanks and cleared another three-foot strip of the Ormoc Trail. And the tanks advanced another three feet.

Fighting during this operation was savage. The men of the Reconnaissance Platoon fired their weapons to burning heat to ward off *Teishintei* detachments intent on throwing mines under the tanks. Corpsman Harvey Perry of Bumwell, West Virginia, carried a wounded engineer down the slope and did not stop his errand even when Jap machinegun fire ripped his first aid pouches from his back. One tank crunched off the edge of the Ormoc Trail. It drowned in mud. Its crew was rescued by another tank—and ten men crowded into armored cubicles which had been built for five. Gunfire then destroyed the mired tank.

The slowness of the advance was blightening torture for the men who fought this battle. The armored column proceeded to the top of the ridge at a pace of three hundred yards a day. But the tanks' cannon destroyed twenty-five Japanese strongpoints defending the pass across Breakneck Ridge.

Three wounded soldiers huddled in a shell hole on the crest of the ridge. They were members of a team which had gained the crest two days earlier. Their team had been thrown back by Japanese counter attacks. Two corpsmen in charge of the wounded had been killed in the withdrawal, and the wounded had been lost among the Japs. For two days they had hidden in thickets and in slime-filled holes. They had experienced the terror of a friendly artillery barrage, and of ant swarms and rats attacking their wounds. When they were discovered by infantrymen protecting the tank thrust, all three were too weak from shock and loss of blood even to speak. The men who carried these wounded to safety over a slope raked by Japanese gunfire were William Dougherty of Atlantic City; Joe Schappert of Covington, Kentucky; Frederick Etheridge of Avenal, California; and Dale Johnson of Manhattan, Kansas. Their comrades safe, the rescuers returned into the fight. Dale Johnson was killed in action.

Leading an assault platoon on another section of the ridge was a young Minnesotan, Lieutenant Evert Rennaker from Fairmont Rennaker felt his heart would burst in the harrowing ascent. His group reached the top. The men fanned out to burn the remaining Japs from their holes. An enemy machinegun fired. The soldiers hit the mud and waited for orders. No orders came. Evert Rennaker had collapsed from exhaustion.

Two soldiers dragged their platoon commander to the nearest command post where aid men were at hand. There Rennaker regained consciousness. "What are you going to do?" he asked the corpsmen.

"You're knocked out," a medic said. "Doggo. We'll ferry you to hospital."

Something in Evert Rennaker rebelled against the idea of rest. He heard batteries of field artillery send crashing salvos toward the mountains. From the embattled heights came the breathless clatter of machineguns. Rennaker thought of his platoon fighting up there on Breakneck Ridge. He brushed the corpsmen aside and staggered out. He panted to the top of the ridge where his platoon was still embroiled with the hostile machinegun. The machinegun fired from a six-foot-deep hole dug at the mouth of a cave.

The men stared at Rennaker as if they saw a ghost. Without a word their lieutenant crawled past them. He crawled toward the machinegun nest with a mute and immense singleness of purpose. He killed the Jap gunners with a grenade. By now he was wounded and bleeding. He jumped into the hole and threw out the dead Japs, one after another.

Down the grassy hillside other Japanese were gathering for a counter assault. Rennaker heard them scream as they came on. His lips tight and his eyes shining through sweat and grime Evert Rennaker, "Item" Company, Twenty-First Infantry, swung around the captured machinegun and made it belch death into the wave of skirmishers down the slope.

In an adjoining sector, to the right of the advancing tanks, fought a rifle platoon led by Albert Wright of little Rock, Arkansas. The platoon was stopped near the crest by machinegun fire. The fire blazed from two spider-holes fifty yards farther to the right. The holes, dug in the shape of upright, thin-necked, thick-bodied bottles could not be reached by the fire of the tanks. Wright led his platoon against the holes. There was but one way to tackle them: to climb on top of them and to destroy their occupants with grenades, dynamite or fire. Machinegun bursts mortally wounded Albert Wright before he reached the holes. But he remained on his feet until the job was done. Then he fell, and the attack continued.

To the left of the Ormoc Trail Captain James Blodgett of Toledo, Oregon, a field artillery observer, kept pace with a company of infantry in the attack. A few yards from the rim of a ravine at the base of the Corkscrew Ridge the company was halted. Hostile machineguns fired from the cover of the ravine and Americans were killed and wounded. Sudden fire from mortars up the slope increased the company's distress. The enemy positions were too close to be pounded by artillery fire without endangering the friendly force. Captain Blodgett, his head pressed close to the ground, heard American machineguns firing some distance away. And abruptly the artillery observer cast all prudence aside and stood up. He shouted to the machinegunners:

"Hey, you guys, come over here."

The gunners came, ducking low through the *kunai*. The artillery officer helped them mount their guns.

"Now," he said. "See that ravine? See that hillside behind it? Give her all the bursts you can."

Through the crashing of Jap mortar shells the machineguns hammered. One hundred and fifty rounds per minute per gun. The Japs pulled in their heads. The machineguns continued to fire while infantry

THE BREAKING OF BREAKNECK RIDGE 169

charged the ravine. When the foremost riflemen broke out in Indian yells, Blodgett waved his hands. "That's fine, boys," he said. "Cease firing."

Night came and the assault battalions dug their perimeters on the summits of Breakneck Ridge. The enemy was reinforcing. Aerial observers reported long troop columns moving north through the town of Limon. Heavy artillery concentrations denied them the use of the Ormoc Trail. But the Japs launched four counter attacks under cover of darkness. All were repulsed.

Chemical mortars rained phosphorus shells on the hillsides and gullies. In the light of the burning slopes and of flares floating from paper parachutes, the machinegunners on the perimeters played havoc with oncrawling Japanese. The conflagration, too, cleared the terrain and opened lanes of fire for the riflemen. Three hundred and fifty rounds of phosphorus and two thousand two hundred high explosive shells roared from the mouths of the mortars during that night. Then infantry again muscled forward.

Somewhere in a factory in America a worker had been careless in fitting a fuze into a mortar shell. On Breakneck Ridge the shell exploded the instant it was fired. Two Americans were killed and seventeen wounded in the premature blast. Among the wounded was Corpsman William Hull of Rock Island, Illinois. He dragged himself around the mud, tending the other wounded until he became too weak to go on.

Five soldiers worked day and night to carry mortar shells from stalled trucks on the Ormoc Trail to their mortar section emplaced on a ridge. They carried more than their own weight in shells down a muddy slope, across a jungle-filled canyon, and up the muddy side of the ridge. Each trip they were harassed by enemy snipers. They skirmished with the snipers while they carried their loads. They were but five of many others: James Huggins of Dillion, South Carolina; Chester Jankowski of Milwaukee, Wisconsin; Charles Bonton of Noroton Heights, Connecticut; Raymond Tonelli of Pawtucket, Rhode Island; and Kenneth E. Cox of Tracy, California.

A Texan, Sergeant Ray Shone, of Denison, spotted six Japanese snipers grouped around the base of an enormous *lauan* tree. His fighting job was that of a platoon guide, and in Shone's Service Record there is a notation which says that his "ability to locate enemy snipers is outstanding." The six snipers under the *lauan* tree had shot down an ammunition carrier. The Texan worked his way through thickets and attacked the snipers from the flank. Five of them crumpled under his marksmanship. The sixth escaped. Shone then went forward to give aid to the wounded ammunition bearer. A sniper's rifle cracked and Sergeant Shone, too, fell in the soggy *kunai*.

The battle for Breakneck Ridge rolled into its tenth day. The men of the Twenty-First knew that they were winning the fight. Exhaustion gave way to a resurrection of the desperate vigor of a spent swimmer who suddenly discovers the nearness of land. Sergeant William Francher of Lakeview, Texas, though badly smashed by artillery shrapnel, held out at his post to keep "King" Company's mortars in action. At the base of Observation Hill, dog-tired John McClelland of San Mateo, California, killed six Japanese who had attacked his platoon from the rear. After ten days and nights of fighting on Arson Hill, chunky, tattooed Leroy F. Hanse crawled atop two pillboxes and killed nineteen Japanese with rifle and grenades. After one company's telephone communications had been smashed, Private William Cheatwood of Buchanan, Georgia, ran two and one-half miles through mud, jungle, sniper and artillery fire to bring telephone wire and hand sets to his company commander.

A rifle platoon working up a gully at dusk was attacked by a company of Japanese who came rushing down the sides of the draw. The platoon fell back to evade destruction. Private Nolen Rogers of Taft, Tennessee, and Private Carl Schneeweiss of Banning, California, remained to cover the withdrawal. Rogers was armed with an automatic rifle. Schneeweiss fired a Thompson sub-machinegun. They held the Japs at a distance until their platoon regrouped and struck the enemy from the flank.

In the fighting for Hill 1525, Sergeant Ricardo Gallegos of Ferrell, Pennsylvania, and Private Roy Adams of Cincinnati, Ohio, blasted Jap defenders from three spider-holes and then held the positions against counter attack until relief arrived. Both were "Able" Company men. Another Adams, also from the "Able" team, dueled with three Japs in a cave, without success. Angered, he went to the rear, came forward again with a flame-thrower and tackled the foe with burning gasoline.

The push down the southern slopes of Breakneck Ridge began on November 13. An all-night cannonade prepared the way. The First Battalion slugged forward six hundred yards to the top of an intermediate ridge. The Second Battalion advanced four hundred yards. The Third Battalion was alerted when heavy Japanese counter thrusts struck the forward teams late in the afternoon.

On November 14 the battalions drove to within 1,200 yards of the town of Limon at the head of the Ormoc Valley. During the day and the following night they repulsed five counter attacks, the last of which ended in a bayonet fight. The Japanese spearhead had penetrated the regiment's defenses. The Japs overran a line of mortar positions. The mortarmen were driven from their weapons. Around the foxhole which housed the battalion command post mortar crews fought their assailants with carbines and knives.

In the command post foxhole sat Captain Hugh S. Crosson. He climbed out of the hole and reassembled the scattered mortarmen. He led them back to the perimeter to defend their weapons. Rain fell in a torrential downpour. More Japs darted out of the *kunai*. They bore knee mortars, machineguns, grenades. They had bayonets fixed to their machineguns. In the uproar of firing and screams Captain Crosson formed a combat patrol of riflemen. He led this patrol to the flank and down the slope with the intention of striking the attackers from the rear.

Standing up in a foxhole and firing his automatic rifle at Japs all around him was Joy Berry of Wapato, Washington. Private Jack Furman of Augusta, Georgia, already twice wounded and on his way to a rest area, seized a rifle and rushed into the fight. A cook named Elon Darby, of Potomac, Illinois, risked his neck to save the critically wounded. Meanwhile, the combat patrol directed by Captain Crosson came up in the enemy rear. The Japanese who had wedged into the American position were trapped. Not one of that group came out alive.

On November 15 and 16 all companies of all battalions attacked the last remaining high ground north of Limon. Engineer and reconnaissance detachments destroyed many pockets of snipers bypassed in the ravines and hollows of Breakneck Ridge.

A company of infantry was dispatched six hundred yards to the rear of Japanese defenses near Limon on a mission of disorganizing the retreat. Led by Lieutenant Theodore Crouch of Owingsville, Kentucky, the company moved out stealthily after sunset of November 15. In a forced march around hills and swamps it circled the enemy flank and dug in astride the route of Japanese withdrawal. At noon, November 16, falling back before the frontal attack, Japanese backed into Crouch's fire. The demoralized survivors fled into the bogs of the upper Naga River.

The enemy had lost the passes over Breakneck Ridge. His main force retreated down the Ormoc Valley for a final stand.

Numerous detachments, pressed away from the Ormoc Trail into the central mountains to the southeast, reorganized and massed to harass the Division's supply lines from Carigara and the Leyte Valley. Japanese artillery manhandled into trackless mountain regions sent salvos crashing over the coastal road.

A battery of field artillery firing from positions near Colasian received more than its normal share of tribulations. There, an artillery duel, a burning powder dump and exploding stores of rifle and machinegun ammunition set the stage for a fire-fighting job which pushed the cannoneers as close to the rim of hell as any man can come and live.

Captain Victor L. Boling of Duncan, Oklahoma, was ducking low under detonations of Japanese shells. Suddenly he heard a crash louder than all others. The crash was followed by a charivari of shouts, and by lesser explosions which the captain's trained ear identified as not from enemy shells. Sheets of yellow-red flame stabbed skyward behind a nearby row of trees. The Oklahoman abandoned shelter to investigate the commotion.

The Japanese had scored a direct hit. A pile of powder charges had been set afire. There were other stores of powder charges nearby. There were quantities of howitzer shells and of small arms ammunition. In the conflagration wounded cannoneers struggled to get away from the flames. The immediate urge of those not disabled was to run away. Shells screamed in at half-minute intervals. Since no one ran—all stayed.

Corpsman James J. Shamany of Sheppton, Pennsylvania, weaved in and out among the flames and explosions to pick up the wounded. He dragged them into an adjoining plantation and gave them morphine to ease their pain.

The battery commander, Lieutenant James H. Will, of Oklahoma City, jumped into the burning gun pit and yanked out several wounded men while enemy artillery projectiles burst twenty-five yards away. Then he organized his cannoneers to fight the fire.

Artillery Sergeant Howard Wagner of South Omaha, Nebraska, jumped aboard a bulldozer. He had never worked a bull-dozer before. But he managed to set it into motion. He piloted the uncouth machine into the blaze and used its blade to push the spreading fire away from the fuzed 155-millimeter howitzer shells lying but a few feet off. Everyone feared that Wagner and his 'dozer would be blown sky-high. Doggedly the Nebraskan pursued his task.

The cannoneers had nothing to use but their hands and their courage. They pounced in and out among the piles of powder charges and carried away the charges as yet untouched by fire. Shells whined through the treetops overhead. The heat was so intense that stores of rifle and machinegun ammunition exploded in sprays of brass and lead. The salvage job done, the cannoneers formed a bucket line to a rain-swollen swamp. They worked until they had doused the flames.

THE BREAKING OF BREAKNECK RIDGE 173

"Back to your pieces," someone yelled.
The howitzers thundered hard and clean.

"On 17 November the Twenty-First Infantry Regiment turned over its positions on Breakneck Ridge to elements of the Thirty-Second Infantry Division which relieved it.... The Regiment moved on foot to Carigara and thence by truck to a bivouac area in the vicinity of Jaro.

"The battle of Breakneck Ridge had been a punishing one for the Twenty-First Infantry. It had lost 630 men killed, wounded and missing and 135 men from other causes. But it had counted 1,779 enemy bodies, and it can be assumed that the slopes of the rough terrain over which it fought held a number of enemy dead not included in that total."

(from the Division Record)

The battle of Breakneck Ridge was won. But General Irving was relieved of his command of the Division. Among the rank and file who had come to admire him as a fearless, able and humane leader of men there were many who felt that their commander had been made a scapegoat for mistakes on the shoulders of higher rank. Had Irving not predicted that the Carigara road, the only overland lane of supplies to Breakneck Ridge, would drown in swamp? The new commander of the Twenty-Fourth Division, who hitherto had commanded troops in Europe, was Major General R. B. Woodruff, of San Antonio, massive, capable, imbued with a boldness that wrung victory from coolly accepted hazards.

As the Twenty-First pulled out to sorely needed rest, there remained two battalions of the Division battling in mountain wilderness miles behind the Japanese lines. They were the "lost battalions" of the correspondents' dispatches. Their names in the Division's code were "Doughboy White" and "Dragon Red."

Chapter Fourteen
DOUGHBOY WHITE

> The Rock of Chickamauga,
> The Nineteenth Infantry:
> Brave her men, steadfast hearts
> Known o'er land and sea.
>
> Forward move her banners
> Down through history.
> Hail our Queen of Battles;
> The Nineteenth Infantry.
>
> *(from "The Song of the
> Nineteenth Infantry Regiment.")*

"DOUGHBOY WHITE, Doughboy White, can you hear me? ... Can you hear me? ... Doughboy White ... Doughboy White ..."

So headquarters of the Nineteenth Infantry Regiment in Pinamopoan called its Second Battalion on the night of November 9, 1944. Since November 4 the Second Battalion had been fighting on the wild slopes around Hill 1525, on Leyte, a thorn in the Japanese Ormoc Valley flank.

"Doughboy White, Doughboy White, this is Doughboy Chief. Can you hear me? Over."

From Hill 1525 the battalion's commander, cool, lanky, sandy-mustached Lt. Col. Robert Spragins answered.

"Doughboy Chief, Doughboy Chief, this is Doughboy White. I can hear you all right Over."

In jungle darkness and mountain mists the walkie-talkies murmured like seasoned conspirators.

"... and due to transportation difficulties the kitchen personnel did not arrive. Last of rations were consumed for breakfast, 9 November. The terrain was steep and difficult, exceedingly punishing for heavy weapons and communications personnel. Heavy rains and high winds became continuous and added to the difficulty of the march. The battalion bivouacked on the western slope of Hill 1525. Wind and rain continued to increase in fury, adding to the discomfort of the troops."

(from a Field Report)

"Doughboy White ... Doughboy White ..

Colonel Spragins received the order to lead his battalion from Hill 1525 to a point 3,000 yards south of the town of Limon and 4,000 yards to the rear of the Yamashita Line. His mission was to throw a blockade across the Ormoc Trail which would prevent the Japanese from pouring reinforcements and supplies into Breakneck Ridge. Colonel Spragins asked for native guides. He also asked for rations. His battalion was under strength from twenty days of fighting since the Red Beach landings, and his men had not eaten for twenty-four hours.

Three native guides arrived with a food carrying party shortly after noon. The food carriers brought slightly less than one ration per man in the battalion. It was all they had managed to pack over the mountain trails.

The battalion left Hill 1525 on the afternoon of November 10. It moved in a southwesterly direction in the wake of a vanguard platoon led by Lieutenant George Whitney of San Francisco. On the march the Californian had surprised and killed a Japanese captain in whose dispatch case documents of high intelligence value were discovered. The battalion marched for two days through constant rain and over a route which was frequently blocked by fallen trees and cliff-like inclines.

"There were no trails and it was determined that the command would avoid all open places and all well-used routes. Concealment was imperative because the unit felt the necessity of reaching its objective without dissipating its strength in combat en-route. This resulted, however, in the pursuit of a circuitous route which taxed the endurance of the men to the utmost. The situation was complicated when native guides proved unsatisfactory and were unable to find trustworthy local civilians.

"With nightfall, 'G' Company bivouacked along a stream bed while the remainder of the battalion set up a perimeter on a high wooded slope. Available rations were opened. The men were hungry. Short rations and long marches were beginning to consume their strength. The men were ordered to make this ration issue last two days. After that the future would have to take care of itself.

"On 11 November, at 0600, a reconnaissance patrol located armed Japanese encamped 300 yards from our perimeter. Another patrol reported strong Japanese outposts 500 yards to the left of our route. They were armed with automatic weapons. A heavily wooded stream bed several hundred yards down the slope was chosen as a concealed route of advance. Leading elements were instructed to avoid contact with the enemy, or else to take steps to prevent the escape of contacted enemy personnel. The battalion resumed its march, cautious to prevent noise. At about 1600 eight Japanese approached within five yards of the column before they were seen. The Japs seemed bent on getting water and did not see the column until well-directed fire caused their systematic destruction. Two were officers."

(from a Field Report)

Sergeant Wesley Greer of Ft. Gibson, Oklahoma, was nibbling away at his last can of cheese when he saw a Jap in the jungle three yards away. In his excitement he took a large mouthful of cheese. He chewed it absent-mindedly while he raised his carbine, took aim and fired. As the Jap fell, Greer forgot about the cheese in his mouth and swallowed it. Later he looked at his almost empty ration tin, muttering that he'd like to know who had taken a mouthful of cheese out of his can while he had been shooting the Japanese.

"At 0700 on the morning of 12 November Colonel Spragins decided to follow a compass course. The guides were merely to pick the trail. At that time the battalion was on sloping ground about 1,500 yards east of the Ormoc Road and some 6,000 yards south of the coast. At 0900 it forded the upper reaches of the Leyte River and moved down a deep gorge, then followed a trail over a ridge to the west. The guides pointed out that it was probably a Jap trail. Seventy-five yards up the trail one of the Filipinos saw a Japanese in a stream bed and fired five shots before the platoon leader could stop him. The element of surprise was thus lost. Our scouts killed the enemy soldier.

"Fifty yards farther the scouts encountered ten more Japanese, apparently sent to investigate the firing. All of these were killed with rifle fire or grenades. Then the leading elements came under fire from positions up the slope."

(from a Field Report)

The vanguard platoon pressed forward through bushes and high grass which limited visibility to about five feet. There was a scattering of giant red lauan and molave trees whose trunks defied even the armor piercing bullets of the Garands. Lead scout was Private Brice H. Green of Raysal, West Virginia.

Silently Scout Green moved through the undergrowth; and suddenly he came upon a well-used trail. He signaled his platoon to a halt. The men crouched low, their rifles held ready for instant use. Green, standing motionless, searched every inch of terrain bordering the trail. From high ground beyond, the Japanese were pouring out a heavy volume of fire. But they were firing blind and their bullets went wide of their mark.

Thirty yards up the trail Brice Green saw a group of bushes strangely uniform in size. These were Japanese, camouflaged to look like bushes. Green prowled forward parallel to the trail. There were more enemies than his platoon could handle. He withdrew to make his report. He had saved his platoon from destruction. But no one mentioned that.

"George" Company's commander, Captain William R. Hanks of Escabose, New Mexico, came forward to investigate the situation. He swung his assault force three hundred yards to the right and then led it against the flank of the defended ridge. Soon mortar fire burst into the skirmish lines. A horde of Japanese stormed down the hillside, throwing grenades. A wild, close-range fight ensued.

Private Joe Druse of East St. Louis, Illinois, killed three Japs with nine bullets at arm's length.

Captain Hanks was running down the trail when suddenly he heard a scream dose behind him. He wheeled and saw a Jap charging him with a bayonet. Hanks fired twice. His assailant rolled dead between his knees.

Sergeant Peter R. Slavinsky of Kulpment, Pennsylvania, saw a grenade plop on the ground two feet away from him. He had one second in which to act before the grenade would burst. He tossed it back in the direction from which it had come, then fired eight shots into a thicket. The result was a protracted groan and the sound of someone thrashing in the brush.

The battalion pushed through stubborn resistance and past many enemy corpses without having lost a man. From forward rang a glad shout. The spearhead had struck upon a hard-surfaced road—the Ormoc Valley Road. It was the only supply line available to Japanese forces fighting on Breakneck Ridge.

"That's fine," one officer said. "We've got 'em by their balls."

Captain Hanks hurried forward. There was heavy firing which came from a hundred yards up another ridge on the far side of the road. There was a steep cut facing the road. It was impossible to scale the cut in a frontal assault. Colonel Spragins decided that a coordinated attack could not be launched without a thorough advance reconnaissance. It was 4 P.M. In two hours it would be twilight.

The battalion withdrew to the head of a ravine east of the road. Night perimeters were established and the men dug in. There was no supper that day. During the night artillery fire from friendly batteries on the coast pounded the Japanese positions. It prevented enemy counter-attacks during the night. Spragins' radiomen carefully adjusted the barrage when shells menaced the battalion's perimeter. A few of the shells burst in the crowns of huge trees near the perimeter edge. All night it rained. In the darkness the outposts could hear the rumbling of wheels on the Ormoc Valley Road—columns of horse-drawn carts moving northward to the Yamashita Line.

"At dawn, 13 November, patrols were sent along the ridges to observe the road and reconnoiter the flow of Jap strength.

"At 0745 they reported sighting a force of Japs moving from the north-west toward our perimeter.

"At 0800 another patrol killed a five-man Jap patrol. Knee mortar shells were falling around our perimeter.

"At 0930 a brisk fire fight developed on the perimeter with enemy forces of unknown strength. Several heavy machineguns and heavy mortars were identified, and several light machineguns. The Japs seemed bent on locating our positions, and determining our strength, for an attack in force. Our 60 millimeter mortars were effective in breaking up the attack.

"By 1100 fighting had died down.

"The men began to look for an air drop of food, medical supplies, and batteries for the radios of our artillery observers. None of the men had eaten for twenty-four hours. The effects of strenuous action over a long period of time made it apparent that if food was not forthcoming, the battalion could not function as it should.

"At 1300 the enemy sprayed our positions with machinegun fire and knee mortar shells, causing some casualties.

"At 1400 'Fox' Company moved against the attacking Japs. Our counter-attack was made without supporting mortar fire because it was necessary to preserve what shells had been carried in by hand. The company ran into a heavy volume of mortar, machinegun and rifle fire and was called back from the direct attack. It was decided that the creeping and crawling method would be best for preservation of our men.

"The airdrop of supplies did not materialize by late afternoon and the battalion prepared to hold its position. As the day ended it became apparent that the enemy had solidly dug in across the battalion's route of withdrawal to the coast. Some mortar fire was directed on the enemy block. A great amount of squealing and noise were heard as our shells struck.

"Our men stripped the hearts from young palms for food. Packs were stripped from the enemy dead and the men munched what rice they could find. Cooking fires were prohibited.

"There was no activity during the night, except that Japs were heard carrying away their dead. Heavy rains."

(from a Field Report)

A soldier was struck in the face by a spray of mortar fragments. He suffered many cuts and holes. None of his wounds were fatal, but both of his eyeballs were punctured. The boy was blind. He would remain blind.

The medic who bandaged the blinded boy's eyes and face knew that many days would go by before they would be able to get back to the coast. Until then the wounded would have to wait in foxholes, covered only with ponchos against the rain.

"Hey, Doc," the blinded soldier asked. "Do you think I'll be able to see again?"

The medic said slowly, "Sure . . . look, one eye isn't so badly hit. Sure, we'll be able to fix up one eye at least... after we get back."

The blind boy was happy. Through his mask of muddy bandages his voice was cheerful. "Oh—that'll be *okay!*"

Day after day of filth, hunger and hardship the medic's white lie kept up the blind soldier's morale. He would see again, would he not? On the long hike back he marched with the rest, and his buddies led him across the ridges and jungle ravines.

Then a Jap machinegun surprised them. The marchers dived into the jungle. All but the blind boy and the corpsman who led him. The blind soldier never knew that he would never see again. A Jap bullet pierced his heart. The corpsman, too, was killed and buried in the jungle.

"On 14 November, before dawn, a single shot was fired into the perimeter.

"At dawn our combat patrols moved out on the ridges toward the Ormoc Road, and another patrol reconnoitered the rear. In one small area investigated, thirteen Jap dead were counted. Their rifles, packs and equipment were recovered. Among the captured items was Jap dehydrated food and rice which our troops promptly consumed. Those still hungry breakfasted on pulp gleaned from small palm trees in the vicinity.

"At 1000 the Battalion Chaplain (Captain Lamar Clark, of Huntsville,

Texas) held burial services for two men who had died of wounds during the night.

"At 1200 patrols returned. They reported having by-passed heavily aimed Jap forces north-west of our positions. The patrols had found enemy communication wires running through a canyon. These wires were cut. Observation of the road showed numerous detachments of Japs moving in both directions. The patrols then discovered that high ground to the west dipped into a saddle toward the road. The sides of the saddle were 150 feet high. A patrol leader reported that the slopes on either side of the saddle could be scaled and that they would provide positions for the blocking of the Ormoc Valley Road.

"At 1345 came the first airdrop of food and supplies ..."

(from a Field Report)

Soldiers weak from hunger watched the transport planes swoop low over the tree-covered ridges. The planes circled, uncertain of the isolated battalion's position. The first drop of food and supplies fell into Japanese lines.

Field radios with near-spent batteries had difficulty in contacting the planes. The second drop was better. It fell fifty yards in front of the enemy positions.

Observers in the circling planes could see no trace of men in the wilderness below. Spragins' soldiers stood strained, oblivious of the Japs. They watched the gray-green planes. The planes floated, their motors muted. Jap machineguns which at first had fired on the transports now held their fire. The planes passed directly over the battalion's positions. Men shouted to the pilots: "Drop it! Drop it! God damn you drop it!"

The third drop of food and supplies went entirely to the Japanese.

The fourth drop fell midway between friendly and hostile lines. After that the planes wheeled. Their motors roared as they disappeared in the rain.

Patrols were dispatched to fight for the supplies. "Bring in the radio batteries at any cost," said Captain Hanks.

The jungle rang with the shots of skirmishers and the rataplan of machineguns. Sergeant Wesley Greer was disentangling a parachute from a case of supplies when a Jap attacked him from behind a tree. Greer slew the Jap and hastened away with the hundred-pound box. Joe Druse raised his score of dead Japs to fourteen. Private John Miller of the Bronx, New York, seized a package of batteries and fought for his life to get them through. An inventory after the "battle for the rations" showed that a few batteries, some medical supplies, sixty-four mortar shells and six cases of rations had been recovered. There were now available two hundred meals for seven hundred famished men.

"On 14 November, at 1400, a patrol returning from the south reported large numbers of Japs combing the hills for our supplies. The patrol found some of our rations and defended them until they could be brought in. All recovered rations provided the men with one third of one meal each.

'That night, friendly artillery, in an attempt to shell Jap positions on heights west of the road, dropped a round into the middle of our perimeter. It killed four men and wounded four. Liaison officers reported the incident and the fire was lifted. Colonel Spragins then decided to attack the hill south of the saddle the next morning without further preparatory fire."

(from a Field Report)

An essential point in Colonel Spragins' plan was never to reveal to the Japanese the full strength of his roadblock force. It was days before the enemy discovered the secret, and before he mustered overwhelming superiority of numbers and weapons against the isolated battalion. In the interval, Spragins achieved his goal—the strangling of hostile traffic on the Ormoc Road.

Patrols moved out at dawn. They ferreted out covered routes of attack upon "Saddle Hill." They spotted a Japanese counter patrol which was crossing the road four hundred yards to the north. Sharpshooters killed all seven members of the counter patrol.

At 8 A.M. the battalion went into the attack. In order not to show his strength, Spragins ordered only "George" Company to consummate the assault. This team was reinforced by machinegun squads from companies "Fox" and "How." The remainder of the battalion lay in hiding, with Major Charles Isackson, of Webster, South Dakota, in charge.

As the assault force pushed toward Saddle Hill, a violent fire fight sprang up in the battalion rear. Japanese detachments who had crossed a nameless tributary to the Leyte River attempted to scale a ridge and strike the battalion from behind. The thrust was repulsed.

In one of the encounters Major Isackson's life was saved by Sergeant Edward Gauthier of San Antonio, Texas. The major stood near a fallen tree trunk eight feet in diameter. The sergeant saw a bush move, and yelled: "Look out!" The major ducked. An instant later a bullet crashed into the tree trunk inches above his head.

Joe Druse of East St. Louis raised his score of dead Japs to seventeen.

The advance against Saddle Hill proceeded. Avoiding the trails, the riflemen cut their way through jungle. At a stream crossing a Japanese sentry noticed the advance and began to run. Two scouts set out to "get the Jap." The Jap was killed.

The spearhead reached the east shoulder of the Ormoc Road. Hanks reconnoitered for a good crossing. Then, stealthily, he deployed his command. A pillbox guarding the road was silenced with rifles and grenades. The leading platoon crossed the road at a rush. It reorganized on its western side under now heavy Japanese fire. The enemy fire came from Saddle Hill.

The spearhead platoon now formed a "beachhead" on the far side of the road to protect the crossing of the main assault force. "George" Company's men crossed the road at a run, one man at a time. They formed a skirmish line and pushed uphill, but were stopped by machinegun fire from camouflaged strongpoints flanking the saddle. Southward along the highway, Japanese bivouacs and supply dumps were visible. A number of "George" Company soldiers were hit. Captain Hanks called for mortar fire on the hilltop positions.

While "George" Company riveted the Japs' attention, Spragins ordered "Easy" Company to assault the northern hump of the saddle. This second team crossed the road at 3 P.M. in swift rushes. It charged up Saddle Hill and put the defenders to flight.

"George" Company disengaged under heavy enemy fire which came from the south, and joined "Easy" Company on the captured saddle. In the rough terrain the evacuation of the wounded was a nightmare. Japanese snipers and machineguns fired relentlessly at the wounded men and at the men who evacuated them. A corpsman working to aid the wounded was killed. Three of the wounded soldiers were killed. Another corpsman helping along a wounded sergeant was critically hit.

At 4 P.M. the two companies dug in on Saddle Hill. From their position they looked directly upon the Ormoc Road. At one point the road was only ten yards from the perimeter. This was called the West Perimeter.

Major Isackson was instructed by radio to have the remainder of the battalion dig in secretly on a ridge on the east side of the highway. This position was called the East Perimeter.

Night fell, dark and menacing. Rain fell steadily on the strained men. In muddy foxholes the wounded were quieted with morphine. But Nippon's gate to its fighters on Breakneck Ridge was blocked.

Radio contact was established with another of the Division's battalions which was hacking away at the enemy's flanks west of the roadblock.* Colonel Spragins discussed the possibility of using the brother battalion's lines of communication to bring in supplies for his own force. But patrols dispatched to make contact with the other battalion returned with their mission uncompleted. They reported masses of Japanese entrenched on the ridges west of the Ormoc Road.

"Shortly before midnight the roadblock bore its first fruit. A number of trucks approached the block from the south. Visibility was nil because of pitch darkness.

"Our heavy machineguns opened fire when the gunners thought that the convoy was in range. Range was estimated by the sounds of wheels. There was considerable commotion, with Japanese squealing, shouting and running up and down the road in the area of fire. apparently the trucks were carrying troops and the Japanese were removing their dead and wounded. The convoy backtracked and did not attempt to force the block. Four of the vehicles were found destroyed.

"Our machinegunners then held their fire. They, as well as the riflemen on the perimeter had been instructed to fire only when they were certain that their fire would be remunerative. Thus the enemy was kept in doubt as to the exact location of the block and as to our exact strength.

"At 0300, on 16 November, a Jap troop column was heard moving north on the Ormoc Road. Our machinegunners opened up when the head of the column had advanced to the point where fire could be brought to bear with maximum effectiveness. An unknown number of casualties was inflicted. There was much confusion on the road. Later small groups were heard to drag away the dead and wounded. Remnants of this column, scattered along the road at daybreak, were picked off by our riflemen.

"Two Japanese 75 mm. field pieces north-east of the block went into action. At 1100 friendly artillery registered counterfire. The perimeter rocked with the blasts, straining the nerves of the men to the breaking point.

"The men had not eaten in 27 hours. Many were so weak that they could not walk from the bottom of the perimeter to the slopes of the saddle. They had lost their sharpness and did not retain enough reserve

---

* This was the First Battalion of the Thirty-Fourth Infantry Regiment, commanded by Colonel Clifford, which had occupied Kilay Ridge in the rear of ?he western sector of the Yamashita Line.

strength to dig in as they should.

"Two patrols were sent out to attempt contact with the First Battalion, 34th Infantry Regiment, believed to be on Kilay Ridge 1,000 yards to the west. The intention was to arrange for supplies and for the evacuation of our wounded through their means of egress. The patrols returned to report that the ridges and valleys between the perimeters were infested with Japanese and woven with well-used trails. Contact was finally made by radio. We were informed that the supply lines of the Thirty-Fourth were strained, that they could not provide rations, but that they would attempt to evacuate our wounded.

"The Battalion Surgeon (Captain Edward L. Croxdale of Villisca, Iowa) was in the East Perimeter and adequate medical attention was not available for the wounded in the West Perimeter. The crossing was hazardous. It was attempted three times, and each attempt resulted in fights with the enemy and in casualties to our own troops.

"The wounded lay in foxholes, exposed to the rain, uncomplaining. But their suffering added to the depression of those still able to carry on. All knew that the number of casualties would steadily increase, with little chance for evacuation.

""Hopes were fanned by a radio report that a carrying team composed of Cannon Company volunteers was fighting its way through the mountains to bring us rations.

"Drinking water was scarce. The nearest supply was at the bottom of a hill to the north. It was necessary to send patrols to protect the earners. Helmets were used for the transport of water because canteens clanked too loudly when the containers struck one another. The first cases of dysentery appeared among our men.

"After artillery fires had lifted with the silencing of the Japanese 75's to the north-east, another enemy artillery piece opened fire at 1300. The field piece was situated about 200 yards southwest of the perimeter. Lieutenant Whitney called for machine guns. The gunners were knocked away from the gun and many Japs were seen to flee the area; 81 millimeter mortars were then zeroed on this position and fired several rounds. Japs were heard to scream. There was no more fire from this field piece for the rest of the day.

"Enemy machinegun and mortar fire continued on the roadblock throughout the day. Our riflemen were active. Sniping at Japanese stragglers on the road continued.

"Also at 1300 an enemy truck convoy attempted to run the block. It was stopped by concentrated fire. Twenty Japanese were killed.

"At 1455 it was learned that the Cannon Company carrying party had arrived in the vicinity with a supply of chocolate ban and cigarettes.

Difficulty was experienced in guiding them to the roadblock.

"At 1500 an airdrop by B-25 planes materialized in the vicinity of the East Perimeter. A part of these rations was recovered.

"At 1530 'G' Company dispatched a six-man patrol to the East Perimeter to escort a carrying party bringing airdrop rations to the West Perimeter. The patrol was led by Sergeant Underwood (Jesse J. Underwood of Camp Taylor, Kentucky). On the way out the patrol engaged in a fire fight and killed three Japs. The patrol then crossed the road and met the ration carrying party. On their return trip, just before they reached the road, patrol and Cannon Company food carriers were caught in hostile grenade and mortar bursts. One man was killed and one wounded. Sergeant Underwood returned to the West Perimeter alone to inform us of the situation. We placed mortar fire and machinegun fire on the Japs. The carrying detail crossed the road, protected by Sergeant Underwood's patrol. Japanese mortar fire then dropped in the West Perimeter, killing two message center men and showering the battalion commander and his staff with earth. Raking hostile machinegun fire wounded several other men on the perimeter. The ration party had lost one third of their load during the fight. The rations secured provided almost one full meal per man, plus ten chocolate bars for each. It was the only meal the men had in forty-eight hours.

"Because of the confusion and oncoming darkness it was decided not to hunt for the lost rations until the following morning. The men had the satisfaction of knowing that they would guard them and eat them later. That knowledge, plus one full meal, gave us a new lease on life.

"The night was relatively quiet. Heavy rains. Some of the wounded men died of their wounds and of exposure. Our cemetery in the West Perimeter is beginning to occupy more than its fair share of the area."

(from a Field Report)

Three Americans went prowling in the jungle for scattered airdrop rations. All three were hungry and they were determined to eat. They scoured the hillsides and ravines, until they saw the gleam of parachute cloth in a tangle of vines. There lay a ration box on the near slope of a gully, and a second box lay on the opposite slope. As the three soldiers approached the first case of food, they saw a group of Japs push through the jungle on the other side of the gully. The Japs were intent on the second ration box which now lay almost at their feet.

The Americans did not fire. At this time food was more important to them than dead Japs. They would not risk to lose it in a fight. They grasped the ration case on their side of the gully and plunged back into the jungle. The Japanese were of the same mind. They, too, secured a box and vanished without firing a shot.

Sergeant Robert R. Wickey of Muscatine, Iowa, also went prowling. But when confronted with the choice between carrying back food or radio batteries—he chose the batteries. Without batteries the battalion would be unable to direct the fire of the Division's artillery on the far side of Breakneck Ridge; and unable to warn their cannoneers if their shells should strike a friendly perimeter.

From their perch on Saddle Hill two scouts looked out across a narrow valley. Beyond the valley lay another ridge. A trail led up this ridge. The scouts saw a lone Jap toil up this trail. The Jap was carrying something that looked like a wooden cartwheel. He was followed by two other Japanese who were lugging the barrel of a cannon. The ends of a pole thrust through the bore rested on the carriers' shoulders. Then a train of other carriers appeared, all muscling parts of a heavy field piece to the summit of the ridge.

The scouts reported what they had seen. A machinegun manned by Sergeant Kleetis Ivey of Careyville, Tennessee, was brought forward and mounted on Saddle Hill. Bursts of long-range gunfire scattered the train of bearers.

When Sergeant Jesse Underwood and his patrol, escorting the ration party, reached the West Perimeter after their encounter with a Japanese ambush, Underwood did not stay. Alone he cut back into the jungle to look for the soldier who had been wounded in the clash. He found the wounded man hiding in the roadside ditch. The road was teeming with Japanese. Underwood rushed forward and dragged his disabled comrade away from the road.

During another patrol skirmish that day, a soldier fell and was left for dead outside of the perimeter. His comrades later heard him shout for help. Private James Gilgen of Chicago went out alone into the jungle and rescued him.

And Joe Druse of East St. Louis raised his score of dead Japs to twenty-three.

"On November 17, at 0700, riflemen on the roadblock detected a force of Japs attempting to filter past the block. Firing was regular throughout the morning. Japs were trying to reach an ammunition dump which they had abandoned near our perimeter. Enemy patrols approached the perimeter from all sides, apparently to test its strength.

"An airdrop materialized shortly before noon. We recovered eighty-three boxes of rations. There was great rejoicing. Some men fell unconscious while eating. Colonel Spragins and other officers and soldiers had given their previous rations to the wounded.

"The rations had fallen near the East Perimeter. Again there was the problem of bringing the West Perimeter's share across the Ormoc Road. The Cannon Company carrying party reinforced by riflemen succeeded in the mission, after a brief fire fight. No batteries were recovered from the airdrop. Our artillery radios were about off the air and the generator of our 284 radio in the East Perimeter had succumbed to rust.

"At about 1530 two Japanese tanks, heavily camouflaged, with boxes of supplies strapped to their sides, moved past. Our bazookas (antitank rocket launchers) did not have a chance to fire. At 1700 these tanks returned and were taken under fire. One tank was hit.

"At 1630 the hostile artillery piece to the north-east shelled the perimeter. It was silenced by fire from friendly batteries. The explosions sprayed the West Perimeter with shell fragments. No further attempts were made by the enemy to move troops or supplies through the roadblock.

"The night was uneventful. Rain."

(from a Field Report)

Sergeant Peter R. Slavinsky of Kulpment, Pennsylvania, led the patrol which carried airdrop supplies into the West Perimeter. Every man in the patrol was heavily loaded. After they had pushed some three hundred yards through rugged jungle land, there was a shout. A Jap leaped from a tree and ran, shouting an alarm. Scouts fired by sound and missed. Then Japanese machineguns and rifles clattered on a steep incline on the left. The patrol dived to the ground. The men crawled into a mud-filled draw where they reformed. But one of the food carriers had been shot through the back. He had fallen across a log and now lay exposed to Japanese bullets which whirred through the underbrush like steel locusts. Peter Slavinsky crawled through gunfire until he reached the log. He pulled the wounded man down to the ground. Then he dragged him into the draw. He was carried to cover on a quickly fashioned bamboo litter.

"On November 18 we received word that the Twenty-First Infantry Regiment on Breakneck Ridge had been relieved by elements of the Thirty-Second Infantry Division. We also received word that a battalion of the Thirty-Fourth Infantry Regiment was pushing through the mountains from Pinamopoan to bring us supplies and to evacuate our wounded.

"At 0730 we sent out a patrol to contact the relief party. Near the Leyte River this patrol came upon fourteen Japs who were cooking rice, and killed them all. Later the patrol contacted the relief force and guided it to the East Perimeter after a fire fight with surrounding Japs.

"This was a harassing day. Friendly artillery shells fell in the vicinity of our perimeter off and on throughout the period, showering both perimeters with shrapnel which caused many wounds. We tried frantically to contact the artillery positions, but the batteries in our radios were gone. Finally a message got through and the fire was lifted about noon. However, later in the afternoon the fire and shrapnel started again. It appeared that our positions were not clearly located because of the inaccuracy of all maps.

"There was sniping throughout the day. A number of Jap infiltration groups were wiped out. Some of them were still trying to reach their ammunition dump. We removed the dump and buried the ammunition behind our perimeter. It consisted of quantities of mortar shells, artillery shells and TNT.

"Twice a day we sent security patrols to a stream at the bottom of the ridge to protect our water carriers. Water was carried in helmets. Some Japs interfered near the watering point. They were killed.

"We still felt that the enemy had been unable to locate our exact positions, or to determine our strength. That saved the lives of a large percentage of our command. Daily the Japs attempted to discover our strength with the apparent intention of sending a force sufficiently large to immobilize us. On two occasions Japanese officers were killed trying to infiltrate our perimeters. By never showing his hand, Col. Spragins was able to kill many Japs in their attempts to erase his command.

"An airdrop was made during the afternoon. It was a poor one. Much of the supplies went to the Japs. We sent out patrols to recover as much as we could. So did the Japs. Two Japs were killed in a patrol fight over rations.

"At 1700 a Japanese troop column appeared on the road. It was dispersed by our fire.

"At 1730 a carrying party came to our perimeter with 33 cases of rations.

"Japanese artillery to the north-east fired into the perimeter. It was silenced by battery fire from our 60 millimeter mortars.

"Then the Jap artillery piece south-east of the perimeter opened fire. Two shells dropped in the West Perimeter, wounding several men, two seriously.

"At 1930 a sheath of friendly artillery bracketed the West Perimeter. One shell went over, one fell short. The third landed in the center, killing five men and wounding nine. One of the wounded men died later. Fortunately, an observer with the carrying party had contact with the unit firing. The fire was lifted.

"During the night Jap tanks passed the roadblock on three occasions, and returned. They apparently carried ammunition to the artillery in the north-east. The last of our bazooka ammunition was expended on them. Some hits were scored."

(from a Field Report)

About a trek of the relief party which marched from the coast through Japanese lines to rescue the wounded men of the "lost battalion," the Division Record states:

"The party left Pinamopoan on the morning of 16 November under the guidance of men who previously had charted a trail to the roadblock positions. The party spent the first night in the mountains south of Pinamopoan. On 17 November it resumed its march over rough terrain, by-passed strong enemy positions and continued until 1600 when an artillery shell wounded one man. An hour later the center of the column was attacked by a force of Japanese. Three men were killed in the ensuing action and eight wounded. Five of the wounded became litter cases and had to be carried the rest of the march. After swinging far around the danger zone, the party bivouacked for the night. On the following morning patrols of the party contacted roadblock patrols in the vicinity of the Leyte River."

Two small advance patrols which charted the relief party's course across the mountains were led by Sergeant Dave J. Boland of Portland, Oregon, and by Captain Brian Walker of Mount Pocono, Pennsylvania. A report by the Oregonian's commanding officer describes the feat:

"Sergeant Boland led a patrol to an Infantry Battalion behind the enemy lines. The climatic conditions during this period were extremely severe and travel difficult. Storms erased all traces of the route of march of the battalion. Since the battalion was completely surrounded, it was necessary for this patrol to pass through the lines of the enemy besieging the hill held by our troops. Despite these obstacles, Sergeant Boland located the battalion. His superior judgment, courage, initiative and quick thinking were responsible for the accomplishment of an urgent mission."

And here is an official description of Captain Walker's patrol:

"Captain Walker personally led a patrol to locate friendly elements that had been cut off and were without communication. The patrol had to go through enemy held territory and was twice challenged by enemy sentries, but skillful maneuvering enabled the patrol to elude the enemy. The patrol discovered and recorded the location of enemy machinegun positions which were later destroyed. It cut enemy communication lines on two occasions. After an eight-hour march the patrol finally located the isolated battalion and re-established communications. On the way back the following day, the patrol was harassed by enemy artillery fire."

"At daybreak, 19 November, Jap artillery to our north-east opened fire. We directed fire on the enemy position. It was silenced.

"At 0800 preparations were made for the evacuation of our wounded. Distribution of rations gave about two days' food per man. Litters were improvised from saplings and sections of parachute cloth salvaged from the airdrops. Most of the wounded had lain in their foxholes for days. Asked how they felt, they simply replied, "Okay."

"The Battalion Surgeon, Captain Edward L. Croxdale, worked without regard for danger or his own physical limitations. During thirty-four days of campaigning, in which the battalion was in almost continuous contact with the enemy, Captain Croxdale was the only medical officer present. It was only through his untiring efforts that many of the wounded were evacuated in such a condition that their lives could be saved. He worked tirelessly, day and night, always without complaint, and under the most adverse conditions.

"At all times food was short, or non-existent. Medical supplies could be obtained only through airdrops. It was necessary for some of the wounded to be treated for ten days inside the battalion perimeter. Operations upon them were performed by flashlight under ponchos.

"At 1030, as we were working over the wounded, the Jap artillery piece to the south-east opened up. We silenced it again with heavy mortars.

"At 1330 the carrying party departed with a burden of 23 litter patients and 27 walking wounded. We wished them luck on their march through the Japanese lines.

"At 1530 the Jap artillery to the north-east and south-east opened up. There was considerable tension among our men. We laid mortar fire on the pieces. We then discovered that the Japs had dug a third artillery position. Our mortar fire succeeded in keeping it silent. However, their other field pieces fired intermittently.

"During our fight with the Jap artillery, four Japanese tanks passed the block running north. We had neither anti-tank mines nor bazooka shells. As the tanks passed they raked the perimeter with machinegun fire. Twenty minutes later they returned, going south. This time they added cannon fire to machinegun fire. One shell cut down a large tree. Another penetrated five feet of earth and exploded in a foxhole. One man was killed, four wounded.

"After the tanks had passed, a column of Jap soldiers approached the roadblock from the direction of Breakneck Ridge. The enemy soldiers moved slowly. They appeared haggard and worn out. After they came into the line of fire, our machineguns opened up. The column was dispersed. The survivors milled in confusion. They attempted to reform, but were again dispersed by our mortar fire.

"During the night Japs on the road threw grenades into our perimeter. Otherwise the night was relatively quiet. Heavy all-night rains.

"Early during the morning of 20 November we received a radio order to withdraw the battalion to Hill 1525.

"Shortly before daylight there was the sound of rifle fire on the perimeter. A Japanese force had infiltrated during the night while most of our men were under their ponchos to escape the rain, with only the guards on the alert. Our men were alerted by the guards. The Japs threw many grenades. Our defense was effective and many enemies were killed. A number of Japs were killed inside of the West Perimeter. The fight continued for an hour.

"Col. Spragins sensed that this attack was but a diversionary move. He immediately reinforced other sectors.

"Before the first attack had ended, a large force of Japs savagely attacked the East Perimeter. The attackers were discovered by an outpost before they reached the top of the ridge. Some of our outposts were killed by Japanese machineguns. As the enemy charged in a Banzai assault he was met with hand-grenades, machinegun fire and mortar shells. Our mortars laid fire on the Japs within twenty yards of our perimeter. More than one hundred Japs were killed. Sniping continued until noon.

"At 0800 a third Jap force attacked another section of our perimeter. Our outposts withdrew fighting. Our mortars went into action to break up the enemy concentrations. They broke with a great amount of yelling and squealing. As the assault closed in, our riflemen killed off the first wave of Japs. The fight lasted until 0900.

"At 0900 a fourth attack struck the perimeter. This appeared to be the main Jap effort. The Banzai sounded on a line hundreds of yards long. The enemy gathered at the foot of Saddle Hill which was too steep for our mortar fire to become effective. The first wave of Japs was killed, but they continued to come. One platoon of "G' Company killed seventy Japanese. At times it seemed that the order for the withdrawal of the battalion had come too late. But after 45 minutes the Japs decided they had had enough.

"At 1000 patrols pushed to the Ormoc Road to secure the withdrawal. 'G' Company acted as the rear guard. The battalion then crossed the road, one man at a time, at a run.

"At 1230 the West Perimeter force had successfully joined the East Perimeter group. Strong Japanese forces were reported to be within two hundred yards. Col. Spragins decided to follow the route of the party which had carried out most of our wounded, on the chance that this party might have encountered trouble.

"At 1300 the battalion moved east toward the Leyte River. The river was raging, swollen from rains and bedded with elephant-sized rocks. The water was too swift for footing. Speed in crossing the river was imperative in that we were still far behind the enemy lines.

"Bamboo vines were tied together to make a staunch rope. A chain of men was formed. The battalion commander crossed the river and tied the vine rope to a tree. The other end of the rope was secured on our side of the river. The battalion commander then re-entered the water to help in the crossing of the helpless wounded. The battalion crossed with the aid of the bamboo rope. The crossing was completed at 1600. A check disclosed that not one weapon had been lost or abandoned, including the heavy weapons, and that all packs were still being carried by the men.

"The battalion moved to high ground and dug in for the night. The night was quiet. Heavy rains."

(from a Field Report)

On that day (November 20) Sergeant Wesley Greer stood upright on the perimeter in machinegun and mortar fire. The morning's Banzai attacks were at their height. He stood upright because he was so better able to direct the defensive fire of his men in the foxholes. Also, he killed three Japs with his rifle and with grenades.

Sergeant Robert B. Hanseen of Scipio, Utah, was a company clerk. But when the Banzai rushes swirled around the isolated battalion, he joined the fight. "By a masterful use of his rifle," his commanding officer said later, "and accuracy in throwing fifteen grenades, Hanseen was instrumental in stopping the assault."

Later, as the battalion moved, an outpost at the foot of Saddle Hill fell in a burst of Japanese machinegun fire. From a distance it was not possible to tell whether the soldier was alive or dead. He had fallen into a gully covered by underbrush. Hanseen volunteered to go into the draw and find out. While he was on his way the Jap gunners fired again. Hanseen was gone for many minutes. When he reappeared, scrambling up the slope, he carried the outpost's tommygun. He reported that the man was dead.

On that day, too, Captain Lamar Clark of Huntsville, Texas, the Battalion Chaplain, walked into a lane of Jap machinegun fire. One bullet passed through the seat of his trousers.

Rifleman Joe Druse had meanwhile raised his score of killed Taps to thirty.

"On 21 November, at 0700, the battalion resumed its march toward Hill 1525. The terrain was difficult and progress slow. After proceeding about 1,000 yards, Col. Sprague was informed by a native that American soldiers had passed here at noon of the previous day. That was the first sign we had of the party which carried most of our wounded.

"At 1300, about 600 yards up Hill 1525, we heard the sound of firing. The column halted.

"A Japanese force had waylaid the carrying party. Heavily burdened with wounded, the party did not have sufficient rifles to deal with the enemy. We joined forces.

"The relief party under Major Carl E. Mann (Clayton, Alabama) brought back twenty-six litter casualties and forty walking wounded. Its entire route was through enemy held territory. There were heavy rains throughout its four day march. There had been only two days' rations available to the party. On two occasions the party received heavy attacks from enemy groups in ambush armed with rifles, machineguns and mortars. There were seven men killed and sixteen wounded in these actions, but Major Mann was able to evacuate all the wounded while protecting the remainder of the party.

"Progress had been slow and laborious. At times litters had to be passed from hand to hand when terrain became too hazardous for routine carrying. The litters could be carried only a short distance by the tired bearers before being turned over to a relief group. Walking wounded had to be frequently assisted over precipices and fallen trees. Some of them should have been carried on litters, but they insisted on walking to ease the burden of the bearers.

"A Filipino volunteer guided us around the Jap positions. We had contacted by radio a friendly force on Hill 1525, and asked them to fire a machinegun burst. The shots sounded close and we had hopes of reaching friendly positions that day. But the tortuous terrain forced us to spend the night in the jungle of the lower slopes.

"Most of 22 November was taken up with moving the litters to the crest. The advance units started at 0700. The rise was too sharp to be scaled by the bearers with their burdens. The litters were passed uphill along a human chain formed by all men.

"By nightfall most men had not eaten for 48 hours. The wounded had been without food for 24 hours. The bearers had given their last food to the wounded. Many of the men were without shoes. Jungle boots had torn and fallen apart. Many wore shoes taken from Jap dead. Some of the shoeless men with bruised and ulcerated feet had to be carried by comrades. There were 153 cases of jungle rot, foot ulcers, dysentery and fever.

"At dawn, 23 November, the column moved out toward Pinamopoan. Patrols reported that Jap forces were active in the mountains between Hill 1525 and the coast. Three companies of riflemen were sent ahead to clear the trail. The litter column followed, and two rifle companies formed the rear guard. Each litter was allotted a carrying force and a group of protecting riflemen. Progress was slow. The litter column drew fire but was able to shift its route and push through to the coast. However, the column of walking wounded was halted. Two of the group were killed and three wounded by knee mortar shells. Enemy fire extended over the greater portion of the trail. A walking casualty and the soldier leading him were killed by a sniper. The walking wounded and some of the litter patients with protecting units then returned to Hill 1525 for the night. One litter patient died during the night."

(from a Field Report)

Corpsman Leo J. Kintana of Martinez, California, was leading two wounded soldiers when the Japanese attack cut the relief column in two. Protecting riflemen fanned out to engage the Japs. On the rough hillside the wounded were unable to move alone. Kintana remained between them. He slung one arm of each wounded man around his neck and shoulders and carried his double burden to the cover of a ravine.

A sniper climbed a tree overlooking the ravine. His first bullet fatally wounded one of Kintana's wards. The rest of the column had withdrawn. Kintana was alone with one dying man and one disabled. He fought it out with the sniper. His fatally wounded comrade had died. Kintana then gave his remaining patient blood plasma to bolster his strength, and led him to the perimeter on Hill 1525.

When Japanese mortar shells killed two and wounded three men in the relief column, Corpsman Richard R. Smith of Atlanta, Georgia, sprang through shell blasts to the aid of the wounded. He bandaged their wounds and gave them sulfa. Then he fought his way alone through snipers' nests to Hill 1525. He returned with a patrol and found the wounded and rescued them.

"On 24 November the column pushed through to Pinamopoan. After their arrival, the men were forced to walk more than a mile to Pinamopoan Point because enemy machineguns prevented the use of landing craft close to the shore. The wounded were immediately evacuated. Two hundred and forty-one of the battalion's officers and men were hospitalized. The men were given their first cooked meal in fourteen days: peas, carrots, bully beef and coffee. It was Thanksgiving Day.

"The battalion killed 606 Japanese during its mission. The men felt that their fire had accounted for many more, although a complete count could not be made because of the nature of the terrain and the fact that the Japs removed their dead whenever they could.

"The battalion rejoined its regiment at Tanauan and at once began to stage for the invasion of Mindoro Island."

(from a Field Report)

Chapter Fifteen
*DRAGON RED**

It took a war
To tear my home apart—and make it more
United than it ever was before.

It took a war
To put the world between my folks and me
Yet knit us dose as any folks can be.

It took a war
To make me stay away, the way I do
And learn the worth of future years with you.

Corporal B. Busch

WITH THE 24TH DIVISION ON LEYTE.—At least once each day, some soldier in this front line division loses his wife thru divorce. And every day at least two other men who have been overseas more than 18 months are informed by the War Department their wives have become mothers. On three occasions this year, two men have discovered they were married to the same woman. While between 400 and 500 divorces a year among approximately 15,000 men seems a relatively low percentage, it must be remembered that by far the majority of soldiers are not married. Causes for divorce boil down to this basic reason: the wives have found somebody new.

(from a dispatch by Arthur Vesey,
Chicago Tribune Correspondent.)

FIVE HUNDRED AND SIXTY Americans met a test of loyalty on wild and lonely Kilay Ridge. Three hundred and fifty came back whole. Through twenty-five days of hardship and death not one wavered in courage and faith.

On November 9, before the final breaking of Breakneck Ridge began, the Division's planners asked themselves, "Where will the

---

* "Dragon"-code designation for the Thirty-Fourth Infantry Regiment; "Red"-code designation for its First Battalion.

Japanese make their next big stand after we have driven them from Breakneck Ridge?"

Aerial photographs showed a long massif of dominating ground four thousand yards south-west of Breakneck Ridge. Geographical maps merely showed a void, with the headwaters of the Naga River springing from this void. Native mountaineers called it *Kilay Ridge*.

The Division Commander pointed at mist-shrouded Kilay Ridge. "There," he said. "We must deny Kilay Ridge to the enemy before he can fall back on it. Seizure of Kilay Ridge will disorganize his entire rear. Clifford, you do it."

Tall, stalwart, adventurous Lieutenant Colonel Thomas E. Clifford nodded. It was a job to his liking. Through the West Virginian's rugged, easy joviality his eyes shone steel-hard. He alerted his battalion, the First Battalion of the Thirty-Fourth Regiment.

The battalion left Capoocan at dawn, November 10, in eighteen amphibious tractors. It was accompanied by a party of artillery observers. The "Alligators" skirted the coast and made an uncontested landing seven miles to the northwest. The battalion pushed up a stream which flowed under a somber tunnel of vegetation, drove inland and reached Hill 827 by noon. After a brief rest the force thrust through unexplored wilderness, counting progress in yards per hour, guided by one of the many tributaries of the Leyte River. By nightfall it bivouacked on a ridge overlooking the river south of the *barrio* of Helen. Roving patrols found no trace of Japanese.

The order for this mission had come suddenly. His battalion reduced in strength to 560 men by twenty-one days of fighting, Colonel Clifford had summoned even cooks and truck drivers to join the expedition. All vehicles had been left behind. Equipment had to be hand-carried. The battalion's anti-tank guns had been left in Capoocan; anti-tank gunners were employed to carry lighter weapons and ammunition. "Dog" Company—the heavy weapons team—had left behind two-thirds of its machineguns and mortars. Its hands were needed to carry ammunition for the few guns and mortars taken on the trek. Rations carried by each man were reduced to a minimum. Food, in an emergency, may be found in the jungle; ammunition never. Maps were soon discovered to be violently inaccurate, and Clifford was forced to rely on the haphazard knowledge of native pathfinders. The terrain was the same wildly broken, dimly trailed, desperately overgrown country which faced other units fighting south of Carigara Bay. The tangle of ferns and vines was house-high. The weather was a nightmare of rain and fog.

A ration drop was scheduled for the morning of November 11. But the hills and jungles were blanketed by dense mists. Unable to find the battalion, the transport planes returned to their base.

That day the column forded the Leyte River and seven tributaries of the Naga River and set up a perimeter near a *barrio* named Agahang. The soldiers spent the evening foraging for wild bananas and breadfruit. Pencils, belt buckles and odd coins were swapped for chickens, potatoes and rice. The forest dwellers were astounded to see Americans. In three years they had barely seen a Jap.

On the morning of November 12, in a pouring rain, the planes identified the battalion's position by the red and yellow smoke from chemical grenades. The planes dropped food and supplies and the column pushed on across a dozen streams and bizarre mountain country to a point two miles south of the village of Consuegra. Simultaneously a force of amphibious tanks skirted twenty-five miles of rugged shoreline and churned up the Naga River. They brought more rations and ammunition. Patrols reconnoitering in native canoes found that the maze of streams defied navigation above Consuegra. At the latter point a supply base was established on the river's edge.

On this day Colonel Clifford was contacted by an officer of a guerilla battalion operating in the mountains [First Battalion, 96th (Guerilla) Infantry Regiment]. The guerilla leader oriented Clifford about his own position and that of Japanese forces guarding the western flanks of the Ormoc Valley. During the later stages of the mission this guerilla force fought bravely to secure the battalion's rear.

Among native volunteers there appeared a husky, middle-aged Filipino. He was barefooted and he wore a battered straw hat. Slung over his shoulder he carried a primitive shotgun. "I want to speak to the American commander," he said.

"What can I do for you?" asked Clifford.

"I want to help. My name is Kilay."

"Kilay?"

The native nodded. "I am the owner of Kilay Ridge," he said. "I know it as I know the lines of my hand. The Japanese have set a price on my head. Now I shall go back with you."

"Fine," said Clifford.

After that they called him Joe Kilay. He was a first-class guide. He fought shoulder to shoulder with the battalion's men—until a sniper's bullet pierced his chest. "Joe" Kilay, Patriot, lies buried now in the lonely American cemetery on Kilay Ridge.

On November 12, Sergeant Donald P. Mason of Frame, West Virginia, led his platoon to occupy a wooded hill. No one expected to find Japs on the hill. But sudden machinegun fire stopped the platoon's right flank. Mason quickly sized up the situation. He told the men on the right to lie tight and to reply the fire. Then he crossed over to his two squads on the left. These he led in a charge to the hilltop.

The Japanese immediately counter-attacked with superior numbers.

"Keep the bums off this hill," ordered Mason.

Three times the Japs attacked; three times they were repulsed with bayonets and grenades.

On November 13, Colonel Clifford split his battalion into two forces. They moved against Kilay Ridge over separate routes. Their advance was swift and quiet. They occupied all dominating features of the ridge without a fight. The top of the ridge was studded with prepared defenses. But not an enemy was in them. It was clear that the Japanese had intended to use Kilay Ridge as a bastion for their further defense of the Ormoc Valley. Clifford's force had caught them completely off guard.

Kilay Ridge is three miles long. Its southeastern tip lies three thousand yards south of the town of Limon. The top of the ridge towers nearly a thousand feet over the Ormoc Road. It is very narrow in some of its portions, with cliff-like sides and jungle-covered precipices, but in places its crest widens to about four hundred yards. The top of the ridge is broken into a series of knolls which delighted the artillery observers. For fifteen miles the Ormoc Valley lay open to their gaze. The Ormoc Road, one thousand yards to the east, was visible in places; but elsewhere other ridges between Kilay and the highway obscured the view. Colonel Clifford decided that it was imperative to prevent the enemy from seizing these intervening ridges. Only then could complete support be given to friendly forces driving south from Breakneck Ridge.

On November 14, the battalion transformed Kilay Ridge into a fortress miles in the enemy's rear. Each company and each platoon was assigned its section of the massif. The summits of the knolls were organized into strongpoints. Trails crossing the ridge were blocked. Reconnaissance patrols ranged near and far to assemble a picture of Japanese positions. Preparations were made for artillery concentrations upon likely avenues of enemy approach.

Scouts were dispatched in an attempt to contact Colonel Spragins' "lost battalion" at the Ormoc Road block—without success.

Then Clifford called for volunteers among his men to conduct carrying parties of Filipinos to and from the jungle supply dump at Consuegra. Champion among these guides was to be Corporal

Lawrence DePaolo, a truck driver from Lodi, New Jersey. On five occasions DePaolo led food and ammunition trains over many miles of extremely difficult terrain controlled by enemy forces.

By the end of the day the Japanese commanders sensed that something was amiss on Kilay Ridge.

Toward evening artillery fire struck the battalion's perimeter. Though rain water half filled the foxholes, Clifford's men ducked low. Through the thunder of shell explosions they listened to the distant rumble of an artillery barrage pounding Breakneck Ridge, far to the north.

Before dawn, battalion outposts heard distant shouting which seemed to come from the direction of the Ormoc Road. And there were the sounds of digging.

"Moles," muttered Clifford, "busy yellow moles."

A combat patrol pulled out to investigate a ridge rising between the battalion's position and the road. They found a company of Japanese. The Japs had dug in there during the night. The patrol slew five sentries and then withdrew to report its findings. Papers taken from the dead showed them to be members of the First Imperial Division. Their ridge position was henceforth known as "Mole Ridge."

Later, other patrols by-passed Mole Ridge. They pushed through to the Ormoc Road. They found no trace of Spragins' roadblock battalion. But they observed a disorganization of traffic on the road which told them that Spragins' men were busy, if unseen.

Not much happened that day. On Kilay and on Mole Ridge the opposing forces sat in mud and eyed each other through a universe of rain.

November 16 was a day of combat patrols. The Japanese knew that Kilay Ridge was in American hands. They massed forces to eliminate the intruders who were a deadly threat to an eventual retreat from Breakneck Ridge. Both sides dispatched spearheads to feel out the enemy's strength.

A patrol led by a cook, Mess Sergeant Jose Carrasquillo, from Long Island City, penetrated boldly to the crest of Mole Ridge. It found the ridge clear of Japs. But Carrasquillo discovered another ridge, eastward of Mole Ridge, and somewhat lower. He observed Japs diligently digging emplacements on this second ridge, which overlooked the Ormoc Road. Carrasquillo named it "Busyman's Ridge." Then the cook returned to Kilay Ridge and reported what he had seen.

Meanwhile the company chewed K-rations.

Colonel Clifford dispatched a taskforce to seize Mole Ridge. It occupied the crest and dug in. In turn it sent a lesser force toward

Busyman's Ridge. A sharp fire fight developed. The second force fell back on Mole Ridge, leaving one of their own dead and carrying seven wounded.

A third spearhead then by-passed Busyman's Ridge in another attempt to contact the roadblock battalion. This was not successful. Several other patrols sent out on the same mission also failed to find Spragins' beleaguered force. All patrols reported fire fights with Japanese detachments guarding the Ormoc Road.

A day later, shortly after dawn, a "Dog" Company patrol cut through jungle in a wide arc to determine Japanese strength on Busyman's Ridge. It was trapped by two Japanese counter-patrols. After a brief and unequal fight it was forced to scatter in a swamp-filled ravine. Only three of the scouts returned: a critically wounded soldier carried by his two comrades. The others were missing and were never heard from again.

Hostile artillery fire falling into the battalion perimeter indicated the presence of a hidden enemy observation post overlooking the American positions. Sergeant Frank Huber, of Milwaukee, led a patrol to ferret out the observers' perch. They crossed two streams and then they came upon an uncertain trail. The trail twisted uphill to a ridge some 1,500 yards from their own positions.

A scout said, "Look!"

Through the undergrowth, parallel to the trail, ran a telephone wire. The insulation of this wire was rust-red.

"Jap wire," said Huber. "Lets follow it."

They left the trail and crept through the brush, following the wire. The wire led into a little clearing. At the edge of the clearing ten yards away squatted a Jap. The Jap was armed with a machinegun and he was peering down the trail.

The scout unleashed a single shot from his Garand. The Jap dropped dead.

"Sit still," whispered Huber. "There must be more around than one."

They waited in silence. Nothing happened. Huber's eyes followed the telephone wire across the clearing—and saw that it seemed to lead into the ground near the gnarled base of a tree. Then he saw something else; he saw a muddy piece of canvas flapping in the wind squall.

Huber crept into the clearing to investigate the canvas. His comrades held their breath. They lay in wait, covering their leader.

Frank Huber found that the canvas was part of the camouflage of a Japanese position. He motioned his patrol forward. They surrounded the canvas. Upon signal they yanked it aside.

There were four holes, and there were two Japs in each of the holes. The Japs sprawled in the mud. Two of the eight wore officers' insignia. Nothing moved. The eyes of seven of the Japs were closed. Only the eyes of one were open in a lifeless stare.

A soldier picked up a handful of mud and threw it into the face of the Jap whose eyes were open. The eyes blinked. Instantly every man of the patrol blazed away into the holes. There was an agony of writhing and yelps and then the shooting ceased and there was only a fading moan. The largest of the holes contained the end of the rust-red wire and a telephone.

Later that day, two companies attacked Busyman's Ridge. There were two hundred Japs entrenched with rifles, machineguns, mortars and artillery. Fifty-six Japanese were killed. Meanwhile, another force of Japanese counter-attacked from the flank and "Baker" Company was cut off from the battalion.

When darkness fell, "Baker" Company was still surrounded. Its commander reported a number of wounded. Three Japanese machineguns were firing into its tight perimeter on Busyman's Ridge. The knolls and canyons between it and Kilay Ridge were loud with the crackling of snipers' rifles.

Clifford called for volunteers. He himself was first to respond to his call. He led the volunteers in a thrust to "B" Company's perimeter on Busyman's Ridge. The firing continued unabated. Clifford assembled the wounded and proposed to carry them back to Kilay Ridge. There an aid station had been established. In the treacherous terrain four men were needed to carry each of the disabled soldiers in relays. The company commander protested that he could not spare so many men if he were to hold the ridge through the night. Clifford thereupon freed four of the litter bearers for combat.

"I'll carry one of the boys," the colonel said.

With that he hoisted a wounded private on his back and led his relief party through a mile of rain forest and sniper fire back to Kilay Ridge.

A battalion lineman, Technician Thurlow Rice of East Boothbay, Maine, heard a wounded soldier cry for help. Hostile machinegun, mortar and rifle fire raked the area. An aid man dashed by in the direction of the cries for help. Rice climbed out of his foxhole to help the aid man carry the wounded soldier to cover. While they lugged their comrade through thickets, the corpsman gave a grunt.

"What's the matter?" asked Rice.

"I'm hit," the corpsman said.

"Jesus Christ," said Rice. "Keep still and let me help you."

Bullets whined through the jungle. There was the flash and crash of mortar shells bursting in the treetops. Rice was down on his knees, working over his two wounded comrades. The aid man muttered instructions. Rice followed the instructions. He disinfected the wounds and bandaged them and the wounded were ready to be moved.

The corpsman said, "There's another wounded guy somewhere. I heard him groan."

Rice crawled through the underbrush until he had found the groaning man. He bandaged him and gave him sulfa and dragged him to the spot where the corpsman lay with the soldier who had been hit first. Just then a long burst of machinegun fire struck among the group. One was killed outright. Another of the wounded was hit three times. A second corpsman rushed forward and Rice helped him to carry the survivors to cover. Thurlow Rice was loyal: loyal to his buddies, to his country, to his wife, Katherine. Death took him a few months later.

In the gray morning of November 18, all machineguns of the battalion were moved from the perimeter to give supporting fire for an attack of Busyman's Ridge. Patrols pushed forward by Captain Edger W. Rapin of Bensenville, Illinois, "Dog" Company's commander, surprised a detachment of twenty-five Japs. The Japs were cooking over two fires. Volleys from Garands ended their breakfast. Seventeen were killed and the survivors scattered in all directions.

But a reconnaissance patrol led by Captain Rapin was ambushed by an enemy force of superior strength. In the first flash of bullets the lead scout died. The second scout fell wounded less than ten yards in front of the ambush—holes dug under the immense trunk of a fallen tree. Machineguns chattered and rifles cracked and nothing could be seen of the firers. The patrol deployed in a skirmish line and held its ground.

Captain Rapin saw that the wounded man was unable to move out of the path of fire. Flat to the ground, the captain crawled forward to rescue his scout. He reached the side of the scout and began to drag him toward a hollow in the ground. Then machinegun bullets struck. The disabled scout was hit again. Captain Rapin was hit.

The wounded captain struggled in desperation to pull the scout to the rear. His own strength was dwindling with the loss of blood. Then he saw that the scout was already dead.

A young Texan, Corporal Arlton Brower, of Avery, now took command of the patrol. He maneuvered the survivors to a spot from where they could fire on the ambush from three yards distance. Captain Rapin was rescued. Corporal Brower then made two attempts to bring back the bodies of the scouts. Sprays of hostile bullets drove him back.

The battalion attacked. Fifty-three Japanese met death. "Charlie" Company relieved "Baker" Company on Busyman's Ridge. "Dog" Company was embroiled in machinegun and mortar fights throughout the day. Two of its corpsmen—dirty, wet and tired as they were—attained the peak of "gallantry in action."

One was Technician Otto Kirchner-Dean, the adopted son of Reverend Dean of Kingston, New York. Kirchner-Dean saved three wounded men from death. One of the wounded was so hopelessly smashed that the corpsman hesitated to move him. Under machinegun fire the corpsman administered two plasma infusions. The wounded soldier lived.

The other corpsman was Sylvester Davis of East Aurora, New York. Japs threw grenades at him as he crawled forward to rescue a comrade. Davis was wounded in the thigh. But he crawled on, leaving a trail of blood, and he pulled the other man to cover.

Private Frank Falbo of Colver, Pennsylvania, had mounted his machinegun behind a log. He was firing steadily at a Japanese position he could not see. His observer on the slope below the log was shot through the hip. The observer shouted for help. Falbo fired another long burst in the direction of the Japs. Then he jumped over the log and rushed down the slope. He quieted the wounded man and after that he carried him to the shelter of the log.

All through the night enemy artillery fire fell into the perimeter on Mole Ridge. Scattered shells harassed the men on Kilay Ridge. The explosions denied them much needed sleep. A steady rain fell.

Silent men dug new graves in the battalion cemetery.

In the bleak dawn of November 19 the Japanese made their first major bid to recapture Kilay Ridge. The attack came at 7 A.M. It struck the battalion's flank with ominous force. In their assault waves the Japanese carried light machineguns and mortars. "Baker" Company's platoons met the brunt of the onset. The Japs attacked with massive fury. Through seven mad hours their charges followed one another like waves lashed by a typhoon.

By 9 A.M. two heavy machineguns had been knocked out of action. The perimeter showed gaps. At this time Japanese detachments began a flanking movement to the right. The battalion's artillery observers crawled to hidden perches in the onrush and directed shellfire by radio.

By noon "Baker" Company was surrounded and desperately in need of ammunition. Two soldiers volunteered to break through the howling ring of Japs. They were Private Fred Finke of Scottsbluff,

Nebraska, and Private Richard Batkies of Quinton, Virginia.

They crept out of the perimeter and slipped through the enemy line, crawling for stretches, rushing from thicket to thicket, lying motionless when Jap assault groups stormed by. They pushed to a knoll where "Able" Company protected the other side of Kilay Ridge. There the two volunteers were greeted with the bark of Garands.

"Don't shoot," yelled Finke. "We are Americans."

The firing stopped and a sullen voice said:

'The hell you say. Who's your officer?"

"Tom Rhem," Finke yelled. "Company "Baker.' "

"Okay," the voice said. "Come in."

Soon they left "Able" Company's line, each loaded down with a hundred pounds of ammunition. They arrived at their own unit while the heaviest Jap attack of the day was under way. Fred Finke collapsed, killed by Jap bullets. Richard Batkies ran along the perimeter, distributing ammunition to the men in the foxholes. Then he returned to his dead comrade. He stared at him as if in mute apology. He picked up Finke's load of ammunition, and again he ran the length of the foxhole line.

On the embattled perimeter an automatic rifle gunner decided to change his position to a spot which would give him a better field of fire. He slipped from hole to hole and then a Jap machinegun sent a burst of slugs through his belly. In a foxhole a little distance away lay Lieutenant Russel Pyle of Newark, Ohio. All day, between fire from his carbine, Pyle had encouraged the men to his right and left. He heard the wounded B.A.R. man scream. He also saw bullets knife into the muck two feet away.

Keeping close to the ground, Pyle inched out of his hole. He dragged the wounded man back into the foxhole and dressed his wounds and covered him with a poncho and that was all that could be done for him. The soldier begged for water; but water cannot be given to men with belly wounds. Russel Pyle picked up the dying gunners' B.A.R. He used it with determination.

Inside the perimeter Corpsmen Duncan Stewart and Michael Murphy patched up all casualties who still could crawl. After first aid was given them, the wounded men crawled out of the battle zone under their own power. Stewart and Murphy then plunged through mortar bursts and rescued other wounded who had been lying in the firing lines. As they were carrying back one of the wounded, Corpsman Stewart was hit Now Murphy worked alone, and he saved them both.

Colonel Clifford prowled about the front to reconnoiter. Toward 2 P.M. he ordered "Baker" Company to fall back a hundred yards to the north and hold there. He reinforced it with "Able" Company teams. Lieutenant Pyle directed the withdrawal. He coolly made the rounds to assure himself that no wounded man, nor weapon, nor supplies were left in the abandoned perimeter.

But there was Sergeant Raymond Kowski of Waterloo, Wisconsin. In the withdrawal Kowski was looking for a friend who had been hit earlier that day. He could not find him. Alone, in loyalty and desperation, he turned back. He ran into the abandoned perimeter to find his wounded friend. He raced along the line of empty, muddy, often blood-stained holes. There was no one in sight. There were only the sounds of Japs scrambling through the undergrowth. Kowski returned on the verge of sobbing.

On the battalion's field map the abandoned knoll bears the name "Easy Hill."

"Loss of manpower was due not only to battle casualties, but to the attrition of weather, terrain and climate upon the battalion. The weather was a constant adverse factor. The Ridge surface became a slick mass of mud and slime. Troops could seldom get dry. They had come on foot, carrying all supplies over uncharted terrain, which taxed their strength to the limit. Rations had been meager, and sleep fitful in sodden holes interrupted by outbursts of sniping and artillery fire. Under these conditions men were unable to properly care for themselves and contracted foot ulcers, dysentery and fevers. Colonel Clifford ordered the battalion surgeon to evacuate only the worst cases, leaving the others to fight with what strength remained them, and often on pure guts."

(from the Division Record)

Clifford felt that every fit man would be needed to defend Kilay Ridge. Before dawn of November 20, he ordered "Charlie" Company to abandon Mole Ridge and Busyman's Ridge. The withdrawal was accomplished without the knowledge of the Japanese.

After daylight a mass of Japs charged Mole Ridge. They found it empty of Americans, but straddled by bursting American artillery shells placed there at Clifford's request. An artillery barrage was also laid on the southern reach of Kilay Ridge ("Easy Hill"). The battalion's observers had crawled to points about one hundred yards from the zone of explosions. But the rain blotted out all visibility. The observers adjusted artillery fire entirely by sound.

At 1 P.M. "Baker" Company attacked Easy Hill to drive the Japs from their toehold on Kilay Ridge. The thumping of mortars paced the infantry charge. "Able" Company, only sixty strong, assaulted a height to the rear of Easy Hill. The attack met heavy gunfire and a curtain of shells from 90 millimeter mortars which had hitherto not been seen in action. The assault units were driven back, and the Japanese counterattacked.

Private Jesse Harris, a corpsman, of San Jose, California, crossed the zone of mortar bursts to rescue a wounded soldier. He went out a second time to save the life of a fellow aid man who had been cut down by shrapnel.

Corpsman Leo McDonnell of White River, South Dakota, had his foot smashed in action. All the same he dragged himself through the scorched thickets to render first aid to the wounded.

Sergeant Donald Watson of Lewis, Iowa, was badly wounded. He did not give up. He remained with his platoon through two perilous hours until a Jap onrush was repulsed.

Private Nelson Coder of Chanute, Kansas, was hit twice that day. He remained in his foxhole and kept his sub-machinegun blazing until he was relieved and ordered to the rear.

When darkness came, Japanese machinegun fire into the perimeter became so murderous that "Baker" Company's men lay flat in the mud, unable to dig their holes for the night. Sergeant James McFarland of Lexington, Kentucky, crawled to an unprotected rise in the ground to direct mortar fire on the enemy guns. In rain and darkness he could not see a thing. He stood up then, to see better. He now saw the red muzzle flashes of the guns, and he told the mortarmen where they should lob their shells. In the fiery fans of exploding shells the Jap gunners ceased firing. They moved away their guns. Now "Baker" Company could dig in. They called for McFarland. There was no answer. James McFarland lay dead in the rain.

Through saturnine jungles trudged a party of artillery observers under the command of Lieutenant James A. Waechter of St. Louis. Darkness overtook the group on the banks of the Naga River. Waechter decided to stop for the night. The men dug shallow foxholes some fifty feet from the west bank of the river.

The night was full of clouds and as dark as the inside of a tomb. There were occasional sheets of lightning, and fireflies meandering among the black barricades of vegetation, and there was the dull croaking of some night bird. No firing disturbed the night.

Waechter did not sleep. The earth beneath him was saturated with moisture. He lay under his poncho and listened to the thin humming of mosquitoes and to the distant growl of an airplane's engine. He thought of home, of the fighting and dying on Kilay Ridge, of the war and whether the whole agonizing mess would do humanity one whit of good. The hours were long and James Waechter looked at his watch.

It was 3:45 A.M. Nearly three hours until dawn.

A shrill cry stabbed through the night like an invisible rocket. It was a cry different from men's dying cries in battle. Waechter flung aside his poncho and reached for his carbine and pressed the safety release and listened. No shots were fired. No outcries followed the first. But there were strange gurgling sounds and then there was a loud splash.

Now Waechter was on his feet. He found one foxhole was empty, one man missing. The others searched the ground and the thickets. No trace of the missing man could be found.

With daylight they searched again. They scoured the ground for tracks that might give a clue to the vanished soldiers whereabouts. They found the mans rifle at the edge of the river. They found tracks in the mud along the rivers edge. A guerilla scout studied the tracks. "Crocodile," he said. "Crocodile come to foxhole, drag boy into river."

The morning of November 21 was quiet. A patrol reported that Japanese were digging new emplacements around Kilay Ridge, apparently for reinforcements.

At 2:30 P.M. scouts sighted two strong columns of Japanese converging on the battalion from south-east and north-east. Clifford dispatched a rifle platoon to the northern end of Kilay Ridge to keep open the supply line from Consuegra.

In the late afternoon a transport plane droned low over the ridge. With fine precision it dropped ammunition, a batch of dry blankets, and litters for the wounded.

The Japanese attacked again at dusk. Their charge swept around "Baker" Company's perimeter and struck a position held by an "Able" Company platoon. The platoon commander, Sergeant Donald Mason, directed the fire even after his hand had been chewed up by shrapnel. Another sergeant, Forest Clark of Webster, Kentucky, plunged through the jungle to bring reinforcements to his now encircled platoon. He saw a Japanese leap out of his path and behind an ironwood tree. Following the rule of "aiming at the middle of what you can see," the Kentuckyman fired. His bullet penetrated the tree trunk and nailed the Jap. But Forest Clark was wounded. He staggered on through the soggy pulp of ferns and rottenness, bent on the completion of his mission. He half slid, half fell down a jungle incline and came face to face with a Japanese patrol wading along the gravel bottom of a stream. The sergeant knew well the simple sequence of jungle combat: You see nothing; you suddenly come face to face with the enemy; the winner is he who scores the first hits. No one really knew what happened, except that Forest Clark was killed before he could bring aid to his platoon.

"Dog" Company's heavy mortars pounded to break up the attack. Closest observation was needed to keep the high explosive shells from falling on friendly troops. Sergeant Guy Brown of Bloomfield, Kentucky, volunteered to do the job. He muscled to the flank of the enemy onslaught. The mortar shells fell clean and true.

The Japs discovered the observer in the brush. They sent snipers to destroy him. Brown dodged the snipers. He continued to direct the doings of the mortars. The assault was broken and repulsed. Guy Brown died later of wounds received in battle.

During the fire fight a man was hit and lost his mind. Hands pressed to his wound he ran about the perimeter, a target to the Japs and an obstruction to the fire of riflemen around him. Corpsman Alfred Smart from Camillus, New York, saw the danger. He sprang out of his hole and pressed the wounded soldier to the ground. Slowly, speaking soothingly, he moved the other to the shelter of a mound of muddy earth. Then Smart discovered that he had left his first aid kit behind.

"I have to get my medicines," he said. "Will you stay quiet now and not get up again?"

The wounded soldier stared at Smart. He said nothing.

"Will you stay down now? Or do I have to tie you up?"

"I'm all right now," the other mumbled.

Again Smart crossed the fire-swept perimeter. He retrieved his kit. He bandaged the wounded man, gave him morphine and sulfa, and then surrendered his poncho to keep him warm and safe from the effects of shock.

That evening more graves were dug on Kilay Ridge. The chaplain's voice was clear and sad.

> Look at your fabric
>   Of labor and sorrow.
> Seamy and dark
>   With despair and disaster,
> Turn it—and lo,
>   The design of the Master!

At daybreak of November 22, Colonel Clifford ordered patrols to probe north and east to test Japanese strength across the battalion's supply line. The patrols discovered an ambush athwart the trail from Consuegra. They ambushed the ambush and then blasted it with machinegun fire. Eleven Japs were killed.

Except for continuous sniping, the day was quiet until late afternoon. "Baker" Company was immobilized by heavy Japanese fire.

The fire came from three sides. At the same time a Banzai assault struck "Able" Company's perimeter.

The ferocity of the attacks grew as dusk approached. At 6 P.M. five hundred Japs charged "Able" Company with bayonets and grenades. Their unearthly screaming rang through the jungle and the dripping *kunai*. It was as if every bush and grass blade and tree stump had joined the pandemonium. By all tactical rules a situation such as developed would call for a fighting withdrawal. But Colonel Clifford had orders to hold Kilay Ridge "at all costs"—and hold it he did.

By 8 P.M., "Baker" Company again was completely surrounded. It was ordered to break out and fall back to the rear of "Abie's" line. The company had lost an officer and two sergeants. There were many wounded. A successful withdrawal was made possible only by a covering wall of machinegun and artillery fire, and by the audacity of Lieutenant Thomas Rhem of Memphis, Tennessee and his platoon of riflemen.

Rhem radioed the isolated company to duck low. He lined up his men. He had them fix bayonets and he gave each man three grenades. They pulled the pins and hurled their grenades in quick volleys. Then they stormed forward with Rebel yells.

It worked. The platoon pierced the Japanese block. A few of the enemy were caught huddled in the darkness, praying. Rhem's "Banzai" platoon killed twenty-five Japs in the charge. It captured five machineguns. And not a man was wounded.

But a litter train of wounded heading for safer ground was ambushed. One wounded soldier was killed.

Private Oronzo Scarcella of Hazelton, Pennsylvania, trotted from foxhole to foxhole. He bandaged four wounded men under fire and then mobilized a squad to carry them to cover. After that Corpsman Scarcella heard that an outpost outside the perimeter had been hit. He made his way through Japanese assault waves and pulled the outpost to safety.

Corporal Paul Lyons of Thomaston, Connecticut, volunteered to act as a litter bearer in the withdrawal. Thus burdened he knew full well that he could not defend himself against attack. The injured man whom he carried was saved. But Paul Lyons was killed by enemy bullets.

The attacks continued into the night. Rain squalls hit Kilay Ridge. The situation became so serious that "Dog" Company's heavy mortars laid a protective barrage yards in front of "Able" Company lines. The indomitable Clifford ordered that ammunition and supplies be hidden in thickets and gullies so that they would not fall into enemy hands in the event of a break-through.

While the evacuation of the wounded was in progress, a Japanese machinegun fired down a black jungle trail. The evacuation party was forced to cross this trail. Sergeant Oliver A. Young of Carlisle, Arkansas, set out to liquidate the Jap gunners. The six-foot-four former University of Arkansas athlete crawled parallel to the trail in the direction of the gun flashes. He found the machinegun dug in behind a big molave tree.

Young snaked his way up the opposite side of the tree. He made sure that he kept the trunk between him and the spears of fire. Then he stood up and pulled the safety pin from a four-second grenade. He reached his long arms around the tree. He counted:

"One dead Jap... two dead Japs..."

With that he let go the grenade. It exploded before it reached the bottom of the hostile nest. Fragments and shreds of human flesh spattered the base of the tree.

Fragments slashed the Arkansan's forearm. . . .

Through the confusion of night fighting Lieutenant Thomas McCorlew of Cleveland, Texas, was searching for "Able" Company's command post. In the blackness of the downpour he bumped into another man. McCorlew put his hand on the man's shoulder. "Say, Buddy," he whispered. "Where's 'A' Company?" A startled Jap wheeled and vanished. McCorlew fired—missed.

Clifford thanked his stars that the Japanese command did not press its attacks on November 23.

The battalion was licking its wounds.

There was an attack at 8:30 A.M., but the enemy appeared to have lost morale in the past days' slaughter. The charge collapsed in mortar fire, which was expertly directed by Staff Sergeant Lester Winkler of Perryville, Missouri.

That day the planes came and two bundles of supplies floated into the battalion position. Japanese observers spotted the place. Machinegun fire and artillery shells furrowed the perimeter.

A patrol pushed through Japanese lines to report the battalion's predicament to the commander of the division driving south from Breakneck Ridge (the 32nd Infantry Division). On the return trip to Kilay Ridge the patrol was cut off. At the same time it was driven to seek cover because friendly artillery bombarded the surrounding Japanese concentrations. But led by Fulton Brightwell of Burley, Idaho, a scout, the patrol reached Kilay Ridge after an adventurous ten-hour trek across far mountains. The message it brought back to Clifford said, "Hold fast."

At dusk enemy reinforcements were observed digging in east of the besieged battalion's lines.

"A strength report of the battalion as of 23 November showed the following men and officers present for duty: "A" Company, three officers, sixty-two enlisted men; "B" Company, four officers, seventy-one enlisted men; "C" Company, four officers, seventy-five enlisted men; Headquarters and attached personnel, six officers, seventy-one enlisted men."

(from the Division Record)

For two days, except for patrol activities, sniping, and intermittent harassing fire from artillery and automatic weapons, Kilay Ridge was quiet. There were skirmishes on the battalion's southern flank. But there was no dangerous offensive action.

On Thanksgiving Day a sickly sun glowed through a pall of clouds. A faint patchwork of light and shadow appeared in the ceiling of jungle and *kunai*. The men looked at the ghost of the sun, and some of them had tears in their eyes. It was as if a ray of hope had filtered into their terrifying loneliness on Kilay Ridge.

In the evening twilight of November 25, "Able" Company's sector was savagely attacked with machineguns, mortars and artillery. The assault was repulsed through the quick thinking of an artillery observer. Lieutenant James Waechter rushed to an exposed knoll which gave him observation of the attacking force. He swiftly adjusted a counter barrage.

An enemy shell exploded nearby. The blast tore Waechter's aid limb from limb. It blew the observer some distance down the slope. Waechter groped, feeling for his bones. Badly shaken, he crept back to his post. He radioed directions until the attack ebbed away in failure.

On November 26 a swarm of Japs dug in astride the supply trail from Consuegra. These Japs were routed in a fire fight by combat patrols.

"On that day Colonel Clifford estimated that a minimum of one reinforced enemy company was operating on his south; at least two reinforced companies on a ridge one kilometer to his east; and a strong but unknown force of enemy troops on the west. If the western force pushed northward, the battalion's route of withdrawal would be cut off.

"Artillery fire fell into the perimeter throughout the 27th. A patrol from the 128th Infantry arrived to report that reinforcements were enroute. The question was: would they arrive in time?

" 'You don't have to tell me that we are in a tight spot,' Colonel Clifford messaged. We know it.' "

(from the Division Record)

In the afternoon of November 27, a massive Japanese assault struck "Charlie" Company's sector of Kilay Ridge. The fight surged up and down the muddy slopes until the thrust was finally repulsed at 8:30 P.M.

During this battle wire lines between the battalion and "Charlie" Company were disrupted. Two men went out in the dark to restore communication, Raymond M. Davis, of Chatsford, Illinois, and Vincent Lyons of Coronado, California.

Davis was a wire chief, Lyons a lineman. In danger of fire from friendly as well as from enemy troops they sensed their way down a crooked trail. Rain and darkness made it difficult to find the break. While one of them searched the line, the other held a sub-machinegun ready. They had searched the line for one-half mile before they found the break. Its repair restored communication with the front line where the counter-attack was still under way. They then patrolled the wire line until dawn.

Two other soldiers who worked alone in the dark savagery were Corpsman Stanley Lokken of Beloit, Wisconsin, and Sergeant Bill Kurdach of New York City. Kurdach, surrounded by fire, sat half buried in slime on the forward hillside, an observer for "Dog" Company's mortar crews. Lokken, who is a family man, abandoned the protection of the foxholes to help the wounded. His night's work ended only when he was critically hit.

The first enemy attack on November 28 came at dawn. While Japanese assault detachments pushed up the slope, Jap machinegun fire and mortar bursts belching from another ridge forced the riflemen to duck low in their holes. Sergeant Irving Greenberg of New York City crawled down the slope and onto a bluff from which he could track the progress of the attacking force. By a system of self-devised signals he directed the counter fire of the mortar batteries. The attack broke before it attained the crest.

The second attack came at 10 A.M. After a close-range fire fight it was repulsed.

The third attack struck in the dark, at 7:30 P.M. This was the Japs' most desperate effort to recapture Kilay Ridge. It began with a barrage of 90 millimeter mortars. The "ashcans" hurtled from the rain-sad sky with the devastating power of artillery. Burning
jungle cast flickering light on fountains of mud, roots and branches driven into ragged geysers by the explosions. The ridge rocked and trembled. Men quaked under the horror of the concussions. In four foxholes six men were smashed by fragments. Still, one man remained

above ground in the barrage: Corpsman John Honeycutt of Rock Springs, Texas. He darted from hole to hole, patching jagged wounds which mortar fragments make.

At eight o'clock heavy machinegun fire from the east joined the mortar cannonade. Simultaneously another brace of machineguns spouted death from the west. The vicious intensity of this cross fire mounted from minute to minute. Jap assault teams were muscling up a gully on the western side of Kilay Ridge. At the same time a determined attack hit "Charlie" Company from the south. Telephone lines from Clifford's headquarters to all company positions were cut.

"Dragon Red" fought back. Every mortar in the battalion pumped high explosives at top speed. By 8:15 friendly artillery was pounding all lanes of approach to Kilay Ridge. By 8:30 "Charlie" Company's squads were in the midst of a bayonet fray with superior numbers of Japanese. By 9 o'clock every man of every unit in the battalion was fighting at close quarters. That was more than a battle for a ridge. It was a battle against annihilation. The night was ugly with flash and crash and cry and blood. Rain fell heavily.

"Dog" Company machinegunners stemmed the twenty-seventh Jap onrush since their machineguns had been mounted on the ridge. Section Leader Jewell Caughlin of Bardwell, Kentucky, urged his crew to do the impossible. Sergeant Frank Falbo of Yorkville, Ohio, singing and cursing, worked over guns that had run hot and jammed, until they functioned again. Private George Meyer, of Brooklyn, fired more than five hundred rounds between dusk and midnight and never said a word. Gunner Michael Crispino of Burkeville, Virginia, poured lead into Japs close enough to be scorched by the muzzle flashes of his killing tool.

By 9:30 the Japanese had driven wedges between the company perimeters. By ten o'clock "Charlie" Company was surrounded.

Private Harry Barnes, whose wife lives in Eufala, Alabama, volunteered to get a communication wire through to the isolated company. Alone, armed with a carbine and a roll of wire, he wriggled away in the dark. He laid four hundred yards of wire through Japanese lines. On the way he heard slurring footfalls in the brush and lay still. A detachment of Japanese with bayonets on their rifles pounced by. Barnes prayed mutely that none would stumble over the wire athwart their course.

Corpsman John Honeycutt heard bursts of Jap grenades in a thicket and then he heard a drawn-out moan. Bent low, he rushed into the thicket.

He found a soldier ensnarled among the roots. The soldier sensed the nearness of another. He lashed out with both feet.

"Hold it," Honeycutt muttered. "I ain't a Jap."

"Something happened," the soldier gasped.

Honeycutt ran his hands over the fallen comrade. He found that the man's arm had been blown off at the elbow. There was the end of a splintered bone and the outpulsing of arterial blood.

John Honeycutt forgot the nearness of the Japs. He forgot the battle and the war and home. In downpour and mud and tumult he worked for four hours. He saved his wounded comrade's life.

The battle pounded through the night. An hour before dawn snipers' rifles still cracked like whips swung by lunatics, and mortar fire still fell in intermittent showers. Rifleman Florencio Ortiz, of New York City, thought he heard something creep into the area held by his platoon. Most of the men in the platoon were exhausted from the all-night ordeal. They lay in their holes like men in a trance.

Ortiz sat up. There were three Japanese slinking past his hole. The Japs were carrying a machinegun. Ortiz sat still and listened. There was the sound of Japs crawling all around the platoon position. He sprang up and threw a grenade at the group with the machinegun. Before it burst, he shouted:

"Japs! Japs!"

He fired the eight rounds in his rifle, reloaded, fired again. Shadowy shapes darted in the gloom, crumpled and panted. The platoon was aroused. The attack was thrown back.

Florencio Ortiz was killed in action on Christmas Eve.

"Captain George E. Morrissey (of Davenport, Iowa) commanded the Medical Detachment during operations on Kilay Ridge, Leyte, Philippine Islands, from 10 November to 4 December 1944. During this period, Captain Morrissey, through his selfless devotion, tireless energy and surgical skill, successfully treated and evacuated all of the hundred and one casualties sustained during twenty-four days and nights of conflict. Working under the most difficult conditions, often without food and water, always under fire, Captain Morrissey ran a medical service that was an inspiration to the entire force, and resulted in an alleviation of suffering that can never be adequately estimated. His medical duties often required his exposure to direct fire. Working at night by flashlight, he frequently made himself a visible target, as snipers often infiltrated into the perimeter. Duty Status: Battalion Surgeon."

(from a Field Citation)

At daybreak November 29, the Japanese were still in force on Kilay Ridge. All perimeters were still under attack. The situation was gloomy, but Clifford was still hitting back.

At 9:20 A.M., lookouts on the highest knoll sighted friendly troops working down the Ormoc Valley from the direction of Breakneck Ridge. Colonel Clifford warned these troops by marking Japanese strongholds in their path with smoke shells from heavy mortars. He followed up the smoke shells with high explosive. The mortar shells, as if bent on some joke, struck two enemy ammunition dumps. The dumps blew up.

At 1 P.M. arrived the welcome word that a relief battalion was slogging toward Kilay Ridge. Combat patrols blasted clear the supply line from Consuegra. Meanwhile, Technician Thurlow Rice of East Boothbay, Maine, and Private Raymond Tingle of Madison, Indiana, crawled through a mile of mucky jungle to repair disrupted wire lines between the ridge defenses. The relief battalion arrived at dark.

On the morning of November 30 the Japanese still held 800 yards of Kilay Ridge. A two-battalion assault swept it clean.

On December 1, Clifford—once an All-American footballer from West Point—received a message from higher headquarters which closed with the following words:

"You and your men have not been forgotten. You are the talk of the island. Army beat Notre Dame 59 to 0, worst defeat on record."

Clifford grinned like a happy boy. (But he never saw another football game. Just before "VJ-Day" we buried his shell-torn body in the muck of Mindanao Island.)

On December 4, the haggard remnants of "Dragon Red" marched back to the coast. They had accounted for more than one thousand dead Japanese in the fighting for Kilay Ridge. When they arrived at Calubian they were greeted with the news that three thousand fresh Japanese troops had landed on the Leyte Peninsula, near San Isidro, five miles to the west. They ate a meal of fresh eggs, and cursing heaven and earth and their own weariness, they slung their rifles and pulled out to meet that new threat. . . .

Since the Red Beach landings seven thousand three hundred Japanese had died in the Division's path.

Among its own the Division counted one thousand nine hundred and twenty-nine wounded, or missing, or killed.

Chapter Sixteen

ANOTHER HALF MILLION COCONUTS

"Most of this fighting is in inconspicuous little actions which nobody hears about—mopping up.

"In Europe when we advance we really capture something. Out here we just capture another island, important though it may be, that looks much like all other islands. As one doughboy remarked after we had cleaned out a small objective—Well, there's another half million coconuts!"

Major General R. B. Woodruff,
Division Commander

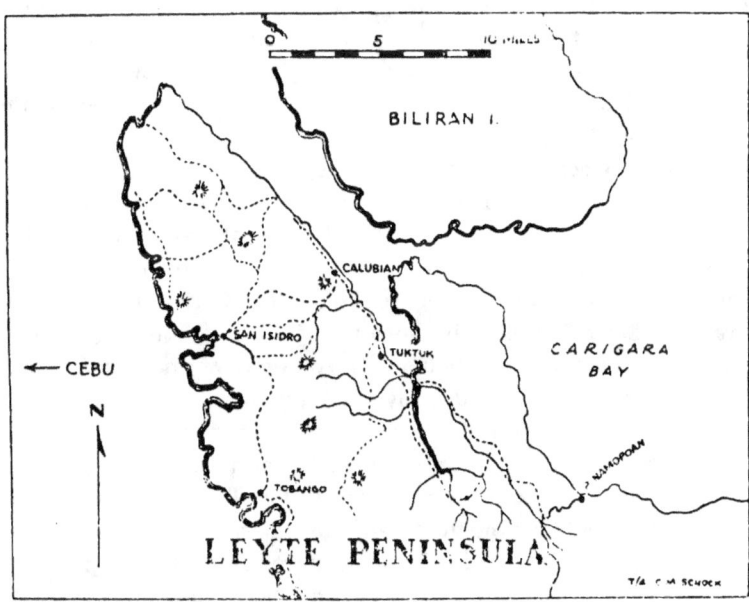

"Where in the name of hell are the trucks?" Quartermaster Lieutenant Robert E. Willet from Atlanta, Georgia, wanted to know.

Yes, where were the trucks?

A convoy winding upward among the hills had been ambushed. The drivers had jumped off, had pursued the waylaying Japs. When the drivers returned, the trucks were gone.

The trucks were needed to move supplies to troops in battle. But the trucks had vanished.

Bob Willet went to find out. With him went Corporal Dolphus Therrien of Manchester, New Hampshire. The two slung carbines, stuck a brace of grenades in their belts, and ventured into Jap-held terrain, through sniper country and over jungle trails. They found the trucks, and a bevy of Japanese encamped around them.

A combat patrol was sent out to retrieve the trucks.

The smallest taskforce unit is the combat patrol. On tropical mountain paths, in villages wedged between a hill and a swamp, in terrain too forbidding to allow for passage of large bodies of troops, in guerilla-type warfare and in "mopping up," the combat patrol becomes an indispensable tool.

"If the Jap, when cornered, would surrender he'd be immeasurably easier to fight," the Division Commander explained to Fred Hampson, the ace front line correspondent of the Associated Press. "But he won't. Tactically you first lick him, then you have to spend days, sometimes weeks and months rooting him out and killing him. Long, miserable days in the jungles and mountains end by burning a few Nips out of caves with flame throwers that have to be carried twenty miles on the back."*

After the Beachhead battles, the sweep across Leyte and the torture in the Ormoc mountains, the Division's forces were divided to prosecute a number of tasks. The Nineteenth and Twenty-First Regiments staged for invasions of other islands of the Philippines. The Thirty-Fourth remained to secure the coast of Carigara Bay. Later it swept the Leyte Peninsula in the north with iron brooms. In this task combat patrols came into their own. As yet there was no place on all of Leyte where a soldier could safely wander unarmed.

From November 8 until December 2 a patrol of company strength roamed the mountain country around Sinayawan. The force was commanded by Lieutenant Benjamin H. Wahle of Helena, Montana. His men lived on cold rations for twenty-five days in the worst of rainy season weather. During this period scattered Jap detachments made

---

* Major General R. B. Woodruff, who previously commanded troops in Europe, assumed command of the Twenty-Fourth Infantry Division on November 18, 1944. Major General F. A. Irving, former commander, took over the command of Eighth Army garrison forces.

sixteen attacks to eliminate Wahle's group. All failed.

On November 9 a new type of Japanese plane came down in a crash landing. Its pilot was killed. An air liaison officer, Captain John Dudney from Echo, Louisiana, decided to strip it of its equipment. But snipers got there first. They set the plane afire, then withdrew two hundred yards to guard the craft until it had burned down. When Dudney saw the flames he broke into a fast run. The snipers fired at him, and missed. In weaving and zig-zag motion, Dudney removed two machineguns and two rapid-fire cannons from the wreck. It took him three trips with a combat patrol to carry off the captured weapons.

On November 10, a group led by Sergeant Thomas Martin of Kai Malino, Hawaii, patrolled a mountain trail three miles south of Capoocan. In the wild fastness around Mount Minoro the patrol came upon a fork in the trail. Sergeant Martin stopped short. He peered and listened. There were only the sounds of falling rain, the breathing of his men, the screech of a cocadoo. A family of monkeys gamboled in the thickets. Martin split his patrol. He himself took the left fork of the trail.

In silence they proceeded among somber barriers of vegetation. They had gone about a thousand yards when a rifle cracked. The scout jumped behind a tree. Other rifle reports joined the first, and then a machinegun hammered.

Martin's scout dropped to the ground. He tried to find the source of the shooting. Where he lay he could see nothing. In a wriggling crawl he made his way to a grassy knoll. Now he saw. There was an enemy observer crouched at the edge of a clump of wild banana. A little farther a company of Japanese was pushing down the trail. The enemy observer spotted the scout and fired. The American returned the fire with his tommygun. Then he withdrew fast, and told Tom Martin what he had seen.

Martin knew that the Japs outnumbered his patrol ten to one. But he also knew that if the Japs were allowed the freedom of the trail they would trap the other half of his patrol.

"Trail block!" he said.

They blocked the trail with all the fire power they could muster. Martin sent a runner to call back the men on the right fork of the trail. Eleven Japs were killed and the patrols retired without losing a man.

Later that day the enemy attacked the Sinawayan base perimeter. He abandoned eighteen corpses after a five-hour fight.

On November 11 another trail patrol was rushed by the same pack of Japs. The patrol's automatic rifle gunner was wounded and the Japanese were closing in. Private Leo Gomolchak from Pittsburgh,

Pennsylvania, grabbed the B.A.R. Japs in adjoining bushes tossed grenades. Gomolchak stood upright, unleashing bursts of automatic rifle fire. That saved the patrol.

On November 15, terrified natives reported that a gang of Japanese had blocked the Colasian-Ormoc trail north of Mount Minoro. The Japs had bayoneted Filipinos who attempted to reach the American coastal zone. The Japs, who were living off the land, forced other natives to procure food. Terror was to prevent their escape to the coast.

A "George" Company patrol investigated. They found a camouflaged trail block. Private Marvin Edge from Rockledge, Georgia, a scout, crawled up a jungle-covered slope. He came within fifty yards of the Jap position. Still he could not pinpoint its exact whereabouts. So he stood up and yelled: "Hey!" Immediate machinegun spurts and grenading were the result. This showed Marvin Edge just where the Japs were dug in. He crawled back to his own lines. A mortar barrage destroyed the trail block.

The impact zone of the mortar blasts yielded twenty-three dead Japanese. But a day later another patrol covering the same trail met vicious fire from the same spot. The lead scout was hit twice. He collapsed on the trail. The patrol leader, Sergeant Galloway from Owensboro, Kentucky, crawled up to the wounded scout and began to drag him away. Again the machineguns clattered, and Galloway, too, was wounded. All the same, he managed to drag himself and his scout into the bushes.

Now "Easy" Company sent out a force to determine the strength of the enemy trail block, and particularly the exact location of its automatic weapons. The scouts were soon caught in the cross fire of machineguns. The patrol leader remained long enough to fix the precise location of the Jap nests. Then he gave the order to withdraw.

All withdrew, except one scout. This scout lay under the eyes of a Japanese machinegunner and he was unable to budge.

Forward again went Private Kenneth Foldoe of Bagley, Minnesota. He worked his way through scorched *kunai* to a point from which he could bring his B.A.R. to bear on the gunner who was shooting at the scout. Presently the Jap gunner swung his gun around and fired at Foldoe. The Minnesotan engaged the machinegun in a duel long enough to allow the scout to scurry to cover. After that Foldoe took to his heels. The patrol brought back the intelligence that the Japs had four machineguns and seventy-five men dug in astride the trail.

On November 18, "Easy" Company set out to liquidate the block for the second time. On the way a soldier died by snipers' bullets. It was found that the wily Japs had shifted the positions of their machineguns overnight. A new reconnaissance was necessary. It was made by Private Kelcie Odom of Gunnison, Colorado.

Odom crawled into the immediate vicinity of the Japs. Then he stood up to draw their fire. When the first shots cracked, he threw himself on the ground and noted the direction from which the bursts came. The Japanese did not like it. They dispatched a sniper to kill Odom. Scout Odom saw the Jap. He watched him until the Jap stopped crawling. "Good-by, Nip," said Odom, and shot him dead.

"Easy" Company attacked the trail block from three sides. It was carried in a hard, uphill fight. The price was a number of American lives. But the majority of the Japs were killed and the survivors dispersed into the jungle.

At one point in the fighting a lone soldier rushed a pillbox and was quickly shot down. Sergeant William Dittsworth of Clover, Pennsylvania, and a comrade crawled almost to the mouth of the pillbox. They slowly pulled the wounded soldier into a thicket. Then they climbed atop the pillbox with grenades.

That same day a band of Japanese popping apparently from nowhere pushed down a half-forgotten mountain path known as the Antipopo Trail. Undetected they reached the vicinity of Colasian.

Now, Colasian was well within the American held coastal zone. A section of the Division's howitzers was passing westward along the coast road. At 7:30 P.M., under cover of darkness, the Japs attacked the artillery team. In the first volley two artillery men slumped off their moving mounts.

"Keep moving, keep moving, don't stop," yelled Sergeant Bill Hammock of East Tallahassee, Alabama.

Hammock was the leader of the howitzer section. Instinctively he preferred to risk his own life to risking the destruction of his howitzers. He kept the howitzers moving. He himself leaped from his mount and fought for the life of his two wounded comrades until help arrived.

The swamp-bound coastal road from Carigara to Pinamopoan proved as vulnerable to flanking attacks from the mountains to the south as it was to the continuous rains. Across this narrow coastal "corridor" moved the bulk of supplies supporting the Ormoc Valley offensive. With combat patrols in action over many miles of wilderness, only one understrength battalion remained to guard this lifeline against enemy attack. The regimental commander pressed the men of his Anti-Tank Company to duty as riflemen and told them to drive the Japs from the Antipopo Trail. The tank-fighters borrowed carbines and machineguns and went patrolling.

They pushed a thousand yards up the trail and attacked the Japs' bivouac. Fire from rifles, machineguns and knee mortars drove the anti-tank gunners back. A second assault was also repulsed. The anti-tank men then lugged mortars up the hillside and put down a mortar barrage. After that they stormed the position. This time not a shot was fired. They found a jumble of Japanese cadavers, sixteen spider-holes, some shallow graves and nine pools of blood.

On the following day the anti-tank gunners moved against the next ridge to the south. Mortar fire drove the enemy from the crest. But the instant the barrage lifted, both sides raced for the top of the ridge. The Japs got there first, but were routed in an all-day fight. For good measure, the anti-tank gunners then occupied a third ridge still farther to the south. However, in the inky, rain-drenched night the Japanese infiltrated through jungle ravines back to the coastal road. There was no way to stop them except to corner them, one by one, and to kill them.

This is the unsung "mopping up"—bitterly fought little actions of which outsiders hear nothing. Meanwhile, at home, dark-suited individuals with telegrams rang door bells in a sorrowful finale.

The Jap fighter was a tricky fellow. He may have been a "bush-leaguer" in the use of artillery. He may have been an amateur of tank tactics. His teamwork was raw. But he was a brave man, not afraid of death. The compulsions of technical inferiority made him a master of night crawling, of digging holes in impossible places, of doing the unanticipated, of wrinkles as dangerous as a copperhead in a flower bed.

Any first Jap attack on a perimeter may be only a diversionary attack. Infiltrating Japs were sometimes dressed to look like women. At other times they might be wearing uniforms stripped from American dead. Japs in ambush loved to let trucks go by, then mined the track over which the trucks were likely to return. The scattered shooting of a few Jap snipers often kept a whole battalion perimeter awake from dusk to 3 A.M.—and then fell silent; but an hour before dawn a suicidal charge would strike the position in the hope that the wearied defenders had dropped off to sleep.

Snipers liked to climb tall trees growing from ravines. Such a perch gave them a good silhouette of troops moving over adjoining higher ground. Other Japs dug their foxholes to face the "wrong" direction; they allowed American detachments to pass, then mowed them down from the rear. Or a sniper would dig a good hole near a mountain trail, bury in it a mine, and then withdraw a little way into the jungle. Soldiers suddenly fired on by the sniper were likely to dive into the convenient foxhole—to be blown sky-high.

There were Japs who left innocent looking sandal tracks in the mud. A patrol following these tracks in the hope of finding one Jap suddenly ran into gun blasts.

There were Japs who started little cooking fires to make Americans believe that there were Japs off guard, eating rice. A patrol intent on surprising the eating enemy blundered into an ambush instead.

There were Japs who squatted a few yards away from American wounded. The Japs shouted "Medic! Medic!" To the corpsman rushing up to help—that was unfailing death.

There was a lone Jap sniper who fired a single shot down a trail to reveal his position. But the patrol lured forward to destroy the sniper was clamped between machinegun fire from both flanks. That happened to a "Fox" Company combat patrol on November 19, near Capoocan. The patrol was saved by Private John Lomko, of Chicago, who had insisted on lugging along a light machinegun. The patrol fell back while he fired. Then he withdrew, dragging his gun. Every few yards he stopped, turned around, and gave the Japs another burst of fire. John Lomko was killed in action.

On November 20, near Calubian, on the east side of the Leyte Peninsula, a patrol lead by Sergeant Jack Wheat of Fountain Run, Kentucky, was waylaid by Japs firing from emplacements which "faced the wrong way." Two soldiers of the patrol crumpled under the hail. The remainder was nailed to the ground. The Japs then made a typical "tactical" mistake. They climbed out of their holes and launched a bayonet charge. Sergeant Wheat's accurate shooting held them off long enough to allow the patrol to fall back into tall *kunai*.

On the same day, in the same manner, another patrol was ambushed in the vicinity of Capoocan. Here it was a "George" Company scout, Private Roy Soden from Shrewsbury, New Jersey, who saved the patrol with twenty-four aimed shots from his Garand.

In the Mount Minoro wilderness, "Easy" Company tangled with a force of Japanese who had harassed traffic on the coastal road. The Japanese were discovered entrenched on a hill. The company attacked. The attack was repulsed. The company reorganized and attacked again. Again it was repulsed. A third attack bogged down in a sudden, swamping rain storm. A fourth charge, following an artillery barrage, attained the hilltop. "Mopping up"; but it cost eleven American lives.

Not far away, also on November 20, a nineteen-man patrol commanded by Sergeant Thomas Turner of Oakland, California, defended another hill against three wild Banzai assaults.

Shortly after dawn of November 21, a patrol moving through hill country south of Colasian came upon the bodies of three Filipino men, four women and two children. All had been bayoneted in the abdomen. Their belongings, scattered about them in the brush, indicated that the group had been fleeing from Jap-held mountain regions. They also indicated that Japs were prowling nearby.

"Easy" Company patrols were dispatched to find and to destroy the Japs. At 10 A.M. a reconnaissance squad heard them talking in the undergrowth. The squad halted, and its first scout crawled forward. Twenty-five yards from the enemy position the scout met machinegun fire. He took off his helmet and propped it into a bush. He then wriggled hurriedly under a nearby log and lay still. The Jap gunner kept firing at the helmet. The scout spotted the emplacement and brought back the required information. "Easy" Company outflanked the Japs. After the skirmish, fourteen dead enemies were found in one spot, eleven at another, and tracks of blood showed that wounded had been dragged into the jungle.

On November 22 another "Easy" Company team went hunting for an enemy artillery observation post. Distant Jap guns had put harassing fire on the coastal road; it was assumed that their observers lurked atop one of the heights bordering the shoreside swamps.

The patrol's scout, Charles Lindenmuth of North Platte, Nebraska, was first to discover the hostile observers. The post was protected by a machinegun. Lindenmuth crept toward the machinegun with rapidity and skill, and suddenly he opened fire. This kept the machinegun out of action. Meanwhile, the other men of the patrol made short shift of the observers' party. The shelling of the coastal road stopped.

But the Japs struck back. During the night, suicide detachments filtered through the inscrutable ravines toward the coast. They seized a section of the road and mounted machineguns in the swamps and on a ridge overlooking the beach. The first supply convoy which passed after dawn was ambushed. The Japs fired on the leading truck, wrecked it, and so stopped the whole convoy. Then they tossed mines to the front and the rear of the stalled column. A by-pass was not possible. Men were hit. A fire fight developed.

Corpsmen endeavored to rescue the wounded. But from both east and west the road was blocked. The attempt was then made to evacuate the wounded by boat. But the boat was driven off by gunfire from the ridge which dominated the beach.

Driving along the road in his amphibious truck came Private Lewis W. Nall, of Blue Jacket, Oklahoma. He heard the shooting and jammed on his brakes and grasped his rifle.

"What's the trouble?" he asked.

"Can't get the wounded out," he was told. "We tried a boat. The Nips shot it full of holes."

"Let me try," said Nall.

He did, with the help of another soldier named Bill Mostovyk. Together they maneuvered the amphibious truck off the road, across the beach and into the water. They swung offshore in a wide circle. Then they churned head on into the trouble spot. The machinegun on the ridge fired angrily. The amphibious truck hit the beach. Its drivers' guns were blazing. Some of the wounded were loaded into the truck. Still firing, the amphibious Samaritans headed out to sea. The remaining wounded were brought to cover by two other volunteers who drove a weapons carrier straight into the firing zone.

To an "Easy" Company platoon was given the mission of destroying the machinegun nest on the ridge. After five fruitless attacks the machinegun was still in place. It was protected by enemy sharpshooters in a ring of foxholes around it. The ridge approaches were a 70° incline, burned clear of brush. Mortar and machinegun fire from the swamps below took no effect. As long as the Japanese gun remained in place, neither the beach nor the coastal road would be clear to traffic.

On November 24 the ridge-top nest was attacked for the sixth time. The patrol assigned to do the job was one decimated platoon, fourteen men strong. The patrol leader, Staff Sergeant Michael Blucas from Ralphton, Pennsylvania, led his men to the base of the ridge, and then up the steep slope in short, daring rushes. A seasoned rifleman needs from three to five seconds to aim his weapon and to squeeze its trigger. No single forward, uphill rush, therefore, could take more than three seconds. In three seconds a man can run ten yards, or climb two, and then drop to the ground before the bullets aimed at him can strike their mark.

In two to ten yard rushes Sergeant Blucas and his team reached the crest of the slope.

But where, exactly, was the hostile nest? Scrubby brush covered the ridge top. To see more than five yards ahead one had to stand up. And standing up, one drew fire.

Two men stood up to draw the Japanese fire. One was Sergeant Blucas. The other was Private Louis H. Baker of Clinton, Iowa. They stood up and the machinegun fired and revealed its position. The machinegun now fired a continuous series of bursts which swept the whole crest. In order to enable the squad to advance, someone again had to stand up to pin down the hostile gunners with aimed, direct shots.

Louis Baker stood up and fired. With eight shots he killed three Japs. Then Baker clutched his chest and fell.

The machinegun continued its deadly rat-a-tat. It was silenced in the seventh assault.

Michael Blucas, too, was killed in action.

Colonel Clifford and one hundred men of the force which had fought on Kilay Ridge were in Calubian when intelligence arrived that three thousand Japanese troops had landed at San Isidro, on the west coast of the Leyte Peninsula. San Isidro lies five miles due west of the village of Calubian. apparently the purpose of this "counter invasion" was to occupy the peninsula for a last ditch stand on Leyte Island. Native refugees told Clifford that the Japs were looting and murdering civilians.

The mud of Kilay Ridge still clung to Clifford's boots. He summoned his officers, including two leaders of a guerilla regiment, a Major Nazarino and a Captain Alejandre.* The guerilla officers assured him that a force of guerillas was on its way to Calubian. This was the crack Ninety-Fifth Guerilla Regiment. But it would take them several days to assemble their men into a striking unit. However, the *barrio* people of the Leyte Peninsula were a militant crew. Colonel Clifford armed local volunteers with captured Japanese rifles. He dispatched an eight-man patrol to block the road from San Isidro. The patrol was ordered to live with the natives, to report all developments, and to fight delaying actions when attacked by superior forces. The situation was perilous.

There existed on Leyte previous to the American landings a guerilla organization of about four thousand armed men. Their mission had been primarily one of intelligence and of harassment. They were of slight help in the Division's battles on Red Beach, the Leyte Valley and on Breakneck Ridge. However, in the sweeping of the Leyte Peninsula, the guerilla units were much in evidence. They patrolled aggressively and brought much information on enemy strength and dispositions.

---

* In a report on the activities of Guerilla Captain Benigno Alejandre of San Isidro, Leyte, Colonel W. W. Jenna, commanding the 34th Infantry Regiment, stated: "Captain Alejandre has been an invaluable addition to our forces and has contributed materially to the success of this campaign. His intimate knowledge of the area ana of the operations of the guerilla and civilian forces since the days of Bataan, combined with a keen insight of Japanese characteristics, has been of inestimable value and has saved many American lives."

They disrupted enemy communications, killed stragglers, and forewarned civilians of impending operations in given districts and villages.

The native village *capitans* used native "trotters" to inform Clifford of every move made by the Japanese. The "trotters" were barefooted boys, armed only with curved bolo knives. They could trot an average of five miles in an hour. The village *capitans* sent their intelligence in relays from *barrio* to *barrio*. When a messenger became exhausted, another native boy grasped the message and trotted on. A typical message was: "To Colonel Clifford. Japs here. Hurry." On one occasion a message was lost when the "trotter" found a sleeping Japanese, cut his throat with a bolo, looted his pockets, and after that went off on a tangent, looking for more.

It was Clifford's plan to induce the Japs to scatter their San Isidro forces, then to prevent them from re-uniting their strength. Their separate detachments could then be defeated one after another. The doings of guerilla patrols soon caused the Japs to occupy the villages of Hubay, Daha, Tabong, Tuk-Tuk and Boho. Signs of unrest caused the enemy to send "security groups" in all directions. In Calubian, Clifford traced all these movements on his battle map.

The first eight-man American patrol to penetrate the peninsula was led by Lieutenant Thomas J. McCorlew of Cleveland, Texas. It boldly entered the outskirts of San Isidro at dawn, December 8, climbed a hill at the rim of the town and there lay in observation for two full days. The Japanese commanders were unaware that a young man from Texas, armed with high-powered binoculars, was gazing steadily through the windows of their headquarters.

The patrol reported on December 9 that five hundred Japs, armed to the teeth, were marching on Calubian.

Clifford bound every man in his force to service as a rifleman. They set out to meet the Japs. Civilians from Calubian were evacuated to Biliran Island, across two-mile-wide Biliran Strait.

Soon a native runner bore word that guerillas were locked in battle with three hundred Japanese at Tobango, five miles south of San Isidro. Clifford called for reinforcements.

Reinforcements arrived at midnight. There were two companies of riflemen, two sections of machineguns and mortars, and two field cannon. The American force on the peninsula now totaled nineteen officers and three hundred and sixty-eight enlisted men.

At 10 P.M. an advance patrol of seventeen men dug in on a grassy knoll near the *barrio* of Tagharigui. The patrol leader, Lieutenant Oakley W. Storey, from Los Angeles, had a feeling that the grass around him was "lousy with Nips." At that time all was quiet. A pale moon shone through ragged cloud flags, and a light night wind stirred the grass in silvery waves.

Exactly at midnight a piercing "Banzai!" rang out. In an instant the patrol perimeter was in a fiendish uproar: flares, fiery stabs, bursts of gunfire and howls of rage. More than one hundred Japanese charged the knoll with fixed bayonets. Through grass and moonlight they had crawled to within fifty yards of the patrol before the Banzai rush began.

The Japs plunged head-on into the fire of the B.A.R's. When a score of Japanese rush an automatic weapon they seem content when sixteen die and four get through. It is as if they embarked on a mad gamble that the automatic rifles would jam. The B.A.R.s did not jam. Lieutenant Storey, wounded four times, spotted a Japanese captain who yelled, "Banzai! Banzai!" The Jap swung a Samurai saber. The Californian met him with a pistol. And the pistol jammed! The Jap officer lashed out with his sword. Storey ducked; he rammed his head into his foe's stomach. He seized the Jap's wrist and twisted until it snapped. Then he seized the Samurai sword. The Jap captain fell, beheaded by his own weapon.

The Japs continued to press their attack after daylight. Standing in the middle of the San Isidro trail a B.A.R. gunner named Orville Schuler from Wathena, Kansas, killed four Japs and wounded seven. Squatting in a foxhole not far from Gunner Schuler was a rifleman named Onnie Johnson from McNinnville, Oregon. Johnson heard the yelling of the Japs who attacked Schuler. But from his foxhole he could not see the attackers. Out he jumped, to a tree at the edge of the trail. That was better. He could see the Japs now. He brought up his Garand and killed three more.

All onsets were repulsed. Clifford's men counter-attacked behind a rolling mortar barrage. Five times they were thrown back. The sixth thrust ended in hand-to-hand fighting. There were seventy-eight Japanese cadavers littering the grass, and much discarded equipment. The equipment was new, and the cadavers appeared to have been fresh and well-fed Japs. A count of noses showed six American dead and ten American wounded.

About three hundred and seventy Americans now held a "front" twenty thousand yards long and five thousand yards deep.

"As numerous small and scattered fights developed on the Leyte Peninsula, new methods of operation were developed. The terrain of the peninsula is composed of low, grassy ridges behind a fringe of high hills along the coast. The grass is not deep, and observation from the highest knolls is effective for miles.

"It was thus impossible to conduct any daylight movements without discovery by the Japanese. We had, however, the advantage of Filipino Scouts who knew every inch of the territory. Hence, night movements became common. Detachments would move out early enough to reach objectives just before daylight, attack in the dawn and men rest the remainder of the day, maintaining observation from vantage points.

"This technique threw the Japanese completely off stride and resulted in the inflicting of many casualties upon the enemy with only small loss to us. Japs were being killed every day."

(from a Field Report)

A one-time accountant from Seaside Park, New Jersey, led a band of guerillas in one of the most adventurous actions on the peninsula. The ex-accountant was Major George D. Willets. The slim, handsome young officer had joined Clifford's battalion only a few days before the opening days of the campaign. The colonel had made the newcomer his executive officer. The job of a battalion executive officer is administration. What Major Willets wanted was action.

He started out at 4 A.M. in a tropical night rain at the head of a patrol of Americans and fifty guerillas. His mission was to isolate a series of hills near Taglawan, which were known to be occupied by the Japanese. In the rain-drenched dawn the little taskforce reached its objective and set up its machineguns. The Japs were unaware of its presence. The former accountant decided to give the Japs the surprise of their lives.

He jumped up and led the charge of his mixed host.

"Hear, all guerillas," he shouted. "Follow me! Long live the Philippines! Long live the guerillas! Long live Rizal, Quezon, Osmena!"

Protected by cross fire from machineguns the guerillas charged, Willets out in front. They reached the crest of the first Japanese-held ridge. Willets' shouting spurred his warriors into a joyous kind of ferocity. The guerillas saw the major hurl hand grenades into enemy foxholes. They saw three Japs die under their commander's grenades. There was a melee of shooting, shouting, throat-cutting, of fleet bare legs, bobbing straw hats and curved bolos in tawny fists. Terror stricken, the surviving defenders sprinted downhill.

Willets ordered the machineguns forward to provide another curtain of protective five. The guerillas charged the second Jap-held ridge. Again they drove the Japanese down the slope in a close quarters fracas.

Not far away, in a shallow ravine, were two abandoned Japanese machineguns. Midway between the guns a dead Jap lay, face down and arms thrown wide. Willets ordered a squad of guerillas to go down and to secure the guns. The guerillas consulted, then shook their heads. They pointed at another hill beyond the ravine.

"Maybe Japs on that hill," they said. "The Japs will shoot when they see us go get their guns."

Major Willets shrugged his shoulders. "Watch that hill," he told them. "When you see Japs, shoot em."

With that the accountant from New Jersey scrambled down the slope toward the abandoned guns. He quickly searched the dead Japanese for documents, but found none. Then he walked to one of the guns, cradled it in his arms, and clambered back to the top of the captured ridge. "You see," he told the guerillas. "Nothing happened."

After that, Willets once more descended into the ravine to secure the second machinegun. The machinegun had disappeared. With it had disappeared the Jap "corpse."

The Japanese then counter-attacked. Four counter-charges were repulsed. A rapid check showed Willets that his guerillas had expended all their ammunition. Whereupon he withdrew his combined force to their original morning positions. On the captured—and jauntily discarded—ridges they left one hundred and twenty-nine enemy dead.

On the night of December 10, Japanese counter patrols assaulted a height known as Guard House Hill, in the vicinity of Calubian. In the surprise sally, carried out in pitch darkness and rain, one American was killed and four were wounded. Before the stab was warded off, Aid Man John Folk of New Kensington, Pennsylvania, dashed across the line of the attacking Japs and hid the wounded. He remained on guard beside his patients for the rest of the night. The Japanese, apparently, took fearless John Folk as one of their own.

One of the wounded soldiers was Private Francis Lockwood from Boyeville, Wisconsin. He had been shot through the leg, but insisted on returning to the fight. He said, "I don't pull my trigger with my toes." He recovered his rifle and rolled off into a clump of *kunai*. From there he fired on Japs dodging past him in the darkness.

The wielders of the iron brooms which swept the Leyte Peninsula worked with rapidity and dash. During the many skirmishes of December 11, Private John Mallon of Bayside, New York, stood upright in the grass to lure the Japs to fire at him and so to disclose their masked positions. He then destroyed three of their nests by walking into them, tossing grenades.

Private Harry Schildt, from Browning, Montana, was wounded by flying shrapnel. He refused first aid and continued to skirmish. His commanding officer then ordered him to go to the rear. After they had bandaged his wound he escaped the corpsmen and rejoined the fight.

During the same day, Lieutenant Robert Caldwell from Turtle Creek, Pennsylvania, conducted his rifle platoon in a hunting trip across many streams, over ridges and through valleys. By evening their day's bag was thirty-nine dead Japs.

Private Santo Magazzi of Bethel, Connecticut, led his squad across an open valley and knocked out a hostile machinegun nest. On the way one of his men sagged in enemy fire. Magazzi returned in broad daylight, peppered by snipers, to rescue his comrade. But he found that the soldier was dead. Magazzi also died in action.

After the capture of a hilltop, Private Dana Wallace from Dunbar, West Virginia, saw a lone Japanese leap out of the ground and charge an officer with a bayonet. The officer was oblivious of the danger. Wallace riddled the Jap. The bullets struck within arm's reach of his startled commander.

Private Paul Garland of Ingalls, North Carolina, a scout, crept up to a Japanese machinegun nest, sprang into the emplacement with Indian war whoops, seized the machinegun and slew its gunners with bullets made in Nippon.

Another machinegun roost had pinned down a whole squad on an exposed slope. The slant-eyed gunners were sure of their kill. For the Division's men it was a situation in which one must give his life to save the whole team from destruction. Private Eugene K. Tupponce of Philadelphia, Pennsylvania, armed with a sub-machinegun, worked himself up the grass-covered slope. And suddenly he stood upright. The others heard the woodpecker rippling of his tommygun. They rushed the Jap roost and destroyed it. Gene Tupponce lay dead, and there seemed almost a smile on his young face.

On December 14, a patrol on a night march became marooned in darkness and rain near the village of Gustosan. Sheets of rain blinded the patrol. Men could not see the rifles they carried in their hands. Gullies between the ridges filled with water. The patrol sat in a huddle, waiting for the deluge to pass. It was near midnight.

At 1 A.M., December 15, a guard of the patrol heard a hoarse grunt in the darkness. He also heard the squishing of boots approaching through the downpour.

"Japs!" he yelled.

The raiders were upon them before any man in the patrol could fire a shot. Their screeching and the absence of firing made the encounter eerie beyond words. It was as if a bunch of werewolves had abruptly popped out of the mushy earth. The Japs had dots of luminous paint on their helmets so that they could recognize one another in the dark. These dots, uncovered when they launched their assault, glowed like darting, unblinking eyes. They also were the Japs' undoing. One man's experience in this Jap-fight was the experience of all. Take Private First Class Eugene E. Madden of Studley, Kansas.

Madden had sat drowsily in the rain, wishing that it would stop. He had fingered in his pocket for a wallet which contained the picture of his girl and a picture of his parents. The wallet had soaked through and the pictures had turned to pulp, and they were mixed with a box of matches and some cigarettes which had dissolved in Madden's sweat and Leyte's rain. Madden felt miserable. Suddenly a screeching Jap jumped on top of him.

Madden rolled over. A Japanese hand clutched his throat, and Madden grasped a wrist and felt that the Jap's fist clutched a dagger. He gave a great heave. He kicked his assailant in the face with both feet. The Jap grunted and thrashed. Madden stood up and kicked at the thrashing Jap. At this point a bayonet sliced into Madden's back.

Madden lunged forward. He felt the bayonet withdrawn with a brutal jerk. Behind him a voice snarled an outlandish word. Madden rolled a few feet. He felt his blood, warm and sticky in the rain. The blood was running between his buttocks and down his thighs. But he felt no pain. He felt stronger than he ever before had felt in his life. His hands found a rifle. He grasped the rifle and lunged in the direction of the alien snarl. He brought up his rifle in a vertical butt stroke. It caught the Jap under the chin, then ripped upward across his mouth, his nose and his eyes. It also knocked off his helmet.

The Jap reeled. There was an outcry of pain. An instant later he charged. Madden felt the bayonet pass inches from his neck. He smashed his rifle butt into the Jap's face. He followed that up with a kick to the Jap's groin. Then he sprang on top of the Jap and both of them rolled in the rain. The Jap had sunk his teeth into Madden's leg. Madden finished him with a trench knife.

All around him his comrades and the Japs were fighting tooth and claw. Madden pitched in. Suddenly there was a shrill whistle. As if by some magic the Japs disengaged. They found and picked up their wounded. Seconds later they had vanished in the night. They left three battered corpses.

After dawn another patrol probed for the Japanese nests. In this probing a scout named Charles C. Puglisi, from Pittsburg, California, found a Jap position hidden on the reverse slope of a ridge. On the way back to his patrol Puglisi was critically wounded by a sniper. But he crawled on and brought back the intelligence he had gleaned. He died before he could receive his Bronze Star Medal, which was sent to his widow, Anna Puglisi.

On December 17, near the *barrio* of Fortuna, Private Donald Ritter of Lewisburg, Pennsylvania, was a member of a combat patrol which had been lured into an ambush by a false report given by a pro-Japanese native. Donald Ritter pushed a machinegun forward and fired into the ambush to enable his patrol to wriggle out of the trap. Donald Ritter was killed in action.

On the morning of December 21, a two-man patrol near the headwaters of the Nipa River, spotted a column of several hundred Japanese moving toward a village named Tuk-Tuk. The two scouts were Private Noel Ellsberry of Perkinston, Mississippi, and Technician Robert Pridemore of Dema, Kentucky. They decided to scale nearby Mount Banao which would give them better observation of the Japanese column. They did not know then that a six-man enemy patrol was scaling the other side of the same mountain.

On the summit they came face to face. The two scouts fired. One Jap fell dead, two bobbed away, wounded. The others ran downhill. But an enemy machinegun opened fire from across a ravine. The scouts were pinned down, but they still were able to pursue the survivors of the hostile patrol with well-aimed shots. When the machinegun jammed they crawled away. Keeping to the ridges they followed the enemy column into its bivouac area. Then they returned and told their officers what they had seen.

That night, combat patrols and guerillas led by Major Willets were dispatched to surround the bivouac and attack it at dawn. Heavy mortars were loaded aboard four amphibious tanks which nosed up the shallow Nipa River toward Tuk-Tuk. At dawn the bivouac was surrounded. The "Alligators" opened point blank fire. Machineguns clattered on the heights overlooking the town. The majority of the Jap force had been caught cooking their breakfast rice. The patrols then charged downhill, led by the indefatigable Thomas McCorlew. Well over a hundred Japanese were killed. The survivors took to the brush and were caught and cut down by other patrols waiting for them on the twisting trails.

Perusal of abandoned enemy equipment showed that the enemy had looted everywhere. Soldiers' sacks were crammed with table linen, silverware, jewelry and other items, including women's brassieres. One dead Jap had even a baby's high chair tied on the top of his field pack.

Another combat patrol reinforced by sixty guerillas pushed

brazenly to the coast of San Isidro Bay, the camping ground of more than a thousand Japs. The mission of this patrol was to split the bulk of the enemy into separate lesser forces. This they accomplished by impudently pricking the main force. There followed a series of forced march maneuvers which drew Japanese pursuit parties to widely divergent points. In their David-Goliath assault the patrol had slain twenty-five Japanese. But one soldier and the patrol leader, Lieutenant Charles T. Dyer of Montgomery, West Virginia, had been killed in action.

Sergeant Bernard L. Purdy of Killbuck, Ohio, now took charge.

"How are we going to get out of here?" he asked himself.

The Japanese were strong in the north, south and east of the patrol. There remained only the sea in the west. This sea, Purdy knew, was not a friendly sea. It was patrolled by Japanese gunboats.

Purdy contacted some native boatmen. They refused to put to sea at night. Not for all the chewing gum and cigarettes in the pockets of the patrol.

Purdy decided to commandeer a ship.

Scouts roamed the shoreline. They found a sailing banca lying high and dry on a beach. Purdy posted guards on both ends of the beach. The rest of his force brought the ship to water after much tugging and heaving. They were helped by a dozen native women who said that they were fugitives from Cebu. All hands then crowded into the leaking craft, Americans and guerillas. The refugee women clamored to be taken along.

"Climb in," growled Purdy. "Only keep quiet."

There were neither paddles nor a sail. Emergency sails were rigged from ponchos. The night was dark. Cloud banks cut off the light of the moon. A brisk wind blew. After two hours' sailing, the silhouette of a patrol craft pushed over the horizon. Purdy doused his sails. No one spoke. No one smoked a cigarette. The patrol boat slunk past them and out of sight.

An hour later a second patrol craft churned by, nearer than the first. Americans and guerillas alike lay flat atop of one another. The native women did the sailing.

Abruptly a brilliant burst of light showered the banca. It was a mortar flare, floating from a paper parachute. The women chattered in fearful confusion. The soldiers quietly cocked their guns.

"Boat ahoy," a voice rang over the water. "Who are you?"

It was an American voice.

Purdy shouted back: "United States Infantry—take it easy."

Aboard the P.T. boat the voice rumbled, "Well, I'll be a son of a bitch."

The Leyte Peninsula was finally swept clear of Japanese by a battalion (Second Battalion, Thirty-Fourth Infantry Regiment) commanded by Major L. Snavely of Lancaster, Pennsylvania.

An artillery barrage cornered and destroyed three hundred not far from Tuk-Tuk. A hundred more were killed near Taglawan. Others were destroyed at Baha, Tobango and on the shores of Arevele Bay. Sergeant Gordon Bailey from Washington, West Virginia, and Private William Daly from Boston, marched into San Isidro and killed sixteen Japs in a house-to-house search. Only one enemy surrendered alive.

In a last gesture of defiance a swarm of Japanese charged with bayonets tied to the ends of bamboo poles. Many others climbed into a tidal cave. In a protest against circumstances over which they had lost control they blew out their innards with grenades.

It was Christmas, 1944.

CHAPTER SEVENTEEN

THE ISLAND RAIDERS

The Island deemed secured, Colonel Verbeck relaxed. A native padre approached him.

"Please," said the servant of the church, "could you do something about cleaning out the Japanese in Lubang town?"

The colonel sat erect.

'What? Still Japs in Lubang?"

"But there are many," the padre said mildly. "They are all over the town."

The colonel called a company commander. He arranged for a force to go in and destroy the remaining enemy.

"Colonel—I don't know . . .," faltered the priest "You see, those Japanese are all dead."

(from a Field Report)

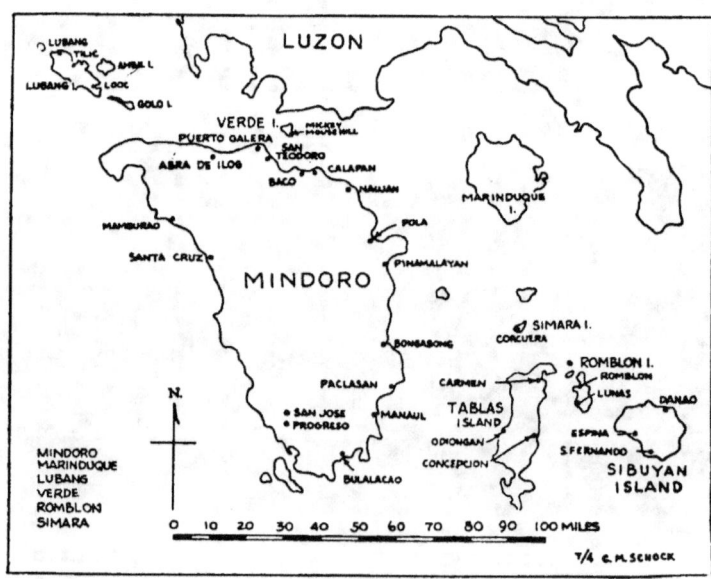

THE ISLAND RAIDERS

IT HAS EVER been the infantryman's lot to experience the worst traits of the countryside he captures. The supposed glamor of life on tropical isles seems somehow hinged to the presence of ice boxes, pith helmets, broad verandahs and saronged shapes; instead the infantryman drank swamp water tasting of chlorine and dead insects, wore hot steel on his head instead of cork, sat in steaming earth holes instead of on cool verandahs. ("Nice" people and the comfort that goes with them seem to vanish everywhere into thin air when infantrymen move in.) Of all the ruined and inhospitable places in the Philippines, the dogface found big Mindoro Island the hottest, dustiest, most boresome and malaria-infested.

On December 15, 1944, the Divisions Nineteenth Infantry Regiment invaded Mindoro at its south-western tip. On the way from Leyte a Japanese suicide bomber crashed into a convoy escort ship, the Nashville. The bomber exploded and the ammunition aboard the cruiser exploded. More than a hundred Americans died, and other hundreds were wounded even before the landing. Infantry aboard the convoy vessels were glum. Everyone expected a hard fight on the beaches of San Jose Bay.

But the landing was unopposed. The assault teams rushed up the beaches and not a shot was fired. Riflemen combed the town of San Jose. They found one Japanese soldier and he was drunk. South of the town a patrol surprised three Jap naval men operating a radio station. The patrol killed one and captured the others. A smiling Austrian missionary emerged from hiding. Father Johann Steiger reported that the Japanese garrison had fled into the mountains when the convoy hove into sight.

The men of the "Rock of Chickamauga" looked at the summits to the north and east of San Jose. The mountains were high, naked, barren volcanic rock. The valleys between the mountains were beds of purple volcanic sand. Upon this promise of exertion the sun beat hotter than the sun of New Guinea.

A few days later the Divisions Twenty-First Infantry Regiment landed on the north coast of Mindoro near the town of Calapan. Here, also, the beach was undefended. Natives reported that the Japanese, after a hurried saturnalia of rape, robbery, and murder, had fled into the hills.

The soldiers of the Twenty-First looked at the hills. They were steep and heavily wooded, and in the distance the peaks rose higher and higher under a gloomy sea of jungle. The sky was gray and heavy with rain. More distant mountains hid their summits in the clouds.

From the first hour of the Mindoro landing, enemy warplanes from

Luzon bombed and strafed the beaches in a daily routine. Japanese warships appeared and bombarded San Jose on December 27. During the nocturnal shelling infantrymen stood up on the sands and watched in awesome silence when they saw an American pursuit pilot crash his Lightning into a Jap cruiser. American bombers from Leyte came to the landing teams' rescue. They sank several Japanese destroyers and drove Nippon's larger warcraft back into hiding. After that the Mindoro campaign wore on through four months of forced marches, mountain raids, heat exhaustion, jungle rot and malaria. Five hundred and ninety-three Japanese were killed by the Division's riflemen on this island. Seventy-three enemies surrendered alive. The first American killed on Mindoro was killed by an angry *carabao*.

Simultaneously with the Mindoro raid, a small Division task-force struck Marinduque, off the south coast of Luzon. Marinduque Island proved to be a well-stocked refuge for rich Filipino and Chinese merchants from Manila. Eighteen forlorn Japs were rooted from their hiding places and killed. Mindoro and Marinduque were the first stepping stones from Leyte to Manila and Luzon. Their control meant domination of the main sea route through the islands. Mindoro's airfields, built hard in the wake of the infantry advance, became the nemesis of enemy shipping in the China Sea.

There was a bitter fight in the town of Paluan, on Mindoro. There was another fight near the village of Bulalacao. But in the town of Pinomalayan, after a band of thieving Japanese had been destroyed, the populace invited the Americans to a banquet. Children and young women fashioned a robe of flowers and they made Private Lawrence Nathan from Highland Park, Michigan, wear this robe. Rifleman Nathan was dazed, for this day happened to be his birthday.

He was led down the village street to a throne-like chair built from bamboo poles. Following him was a parade of dancing, chanting men and women, the beating of drums, and strumming of guitars. Nathan was seated on the throne. The mayor of the *barrio* approached the throne and placed a crown of hibiscus flowers on the soldiers head. Then he pronounced him "King of Pinomalayan." Nathan grinned. Coached by the sinewy school mistress, the natives sang "God Bless America." The mayor then asked the "king" to sing. After a brief pause Nathan broke the silence with a raucous version of "I Want a Paper Doll That I Can Call My Own."

The seven hundred Japanese who were on Mindoro were utterly surprised when the invasion struck them. Their garrisons in the coastal towns were unable to unite into a striking force. They abandoned the towns and took to banditry in the mountainous interior. They had no food, medicines, or contact with Japan. Their groups broke up into lesser groups which plundered, raped and burned almost at will. Mindoro is vast and wild. Much of its interior has never been explored. Guerillas were unable to cope with the machineguns of Jap marauders. For the Division's patrols it was slow, painfully difficult work to corner these bands where they could be destroyed.

The task was complicated by numerous guerilla bands operating with a sort of Robin Hood independence. Guerillas established concentration camps for all those who did not agree with them. The formula was to accuse their victims and rivals of collaboration with the Japanese. Roads were few and far between; supply lines were dependent on native carriers or animal pack trains. There was much confusion in the towns as temperamental faction leaders quarreled over offices of power and charged one another with being Jap spies.

Through this atmosphere of local squabbles and confusion moved American combat patrols and Signal Corps crews intent on securing Mindoro as a base and nerve center for decisive undertakings in the future. Typical of countless exploits by small groups during the West Visayan campaign is the story of Sergeant Joe Nicksich of Pueblo, Colorado.

Six feet of upright bone and muscle, dauntless cheer and panther strength, this one-time mill worker led a crew of onetime farmers, painters and welders on a five weeks' trek through unexplored desolation. They vanished into Mindoro at San Jose in the south, and nothing was heard of them until they materialized again at Calapan in the north. Their mission was the extermination of Japanese banditry in the interior.

Joe Nicksich was the leader of a mortar section—two mortars and twelve men, reinforced by a pitch-and-toss assembly of guerillas— detached for "special duty." Nicksich liked adventure. He also liked mortars. On Red Beach in Leyte he had been the first soldier of the invasion who captured a Japanese mortar and turned it against the foe. To his mortarmen he said, "We're going on a junket. We're going to travel light."

He supervised the cleaning of their mortars, and he drew their store of shells and rations, and then he broke down the whole load into "one man carries." His picturesque taskforce traversed the belt of palms and meadow lands on the coast, and pushed in single file into the mountains beyond: native warriors in the van, then Nicksich at the head of his mortarmen, followed by a carrier train. Another detachment of guerillas protected the rear.

They trudged on, day after day. They followed the dry stream beds and the saddles, lugging their mortar tubes, their bipods and butt plates, their ammunition load and jungle packs through dust and sunlight. They crossed vast expanses of volcanic sands; they panted over razorback ridges. On the rainy northern half of Mindoro they pushed through thickets, and virgin forest and across many swollen streams. Nicksich was well aware of the vulnerability of his slow-moving column. An unseen enemy machinegun could have erased his caravan in a matter of minutes. But the sergeant was ever alert. In open country his scouts were a mile out in front. Flank patrols moved silently along the hillsides to his right and left. Here and there they sighted Jap food-stealing parties or a secret Jap bivouac—things they had set out to find. But not once were they surprised.

At times they traveled astride lumbering *carabao* oxen. The massive black beasts, progressing at about one mile an hour, were wont to halt at every stream to wallow in mud. Nicksich and his aides eliminated many of these stoppages by carrying helmets full of water and mud. Whenever the water buffalos showed intentions of meandering off their course, the mortarmen doused the animals' big heads with water and administered mudpacks—and the *carabao*, appeased, proceeded.

At other times Nicksich and his crew pushed on, riding shaggy native ponies, or in ancient two-wheeled carts supplied them by *barrio* patriots. But most often they walked. To the villagers along their plodding course they were the vanguard of liberation from banditry by demoralized Japanese and gangs of "good neighbors."

"Japs over there."

A tawny arm pointed to a sector of the purple ranges. Sometimes such intelligence would come from women visiting friends in a neighboring *barrio*. At other times it would come from children playing on the porch of a bamboo hut; or from a farmer whose pigs had been stolen at dawn.

Barefooted scouts prowled forward. Dusk falling, and their bellies full, the Japs became careless. Again and again the Coloradoan and his haphazard force surrounded groups of loafing Japs, shredded Jap delusions of safety with sudden mortar barrages. Then came hails of lead followed by a fleet guerilla charge. The Japs were buried and Nicksich handed their rifles to farmers' sons who had never held a rifle before.

The new guerillas would nod fiercely and brandish their weapons. Nicksich would show them how to load their rifles, how to operate the safety mechanism, how to aim and to fire.

After an hour of such basic training the expedition would move on to other tasks.

On one occasion Nicksich's force raided a *barrio* and killed forty Japs who were too drunk from sake to run, but not too drunk to fight. But then another force of sixty Japanese came down a ravine. Nicksich sealed off the mouth of the ravine with a pattern of mortar bursts. The Japs, too, had mortars; they set the village afire.

Nicksich rallied the fleeing villagers. Men, women and children helped the guerillas to carry mortars and ammunition to the hillsides flanking the ravine. Caught in a cross fire of mortar shells and rifle fire, the Japanese dispersed. The villagers celebrated among the smoldering ruins of their homes.

Bamboo houses are easily rebuilt.

Village communities received the wandering mortarmen with jubilation. Crusted with sweat and dust as they were, they were promptly dragged to feasts. Suckling pigs roasted over backyard fires. Chickens long hidden in caves were brought to light and killed. There was fruit, and fish in the streams. Householders presented palm wine in bamboo log containers and with smiling dignity. Then the night was one of well-being. Old and young strummed guitars. Girls danced with guerillas until dawn. There was love-making in the huts. Two hundred yards out the sentries watched, motionless and wide-awake.

When Joe Nicksich's expedition arrived at Calapan, they heard of Jap trouble on the small island of Verde, ten miles to the north.

The Japanese had shipped artillery to Verde Island. The heavy guns were mounted on a height named Mickey Mouse Hill, and they were a threat to shipping through Verde Straits which separated the smaller island from Mindoro. The Japs there also had a radio station which spied on planes and ships moving in the direction of Luzon.

On February 23, 1945, a taskforce of Nineteenth Infantry Regiment teams and guerillas had invaded Verde. They had scoured the island, fought a number of skirmishes, and departed two days later, leaving local guerillas in charge.

The guerillas soon messaged for help. Their message spoke of Japanese artillery and machineguns in action, against which the lightly armed natives were helpless. Joe Nicksich and his mortarmen were ordered to go to Verde to knock out the enemy artillery on Mickey Mouse Hill.

The sergeant asked for a ship to carry him across. No ship was available. "Get some canoes," Nicksich was told, "and paddle across."

The Coloradoan and his crew requisitioned two hollow-log canoes. They loaded their mortars and ammunition, filled the canoes with guerillas, and paddled off.

The night was dark and windy. Approaching Verde the mortarmen heard the booming of a heavy surf. In the darkness the canoes were thrown athwart the seas. The craft's outriggers were knocked away by the surf and the craft capsized. Mortarmen and guerillas swam to the beach. Their weapons had spilled into ten feet of water.

Joe Nicksich scratched his ears. His mortars were gone.

But as though his curses had been prayers, help appeared. A local guerilla chief, saturnine and squat, emerged from the jungled hillside. "Let me help you," he said.

He disappeared, and soon he returned with a swarm of young men. "Divers," he announced.

Divers they were. Within an hour they retrieved every weapon and every shell that had been lost in the sea. Then they all crowded around Joe Nicksich.

"Fix the Japs," they demanded. "We show you where the guns are."

Nicksich laughed. "Take it easy," he told them, "and don't make so much noise."

"Will you fix the Japanese guns?"

"I shall fix them," Nicksich promised.

They camped in a gully. On February 28, also by native banca, there arrived Major George W. Dickerson of Warrenton, Virginia. He assumed command of "all American and Guerilla forces on Verde Island."

An air bombardment of Mickey Mouse Hill was planned for 11 A.M. Nicksich's mortars were to mark the target area with smoke shells. But on their canoe voyage from Mindoro wind and currents had carried the mortarmen off their course.

The landing had been made at the wrong spot. The mortars could not be carried into position in time to fire the smoke shells.

Promptly at 11 A.M. the planes winged in over Verde Island. They bombed the wrong hill.

Major Dickerson posted guards on strategic shore points and trail crossings. Then he led his mortarmen and guerillas through rugged jungle to a point eight hundred yards from Mickey Mouse Hill. It was a night march by compass, through inky darkness. The taskforce arrived at midnight and camped in a ravine. Plans for the next day's action were discussed. A mortar barrage was to be placed on the Jap artillery positions and the guerillas were to charge the hill.

In his Field Report, Major Dickerson relates:

"At daybreak on 1 March the mortars were set up and an observation post established on the forward slope of a hill overlooking the Jap position. The enemy guns and installations were cleverly concealed, and we could not locate them through our field glasses. The guerilla leaders were then called forward to point out the Jap positions, but even they were in doubt as to their exact location.

"Our observation post became like a beehive. The crowd of Filipinos anxious to help us made a large volume of noise. Evidently we were spotted by the Japs, for we were soon under fire from one of the belching bolt machines, canister ammunition. We were now able to pin-point the 75 millimeter gun and immediately began bracketing in on it with our 81 millimeter mortars. Smoke was used until we got the proper range. As we fired for effect, we could see that the mortar shells were right in there. One direct hit was scored on the breech of a 75 millimeter gun just as she spit another shell of lead balls. The crew could be seen blown into the air.

"Our explosive shells hit one of the Jap ammunition dumps, and the entire hill seemed to explode as fire raged through the camouflage and grass quarters, exploding more ammunition. Sergeant Nicksich yelled with pride and joy.

"Orders were issued to the guerillas to attack Mickey Mouse Hill while the mortar barrage continued. As the fighting men approached the position, the mortars ceased fire, and the guerillas came under small arms fire. The troops did not take cover, nor did they advance; they just stood at the base of the hill excitedly discussing the situation, with their straw hats and colorful clothing giving their position away. The advance had stopped. The Japs were frantic and fired wildly with little effect. It was the opportune time to attack. . . .

"As we left our observation post, a second 75 millimeter gun began firing; this was the first time that this gun had fired that day. We made a mad rush for the base of the hill. The gunner seemed to be tracking our small party because the shells were bursting to our rear. We dived into a ditch as a volley of canister came up through the brush toward us. A civilian, who was carrying my pack, was not as lucky as we; he was hit in the chest and died on the spot. From the ditch we could see that our observation post on the hill was receiving a terrific pounding point-blank; both from high explosive and canister shells.

"Our guerilla troops could not be located; they had disappeared in the brush. The exact location of the second 75 millimeter gun could not be determined; so we decided to get the hell out of there. ..."

They found their observation post plowed-up by shell explosions. Sergeant Nicksich and his aides crawled out of a stream bed where they had lain in water, only their faces showing.

"Anybody hurt?" the major asked.

Nicksich counted noses. "No," he grinned.

They prowled up a hillside and established a new observation post.

They mounted the mortars and brought the second hostile field piece under fire. Scouts searched the countryside to corral the panicky guerillas.

At nightfall the guerillas reassembled. They seemed a downcast, disillusioned lot. "Why not give these babies a pep talk?" Nicksich suggested. "Cheer up the gallant chargers."

Major Dickerson made a speech. Sergeant Nicksich made a speech. Then the guerilla officers made speeches. The guerillas replied with fierce mumbling. They made the sign of cutting throats. They waved their ancient rifles. However, one native officer and his two squads had not joined the meeting. He and some of his men had malaria, and they insisted that they were too sick to fight.

Sentinels were posted. All others stretched out to sleep on the gravel of a stream bed. The night was clear and brilliant with stars. But an hour before midnight everybody was awakened by the bursts of 75 millimeter shells. The Japanese on Mickey Mouse Hill were shelling the adjoining slopes and beaches at random. The scattered cannonade stopped promptly at midnight, and the remainder of the night passed undisturbed.

At 7 A.M., on March 2, Major Dickerson deployed his motley force for the attack. The mortarmen surrendered their carbines to the guerillas. "That," reported Major Dickerson, "gave them great confidence and put them in a happy frame of mind."

Nicksich crawled toward the Japanese positions to find a spot from which he could direct the fire of his mortars. He halted when he heard the chatter of Jap voices, then withdrew to a nearby knoll and relayed his fire orders.

The first shells destroyed the camouflage and brought the gun into full view. Soon high explosive projectiles struck home. Ammunition fires blazed. The guerillas spread out in skirmish lines surrounding the base of Mickey Mouse Hill.

At 11 A.M. Nicksich dispatched two colored smoke shells. They were the signal that the barrage had ended. This time the guerillas charged in true infantry style. By 11:30 they tangled with survivors on the crest and cut them down.

"While mopping up," reported Major Dickerson, "there was a snappy little fire fight when two guerilla patrols clashed; however, it made them wiser soldiers."

Among the Japanese equipment captured on Verde Island were three field guns, more than one thousand rounds of artillery ammunition, five hundred hand grenades, one hundred thousand rounds of rifle and machinegun ammunition, mines, rifles, bayonets, pigs, chickens, flour, sugar, rice and sake. The captured armament was distributed among the guerillas. The captured field guns proved to be of French design, American made. Eighty-two Japanese were killed on Verde.

During the early months of 1945, other raiding parties of the Division invaded and seized other islands in the seas adjoining Mindoro.

Sergeant Ernest E. Payne of Takamah, Nebraska, led a patrol to Culian Island.

On March 3 a five-man patrol led by Lieutenant James Jarret of Cutbert, Georgia, and by Sergeant Dave Boland of Portland, Oregon, secretly landed on Simara Island in the Sibuyan Sea. Their mission was to ferret out the secrets of the Jap force on Simara in preparation of an American assault. They prowled about the island for two days, counting Japanese and noting the disposition of their strength.

A Nineteenth Infantry Regiment taskforce invaded Simara at dawn, March 13. By March 17 the island was secured. The Japanese garrison sought refuge on a hilltop. The liberation taskforce surrounded the hill at dusk, and dug in for the night at its base. But in the darkness the Japs harassed the besiegers with fire from four machineguns and with scores of grenades.

The riflemen did not like it. "If we do have to sleep in grenade range," they agreed, "let's sleep it out on the hilltop, not on the bottom."

Through the moonlit night they stormed the hill.

One hundred and one Japs were killed on Simara. Twenty-one others committed hara-kiri by grenade.

The invading taskforce lost ten soldiers killed in action, and seventeen were wounded.

Simultaneous with the seizure of Simara, a rifle company commanded by Captain Dallas Dick, reinforced by one company of guerillas, invaded the island of Romblon.

Deep green and wildly picturesque Romblon had become a refuge for scattered Japanese remnants from other islands. To keep their presence on the isle a secret, the Japs had burned all native craft and decreed death by bayonet to all islanders caught in the attempt to flee. Already they had bayoneted some seventy civilians.

The Division's taskforce landed stealthily during a torrential night rain. It traversed the black hills and valleys in a forced march, occupied the heights surrounding Romblon Town at dawn. Sudden machinegun and mortar fire caught the Japs at breakfast. Thirty were killed fleeing from their stolen houses. The survivors fled to the jungle-clad hills. Six weeks of arduous patrol pursuit followed.

One hundred and forty-nine Japanese soldiers died on Romblon. Eighteen soldiers of the liberation force were killed in action. Tablas, Carabao and Sibuyan Islands were freed in swift succession. Two companies of the Division's riflemen were flown to Mindanao to seize an airfield in advance of American landings near Zamboanga. Commanded by Major Roy Marcy of Walla Walla, Washington, they landed at Dipolog, deep in Jap country, and occupied the field. It was used by Navy Corsair planes supporting the scheduled amphibious assault.* These air-borne infantrymen were the first American soldiers to invade Mindanao. Their skirmishes took them through country inhabited by headhunting savages. Poisoned arrows, crocodiles, monkeys and boa constrictors are among the souvenirs they collected on their way.

And then there was Lubang....

Look at Lubang. It is twenty-five miles long and nine miles wide. It lies plumb at the head of Verde Island Passage between Mindoro and Luzon. Control of Lubang meant control of the shortest shipping route between the Sulu and the South China Seas, the shortest route from San Francisco to Manila. It is what generals call a "strategic" isle. Also, it had two air fields and a radio station.

To Lieutenant Thomas R. Campbell, an ex-salesman from the White Bear Lake country of Minnesota, fell the task of reconnoitering Lubang. Colonel W. J. Verbeck of the Twenty-First Infantry Regiment considered him the right man for the job. Short, chunky, and afraid of nothing, Campbell agreed.

What did they know of Lubang Island? They knew what their map told them: Tropical rain forest surrounding central mountains some 2,000 feet high; a series of deep inlets on the island's northern shore with the town of Lubang near its tip, and Port Tilic roughly seven miles to the east; rice fields spreading inland to the jungle-matted slopes. There would be no rain, but a bright moon in a clear sky.

The planners also knew that an enemy force held Lubang. But the strength and location of the foe—Campbell's mission was to find that out.

He set out in a power boat a week before the scheduled assault.

---

* The American landings at Zamboanga were effected by the Forty-First Infantry Division two days after the Dipolog air field had been seized by two companies of the Twenty-First Infantry Regiment.

Three infantrymen and two native scouts were his companions. They carried light weapons, food, a radio. Mindoro's Cape Calavite fell astern. The sea was calm. A night wind helped to subdue the purr of the patrol craft's engines.

The blacked-out boat slipped into Tagbac Cove, not far from Lubang town. Under the stars the shore loomed black. Crouched low on a rubber raft and dipping their paddles with care, the six men made their way toward the beach.

No trouble disturbed the stillness of the night. The invaders knew the hazard of moving about in the darkness of a hostile shore. A cough, a slipping foot might mean disaster.

The silhouettes of palms stood sharp against the early morning light when the patrol approached some native huts.

The Filipinos showed terror and amazement at the sight of Americans on their flimsy thresholds. More than one of their people had lost his life under a saber for words or deeds which had displeased the Japanese.

Would the people of Lubang help the Americans to discover the secrets of the Japanese? The Filipinos were not sure. They were farmers, fishermen—not conspirators. They did not make this war and they wanted none of it. To them, the chief difference between Japanese and Americans was that the Japs stole food while the Americans brought along their own.

"No fear," Campbell assured them. "Americans have taken Manila. Americans have punched into Bataan."—Aye, men from his own division, the battling Twenty-Fourth.

Manila? Bataan?

It was wise to side with the winner. Slow smiles crept into the tawny faces. "But do you speak truth?"

"Absolute truth," said the man from Minnesota.

Some of the people of Lubang would help. They would be guides. They would tell the inquisitive lieutenant what they knew about the Japs.

The day was laden with busyness and stealth. Native scouts guided the patrol past enemy detachments. The Americans reconnoitered the island's air fields, studied strongholds, landing beaches, routes of approach. No day of fishing on White Bear Lake could have yielded a richer harvest than Campbell's secret exploration of Lubang. At times they heard the enemy's footfalls and chatter. Then patrol and guides would melt into the undergrowth and breathe silently until the enemy passed by.

Again night covered Lubang. The Americans returned to the beach.

They must rest. But where?

A dusky patriarch grinned, "Come with me."

Follow him? Safe enough, Campbell decided. The fellow did not act like a "Quisling." The old Filipino led them to an overgrown gully at the edge of a garden patch. It was a perfect hideout.

In this secret draw, the guide explained, his people had hidden their young women whenever *sake*-happy Japs came searching for girls and loot.

Next morning a guerilla volunteered the information that a lone Jap soldier lived with civilians in a hut not far away.

"Are those people friendly with the Nips?"

No—but what could they do if a Jap chose to camp under their roof?

Campbell knew of plenty they could do. For instance, they could entice the Jap to a covered spot near the gully where they were wont to hide their women. How? Let the girl he was after give the scoundrel a smile and say, "Come."

It was a thunderstruck Jap who saw Americans break out of the bushes. The girl laughed, and vanished. Campbells men secured the enemy and tied his arms. A job of questioning followed.

Later that day they left their prisoner to a bolo-knife guard. Circling the populated valleys, they penetrated into the hill country beyond, exploring mountain trails the enemy might use in his attempt to escape when the assault force would hit Lubang.

Their second night on the island again found Campbells patrol crouched at the silent beach. It was time to leave. Some whisper of their foray had come to enemy ears. They uncovered their rubber raft and pulled out through phosphorescent darkness to the patrol boat hovering offshore. And none too soon. Japanese combat groups scoured the countryside for the spy party soon after its departure.

Two days later Raider Campbell returned. This time he landed near Port Tilic, the spot he had chosen for the attack which was to put the Stars and Stripes over Lubang.

From vantage points in the undergrowth he observed the enemy garrison, counted its strength and weapons.

"Look at the stinkers swipe chickens out of a *kampong*," Campbell growled. The Japs had a chicken picnic. The Minnesotan was tempted to kill the cooks and take the chicken. But he lay still.

Through forty-eight hours the Americans clung to their posts. They ate cold beans, smuggled water from a spring frequented by Japanese, fought off mosquitoes and the most persistent flies in the world.

Campbell knew all he needed to know. There was a brief conference in a clump of *kunai* grass not far from the beach.

"Next time we come," said Campbell to the native headman, "it's the goods. Have patriots ready to lead us over the mountains."

The headman nodded.

"You shall have horses," he announced.

"Horses?"

"Horses to carry you over the mountains."

Campbell grunted.

Once more he departed by rubber raft, boarded the power boat lurking in the moonlit offing.

Upon the information he brought back to Colonel Verbeck the plan for the assault was built.

Thirty-six hours before the time of the attack, Raider Campbell made his third incursion into Lubang. With him went a combat patrol of fourteen hand-picked infantrymen, armed with sub-machineguns, carbines and Garands.

Two lights glowed from the beach: the guerilla signal that it was safe to land. A ripe moon had risen over the dark ridges, and there was the saturnine mutter of the surf. Wading ashore Campbell was confronted by a lean youth with curved knives at his belt and hair covering his ears in black confusion.

"Christ," said Campbell, "Who are you?"

"We are ready," whispered the boy, his belly-muscles rippling.

"Fine," said Campbell, and then spontaneously, "Why don't you get a haircut?"

"The horses, too, are ready," said the guerilla. "I and my friends have sworn not to cut hair until the last Japanese in the islands is dead."

"Good enough," growled the American. "We have brought rifles for your friends."

"How many?"

"Forty."

The patriot was pleased. Soon they moved inland. Through the rest of the night and all the following day they remained in a cluster of bamboo huts at the edge of a swamp. Japs passed nearby, singly, more often in groups. The croaking of bullfrogs and the chirping of cicadas filled the air and bats flew silently about the huts. And during the day not more was to be seen than a few women beating rice in wooden mortars, children playing, and an old man carving a paddle for his canoe.

All the same, Campbell was busy. Runners were dispatched to Port Tilic to warn the inhabitants to filter into the hills after sundown.

Scouts went into Lubang Town to spy and mark all houses occupied by Japanese. The plan was simple: The invasion would hit Tilic Harbor. Campbell's patrol would create a divertsion in Lubang Town to draw the enemy from the spot chosen for the landing. Fine—but why not go into Lubang this very night? Kill the Japs, take over, and then tell the colonel, "Here is your blasted island." What was wrong faith that?

His men nodded their appreciation. Campbell called for the horses. He stared at the mounts. "Horses!" In the dark they looked to him like a crossbreed between llamas and razorbacks.

Fourteen foot-slogging infantrymen mounted their "razorback" steeds. Afoot, they grumbled, they could make better time than any island "horse" could carry them. But if the lieutenant wanted to ride ... Hell, what Campbell could do, they could do as well.

Across the mountains of Lubang, in single file, rode the first horse-infantry of the Pacific war. Out in front was the longhaired guide, his bolo knives augmented by a potent Garand. Close at his heels rode chunky Campbell. The guerillas moved noiselessly through the flanking jungle. Through the stifling forest gloom the rear horseman fathomed the trail less by sight than by the smell of the ponies trudging in the vanguard.

At 9:30 P.M. the patrol emerged in the rice fields. At 10 P.M. they reached the outskirts of Lubang town. Campbell signaled, "Halt."

The dogfaces sighed. Their bodies ached from their unwonted ride. They slipped from their mounts and felt better.

Hugging their Garands, the guerillas fanned out into the dusty streets. They surrounded each house which harbored Japs. The infantry followed.

At 10:45 pandemonium engulfed Lubang Town.

A sentry shouted, heaved a grenade, was killed by a shot fired at arm's length. Guerillas pounced into the huts. The night rang with a macabre crescendo of howls. Japs darted from doorways, jumped from windows, crawled beneath the houses, dashed wildly down the moonlit streets. Grenades tossed through windows erupted through palm-thatched roofs. There was the tearing sound of sub-machineguns spouting and there was the dry bark of the Garands. The guerilla leader and his hirsute friends worked with butts and jungle knives. A Jap screamed under a blade that cut his throat. A few fought back. Campbell kept moving, directing his men. Three times grenades burst plumb on spots where he had been standing seconds before.

At 11 all resistance ceased in Lubang Town. The enemy dead sprawled in the streets, in the huts, under the huts. The patrol moved out.

"Back to the ponies," was all that Campbell said.

In silence they rode through the night toward Port Tilic. A red glow hung in the sky. They arrived above Port Tilic at 2:30 A.M., ready to attack. But the guerillas, as usual, had disappeared. "Damn," said Campbell. "Might as well take it easy." They curled up in the brush and slept. When they awoke it was dawn. Warships dotted the horizon. A naval cannonade set Tilic Harbor afire. When the shelling stopped, Campbell said, "Let's move in."

They combed the town of Tilic before the taskforce hit the shore.

Weeks of bitter mopping-up fatigue followed. A battle patrol led by Lieutenant Bob Carmody of Pittsburgh skirted the island in canoes, then struck inland and blocked a number of mountain trails. A score of fleeing Japs died in the ambush.

Another patrol discovered sixteen Japanese "Q-boats" tied to a ramshackle wharf. Each of the suicide launches had been booby-trapped with torpedoes. But the traps were disarmed, and infantrymen used the launches to exterminate enemy groups holding out in coastal villages which could not be reached by overland trails.

One patrol of four was lost in the mountains of Lubang. A rescue patrol of three set out to find them. Colonel Verbeck gave way to his flair for adventure and made himself the leader of this patrol. Roaming the hills they encountered a tough bunch of Japanese. One man of the rescue party was shot to death. A Jap bullet pierced the colonel's shoulder. With a fine smile, Verbeck asked the combat reporter covering the operation not to write a story about his wound. ("What will folks think of me when they hear that a colonel leads a three-man patrol, hey?") The lost patrol of four was found days later; all four soldiers had been killed and mutilated beyond recognition.

Meanwhile, a cowboy from Wyoming named Raymond Lund, rounded up six native horses to carry telephone wiring equipment across Lubang Island. Lund had trouble. At times he carried the horses' loads. At other times he was chased by his angered steeds. Crossing mountain rivers, he was forced to unhitch all equipment and to lug it across the river himself in hundred pound loads. He then returned to lead each horse through the current. When Lund emerged on the other side of Lubang, he came alone and afoot. He had laid forty-three miles of wire in three days. And all of his horses had died on the way.

Eight Americans lost their lives on Lubang; eighteen were wounded. Two hundred and twenty-seven enemy corpses were counted on the island. Six Japs were seized alive.

CHAPTER EIGHTEEN

RETURN TO BATAAN

"Zig-Zag Pass was not lightly named. There is no map to show but half the twists and aides, the dips ana rises, the strong slopes, the cliffs and gorges that make it hazardous and difficult fighting ground. Each turn masked the road beyond. Having passed one turn, the road was visible only to the next .
The Jap was getting rough. ..."

(from the Historical Record of the Thirty-Fourth Infantry Regiment)

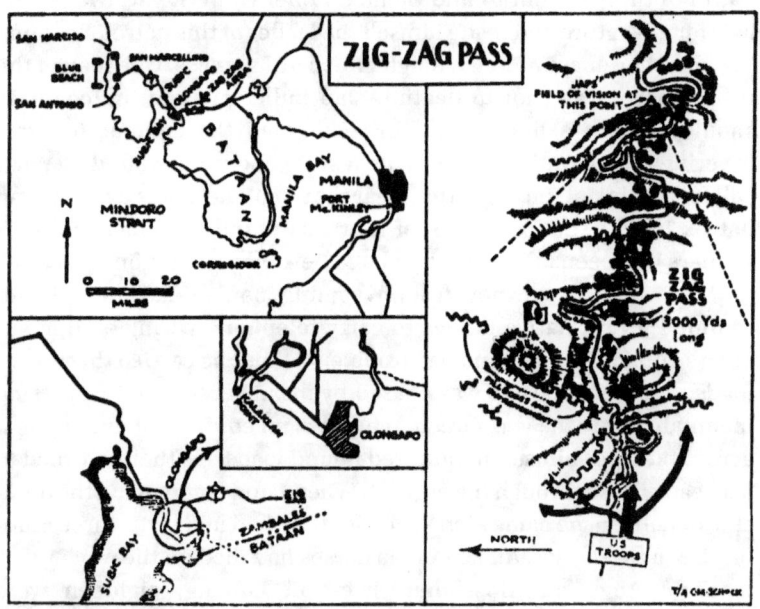

EIGHT YEARS before the Japanese stole the Philippines, an American major surveying Zig-Zag Pass, Luzon, voiced the opinion that "a small force taking advantage of the natural defenses could hold Zig-

Zag Pass against any size force until hell freezes over." But now the Japs held the pass. They held it with thousands of first line troops, and they had had three years in which to dig their defenses.

While other elements of the Division scoured Mindoro, the Thirty-Fourth Regimental Combat Team fought with a taskforce* ordered to seal off Bataan, to deny this natural stronghold to Jap forces driven southward by MacArthur's invasion of Lingayen Gulf. From the town of Olongapo on Subic Bay a highway winds eastward to Manila. This is Highway 7. Where Highway 7 crosses the base of Bataan Peninsula, it twists upward through a mountain pass, a nightmare of hairpin turns and sight-blocking spirals: Zig-Zag Pass, the mission's key objective.

Two hours before dawn, on January 29, 1945, the convoy of war-spawned ships anchored seven thousand yards off the west coast of Luzon. Phlegmatic mine sweepers cleared the waters fronting the invasion beaches. Helmeted men crowding the decks of ships studied the shore. Low tide was at 7:09 A.M. The sun rose clear and brassy at 7:30. The sea was calm, the surf light, the beaches undefended.

Beyond the beaches the mouth of a valley rose into a saddle to the east. South of the valley mountains loomed. Field glasses revealed a twisting road cut into the promontories of Subic Bay, and the wreckage of blasted bridges.

Around the larger ships the swarm of assault boats drew nervous wakes in the cobalt. Destroyers hovered offshore, watching for the geysers in the sea that would mean the beginning of battle. Aboard the transports, ward rooms were transformed into surgeries. Doctors stood idly watching, waiting, their clean hands in the pockets of their clean smocks. A canoe bearing three natives passed the bow of a destroyer. It hoisted sail and made for shore. Someone on the bridge bawled a query about the canoe. Nobody did anything about it.

Through the loudspeakers a calm voice said: "The surf is low. The landing is dry. The first waves have gone ashore. They are moving in standing up. They were met by natives waving American flags."

There were no Japs on "Blue" Beach, where the assault teams of the Thirty-Fourth struck. Ashore, gaunt in the midst of a riotous native crowd, stood a bearded man in tattered khakis. He was armed with an ancient .45 pistol. He held an old straw hat in his hand and said nothing. His eyes were somber, and shining with tears. He was Captain Joseph Craine, United States Army. For three years he had made single-

* This taskforce consisted of the 38th Infantry Division and the 34th Regiment of the 24th Infantry Division. Since this volume deals with the battle record of one infantry division, the narrative will be limited to the activities of the 24th Infantry Division teams in the battle for Zig-Zag Pass.

handed war against the Japanese in the mountains of Zambales Province. Each night in prayer he had reaffirmed his faith that some day American troops would come back to Luzon.

Now they were here.

A battalion commanded by Major Harry L. Snavely of Lancaster, Pennsylvania, spearheaded the drive into Bataan. It was found that trucks could not be landed on Blue Beach.* So Snavely led his men in a forced foot march through southern Zambales. The day was dry and hot. The sun-baked roads followed long-dried stream beds. The vanguard passed the village of San Antonio and struck Highway 7, which had a solid crown. Though many sagged from heat exhaustion, Snavely's infantrymen traversed San Marcelino and Castillejos. They pitched bivouac at dusk without having met a Jap. In seven hours, loaded down with weapons and equipment as they were, they had slogged forward seventeen miles.

Hard on the heels of the vanguard battalion toiled communication parties under Lieutenant Anthony Roozen of Mankato, Minnesota. On this day, and throughout the campaign, their telephone wires followed the attack teams as a tail follows the dog.

At the same time a lone sergeant mobilized a swarm of natives to establish an ammunition dump on Blue Beach. When the trucks arrived, the sergeant had them loaded, and then he guided his ammunition convoy to the spearhead battalion. After that he returned to the beach and moved the remainder of his dump sixteen miles to Castillejos. It was an uninterrupted 48-hour grind. Yet, the sergeant stood guard over his ammunition stores all through the following night. "It was a matter of conscience," he said. His name: George Shattuck, from Minneapolis.

The goal for January 30 was the town of Olongapo at the approaches of Zig-Zag Pass. Guerilla guides reported for duty before dawn. Patrols found bridges along the highway burning. The assault teams ate a K-ration breakfast in starlit darkness. The advance continued at 8 A.M.

Between the advance battalion's bivouac and Olongapo lay the village of Subic.

But where were the Japs?

On the previous day Filipinos had reported the presence of strong Japanese detachments in Subic. The spearhead entered Subic at 9 A.M. There was a tomb-like silence among the unpainted huts and buildings. Rust covered the corrugated iron roofs. The battalion searched every house. Subic was empty of life.

* Landing ships bearing trucks were detoured and finally landed their vehicles near San Miguel.

The march on Olongapo continued at 11 A.M. The bridges across the Matain and Matagan Rivers were still afire. Infantrymen forded the streams, wary of ambush.

At the next river—the Kalaklan—the Japs were ready. They had chosen their position well. They had fortified a cemetery which overlooked the highway. A pillbox commanded the Kalaklan River bridge. On the other side of the road, around the lighthouse of Kalaklan Point, they had dug machinegun bunkers and trenches. Cliffs dropped from the road shoulder to the sea. Guns on the lighthouse promontory covered the cliff sides. At low tide a narrow strip of sand skirted the base of the cliffs.

"Item" Company led the assault. One platoon ascended the hillside and approached the cemetery in a bear crawl. Another platoon muscled down the cliffs and toward the lighthouse bastion. A third group advanced toward the bridge.

A solitary Japanese crept onto the bridge from its southern end. His mission, apparently, was demolition. From eight hundred yards away the muzzle of a Garand traced his movement. Steady behind the Garands sights peered the eye of a Yankee sergeant. The Garand barked. The Jap dropped in his tracks. The sergeant fired again to make sure.

That opened the battle for Bataan. From among the graves machineguns spat. Gunfire rattled from the rocks of Kalaklan Point. The pillbox at the bridge belched steel. The platoons attacked in a concert of fire and movement. Men were hit, staggered to their knees, then sprawled. The attack did not halt.

The cemetery was quickly taken. Bullets chipped fragments from tombstones. A scout fell wounded across a grave. From other graves Japs fired at the fallen scout. Sergeant Walter Orzepowski of Bayonne, New Jersey, turned his Garand on the snipers. As they dodged away behind the monuments, Orzepowski rushed forward and pulled his scout to cover.

Tank-destroyers ground forward. They blasted the pillbox at the end of the bridge. Then they turned on the lighthouse bastion, where resistance was stubborn. Logs, rocks, dirt flew into the air, and with them the wreckage of a machinegun and its gunners.. Riflemen closed in.

Private John Deeghan of Renova, Pennsylvania, rushed an enemy emplacement, shooting as he ran. He followed up with a grenade, then with grit and muscle. He killed one Jap, wounded two, and two others scurried down the cliffs. Rifle bullets sent them tumbling into the sea.

A machinegun burst caught a scout through the hip. He floundered on the rocks, in view of the remaining Japs. Sergeant Roger Guilliam of Defiance, Ohio, and Private Victor Hinze of Racine, Wisconsin, hurried to his aid. Machinegun and rifle bullets struck sparks from the rocks about them. Lying flat on their bellies they bandaged the injured scout, and the only words said were, "Now... roll him over... gently, gently..."

To the rescue of another wounded soldier sprang Private William Rose of Connersville, Indiana. Bullets twanged in front of his feet, pinned him down. Rose lay on the rocks, his hands stretched toward his helpless comrade. "Andy," he shouted, "Andy, I'm coming." The battle-injured soldier did not answer. Bill Rose jumped up to hasten to his side. Jap bullets ripped their lives away.

Black smoke climbed over the hills. The Japanese had put the torch to Olongapo. Engineers removed dynamite charges from the Kalaklan River bridge. Booby traps and land mines infested the Olongapo road. The town was gutted. The Japanese destroyed everything that could be of use to the taskforce. American artillery destroyed everything that could be of use to the Japs.

The vanguard battalion moved through the burning town. Once an American naval base, it had become a corpse. There was an old-type Yankee helmet lying in a garbage-littered yard. There was a German-made Diesel generator in the shower room of a demolished tennis club. There were the old Spanish towers, crumbling and black. The Japs had converted them into a prison full of dirty, tiny, suffocating cells. And there was also Kiochiro Kusumi, an aged Japanese, who had once been a cook for a unit of United States Marines. He had lived in the hills for many months, a fugitive from his compatriots.

"I lived in Olongapo thirty years," he said. "I no like de Japs." Olongapo smoldered for many days.

On January 31, the riflemen secured the approaches to Zig-Zag Pass. "Able" Company set out to block the junction of a lesser road with Highway 7 in the rear of enemy outpost positions.

Where the highway crossed looping reaches of the Kalaklan River, two bridges had been demolished. Engineers had built emergency bridges during the night, and bulldozers had scooped out fords for the heavier traffic and paved them with gravel taken from an old railroad bed. Some distance to the east the Japanese provided illumination for the engineers by setting fire to an oil dump. The enemy attempted to disturb the construction. Guards opened fire in the darkness.

The mountains through which Zig-Zag Pass is cut rise abruptly from the Olongapo Valley. A roaring vegetation flanks the road and the river.

A narrow gauge railway has been hewn out of the rocky slope above the road. To the south high ground ended in a twin-peaked ridge.

One "Able" Company force seized the twin-peaked ridge. Another moved forward astride Highway 7. The assault teams found well-built fortifications—unoccupied by Japs. But from high grass along the abandoned railroad bed to the right of the road lanced rifle fire, machinegun sprays and grenades. An officer and a soldier of the advance party collapsed. The others hurried off the road and into cover.

Counter fire was ineffective. The Japs were entrenched in strength, on high terrain, but not a Jap could be seen. The vanguard fell back. Phosphorus shells lobbed from American mortars set the grass along the railroad bed afire.

"Able" Company's commander decided to by-pass the resistance. Scouts found a trail which circled the twin-peaked hill. The company swung around the enemy block, forded the 300-foot-wide Kalaklan River and seized its objective, the road junction. On its way it passed two Japanese machinegun installations unobserved. The enemy gunners were watching the highway to Manila . . .

A patrol set out to explore the surrounding terrain. It skirted a ravine, unaware that the ravine was alive with Japanese. The Japs allowed the leading scout to pass. They raked the body of the patrol with mortar shells and machineguns. Simultaneously a sniper shot at the scout.

The scout was Private Ben Guzman of Centerville, California. The first bullet pierced his leg. Guzman rolled behind a tree. He tried to locate the sniper. Underbrush obscured his view. He crawled away from the tree toward another tree which stood on higher ground. Again the sniper's rifle cracked. Ben Guzman was shot through the shoulder. He was faint from loss of blood, but he was furious. Also, he knew that if he remained where he was the sniper would shoot him again.

He could hear two Japs shouting to one another in the thickets. Ben Guzman crawled to a third tree, still searching for his sniper. He could not see him. But again the sniper's rifle cracked. Guzman winced. A third bullet had hit him; in the leg, inches from the first. He groaned with pain and frustration. Then he heard the sniper laugh.

The laughter came from a clump of grass on a small rise twelve yards away. Ben Guzman rolled into a bush. He dragged himself forward on one hand and one knee and circled the sniper. He reached the fringe of the clump of grass. He tossed a grenade. He sprang to his feet, lurched toward the Jap. The sniper was stunned from the concussion. Guzman pumped him full of bullets—and collapsed atop his dead assailant.

Across the highway three soldiers advanced to rescue their scout. They tangled with other snipers in the thickets. They found Ben Guzman and guarded him until a corpsman could arrive.

"Able" Company's road block held. Infantry battalions and tank platoons passed through on their way to Zig-Zag Pass. Long stretches of Highway 7 were now under continuous enemy machinegun and mortar fire. The sparring was at an end. The foe gave battle.

While "Able" held the road, "Easy" Company occupied Olongapo Harbor. "King" and "Love" Companies crossed the harbor slough to seize a promontory named Maritan Point. They came to a river mouth too deep to be forded. The riflemen commandeered all native canoes in the neighborhood and crossed the river. "Love" Company—in the style of the Indian wars—attacked Maritan Point in a fleet of canoes.

Anti-Tank Company teams dug mines from the captured portions of the Manila Highway. Cannon Company defended Subic Bay. Guerilla detachments roamed on spying missions. Neil Wood, from Bogalusa, Louisiana, and Frank Weeks, from Oklahoma City, led carrier trains with food, water and ammunition to the front lines. Though half the men in their parties succumbed to heat fatigue, they again and again hiked through the firing zones to consummate their job. On their return trips they transported the wounded and the dead.

By the end of the day the American command knew that there were some 5,000 Japanese in Zig-Zag Pass. The Japs were malaria-ridden, but well equipped. They had plenty of artillery and their morale was high....

The regiments of the 38th Infantry Division pounded into the maw of Zig-Zag pass.* The tide of battle surged uncertainly up and down the savage slopes. Ambulances churned in relays between the field hospitals and the front. Truckloads of dead rolled back for military burial. The Thirty-Fourth Regiment, meanwhile, was held in reserve.

To be "in reserve" does not mean to be at rest. During the night of February 1, enemy artillery shells struck the perimeters. There was intermittent sniping on all positions.

Two Japs approached Kalaklan River bridge in a canoe full of explosives. Guards killed one. The other jumped into the river and disappeared.

In the dead of night a suicide detail of four Japs rushed into the "Baker" Company bivouac and hurled explosives. Three escaped in the confusion. One was shot to death.

---

* The regiments of the 38th Infantry Division which made the initial, costly assaults on Zig-Zag Pass were the 152nd and 149th Infantry Regiments.

Again, at noon, February 1, a mountain outpost encountered a lone Jap armed only with a knife. The Jap insisted on storming the outpost. He was killed.

At Maritan Point "Love" Company's riflemen boarded their canoes and adventured down the coast. They found a camouflaged radio station operated by a grinning guerilla. He informed the Americans that native patriots had cut off the heads of the Japanese garrison. The Americans were satisfied; more so when they heard that their random excursion had made them the first American troops to return to the peninsula of Bataan.

Patrols scoured the coastal villages. They killed twenty-four Japanese in scattered clashes, and they lost eight wounded and three men killed. Elsewhere, five hundred of the regiment's riflemen unloaded supply ships on the beaches. While working in the night they watched the fireworks of tracers, artillery flashes and the glare of explosions over the mountains of Zambales.

New orders arrived in the small hours of February 3: the regiment was to relieve the 38th Division in the storming of the Pass.

The regiment advanced into Zig-Zag Pass in a column of battalions. They crossed the Santa Rita River. They passed wooded mountainsides and remnants of abandoned logging camps. Zig-Zag Pass swung south in a great loop. This "mother" loop was sinuous with eleven minor loops, each of which changed the direction of Highway 7. Each loop of the road provided the Japs with an almost perfect defensive position. On the left a hill mass towered over the highway in five nearly perpendicular noses. On the right the ground careened into deep gullies. The heights and the precipices were covered with jungle. Toward the end of the "mother" loop, Highway 7 dropped down a sweeping gorge. Jap strong points burrowed deep into the heights commanded every yard of the way.

At 10 A.M., "Baker" Company, striking across jungle between two loops of the road, radioed that it had entered a zone of hostile mortar fire. Japanese machineguns firing from natural bulwarks stemmed the advance. Lieutenant Tom Rhem, the company commander, was shot through the hip, but remained to direct his troops in the fight until nightfall.

Other companies reported hostile artillery concentrations. The whole American end of Zig-Zag Pass was rocked by the explosions. There had been no warning, no sensing to find the range. The enemy field guns were zeroed on the loops. The bursts were sudden and accurate. Trucks were destroyed by direct hits.

The advance stopped. Counter-batteries thundered.

The vanguard companies left the highway in an attempt to circle the impact zone of the barrage. "Charlie" Company climbed over one of the "noses" and knifed into enemy entrenchments on the slope beyond. Its first thrust was repulsed by interlocking bands of machinegun fire. Some wounded men were left lying between the Jap holes. Private Bernard Schneller, from Carlton, Oregon, moved up and down the killing line and helped away the wounded. In his platoon every third soldier had been hit. Sergeant George Parsons from Charleston, West Virginia, stayed inside the Japanese lines to guard the wounded who could not be carried out.

Jap gunners in a pillbox had singled out Parsons as their target. Parsons' alternatives were to run for his life, or to lose it staying with the wounded. He stayed—and lived. To the rescue came Private Ed Gonzales, who called the deserts of New Mexico his home.

Gonzales rushed the pillbox. He fired his sub-machinegun through the ports of the pillbox until a Jap bullet brought him down.

"Baker" Company cut through rain forests parallel to Highway 7, driving Jap defenders from the roadbed. "Able" Company thrust in a wide flanking movement to the east. They worked through jungle and over mountains, guided by compass. The terrain was confusing. Once a man was more than a few feet away from the road, orientation became a matter of guess. "Able" Company circled cliffs and ravines, and was thrown off its course. Its only contact with the battalion was by a field radio in the hands of Private Zeno Reitmeyer of Madison, Wisconsin. The company remained isolated and surrounded by Japanese for two days. Radioman Reitmeyer was on duty every hour of that time. Meanwhile, on the battle maps, the location of "Able" Company was marked, "Unknown."

By 4 P.M., both "Baker" and "Charlie" teams were locked in a bitter fire fight. Of the enemy little or nothing could be seen. He fired from caves and tunnels and shrub-masked holes. His artillery thundered from positions more than a thousand yards beyond the far side of the "mother" loop on Zig-Zag Pass.

The Japs had mined Highway 7. The mines were buried in the roadbed. Detonating wires led through underground pipes from the mines to foxholes in the adjoining jungle. Japs waited in the foxholes. At other places the Japanese had felled trees across the road, augmented by nests of dynamite designed to blow up anyone attempting to remove the obstacles. At 5 P.M., guerillas reported that a force of one thousand Japanese reinforcements was moving in over a woodland path known as Telegraph Trail. The attack was stalled. All companies dug in at dusk and held on. Night brought on a counter attack, and over Zig-Zag Pass artillery duelled until dawn.

On the morning of February 4, "Able" Company radioed that it was beleaguered on a mountain slope ("Familiar Peak") and unable to fight out of the trap.

At 10 A.M., in the wake of a rolling artillery barrage, the battalions resumed their winding, uphill push on Highway 7. "Easy" Company was the vanguard. It rounded a "2"-shaped curve and met machinegun fire. The company was pinned down. To its right, "Baker" Company was also nailed to the ground. Both tried maneuvering to the flanks. But each movement they made drew fire from a different direction. There was intensive sniping from a gully in "Easy" Company's rear. The terrain was so narrow and the curves so sharp that the following battalions could not deploy to fight. One team of riflemen endeavored to rout the snipers from the gully. It was repulsed by bullets from other snipers lurking on higher ground. The vanguard radioed for shell fire.

The cannoneers worked with precision. The first round landed on the road a few feet beyond the Jap position. Another blasted snipers from a knoll. Then another squarely hit a hostile machinegun emplacement. The shells whistled hazardously close to the treetops under which "Easy" Company held its line.

A colonel and his liaison party were taking cover in a ditch on the left side of the highway. At this moment an artillery shell aimed at the Japanese two hundred yards in front caught a branch of a nearby tree. Seconds of silence followed the shattering roar.

Then there were screams. The colonel raised his head from the dust and quietly remarked, "I got it."

Major Harry Snavely, battalion commander, led "Fox" and "George" Companies in an enveloping movement to knock out hostile strongpoints from the rear. But again there blazed well-aimed fire from all directions.

At this time, "Charlie" Company made slow but steady progress on the southern flank of the road. The battalion commander slogged with the advance elements. Suddenly rifle fire crackled from ground slightly higher, not many yards away. "Don't fire, these are our troops," the commander shouted. Scarcely had he spoken when a grenade thrown at him exploded beside his head. His face was lacerated, his arms and chest pierced in many places.

By the road, twenty minutes to the rear, sat the crews of several tanks, waiting for a mission. The tanks were called forward. At 4 P.M., they assaulted the strongpoints blocking Highway 7. The leading tank lumbered around a bend and sprayed the hillside with machinegun slugs. But the Japs refused to fire on the tank. They fired on the riflemen beyond. Searching through his periscope the tank commander was unable to spot the enemy position. A tank "buttoned down" for battle has only a small field of vision. The tank commander selected a promising knoll, swung his turret into line, and dispatched a 75 millimeter shell. It was a true hit. A hidden pillbox blew up in death and ruin.

It was as if the tank's gun had been a match held to an immense reservoir of TNT. Out of the blue sky an avalanche of mortar and artillery shells descended on the American troops in Zig-Zag Pass.

Gun after gun spat steel and high explosive with resolute accuracy all along the curving road—and into every position American troops held or had held during the day. The barrage continued far into the night. The Japanese were not guessing. They knew.

Under the blightening horror of the barrage the assault team gave way. The many dead on the highway were torn to bits by a succession of explosions. The wounded lay writhing with jagged holes in their chests or bellies, with an arm or leg shattered, or with broken bones. The day's thousand-yard advance was made for naught.

Nearest to the Japanese position lay a squad of riflemen under the command of a private, Jack Davies from White Plains, New York. The squad leader had been hit and Davies had taken over. In the agonized withdrawal he kept his squad in line and fighting until the last cartridge on hand had gone its way.

In another unit Sergeant Eric Erickson of Blairstown, New Jersey, saw his platoon leader and two aides blown to pieces in the hellish descent. Half of the other men in the platoon were wounded. Erickson grasped command of the demoralized platoon. He organized the fit survivors into Utter teams and quietly covered the evacuation of the dying and the wounded.

Private Harry Potter, a scout, remained calm when panic seized his group. He had spotted a nest of Japs. He killed one and continued to fire at the others until his gun jammed in his hands.

Sergeant Layton Ernst of Eyota, Minnesota, lugged smashed-up mortarmen to safety.

Sergeant Edward Benik of Moquah, Wisconsin, saw six members of his machinegun section cut down by fragments. He put the survivors to fashioning litters from rifles and ponchos and led the transport of the wounded to the rear.

"Fox" Company, on a roadside hilltop, was dispersed by the barrage. The men fell back wildly, alone or in scattered groups. But four riflemen remained on the hilltop through the night to guard the wounded. (Their names are on their regiment's honor roll for all time to come: Sergeant Jere Kuehn of Parkdale, Arkansas; Private First Class Howard Herman of Seattle, Washington; Private First Class Mariano Chavez of Los Limas, New Mexico; and Private First Class John Lynch of Clarksburg, West Virginia.)

Driving a six-wheel truck loaded with rations was Private Lorne E. Curtis, from Eldred, Pennsylvania. He had left Olongapo at 4 P.M. and he was driving toward Zig-Zag Pass. Except for a scattering of snipers the road seemed clear. Curtis eased his truck around mines, shell holes, fallen trees and occasional corpses, and everything was fine. Suddenly there was a snarl in the air, followed by an explosion and a cloud of black smoke on the road ahead. More shells followed the first. Curtis maneuvered the truck into a ditch. He jumped out of the truck and ducked in the ditch.

But Lorne Curtis was bothered by the knowledge that his comrades up front had not eaten since early morning. It was his mission to bring them their rations. He climbed out of the ditch and back into his truck. He started the motor. He whispered a prayer and then he eased in the clutch. His truck rumbled on through the artillery barrage.

He reached the furthermost battalion command post and delivered his two tons of rations. The thunder of bursting shells was near and continuous. Curtis heard the whirr of fragments crashing through vegetation. The battalion adjutant leaned over and shouted into the truck driver's ear.

"Up front the wounded are piling up. We can't get them out by hand."

Curtis dumped the rations from his truck and headed to the firing lines. He backed his truck through a series of mines and then he had to stop because the road was littered with bleeding men. He loaded sixteen wounded soldiers into the truck and drove back down the blasted road to Olongapo where a field hospital had been established.

At the 18th Portable Field Hospital the wounded arrived in loads. The trucks and jeeps and ambulances dripped blood. Six doctors, on the verge of exhaustion, toiled like titans through forty-eight hours. Shells make uglier wounds than bullets. Captain Alan Tigert patched up one man whose heart pulsed uncovered in his split-open chest. And out at the half-abandoned front, tinder shellfire, in a caldron of dirt and sweat and noise and tattered flesh, toiled the battalion surgeon, Captain George E. Morrissey of Davenport, Iowa: hands steady, and a stranglehold upon his jangled nerves.

The punished remnants dug in for the night. Men drugged with fatigue cleaned their weapons. Here and there a rifle blurted into the gloom beneath the stars. Sleep was fitful; wakefulness poisoned with bleak fear.

A field report sent back at dawn, said, "No activity, night of February 4-5."

The cooks were awake and at work before sunrise February 5. They lit their field stoves in defiance of snipers. At dawn the men of the assault teams rolled out of their foxholes. They shook themselves awake and mopped faces and necks with a few ounces of water from their canteens and cursed the war and the Philippines. They drank hot coffee and ate a fat mess of dehydrated eggs; after that they were ready. Their advance crossed bitterly familiar ground.

The Third Battalion pushed to the ridge from which they had been driven the previous day by the barrage. Patrols forged to the crest. In the final climb the scouts pulled themselves up with the aid of roots and vines. Japs held the crest. They opened fire at a range of ten feet and chased the spearhead back to the lower slope. Then flame throwers and bazookas were brought into play. Documents taken from enemy dead identified them as members of the Osaka Infantry Regiment.

Offensive movement was resumed on Highway 7. The Thirty-Fourth Regiment held the center. Other elements of the task-force advanced to the right and left of the road. They rounded a bend and the shoulder of a mountain. The sun hurled flamboyant javelins. Japanese mortar shells plummeted from the brassy sky.

On the roadside a company commander and two sergeants discussed a shortage of equipment. A mortar burst ended the discussion. There was a flash, a roar, and blood tinting the dust. The company commander was critically hurt. The supply sergeant, Leo Heck of Cedar Rapids, Iowa, was hit in his left arm and in both legs. The second sergeant, Lewis Downey of Muskegon, Michigan, had gone off to pee and was unhurt. Downey carried his fallen commander to the rear, followed by Heck who dragged himself through the dust.

By 9:30 that morning the dragon of Nippon again whipped his tail in fury. He caught the Yankee Dragon Regiment squarely in the face. It was pinpointed, unendurably concentrated artillery fire. It was machinegun fire from the flanks and sniper fire from the rear.

Friendly field artillery replied. Shells from both directions cut the morning air to ribbons. "Charlie" Company's commander was wounded for the second time in two days. His first sergeant was knocked senseless by concussion. Fifty men and all officers but one were killed or wounded. Riflemen clawed into the hard earth of Zig-Zag Pass. Major Snavely, reorganizing his command, urged them to hold on.

Joseph O'Malley, a mortarman from Newark, New Jersey, had a bead on a Jap machinegun. He mounted his mortar in a shallow shell hole and silenced the gun. There were friendly machineguns hammering nearby, and the hammering suddenly ceased. O'Malley discovered that every member of the friendly gun squad had been hit by shrapnel. "Hey Joe," he said, "take over." He turned his mortar over to his assistant gunner. He crawled across the road to the silenced machinegun emplacement. He rolled the disabled machinegunners into the shelter of a shell hole and then he manned the machinegun himself. The gun hammered until another Jap shell blew O'Malley into the road.

Direct artillery hits roared into a ravine where a detachment had taken cover. The ravine echoed the cries of the dying. Technician Dallas Johnson of Windom, Minnesota, had his knee smashed by shrapnel. A few feet away a corpsman was working over a soldier who was hurt worse; compound fractures. Johnson cursed his knee and crept over to help the corpsman carry the other wounded to an ambulance on the road.

Amidst the desolation of high explosive and shattered lives Chaplain James J. Moran, from Shaker Heights, Ohio, administered the last rites to the dead. In the enormous thunder of the detonations his voice was austere and calm. *"O Lord, let Thy mercy be upon us: As our trust is in Thee ... Hear my prayer. O Lord ..."*

With a solemn "Rest in peace, comrades" he turned away. And then James Moran laid hand on the litters and helped to transport wounded men to ambulances on the road.

A little way off another battalion chaplain, Captain Kingsley W. Hawthorne of Belmont, Massachusetts, spat into his hands and pitched in. In the hard clamor of mortar and machinegun fire he took command of the evacuation of casualties. He directed men in the task of dressing wounds. He administered morphine to men screaming with pain. He gave sulfa, he carried litters, he spoke words soothing and confident and firm. He did not leave the death-raked highway until the last of the wounded had been carried to shelter.

Toward noon a flight of high explosive shells howled over the hills and landed in the center of a battalion command post. The shells struck the trunks of trees directly over the foxholes. The sergeant major, the operations sergeant, staff officers, radiomen, telephones, battle maps and weapons flew to the four winds.

Threading a course through shell craters and wreckage was a jeep and a trailer driven by Private James McFee of Parkersburg, West

Virginia. Jeep and trailer were loaded with mortar ammunition. McFee saw the wounded covering the roadside. He stopped. Around him shells whined and burst. McFee jumped from the jeep and helped the fallen. But abruptly he was in the grip of an awful fear; what if a shell should strike his jeep and trailer? The ammunition would blow sky-high. More men would die in the explosion. He sprang back into the jeep. The jeep was parked in a deep rut. McFee coaxed and worked for ten minutes before he extricated it from the trap. Then he drove out of the shelling. Minutes later a 90 millimeter mortar shell burst where jeep and trailer had been ...

At the height of the artillery slaughter there was such a shortage of aid men that Sergeant Ernest Dillingham, from Elmore

City, Oklahoma, hastening from hole to hole, pressed riflemen into service as corpsmen. When medical supplies were exhausted he led a party to the destroyed command post to look for more. The earth in front of him erupted. Ernest Dillingham sagged to his knees. Both hands clutched his abdomen.

It was as if the mountains of Bataan reveled in brutal laughter at the Americans1 plight. The Jap cannoneers did not have to test the range. There was neither bracketing nor registration. Their shells sped straight to the target, multiple bolts from the blue. There was no room for evasion or maneuver. From their observation posts on the high mountains enemy observers had a perfect field of vision of every loop of Highway 7. They sat there "looking down the throats" of the men of the Thirty-Fourth, counting the rifles and trucks, watching and waiting for the Americans to enter prepared fields of fire, then cutting loose and watching what happened and correcting the errors and starting in somewhere else. Of the Japs and their mountain batteries nothing could be seen from the bottom of Zig-Zag Pass.

The battalions fell back and dug in again and the enemy barrage dogged their retreat and thundered over the perimeters all night. Men dug their foxholes deeper and huddled low. Calls for aid men were like whimpers in a hurricane.

Sergeant Leroy Johnson of Orange, Texas, went forward with a captured knee mortar and a sack full of shells to ward off a band of snipers.

Technician Kenneth Seitner of Dayton, Ohio, shouldered into the shell bursts to drag out the wounded. A shell found him. He died quickly.

An outpost on a ridge above the perimeter dissolved in a direct hit. A soldier came running downhill, terror on his face. His comrade up there, he said, was bleeding to death. Without a question or a second's preparation a surgeon, John Kemodle of Durham, North Carolina, aided by two volunteers, crawled out into the murder night. They crawled three hundred yards up a black mountain trail overgrown with vegetation. They found the wounded sentinel and saved his life. They also found the ridge acrawl with snipers. They remained on the ridge until daylight. They lay on top of the ground because the sounds of digging would have signaled their location to the snipers.*

Dawn came.

A message sent by the commander of the Thirty-Fourth Regiment to higher headquarters read:

"I AM CONVINCED THAT THE JAP POSITION CANNOT BE CRACKED UNLESS THERE IS A WITHDRAWAL TO A POINT WHERE ENTIRE CORPS ARTILLERY AND ALL AVAILABLE AIR WORKS IT OVER WITH EVERY POSSIBLE MEANS FOR AT LEAST FORTY-EIGHT HOURS. MY FIRST AND SECOND BATTALIONS HAVE SUFFERED TERRIFIC CASUALTIES, AND IT IS BECOMING QUESTIONABLE HOW LONG THEY CAN HOLD UNDER THE POUNDING."

The troops—and the pounding—both held. So did the wisdom of the recommendation.†

---

* First Lieutenant John R. Kemodle's helpers were Staff Sergeant Willard R. Harp of Durhamville, New York, and Technician James R. Carter of Ennenton, South Carolina.

† On February 6 the Thirty-Fourth Regiment was relieved on Zig-Zag Pass by the 151st Regiment of the 38th Infantry Division. On F^ruary 7, Japanese positions on Zig-Zag Pass were bombarded with 4,000 demolition bombs ana 1,320 gallons of Napalm. The process was repeated on February 8th, 9th, and 10th. Zig-Zag Pass was then stormed by the regiments of the 38th Infantry Division. After fourteen days of fighting the whole length of Zig-Zag Pass was in American hands. Thus, Japanese armies fighting in the north were denied a retreat into Bataan Peninsula. Soon thereafter a message was received which read: ". . .JAPS WERE OBSERVED WITHDRAWING FROM BATAAN TO CORREGIDOR VIA SMALL NAVAL CRAFT."

CHAPTER NINETEEN

WE STORM CORREGIDOR

"If the majesty and power of Our Empire be imperiled, you must share with Us the sorrow..

(from a Japanese Imperial Rescript)

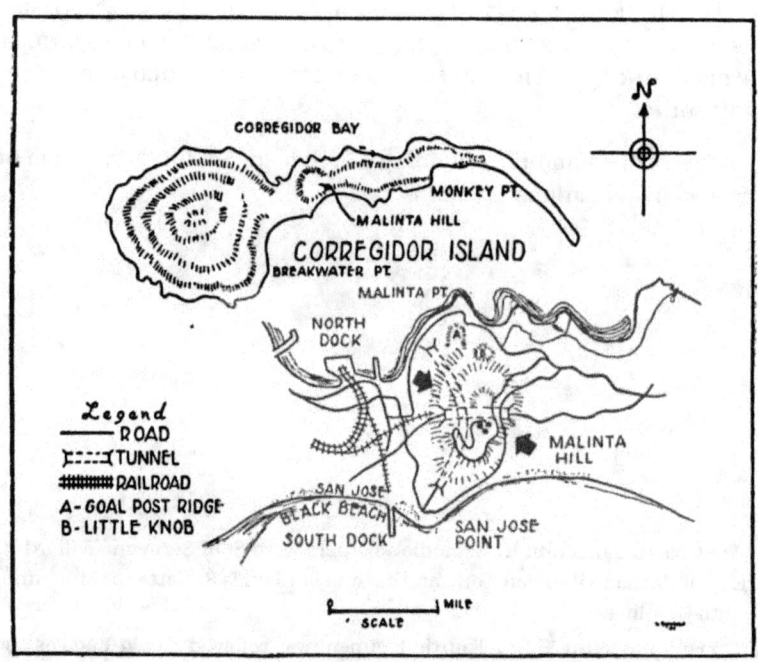

WHEN WE HIT Corregidor's Black Beach with the first wave, not much happened. Through a scattering of rifle fire we streaked across the chewed-up sands and on up the rock-bound side of Malinta Hill, knocking off a handful of Japs on the way. We dug in on that hill and there were a lot of Japs and guns and dynamite in the tunnels beneath us. We had occupied the height that divides Corregidor in two like a buckle on the belt around the waist of a big-breasted woman, and we had not lost a single man. Captain Frank Centanni, commanding "K" Company, looked around.

"I'll be damned," he said.

Before two days had passed that captain of ours was dead and covered by enemy fire so that we could not even recover his body. The hill was full of howling Japs and battle noise that'll ring in my ears as long as I live. The tunnels below us turned into belching volcanoes and the limestone rocks dripped with American blood. A hundred and sixty-one of us moved in. Ninety-three came out. "K" stands for "King" Company, though when we got through we felt more like kindling wood than kings.*

We knew what soldiers can and cannot do. War had thrown us together whether we liked it or not; and war had crushed our illusions into the mud. We slugged it out with the Jap in Hollandia. We killed and buried him wholesale on Biak. We fought for seventy-eight days straight on Leyte. We led the drive into Bataan and we caught hell at Zig-Zag Pass. Right after that we were alerted for the storming of Corregidor. To every one of us still alive Corregidor is not a spot of glory, but the echo of a nightmare in hell.

The "Rock" did not look good to us even on the map. We knew that we were heading for one of the toughest jobs in any war. We were going to have help, but it was one of those combinations that has to work perfectly, or end in disaster.

"K" Company moved into Mariveles at the southernmost tip of Bataan on the day the 151st Infantry carved out a beachhead there. We came ashore wading hip-deep with rifles held high.

Mariveles. Its the spot where MacArthur's men made their last heart-breaking stand before the men of Nippon hoisted the rising sun banner over Bataan. It's the spot where the "Death March" began. Remember? All the same, the guys on the beach of Mariveles were in no mood to dig back into history. All of us were looking down the inlet and out across the maw of Manila Bay. The sun glowed low on the horizon, blood-red. Out there, five miles to the south, Corregidor lay brooding in the twilight.

How we studied that Rock! Its massive western half, called Topside,

---

* Fortress Corregidor was invaded by a U.S. taskforce on the morning of February 16, 1945. The parachute invasion of the island's "Topside" was accomplished by the 503rd Parachute Infantry Regiment. The invasion of the soutnem beaches of Corregidor was the work of the Third Battalion, reinforced by Company "A," Thirty-Fourth Infantry Regiment, Twenty-Fourth Infantry Division. This narrative deals in the main with the activities of one company of the invasion force—Company "K."

lay on sand-colored cliffs thrusting out at Battery Point. A low, slim saddle—the womans midriff—led over from Topside to jutting Malinta Hill, which in turn was fronted by a promontory called Malinta Point; and tapering eastward from Malinta Hill lay the other half of the island: Engineer Point, Artillery Point, Infantry Point.

Our mission was to take Malinta Hill and cut the island in two: keep the Jap forces in the east from interfering with the cleanup of the Topside massif in the west—the paratroopers' play. We didn't envy them. The longer we looked at Malinta's ramparts the more the hill seemed to us a furuncle ready to spurt poison under the push of a finger. The battalion commander, Lieutenant Colonel Edward M. Postlethwait (Warren, Minnesota), was looking, too.

"I hope it works," he said.

We dug holes in the sand and slept as soldiers sleep—dropping off quick, but alert to the softest call. The clatter of machinery nearby did not disturb us. Somebody was loading assault equipment into landing craft: tanks, tank-destroyers, bulldozers, ambulances, a big truck loaded with TNT. That was for blowing up the tunnels.

The usual number of little things happened. One of the tank destroyers broke an oil line. It stuck lopsided in the surf. There was a flurry of curses and a clanking of chains. The thing would not budge. They borrowed another from the 151st.

We were awakened at 0530. A good wind rustled through the scrub and the night was full of stars. Already it seemed hot. Just fastening the pack and opening ration tins in the dark brought out the sweat. Loading began a half hour later.

One by one the landing craft pulled up to Mariveles jetty. Troops filed aboard, quiet and orderly. The rifle squads. Machinegun crews and mortarmen lugging their weapons. Bazooka-men with their stovepipes across their shoulders. Flamethrower operators glum under the weight of their tools. They climbed aboard and squatted, tightly packed. Each man packed grenades, atabrine and two canteens of chlorinated water. Smoking was out until daylight.

Last in, first out. "King" and "Love" Companies loaded last.

Dawn broke, pearly and big. Wind clouds stood over the horizon. Corregidor lay as silent in the twilight as a huge tomb. By now the Japs were watching us through their glasses. Some of us lit cigarettes. Light was passed around to others. You could feel the fellows wondering what yonder Japs were cooking up for our reception. The wind blew from the south. Some thought they could smell Nips five miles away.

The sun came up and the boats vibrated with the steady rumbling of their engines. As we moved out—very slowly—small dots drifted up with the wind, came nearer, became formations of bombers. We saw them circle the Rock, lazy-like and distant. Over the white-yellow cliffs of Corregidor blossomed sudden little shapes, like flowers pushed up out of a magic garden. Petals of smoke; bombs bursting. Soon the planes were as thick as sailboats at the starting line of a regatta. We looked for ack-ack, saw none.*

Rolling across the bay was the thunder of many explosions. Warships appeared and moved in close. Steel pitched into the Fortress' gun positions. The cruisers and destroyers were as casual about it as the planes. By 0800 a heavy pall of smoke covered the island. Peering over bulwarks as we drew closer it seemed to us that every foot of surface up there had been put through a giant sausage grinder. The smoke was so dense that we could not see the flashes of bombs and shells striking home. Diving planes vanished in the black welter and then zoomed out of it with screeching motors.

0830: another series of dots drifted up from the south. They came in fat formations and slower than the bombers. They were black planes, transports loaded with paratroops. They lower their flaps and barely maintain flying speed when they drop their men. In twos and three they floated in over the Topside plateau and paratroops floated out. Cross winds gave trouble. Many troopers came to grief on the cliff sides. But most dropped out of sight into the smoke.

We waited and listened, but everything seemed quiet up there. We had been circling all this time through choppy seas and now hovered off the southern beach which links the tunnels of Malinta Hill with the Topside forts. Black Beach this strip of sand was called. It lay open to crossfire from the flanking heights. We ducked and sucked in our guts as the motors pounded into high. The rocket ships cruised in close, pasting the cliffs as they went. Then we made the run.

We hit the beach two platoons abreast on a two-hundred-yard front. The ramps creaked down and we rushed ashore—through swarms of big, blue-bodied flies. Millions of flies.

At this spot the island is only five hundred yards wide. The sand was churned into an irregular pattern of craters. A band of land-mines followed the water's edge and another band of mines lay parallel to it some thirty feet inshore. Some of the mines were connected by trip wires which would set them off if somebody stumbled. We kept going fast, leaping across the mines and the wires and holes in the sand.

There was a fantastic silence. The engines of landing craft chugged

* Advance intelligence on Japanese armament reported 18 heavy coastal defense gun positions, 14 anti-aircraft installations, and countless caves and machinegun emplacements around Malinta Hill, San Jose and South Dock.

to keep their boats' snouts anchored to the beach. Shouted commands sounded silly in the stillness after the barrage. The bombs and shells and the rockets had driven the Nips from their guns. A spattering of rifle fire welcomed us. That was all.

We double-timed through sand and flies. The morning sun was blazing. We traversed a belt of what had been concrete buildings. The buildings were razed. There wasn't a piece of wall more than a foot high. The rubble lay not in piles, but scattered and flattened in crazy confusion. We dashed across that. About two hundred yards inland we swerved to the right on up the cliff-like face of Malinta Hill. We climbed like hell-bent apes.

Once on top we felt pretty lucky. Violence rocked the beach behind us. Recovered, the enemy had remanned his guns. Right and left the hillsides spewed fire. Fifties tore through the landing craft and thirties hammered the plates and the ramps. Mines popped. Pieces of jeeps and tanks and tank-destroyers were flying in the sunshine. But a tank and a self-propelled gun crawled up the beach and plugged away at the pillboxes.

It was a tough climb up Malinta Hill. Mostly we were on hands and feet, like goats. The equipment on our backs seemed to weigh a ton. The company commander sent the Third Platoon around to the promontory called Malinta Point, just north of the big hump. The rest of us kept going, three hundred feet up.

We saw a tunnel entrance with a sand bag barricade. That was the Hospital Tunnel. One squad went over and fired rockets to neutralize Jap guns in the tunnel mouth. Two squads took position just above the entrance to watch it. Their business was to keep the Japs inside or kill them if they came out. There was a cave halfway up, just off the trail. A squad was sent to clean it out. The cave was empty. We gained the top without losing a man.

Except for a mat of sun-scorched grass and thin bushes the summit was bare. Not a speck of shade. Protruding from the crumbling limestone were the vents for the tunnels below. "Grenades!" Our men pulled pins and dropped grenades down the shafts. The bursts were muffled and far away. Then there was a yell and some shooting. Someone had found a cave and in it was a large searchlight. Behind the searchlight crouched four Japs. They squealed and died.

Meanwhile, the Third Platoon kept moving north toward Malinta Point. They rounded a curve of rock and met fire from the Hospital Tunnel. They slithered past in a hurry, leaving those tunnel guns between themselves and their battalion. They darted through the rubble of ruined buildings and came face to face with the mouth of

WE STORM CORREGIDOR 273

another tunnel—this one opening to the northwest. They fired bazooka rockets into the tunnel and hurried on their way. They reached Malinta Point and spotted a few Japs in a cave. The Nips vanished in the inside of the cave, leaving three anti-aircraft guns at the entrance. Our men kicked over the guns and left a patrol to cover the cave. The rest climbed up Malinta Point and dug in—as much as you can dig in hot rock.

Malinta Hill was unnaturally quiet. The top was covered with big, blue flies. The flies buzzed around us like locusts. A hundred pounced to suck your sweat for every one you killed.

Down on Black Beach things did not go so well. A tank was knocked out by a mine. A tank-destroyer went to hell. An antitank gun, the jeep that pulled it and the men in the jeep were blown in all directions. "Mike" Company was hit in the boats before they reached shore. Nip machineguns fired from San Jose and from Breakwater Point. "Mike" Company lost more men by mortar bursts as they raced up the beach. More steel killed two staff officers. "Item" Company rushed across the narrow middle of the island toward North Dock. More ships, more men kept coming ashore. You could see them unload their ships under mortar blasts and you wondered how they got away with that. Fire from the Hospital Tunnel under Malinta Hill was heavy. The Hospital Tunnel was the biggest of all the tunnels. It's the spot from which General Wainwright surrendered to the Japs three years before.

Down there on the sweltering beach Captain Joe Richards (Portales, New Mexico) walked around collecting his scattered squads. Corpsman Sam Schneiderman (Bronx, New York) was squatting under machinegun fire, trying to patch up an officer who got it badly. Another aid man, Florian Bauman (Buffalo, New York) maneuvered a jeep full of medicines and plasma through the mine belts. Two supply boats were driven twice off the beach by enemy fire. The coxswain of one was killed. The captain of the other was hit and so were fifteen men on the boat. Corpsman Raymond Backlund (Chicago) jumped around, stopping blood-flow and treating the hit men for shock. Backlund brought one of the boats inshore and helped to unload it, with lead slapping the sand around him.

Jerry Rostello (Haledon, New Jersey), a motor sergeant, had his leg mangled by shrapnel. All the same he kept moving, pulling dead men out of jeeps and trucks among the mines, and getting the trucks to a safer place. Lieutenant Pete Slavinsky (Kulpmont, Pennsylvania) was busy mounting machineguns at the edge of the beach. Corpsman Harold Asman (Braddock, Pennsylvania) lugged wounded buddies down the sheer slope of Malinta Hill. So did Aid Man Russell Hill (Bartenville, Illinois). They bedded the wounded on litters in the sand, and applied the splints and the tourniquets and the bandages, sulfa and morphine, ducking the bullets and fighting off flies all the while. Sergeant Don Wood (Reedy, West Virginia), one of the best mortarmen in the world, saw four Japs toss grenades from a shell crater. He killed two of them with his rifle.

Two landing craft loaded with vehicles hit the beach and all vehicles promptly hit mines and blew up. Lieutenant Bill Skobolewsky (Nanticoke, Pennsylvania) went to work marking out a safer path among the mines. He took the chance of machinegun bullets setting off the mines around him. He crawled from mine to mine and marked them with little sticks and after that he marked out a path through the mine field with white tape. They later counted the mines he had marked—there were 216.

On top of Malinta Hill the strange quiet lasted all afternoon. "King" Company held the north end of the hill. "Love" Company occupied the southern hump. From where we sat the whole island lay beneath us like a living map. Everywhere was smoke and commotion except on top of Malinta Hill. But the heat and the flies gave us a hard time. Besides, a man feels peculiar when he knows that the insides of the hill on which he sits are jam-packed with Japs and dynamite.

Our mission was to keep the Japs in the tunnels; to let no Japs run from one end of the island to the other. To make the block complete, two squads pulled out to occupy two rises in the ground between us and the Third Platoon on Malinta Point. On one of these knolls the men found a cable hoisting contraption which resembled a football goal post. They called it Goal Post Ridge. Let's call the other one Little Knob.

Three men were sent to block the road which runs east-west past Malinta Point. These men stayed at their post for eight straight days under almost unbearable conditions. They stayed there from February 16 to February 23. They fought off eight night attacks in this time. In the eighth attack they killed twenty-three Japs who tried to Banzai them with rifles, bayonets, pistols, sabers and grenades. Each of these three men lost twenty pounds in a week. You should know their names. They might mean little to you, but they mean a lot to us: Sergeant Lewis Vershun from Britton, Michigan. Private Emil Ehrenbold from Hutchinson, Kansas. Private Roland Paeth from Bay City, Michigan.

To get back to Malinta Hill: That first afternoon we strung telephone wire from Malinta Hill to Malinta Point by way of Goal Post Ridge and Little Knob. Nothing more was to be done than to watch the fighting on the beach below, and to join in once in a while with a burst when Japs poked their heads out of the tunnels. By 5 P.M. most canteens were empty. Some grumbled about their thirst. So came darkness.

The silence was torn asunder by a burst of firing just before midnight. First there was rifle fire and the rapid stuttering of tommyguns, then the pounding of heavy machineguns and the thumping of mortars. Shouts and the sound of men scrambling over rocks somewhere downhill. The wires were cut and communications with the Third Platoon went out. Mortar fire fell on Malinta Hill. Around us and among us jerked the glares of bursting shells. Men were hit. Medics were busy. We could see

A voice growled, "Something's climbing up the hill."

Through the commotion came a crunching of footsteps, a panting and groaning.

"Let 'em have it."

"Hold your fire."

An angry whisper in the dark. Someone sobbing with pain.

Laboring up from little Knob was Private Rivers P. Bourque of Delcambre, Louisiana. He had thrown away his pack but he still had his rifle. On his back he carried a comrade whose leg was shattered. Every few steps he halted to help a third man along whose hand was dripping blood. We dragged them up the last yards.

"What's wrong down there?"

Bourque sat down. He stared at the ground and panted. Jap mortar fire beat a witches' tattoo. Malinta Hill and all Corregidor blurted battle.

"Down there—We've got to send them help."

"What's going on?"

"Surrounded..."

Through stabbing flame and flying steel Bourque's words drifted like a faint dirge. His squad had spotted an enemy force deployed to push through between the ridges to attack the crowded beach. Bourque's squad had opened fire with an automatic rifle, a tommygun and nine Garands. The Japs had rushed forward over their own dead. Grenades killed five men in Bourque's squad. Four others were badly wounded. Two of the wounded had to remain behind, tended by Private Cassise of 3302 Canton Street, Detroit, Michigan. He had crawled through prancing death and given first aid to the wounded, then hidden them as best he could. Cassise was still down there among the Japs.

A little later came two men from the squad on Goal Post Ridge. They were cool and angry. They said the Japs had tried to storm Malinta

Point. But the Third Platoon there had held out in good shape. On Goal Post Ridge things were different.

The Nips had swamped their squad in the dark and killed or wounded all but two.

To leave the wounded buddies behind them in the night had been the hardest task of their lives. But one infantryman had elected to stay with the wounded, to tend them and to defend them. That boy was Clarence Baumea, whose mother lives in Adrian, Michigan.

Much happened that night. Soldiers of one "Able" Company platoon, stationed near the water, saw a great hunk of the cliff above them lurch away and down in the dark. We all heard the deafening noise and wondered what it was. The Nips had mined the cliff with the idea of burying "Able" alive. But the Nips had filled the cliff so full of explosives that the mass of rock flew clear over the heads of the troops below and banged into Manila Bay.

Soon "Abie's" riflemen heard splashes in the water. There were little whirlpools of phosphorescence. At first they thought it was porpoises gamboling. But they took no chances. They fired. They heard screams. It was a bunch of Nips trying to swim around San Jose Point with waterproofed packages of TNT strapped to their bellies. "Able" Company killed twenty-three of the swimmers.

A soldier checking a broken telephone wire slipped around a rocky nose and suddenly found himself in front of one of the tunnels. Nine Japs came popping out of the tunnel. The lineman, Jack Sparkman (Littlefield, Texas) backed off the way he had come. The Japs followed him, skirting the rock in single file. Jack Sparkman grew desperate. Finally he yelled,

"Ain't there anybody who kin shoot those Japs?"

Gunfire from somewhere answered his plea. Sparkman heard the slugs whizz by his ears. They killed five of the Nips and the others dodged back into their tunnel.

Up the cliffs of Malinta Hill came two anti-tank gunners with water and ammunition. The water was for the wounded. Snipers took shots at the two as they climbed. The two soldiers crept from rock to rock, a few feet at a time. One pushed up their loads over his head and the other pulled them up with a rope. Corporal Nino DiGregorio (Wappinger Falls, New York) and Private Francis Titus (Arcadia, California) made the trip four times. Each trip they carried back a wounded man, or rather lowered him down the hillside with ropes.

We on the hilltop felt bad about our wounded buddies on Goal Post Ridge and Little Knob. It's the worst feeling in the whole world. The coward in you comes out. You want to go and you don't. What if it were *you?*

We all wanted to get those wounded out. Our captain did too. But the odds were too great. He couldn't risk any more men. His mission was to hold the hill. It was tough but that's the way some hands are dealt. Then it was too late. Determined to clear the way to the beach the Nips now flooded out of the tunnels in force. They assaulted Malinta Hill.

The night exploded in fury and death. First came a concentration of mortar fire. Five men were hit by fragments from the "Flying Ashcans." Then came the assault, in two waves a-chum with the insane savagery of a Banzai charge.

We let them come to within ten feet of the top. Then we opened up with all we had. It was like a massacre in a lunatic asylum.

The cliffside which the Japs scaled was so steep that the first who were hit fell into the faces of their fellows farther down. We sent scores of them tumbling down. Japs pitched end over end into the gorge below. The hillside seethed with Japs. Their mad yelling hurt our ears more than the blasts from rifles and machineguns. They kept coming. In close-in fighting one of our squads was pushed toward Goal Post Hill, ran into a solid wall of fire and lost five men, including its automatic rifle gunner.

There were shouting Japs ten feet from our perimeter. You could see them briefly in the blue light of flares: eyes gleaming under helmet rims, one hand grasping the bayoneted rifle, the other clutching a grenade. Some had double-barrelled shotguns. Corporal Daniel Smith of Bellevue, Pennsylvania, hurled grenades, saw them crumple a flock of Japs like paper dolls. Another Pennsylvanian, Private Adolph Neamend of Bethlehem, emptied his Garand into the wide-open mouth of a howling Jap, or so it looked. Another Jap tossed a grenade pointblank at Private Ray Crenshaw of Clinton, Oklahoma, and Ray kicked it aside and gave the Jap his due.

This fray lasted for an hour and a half. Don't tell me the Jap is inferior. They were able and brave. But they, too, have their saturation point. They sank away in the dark and with them they took some of their dead. The rest of the night both sides licked wounds.

Sergeant Willard Harp from Durhamville, New York, and seven fellow medics piloted six of our litter cases down the cliffs and past the tunnel mouths. Corpsman James Carter from Ennenton, South Carolina, and another aid man rescued a wounded comrade who had fallen down the slope. On the way Carter's companion was killed by a Jap machinegun.

Came dawn, and another fly-cursed day. The bodies of dead Nips hanging in the rocks below us began to smell soon after the sun came up. You could not see their faces for all the flies. Some wounded groaned, with the hot sun and the flies in their wounds, and we killed them to help them, but their smell became as bad as their groaning.

Malinta Hill was quiet. Elsewhere the fighting had picked up again after sunrise. Our captain dispatched an eight-man patrol to secure the wounded on Little Knob and Goal Post Ridge. We watched the patrol slide down the hillside and move past the harvest of cadavers. It reached Little Knob all right. One of the wounded men there was still alive. The others had died during the night.

The patrol regrouped and pushed toward Goal Post Ridge. They had not gone thirty yards before they met an ambush. Four men fell in a squall of bullets and grenades. The survivors fell back to Malinta Hill.

Our captain was gallant and humane. He could not sit still with the thought that there were wounded members of his team down there, helpless at the mercy of the Japs. He called for volunteers and he himself volunteered to lead the patrol.

We wished him luck. He grinned.

We covered them as they went down the slope. Crawling and creeping they proceeded to the point where the first patrol had met disaster. They passed that point without drawing fire. They had gone halfway to Malinta Point. Then lurking Nips opened up with rifles and lobbed grenades.

Captain Centanni was out in front. A bullet killed him where he stood. His men poured instant fire, killing four Japs. But three enemy grenades exploded almost on top of the captain. The men crept to within inches of their dead commander. But the Japs kept his body covered by fire and the boys couldn't bring him back.

Sergeant Bill Scott (Garnett, Kansas) carried a wounded soldier from Goal Post Ridge to Malinta Hill. On the way he was shot by a sniper, but he finished his mission without asking for help.

Early that morning Jap demolition teams tried to sneak through "Mike" Company ranks to Black Beach. The machinegunners on the perimeter worked with carbines and grenades and fifty-nine Nips died in the rubble of flattened buildings. These Japs wore the uniforms of Imperial Marines. Some of them were armed with big, American-made shotguns shooting loads of rusty scrap.

The Japs had slipped out of one of the tunnels in Malinta Hill. A

"Mike" Company platoon went out to seal the tunnel. The platoon was quickly surrounded by stronger Japanese forces. Mortars were needed to blast them out of the trap. Sergeant Marion Veal (Hardwick, Georgia) clambered over the rocks to Malinta Hill with a telephone and a wire line to a point from which he could see the Japs around the tunnel. Another observer laid another telephone wire up the western side of the hill. Three others had tried that before, and all three had been shot by a machinegun. Sergeant Arnold Kuyper (West Bend, Iowa), did the job in good shape. After that the mortarmen laid their eggs true among the Japs.

Down by the North Dock, "Item" Company platoons dug and blew and burned the enemy out of a dozen holes and caves. After a hard day's flamethrower work their score was thirty-one.

"Able" Company soldiers accompanied some tanks which battered the entrance of the Hospital Tunnel. They helped to keep a host of Japs inside and stewing.

"Love" Company dispatched a patrol with a trunk full of TNT to blast two caves on the eastern side of Malinta Hill, just below the crest. The first cave was quickly sealed with the Japs chanting inside. The patrol then moved to the second cave and installed the rest of the TNT. The charge was too big. Instead of being sealed by the blast the cave was blown wide open. The Japs rushed out. Our sharpshooters cut them down.

After that the patrol found a field gun and knocked it out. This gun bore the marking: "Edgewood Arsenal."

Sergeant Herman Taylor (Russellville, Kentucky) carried a load of fresh ammunition two hundred yards over the rocks. Lieutenant Kenneth Yeomans (West Somerville, Massachusetts) and his platoon specialized all day in fragmentation charges and white phosphorus grenades. They burned twenty-five Japs to death.

On the same day the commanding officer of the Division taskforce shook hands with the commander of the paratroopers fighting on Topside. It was like Stanley meeting Livingstone in the Congo.

It was now 1400 February 11, and the sun oozed heat. Gun barrels and helmets became too hot to touch. We kept wondering why it was so quiet on Malinta Hill. We also kept wondering what had happened to the Third Platoon, marooned out there on the promontory.

Contact was finally made by radio.

"This is Joe Blow to King Three. King Three, tell me your situation."

"King Three to Joe Blow ... We're okay ... Over," they answered.

"Joe Blow asks have you had any trouble ... Over."

'Two attacks. We have three walking wounded. Not bad ... Over."

"What are you firing at ... ? What are you firing at ... ? Over."
At the other end somebody chuckled.
"Just good clean fun, we've got ..."
The Third Platoon explained: They had a bead on a distant water well, on the eastern end of the island, and the Nips seemed to have become mighty thirsty. They kept dashing up to the well with jugs and the marksmen of the Third Platoon were picking them off.
"Good. Sit tight."
"We're sitting all right."
"Roger—out."

Orders were to hold Malinta Hill and the other position as bulkheads denying the enemy a pooling of his strength. Already our battalion was spread so thinly that no reinforcements could be spared for Company "K." So we reorganized our decimated squads. We dug in deeper to meet another night. The sun beat down on us with devouring power. The pale rock reflected the heat and drilled it into our brains and bones. Some men collapsed. A few lost heart and hid their heads like whipped dogs.

We asked the battalion for water.

"No more water," was the reply. Nips on a suicide mission had demolished the water purification units during the night. The nearest water was five miles away in Mariveles and must be transported by barge. More and more the belt buckle on the island-woman's midriff—Malinta Hill—became to us the navel of a leprous whore. Another night towered over the mountains of Luzon.

Down near the beach a lone Jap with a mine crawled under the Red Cross wagon and blew up the wagon and himself as well. The Red Cross man came running. His wagon, his cigarettes, his soap, coffee, cokes, toothpastes and magazines were one big mush mixed up with minced Jap.

A mortar barrage fell at 2330. At midnight the Japs attacked. They threw in everything they had. Again they scaled that impossible cliff in a death-seeking, death-dealing frenzy. They had made up their stubborn minds to claw out a passage that would let them join their well trounced Topside garrison.

Lieutenant Albert S. Barham, a Texan from Eastland, was the first to hear them pussyfoot up the slope. Barham had won his commission fighting at Leyte. He launched some flares. The hillside swarmed with crawling shapes. We looked right into their faces, twenty feet below us. Our fire transformed their stealth into a crazy rampage. They were like demons running amuck, half tiger, half baboon.

I've never heard so many grenades thrown in so short a time. When we ran short of grenades, "Texo Barham had been hit in the face. But he ducked through the uproar to where Company "Love" had its perimeter. I never saw a man sprint so fast on all fours. Sergeant Herman Taylor helped him. Soon they came back with more grenades. For this time the Japs had enough. They scrambled downhill and vanished in the dark. Some twenty of our men were hit. But we had killed plenty. One of the few who did not kill a Jap was Corporal Edward J. Stachelek of North Adams, Massachusetts. While grenade fragments and bullets ripped the night, he slipped from hole to hole to tend the wounded. Then he was wounded himself.

"Take it easy," we told him. "Let somebody else carry on."

"No," said Aid Man Stachelek, "my mission, ain't it?"

And he went right ahead with sulfa and bandage kit, as did another corpsman, Frederick Lederer, who has a wife in Saint Joseph, Missouri.

Just then the moon rose over Manila Bay like a fine orange. It outlined our positions on top to observers around the base of the hill. Lying wounded in a foxhole, Lieutenant Henry G. Kitnik (Broughton, Pennsylvania) was swearing at the moon.

"Hank" Kitnik had taken command of "King" Company when our captain was killed by grenades. But "Hank" was hit in the back of the head and in the arm, and so another Pennsylvanian, Lieutenant Robert R. Fugitti (Philadelphia) took over.

Besides the indestructible Barham, Bob Fugitti had only one officer left, Lieutenant Albert J. Cruver of Seattle. Through the moonlight they crawled, counting the fit.

"How many in the Second Platoon, Al?"

"Eight," reported Al Cruver.

"First Platoon?"

"Nine," came a muffled reply. "Grenades are all gone."

"Christ, what a mess."

The Weapons Platoon reported only eleven men fit for action. Headquarters had ten: linemen, messengers, supply crew, cooks, all of them fighting with the rest.

Thirty-eight men and three officers to hang onto Malinta Hill. "I'm going to get some more grenades," Tex Barham announced—and off he went, bandaged head and all.

We pulled our men closer together to tighten up the mangled line. We waited through the longest minutes of the longest night that ever straddled the Philippines. A few canteens of water were carried up from the beach. The carrying party had trouble with snipers. Only the wounded got water. The rest of us chewed our tongues. A shadow bobbed up in the dark.

That was Barham, coming back with eight more grenades.

The minutes wore on.

"What time is it?"

"Same time as this time last night."

"Hey, what time is it?"

"Oh, pipe down."

"What time is it?"

"Banzai time."

"Has anybody got the time?"

Every five minutes someone asked about the time.

The Japs attacked at 0300. First there was ferocious mortar ° then the frantic yelling, the hot bloody sweat, the bullets and grenades, the kicks and cold steel, the wordless rage, the whole twisted monstrosity of killing in the dark. That went on for an hour before the enemy streaked back downhill where he belonged. Five more of our men were hit.

Again we reorganized, now thirty-three of us, sat tight, sweating out the dawn.

One hundred and fifty Jap cadavers stared up from the limestone cliffside.

With daylight a carrying party came through with water and rations. They took away the wounded. Then another company relieved us and we dragged ourselves down to the sweltering beach. There was a bevy of medics dealing out "something to quiet your nerves."

"Make mine rye," cracked a kid with blood in his hair.

They gave us capsules.

We flopped into the sand and slept, sweating while we slept, with firing loud a couple of hundred yards away, among millions of flies and the stench of dead men decomposing in the sun. Warships stood offshore, shelling the cliffs around Breakwater Point.

The battle for Corregidor was not finished when we woke up to a meal of canned frankfurters, canned sauerkraut and dehydrated potatoes. The whole rutted island was still heavy with trouble.

"Item" Company cleaned out the North Dock area for the second time. One of the squads ran into grenade ambush among the rocks. Sergeant Owen Williams (Chicago, Illinois) cried a warning. The squad ducked and was saved. But Williams' warning shout had given his position away. He dropped mortally wounded.

"Item" Company swept forward. They killed forty Nips and captured two machineguns.

"Love" Company men cleaned out caves and tunnel entrances around Malinta Hill. They blew up three naval guns mounted in rock bunkers. They also destroyed a huge fourteen-inch cannon. The men of "Love" changed the name of their company to "Lucky." In five days of fighting on the hill they had not lost one man.

The Japs were still firing doggedly from Engineers Point. Elsewhere our tank-destroyers smashed pillboxes which the Nips had built in an old ice plant between Topside and the Hill.

At one time word came through that the portable hospital treating wounded paratroopers on Topside had used up all its plasma and whole blood and needed more. That hospital was two miles from Black Beach. Two men on a tank-destroyer volunteered to slug through with more plasma.

They stowed the life-saving stuff under their cannon and roared off along a winding road. Enemy machineguns near the ice plant beat against the armor of the SPM.

Through the sight slots of the tank-destroyer Sergeant Bill Hartman (Peoria, Illinois) and Corporal Mike Nolan (New York City) saw a shell-wrecked bridge ahead. The bridge lay askew and there was a jagged gap. Their self-propelled cannon weighed twenty-three tons.

"Give her the works," said Hartman.

Either the bridge would hold, or it would not.

The tracks ground over the jagged gap, lapping over four inches on each side of the span. The bridge groaned—and held.

Past shredded clumps of vegetation and a line of pillboxes the tank-destroyer reached its destination. The medics took the plasma and hurried away. Others unloaded a few cans of water which happened to be aboard the mount.

"Sure wish you had brought us some more water," a doctor said. "We've none up here."

"We'll bring it, Doc," said Hartman.

The wrecked bridge groaned and held and the paratroopers got their water. Back on the beach Hartman and Nolan drove toward a gasoline dump to tank up. Before they reached it their motor bucked and stopped. A connecting rod had broken. Bill Hartman stood among swarms of flies and stared at his mount. Its name, big and white, was SAD SACK. Mike Nolan counted the bullet scars on the armor. He stopped after counting two hundred.

On February 19 our mortars put three hundred pounds of high explosive on Goal Post Ridge where our gallant captain had been killed.

February 20 we spent thinking up ways of finishing off the Japs in the big tunnels of Malinta Hill. We knew that there were hundreds of them holding out in the tunnels. At night they came out to raise hell; at dawn they crawled out of our sight and reach. We tried this and that. "Love" Company men threw smoke grenades into a tunnel in the hope that the rising smoke would curl from the air vent that serviced it. The vent could then be blocked and the Nips' air supply cut off. But the smoke stayed in the tunnel. So did the Japanese.

There was a threat in the cavernous bowels of Malinta Hill that had us all on edge. A captured list of supplies in the Hospital Tunnel showed that there were stowed away inside the hill 35,000 artillery shells, more than 10,000 powder charges, more than 2,000 pounds of TNT, some two million rounds of rifle and machinegun ammunition, 80,000 mortar shells, more than 93,000 hand grenades, 2,900 antitank mines among many other parcels of war.

At 9:30 P.M., February 21, the Japs blew up Malinta Hill.

First there was a rumbling noise. It sounded like freight trains thundering beneath the rocks of Corregidor. Then there were mighty explosions and the island trembled. Sheets of flame shot from the tunnel mouths. Flames belched through the summit of the hill. A crumbling hillside buried alive an "Able" Company detachment on a roadblock below. Sections of road were blown out. Rocks and wreckage and clouds of Jap bodies sailed high in the mellow night. From other places Jap machineguns were firing wild into the flanks of Malinta Hill. About fifty Nips, in a column of twos, marched out of a tunnel as if they were on parade. Our machineguns mowed them down. Other Japs came dashing out of other tunnels. Our guns kept barking.

Two nights later they tried again. Rocks crumbled and fire belched from every hole in the rocks.

Our engineers went to work to carry the job to an end. Quantities of gasoline were set afire in the remaining tunnel mouths, and the entrances were then sealed by blasts. For days there came dimly out of the tunnels the sounds of shouting, of mass singing, of muffled pistol shots and grenade explosions. Then silence.

CHAPTER TWENTY

THUNDER TO DAVAO
(The Notebook of a Cross-Island Campaign)

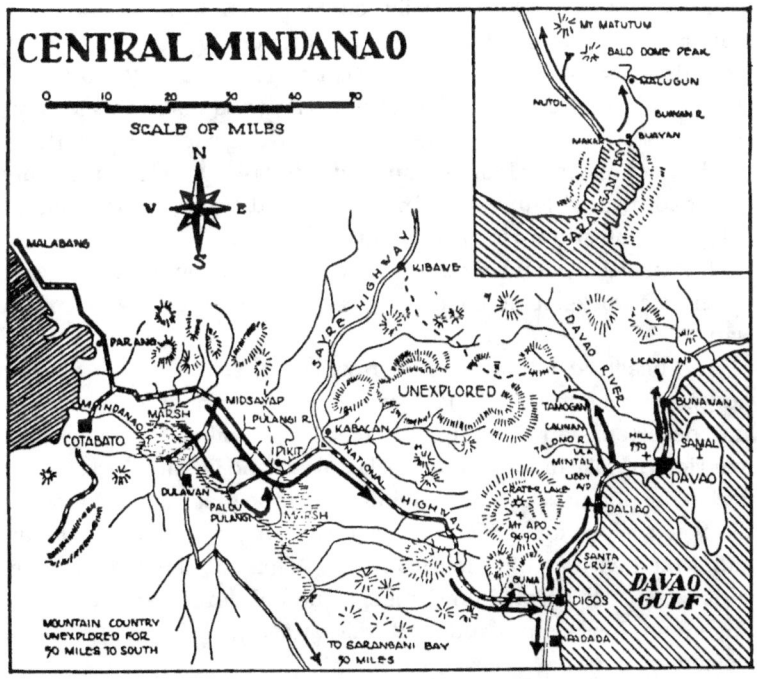

THE DIVISION struck Mindanao like a thunderbolt. It struck with a hundred ships, with thousands of men, scores of field guns, hundreds of trucks. It struck where the Japanese least expected it to strike: at the town of Parang, in Moro Gulf, at dawn, April ty, 1945.

The Division convoy had steamed out of San Jose harbor, Mindoro Island, at 1300, Friday, April 13. Original plans had called for an invasion of Mindanao at the harbor of Malabang. However, a radio message received on the way had brought intelligence that the Malabang area had already been liberated by guerilla forces. Whereupon General

Woodruff boldly changed his plan of invasion while the convoy was still on the high seas. Instead of landing at Malabang, he struck Parang.

The Division's goal was the city of Davao. At that time the bulk of an estimated 50,000 Japanese troops defending Mindanao were encamped in the Province of Davao, one hundred fifty miles east by trail from Parang. The naval base of Davao and the surrounding countryside has been for decades a hub of Japanese colonization. After the fall of Manila it was Nippon's last major bastion in the Philippines.

Broad valleys, high mountains, belts of jungle, lay between Parang and Davao. More than fifty streams and rivers obstructed the Division's advance. They flowed through wild country inhabited by Mohammedan Moros; and by tribes still addicted to head hunting and cannibalism. Maps depicted large expanses of the country in white patches and the legend "Unexplored." The "National Highway" to Davao was mostly a one-lane track with a thousand-and-one twisting curves. The Japanese had burned or blasted more than a hundred bridges along the route. They had planted hundreds of mines, plotted scores of ambushes to delay the fantastic cross-island rush.

The Division pounded across Mindanao, from Parang to Davao, in two hectic weeks. It set an all-time record of mile-eating in tropical warfare.

The beach at Parang was narrow, black, steep. Jungle-covered ridges arose a hundred yards inland. The town of Parang was wrecked and deserted. Jap demolition, American bombs, Jap vengeance, American naval cannonade and rocket blasts and infantry invasion had driven the populace into the mountains. As the first waves stormed up the beach, a lone figure met them: a brown, sinewy woman clad in rags and armed with an old American rifle. When she saw the Division's code letter "V," painted on the jeeps and bulldozers, she raised two fingers of her right hand and said gravely, "Victoree—you are welcome."

On that first day the Division seized Parang, Port Baras, Malabang air field, and a thirty-five mile stretch of the coast. Assault companies forded three rivers and slogged five miles inshore. A 240-foot bridge across the Ambal River had been burned. Infantry waded through shoulder-deep with all weapons and ammunition that could be carried by hand. An amphibious reconnaissance group skirted southward along the shore and entered the gloomy estuary of the Mindanao River. It reported "many crocodiles but no Japs." Combat engineers fell to and built new bridges almost overnight.

A soldier from New York and another from California slew the first two Japs of the new invasion. Sergeant Robert McKenzie of Syracuse and Sergeant Paul Salas of Richmond probed through a coastal swamp. They chanced upon a slit-like opening in the vines. Peering up at them were two Japanese armed with rifles and a copra sack full of grenades. The New Yorker fired and killed one. The Californian heaved a grenade and killed the other. "Good work," an officer commented.

"Reflex action," said Bob McKenzie.

The first casualty in the invasion was Brooklyn's Colonel William J. Verbeck. It was his fourth wound received in battle. The colonel had dipped a helmet full of water from a stream and he was washing his face in front of his regimental command post. In a nearby wrecked building lurked a sniper. The sniper fired as the colonel bent forward to rinse his face. That saved Verbeck's life. The bullet plowed a flesh wound across the officer's back.

Under a palm, digging beef from ration cans, sat three scouts with tommyguns. They heard the shot followed by their colonel's oath. A second later the Jap pitched head first out of the ruined building. A corpsman had jumped from an ambulance and shot the sniper. Submachine bullets riddled him before he struck the ground. Almost simultaneously, the Division Commander, General Woodruff, stepped into a spider-hole and came out swearing and with cracked ribs.

The first Americans to die in the last campaign of the Philippine war were victims of accidents. One night a green replacement crawled out of his foxhole to pee. A soldier in a neighboring hole saw movement in the dark and shot him dead. On another advanced night perimeter a soldier thought he heard a noise in a clump of bushes. He tossed a grenade. The grenade struck a palm trunk and bounced back into the thrower's foxhole, where it exploded and killed him. A rifle squad had cornered four Japanese in a cave. The Japanese killed themselves with grenades. That same day, as the squad proceeded through an *abaca* field in single file, an eighteen-year-old infantryman committed suicide while marching by slipping a cocked grenade down the neck opening of his shirt. The blast tore him to pieces; it also killed the American marching to his immediate rear.

Lieutenant John Ebbets of Miami, Florida, poked around the ruins of Parang. In a half-smashed cubicle he found five carrier pigeons. Two had been killed by the concussions of the preparatory rocket barrage.

Three were alive, but stunned. All of them had messages attached to their legs. John Ebbets called a Nisei soldier to translate the messages. The text of all was identical.

"The Americans are here," it said.

That evening John Ebbets and the Nisei brewed pigeon stew. Both men were later killed in the storming of Mandog Hill, north of Davao.

An eighteen-ton tank-destroyer rumbled over the ramp of a landing craft. Its weight pressed the landing boat away from the shore. The big machine toppled into twenty feet of water. Inside, Corporal James Gibson from Oklahoma City tackled the problem of escaping death by drowning in an armored coffin. He came out alive. Three bulldozers towed the sunken destroyer ashore.

Through bizarre mountain passes the battalions thrust inland. The cross-island road, long unused, twisted like a corkscrew through a dark welter of jungle, immense trees, ravines, cliffs, tangled stream beds and inscrutable mountain sides. The sun blazed, and among the sinister ramparts of vegetation and house-high grass there stirred not the ghost of a breeze. Cases of heat exhaustion among the spearhead elements approached a hundred a day. Names like Simuay River, Tumbao, Dulauan, Lake Lanao were heard, passed and forgotten. An amphibious assault group seized the harbor of Cotabato, the Moro capital south of Parang.

Throughout the Mindanao River country the guerilla organizations were strong. They were led by a former mining engineer, Colonel Wendell Fertig of Boulder, Colorado. Fertig had fought on Bataan when the Japanese invaded the Philippines in 1942. After the American surrender he had escaped by native *banca* to Mindanao and had become the driving brain behind guerilla doings in the islands' southwest.

Enemy resistance in the first days of the Division's drive was sporadic. Bridges burned. Ambushes flared. Nothing more. Nippon's commanders had never reckoned that the drive on Davao could be made from the west, over abandoned mountain roads and half-explored wilderness. All fortifications and fire lanes along Mindanao's "National Highway" faced east.

They all faced the wrong direction.

Sweating through a meadow of sword grass a four man patrol led by Sergeant Joseph Buckovich, of Brooklyn, followed a fresh-made trail. They came upon five Japanese. The Japs had been outraced by the

American advance. Haggard and weary they lay asleep under a tree. A volley killed the sleepers.

Then Buckovich heard a rustling in the grass beside him. A sixth Jap was trying to creep away. Joe shot him through the head.

"This field is crawling with Japs," he said slowly. "Let's give her a good spray."

Every man in the patrol opened rapid fire. Bullets swished through the grass in all directions. There came screams and Japs charging in frantic groups of two and three. A bullet knocked the rifle from Buckovich's hand.

When it was over they counted. There were eighteen corpses.

Lieutenant Robert Drennan of Rock Hill, South Carolina, was passing through a mountain *barrio* at the head of his platoon. A shaggy native accosted him. The Moro waved a paper in front of the officer's face.

"What's that?" asked Drennan.

"You from Nineteenth Infantry?"

"How do you know?" Drennan demanded.

"Please read the paper, sir," the native said.

Drennan read. It was a discharge certificate from the Nineteenth Infantry Regiment, issued in Hawaii, in 1924, to Private Maximo Cabayan.

The islander pounded his chest. "I am Maximo Cabayan," he announced. "I weesh to serve my old outfit."

Bob Drennan made him an interpreter and scout.

A Nineteenth Infantry battalion commanded by Lt. Col. Joy K. Vallery of Lincoln, Nebraska, came to a raging river in the middle of a rain-filled night. Engineers had improvised a foot bridge one hundred feet long. The nine hundred men of the battalion negotiated the crossing one by one. For the first fifty feet they inched along a log, with another, higher log serving as a hand hold. For the next fifty feet it was the same, except that the hand hold disappeared. One steel helmet was lost.

The river, it was found later, was the home of many crocodiles.

A bridge guard crouched in the rain. Peering over the rim of his hole he could discern the road only as a dim ribbon which vanished in darkness five yards away.

Suddenly a grenade exploded at the water's edge.

Corporal J. W. Owensby took no chances. He had in his belt twelve clips of ammunition—ninety-six rounds. He spent the hours until dawn firing down the roadside ditches. His shots went into complete darkness. At dawn he found a dead Japanese three yards from his foxhole.

Sergeant Charles Worthington of Compton, Kansas, wanted to take a prisoner. His platoon slogged down the road which at this spot spiraled into a canyon. Scouts ranged ahead. Ahead and below them lay a stream bed.

Abruptly the lead scout stopped. He had seen a bush by the stream bank jerk to cover behind a large tree. It became a question of who ambushed whom. The patrol moved stealthily through flanking thickets. Its men then waded along the stream. They pounced on the enemy from the rear. Two Japs were killed. Three committed hara-kiri by grenade. One ran.

Charles Worthington chased the running Jap. He wanted a prisoner. His pursuit was so rapid that he could not come to a quick halt when his quarry suddenly turned and cocked a grenade. Worthington swerved sideways and pitched headlong into a swamp. He held his breath and waited for the grenade. But the Jap had other intentions. He held the grenade to his stomach and bowed. The grenade exploded.

Machinegunner Arthur Imm of Long Island, Kansas, was a night perimeter guard for a battery of field artillery. He sat in a shallow foxhole at the edge of the cannoneers' bivouac and stared into the darkness. Forty feet away the jungle stood like a mysterious wall.

A half hour before midnight the gunner felt that something was moving in front of him. He trained his gun and fired a burst of six rounds.

A bird screeched. Nothing moved.

Next morning he found a Japanese soldier with six holes in his neck. Strapped around the dead man were two land mines, eight grenades and a bangalore torpedo four feet long. The cannoneers now call their guard "Dead Eye Imm."

Sergeant Robert Savidge of Los Angeles led a detail carrying rations to the perimeter of a spearhead patrol. One of his men detected movement in the jungle twilight. They all threw themselves flat on the ground, their rifles ready. Something was prowling through the foliage.

"Holy cats," whispered Private Francis Ridge, of Sacramento,

California, "I can see 'em. They're camouflaged with fur coats."
He pointed, and Robert Savidge followed the direction with his eyes.

"Dope," he said. "That's apes."

When the ration detail reached their destination after a five mile march, scouts of the spearhead patrol recounted how "some kind of man-sized monkeys" had set off booby traps around their perimeter during the previous night.

In the advance across Mindanao the Division's vanguard bypassed many Japanese detachments. The Japs, when overtaken, faded into the flanking jungle. Ten yards away from the trails they were safe and unseen. They then slept during the day and banded together for raids under cover of darkness.

Sergeant James Keeses of Winchester, Ohio, marched with a patrol which had traversed fifteen miles of jungle in a search for Japanese bivouacs. On the third night of their mission the patrol was attacked. The attacking Japs wore knee-length nets entwined with leafy twigs. In the dark the keenest eye could not distinguish them from bushes. They crept to within ten feet of the patrol's camp before they jumped up and rushed with shrill cries. Two Americans were bayoneted before the fire power of automatic rifles could be brought to bear.

Hard in the wake of the trail-blazing infantry and combat engineers rolled trucks, ambulances, bulldozers and artillery; and with the artillery came the Cub planes of the artillery observers. But with each nightfall all traffic stopped and all units dug foxholes and posted perimeter guards. The holes of the perimeter guards were separated from one another by but a few paces. Still, Japs managed to creep through at night.

Lieutenant Robert Price of Skiatook, Oklahoma, was an artillery observation flier. He parked his Piper Cub inside the perimeter and went to sleep beneath an artillery truck.

Toward midnight he heard a flurry of footfalls. Price grasped his pistol. A moment later a bomb exploded. Debris fluttered out of the night. The officer saw three shadowy figures run past the truck. He emptied his pistol. Two Japs dial. The third escaped. The Piper Cub plane was a mass of brightly burning wreckage.

One morning a guerilla wearing a Notre Dame University basketball shirt and an American Legion cap walked into an advanced perimeter. He told the commander that he knew of an enemy bivouac two miles off the Division's left flank.

"How many Japs?" he was asked.

"About three hundred," he said.

It seemed a worthwhile artillery target.

But the guerilla was unable to pinpoint the location of the bivouac on a military map. It was decided to send him aloft in a Cub plane. A sergeant from Portland, Oregon, guided the native warrior into a plane. They took off from the road. In the flight over the mountains the guerilla became violently sick. His face turned green. Fright wrinkled his face as the Cub swept low over the tangled wilderness below. He also became enormously excited.

"If you touch the controls," the sergeant warned, "I must knock you out."

The guerilla calmed down. He motioned the pilot onward with expressive hands. Then his eyes gleamed. He had spotted the bivouac.

The sergeant radioed. Shells screamed over the jungles. The guerilla rolled with laughter when he saw the Japs flee like hares from the area of explosions.

"If you don't sit still," the sergeant warned him again, "I must knock you out."

The company slogged through the seventh hour that day on their forced march on Davao. The faces of the men were drawn and their uniforms were black with sweat. Packs were heavy and weapons heavier. The muzzles of a hundred rifles and sub-machineguns were pointed at the barriers of jungle while their bearers marched.

Scouts signaled a warning. There was a faint crunching in the thickets. The company swarmed off the road. In two seconds the road was empty. Fingers rested on triggers of a hundred rifles and sub-machineguns.

Out of the forest stalked a lean, barefooted woman. About her were five skinny children. The legs of all were covered with sores. The woman looked steadily up and down the empty road, at the gun muzzles in the roadside ditches.

"Don't kill," she said. "Only medicines I want."

The soldiers relaxed. They sprawled at the edge of the green barricades and rested while their aid man, Albert Wright of Seattle, treated the jungle rot on the skinny brown legs.

> "Movement is very difficult due to intense heat in the high grass which has overgrown the road. A distance of twelve road miles was covered during the period."

(from a Field Report, April 20)

Where the trans-Mindanao road crosses the broad Mindanao River the mountains and jungles give way to a wide central valley. There are rolling expanses of *kunai* grass, palm plantations untended for years, banana groves and *abaca* fields denser than any jungle can be. At the junction of road and river lies Fort Pikit.

On November 19 planes ranging over Fort Pikit were greeted by machinegun fire. Observers saw that the big steel bridge was blasted, its span sunken in the river. The planes strafed the fort and its surroundings with incendiary shells. When they departed the fort was burning, adjoining barracks were afire, and a Jap supply truck had gone up in flames.

That day, in the march on Fort Pikit, the Nineteenth Infantry vanguard skirmished with twenty-five Japs and killed eighteen. They captured three trucks. The trucks had been camouflaged to look like bushes. At nightfall the advance guard engaged a band of thirty Japs in a fire fight. The ambush was destroyed. Thirteen enemies were killed.

Twenty-First Regiment patrols contacted eighty Japs near the village of Lomopog and killed eighteen. Canoe patrols in the estuary of the Mindanao River killed two more.

Two Americans died in action that day, and five fell wounded.

A day later the Nineteenth Regiment crossed the Libungan River. The bridge had been burned. The river is three hundred feet wide and too deep to be forded. The riflemen built rafts. A team of swimmers carried a cable to the far bank and the regiment crossed the river on cable-drawn rafts. In a fire fight three Japanese trucks were wrecked. Five trucks were captured intact. Of these five, three were found booby-trapped with grenades. The traps were disarmed. The trucks were put to immediate use, U.S. ARMY *. * DONT SHOOT chalked onto their sides.

Infantrymen seized the town of Midsayap. They captured two hidden supply dumps which contained mortar and artillery ammunition, grenades, two hundred American rifles, motor fuel, dynamite and twelve tons of rice.

Reconnaissance groups of the Thirty-Fourth Regiment captured Fort Pikit in a surprise thrust up the Mindanao River. On shallow-draft barges they mounted captured Japanese machineguns, cannon and rocket guns salvaged from wrecked American planes. They piloted these "home-made" gunboats up sixty miles of crocodile-ridden river courses, past dark swamplands and over muddy shallows. They appeared off Fort Pikit like men from Mars, all armament blazing. Their radio message astounded the Division's planners.

"Stormed Fort Pikit," the message said. "Hoisted flag. Awaiting infantry."

Soon a fleet of landing craft was on its way upstream from Cotabato to ferry heavy equipment across the Mindanao River. The whole Thirty-Fourth Infantry Regiment marched seven miles to a river town named Paidu-Pulangi. On the way some of the riflemen swapped rifle ammunition for fine Moro swords. The proud and never-conquered Moros used this ammunition to shoot Americans and Japs alike. In Paidu-Pulangi the regiment boarded ocean going assault ships (LCI's) and pushed upriver to Fort Pikit. General Woodruff boldly accepted hazards that would have frightened off a more cautious commander. The trip was an adventurous exploitation of the river highway in spite of sand bars and many hairpin turns. The ships' sides plowed the flanking jungle and the Navy crews had the novel experience of sweeping jungle foliage from the decks of their ships. At one spot gunners detected movement behind a promontory in the river. They promptly opened fire. Around the bend an Army gunboat was surprised by the sudden overhead bursts and quickly replied in kind. The Army-Navy duel ended when the ships met head on in the bend of the river.

Unloading at Fort Pikit, the men of the Thirty-Fourth Regiment—who two months earlier had stormed Corregidor from the sea—became the overland battering ram of the Division. They swept twenty miles eastward and overran Kabakan on April 22. Kabakan is the cross-roads of the east-west and north-south highways of central Mindanao. Blasting ambushes, circling burning bridges, and fording rivers the riflemen speared eastward out of Kabakan and penetrated Saguing, thirty miles from Davao Gulf, on April 24, far beyond the reach of supporting artillery. They pushed through immense swarms of locusts. Through whirring insect clouds they approached a bridge which seemed intact. The Japs blew it up into their faces.

A Moro wearing a wine-red turban and a magnificent curved gold and ivory dagger wandered into "Fox" Company's perimeter. He asked to see the "commandant."

"Any Japs?" the company commander asked him.

"Yes, sir." The Moslem pointed toward the river. "Two thousand yards from here I see seventy-five Japanese soldiers, sir."

"What were they doing?"

"Some cook rice, some sleep. They make me chop wood."

"What's the place like?"

"Bamboo," the Moro said.

"Fox" Company was alerted and pushed toward a bamboo forest on the south bank of the Mindanao River. Stealthily they surrounded the bamboo. But abruptly mortar shells rained from nowhere. The shells covered every square yard of the bamboo grove with a checkerboard of explosions. "A trap," the company commander growled. "Where's that native bait?" The Moro had vanished.

As the company withdrew from the barrage a howl arose out of an expanse of sword grass on its right. A company of Japanese rushed out of the grass in a flanking attack. The Japs charged with bayonets fixed, with grenades, spears and sabers. "Fox" Company quickly fell back to safer ground.

On the left flank, a 36-year-old German-American, Private William Roepke, of Philadelphia, did not hear the command to retreat. He lay behind a bamboo tree and held his ground. At the time he did not know that many Japanese were armed with captured American rifles. He heard the heavy barks of the Enfields and he was happy.

Roepke was of a stalwart breed. His blond mustache bristled. He held his post for three hours and then the yelling and shooting stopped. After another hour he became aware that his company had retreated and that he was alone in the rear of the Japanese lines. He stood up to peer through the underbrush and what he saw was Japs. He ducked low and did not move from the spot.

Morning wore on into afternoon and the sun covered the land with brooding heat. Roepke drank the last water in his canteen and waited. He was thirsty. Thirst waxed into torture. He could hear the Japanese jabber among the bamboo and *kunai* but he could not see more than four feet in any direction. The sun set and the Japs pitched camp and Bill Roepke found himself marooned in the middle of an enemy bivouac. He heard the Japs kill chickens and cook rice and defecate, and he heard them clean their weapons. Darkness fell and Roepke did not dare to move. Each hour the enemy guards exchanged hissing cries to assure each other that they were awake. Enemy patrols came and went. Roepke was exhausted and half out of his mind from the day-long hammer blows of the sun upon his helmet. Heavy rains fell during the night. Bill Roepke buried himself in mud and rested.

Came dawn and another day. The lone soldier was ragged and dirty and hungry and he felt a pile-driver pounding in his brain. His cocky blond mustache was gray and drooping.

He decided to shoot his way out. He stood up and staggered toward the river through grass thickets eight feet high. He passed groups of Japanese squatting in his path. But he could not bring himself to shoot at them unless they first saw him. "Hallo," he said roughly. The Japs turned, startled, and Roepke fired. He killed thirteen Japanese before he reached the river.

He dived into the river and let the current carry him away. He knew that there were crocodiles in the river. He lay there, floating on his back, looking at the sky, and tried to drown his fear by singing German songs. A native in a canoe rescued him. The Filipino paddled him to the nearest camp. Soldiers on the perimeter stared at the gaunt apparition.

Bill Roepke stumbled between the line of foxholes and collapsed.

"I ate a lot of Yaps for breakfast," he mumbled.

A Jap bombing plane appeared over Division headquarters at 6 A.M. and went into a dive. The general and his aides were awakened by a roar of machinegun fire. The plane swept away, circled, dived again. Again it was driven off. The enemy pilot then spotted a team of wiremen stringing telephone wires along the roadside thickets. He dived on the wire party and dropped a 500-pound bomb.

A crater opened in the road.

There were many craters in the road, put there by American planes bombing columns of fleeing Japanese and by Japanese mines. The Japanese, knocked off balance by this stormwind advance "from the wrong direction," were fleeing toward Davao. The Division's pace gave them no time to build fortifications facing west. The road was lined with cunningly hidden emplacements, but they were useless to the Japs; their fire lanes pointed east, toward Davao. The fleeing Japs left burning bridges, burning barracks, burning supply dumps and burning trucks.

A group of Japanese civilians trudging toward Davao was overtaken by footsore patrols. There were thirty. There were twenty thousand more in Davao. Among those caught there was a mother with six children. "Americans," the mother asked, "after you have killed me, will you take care of my children?"

An artillery corporal reached into his pack. "Here, lady," he said. "Better take these rations. Your kids look hungry."

Mines!

Between Fort Pikit and Davao the Japanese had mined the road with many hundreds of aerial bombs. The bombs were buried so that only an inch of their noses showed above ground. Wires attached to the detonating mechanism led forty to fifty yards to foxholes dug in the flanking jungle. And in each foxhole sat a Jap. A tug upon the wire would set off an explosion violent enough to blow a hundred men to death.

The first bomb-mine encountered was made to naught by Jap eagerness. A squad led by Sergeant Clifford Barnes of Oakfield, Wisconsin, received sudden machinegun fire from the front. In a split second the soldiers sought cover. It was only a moment later that other Japs pulled a hidden wire and detonated a bomb buried thirty yards ahead of Clifford Barnes. The members of the squad were stunned by the concussion. But except for bruises caused by flying pieces of road and vegetation they were unhurt.

Barnes silently thanked the enemy gunners. Had they not prematurely opened fire, his squad would have been caught standing upright on the road. Not one would have escaped alive. He heard a Japanese officer in the bushes berate his men for yanking the wires too soon.

Now mortars accompanied the vanguard platoons. Their shells set the roadside jungle afire and drove the wire pullers out of their holes. Combat engineers marked buried bombs with bits of paper propped on sticks, and past them and around them the advance rolled on.

The Japanese on the road to Davao were of many units. Japs name their fighting teams after their commanders. There was the Harada Unit and the Suzuki Unit. There were members of the Tanaka and Watari Units. There were first line infantry troops, the 100th Imperial Division, Japs from labor battalions, the crews of sunken naval vessels, Imperial Marines, native conscripts and volunteers from Davao, and aviation personnel fighting as foot troops.

Hidden in grass huts and tunnels patrols captured nineteen cases of hand grenades, seventy naval torpedoes, forty aerial bombs, twenty-two mines—the first of vastly larger hauls to come.

General Woodruff had reason to be satisfied. Satisfied with his men and with himself. Hard-striking troops giving their utmost; audacity of command and bold self-confidence; those were the elements which made possible one Division's apparently foolhardy dash across an island manned by the numerical equal of three enemy divisions. The corridor carved out of Mindanao was less than one mile wide. Communications and supply lines from Parang were long, vulnerable and only thinly held. Night ambushes on rear communication lines became a common occurrence. But it was no rarity in this campaign to see patrols of riflemen dart off the road to make room for a speeding jeep driven by their commanding general deep in Jap country; a jouncing little car, the burly, dusty, mustached Texan behind the wheel, three bodyguards with sub-machineguns perched on the remaining seats.

Not to be outdone by the general was the Division Chaplain, Major Paul Slavik of New York. He, too, drove his own jeep, ever on the move to "visit the men up front." One Sunday General Woodruff's car was stopped by a burning bridge. On the far end of the bridge stood another jeep, the chaplain's, and arms akimbo, the two men exchanged greetings across the blazing timbers.

"Chaplain," rumbled the general. "I see you in the damndest places! How'd you get across?"

"This bridge was all right when I drove over it a little while ago," the chaplain said.

The general sought a by-pass. He nosed his jeep down a steep bank, half rolling, half sliding, and miraculously made it climb the other side.

He asked the chaplain, "See any Japs?"

Slavik shook his head.

Woodruff wiped the sweat from his face. He stepped on the accelerator.

"What a hell of a way to spend a Sabbath," he growled. Seconds later the chaplain saw him vanish in a cloud of dust in the direction of Davao.

In a clear mountain stream, beneath the charred and still smoking bridge, a combat patrol of twenty stripped to bathe. The soldiers left their clothes and their weapons on the bank and plunged into the water.

Without warning, without as much as a splash, a lone Japanese slipped around a nearby bend in the stream. His light machinegun spat lead.

The bathers scattered into the underbrush. All were naked. Some were covered with soap suds. None was armed.

It did not occur to the lone Jap that twenty American rifles lay unguarded only a little way off. He stopped in the stream bed and sprayed the thickets. That gave two of the bathers a chance to crawl to their rifles. The Jap died.

Soldiers speaking:

Private First Class George Mahnke, Napoleon, Ohio: Nips are stubborn unto death. I was on patrol and we were stopped all of a sudden by mortar fire which came from a banana plantation. After about twenty shells the Japs stopped firing their mortars. They came rushing at us in a bunch, yelling, swinging their bayonets and shooting their rifles. We broke up the charge with our own fire. But after a few minutes they charged again, yelling "Banzai!" Our B.A.R.'s mowed them down. Instead of going back to their mortars the fools rushed us a third time. The last of the lot died feet in front of our firing line. We counted forty-six dead Nips. We had one man wounded by a hand grenade.

Private First Class Joseph Reed, Adrian, Michigan: I was the lead scout of a ten-man patrol. I came to a quick-flowing river and stopped. The bridge was out and still smoking. I lay there for a minute or so and studied the bushes on the far bank. Japs like to set up ambushes at river crossings. They let the scout pass and wait until the body of the patrol is wading in the middle of the river. Then they cut loose. Sure enough, there was the muzzle of a machinegun sticking through the leaves. The Japs saw that I saw them and they opened fire. My patrol leader was hit. We then called for mortar fire on the machinegun nest. The shells set the bushes ablaze and the Nips disappeared.

Sergeant Eugene Rink, Huntington Park, California: I was guarding a bridge in the night. It was raining hard. I felt a blinding glare when a Jap rifle butt came crashing down on my helmet. The Jap thought I was dead. First he kicked me. Then he stepped over me and crept onto the bridge. But the rain beating in my face brought me out of the daze. I shot the Jap and then I raised my head and listened. There was a rustle in the brush and it wasn't the rain. I let fly with a grenade and I heard somebody groan. Before morning a third Jap came around. I shot him. By dawn I had a pretty bad headache.

Cannoneer John Lozinak, Ecldey, Pennsylvania: My artillery battalion displaced forward every day. The supply line up from Moro Gulf was a hundred miles long, with the jungle on both sides still filthy with Japs. They liked to creep up to the road-side with sacks of dynamite to blow up our ammunition trucks. One day I was patrolling a five-mile stretch of road in a jeep. A Moro came up to me and said: "Jap officer hide in cave over there." He pointed. I went over to the cave, and hollered for the yellow-belly to come out. Nothing moved. I threw a grenade into the cave. When the smoke cleared away I crawled into the cave, my tommygun at the ready. There was a pistol shot and I let the Nip have a long burst. The cave was full of mines. I can't figure out why they didn't blow up when my grenade went off. I got a Jap saber out of it, a bit shot up, but still good.

Sergeant Paul Brennan, Great Kills, New York: I was riding an ammunition truck behind our lines. We were rounding a bend in the road when suddenly three Japs jumped out of the bushes and threw a mine in the path of the truck. The mine exploded. One of my buddies was blown off the truck. A front wheel was blown off and sailed fifty yards through space. We dived off the truck and into the jungle and every second of it we fired wild in all directions. When things quieted down we looked around. There were nine dead Japs in the bushes.

Private David T. Aldrine, Paola, Kansas: I was with a four-man patrol in the jungle. With us was a Jap-speaking guerilla guide. Near a river a machinegun fired in our direction. The Nips did not see us, they fired by sound. The guide and I wriggled forward and I killed the Jap gunner with two shots. Then we heard somebody shout an order. I asked our guide, "What did that Jap say?" The guerilla translated: "Squad to the right, squad to the left, advance!" So I started shouting too. "Send up the company," I shouted. My two buddies in the rear caught on. They repeated the shout. "Send up the company." The Japs thought a whole company was coming for them. They stayed where they were and we could hear them digging in a hurry. That saved our patrol.

Lieutenant McCullough B. Lewis, Los Angeles, California: I was returning from the front with a convoy of three trucks that had taken up hot food for the men. We came to a spot where the jungle grew over the road like the top of a tunnel. A Jap ambush squad threw a bangalore torpedo out of the jungle in front of the lead truck. The truck ran over it. The torpedo failed to explode. Nine of us piled out of the trucks and went after the Japs. I shot two. Then a grenade blast knocked me down. When I raised my head I saw the muzzle of a Jap rifle one foot away from me. It was pointing at my heart. I stared and the hammer fell. A click. Misfire! I did not give the fellow a chance to pull his bolt for a second shot.

On April 27 the Division vanguard penetrated Digos Town, not far from the Gulf of Davao. They crossed several streams before they met bitter resistance. The bridges across all streams were "out." One was destroyed by shell fire; one was found burning the third, spanning the Digos River, had been craftily mined. Its timbers were almost sawn through, and seven mines had been attached to the cuts.

The road was heavily mined with aerial bombs. One of the mines blew up an armored reconnaissance car. Another mine, booby-trapped with a fountain pen, was set off fifty yards in front of the assistant Division commander's speeding jeep. General Cramer escaped unhurt. In turn, American planes bombed two Japanese truck convoys heading toward Davao under cover of darkness.

Ninety-four Japanese were killed on the approaches to Digos. The survivors fled toward the coast. Said one footsore infantryman: "I wish the Nips would stand a bit longer so that we could get some rest."

South-eastern Mindanao has long been a center of Japanese

influence. Before the Division's sweep, hordes of Japanese civilians were fleeing pell-mell toward Davao. Observation planes reported long, ragged columns trudging eastward. The enemy civilians had stripped their dwellings and left them burning. They had killed all their livestock. In some of the half-burned huts and barracks roast chicken stood untouched on charred tables. Among captured equipment that day were fifteen trucks loaded with rice; hundreds of grenades; cases of sake, sewing machines, spears, war clubs, knives and pictures of Nipponese glory.

A jeep occupied by three artillery officers bounced around a road bend and collided head on with a Japanese troop truck heading in the opposite direction. There were some fifteen astonished Japanese in the truck. The officers scrambled out of the jeep and dashed into the jungle. After a wild volley of shots the Jap truck turned and sped the way it had come. The officers climbed back into their jeep. They continued on their mission of finding new firing positions for their advancing artillery.

Dawn broke over the roadside foxhole.
"See that Jap I got last night," said Private Clarence Ralph of Fisher, Illinois.
His comrade peered over the rim of the hole.
"Hell," he said. "You got two."
"Nope, only one," said Ralph.
"Well, there are two Japs lying out there."
"Then one of them's alive."
Clarence Ralph raised his rifle. A much-alive Jap jumped to his feet and charged with a grenade. Ralph fired eight shots in swift succession. His score was two.

Communications Sergeant Tom Saunders from Somerset, Ohio, knew that Japs liked to cut telephone lines at night, then lie in ambush to kill the linemen who came to repair the break. So Saunders sent a guerilla scout ahead to investigate the terrain adjoining the break. Moro guerillas are the finest jungle fighters in the world. In noiseless and skilful crawling they outdo the most skilled Jap. The scout reported four Japanese lying in ambush. Saunders and his telephone crew circled the spot and shot them to death. In the enemy emplacement they found bangalore torpedoes, rifles, mines and seven wires which ran to seven 500-pound bombs buried overnight along the road.

Guarding one of the many makeshift bridges at night, Corporal Melvin Norwood of Glencoe, Alabama, heard a slurring noise at the edge of his foxhole. Norwood reached for the safety release of his automatic rifle. He touched the wrong release and his cartridge magazine dropped from the weapon instead.

With one cartridge in the chamber of his B.A.R., Norwood released the safety and fired. A Jap soldier crumpled so close that his head hung over the rim of the bridge guard's foxhole.

Hearing the shot, other Japs sprang up and charged. But Norwood had had time to reload. The B.A.R. clattered as only a B.A.R. can clatter in a dark night. The attackers faded away. At dawn there were three—dead.

The Moros of Mindanao remained a question mark throughout the campaign. Fine silversmiths and sword makers, they are also expert killers. They are the proudest, most untamed, most self-confident people of the tropical mountains. Like most Mohammedans they have little fear of death. They made war on Filipinos, Japanese and Americans alike. A Filipino guerilla party stalking a Japanese bivouac was ambushed by Moros. The Moros killed the Filipinos and cut off their heads. Then they took the weapons they had captured from the Filipinos and used them to kill Japs.

There was a Moro who, having heard of vitamins, liked to eat the livers of the Japs killed in battle.

The Moros are also an extremely moral people. Their code forbids a stranger even to touch the hand of a Moro woman. On the road to Davao a battalion surgeon gave this advice: "Keep your penis in your pants and the Moro will keep his kris inside his sheath."

Among other tribes on Mindanao are the Manobos. They are wild pagans, tree dwellers with no reputation for peaceful ways. They are stalwart, meat eating people. Their hair is long, their teeth filed flat.

There are the Bagobos, a primitive pagan tribe of the unexplored hinterland of Davao; before American artillery came their way they dwelled on the slopes of towering Mount Apo.

There are the Negritos, small, pitch-black, with broad heads and thick lips, and armed with blow-pipes shooting arrows poisoned with the juice of upas trees.

And there were the Japanese of Davao. Long established in the Philippines, they were Japanese loyalists at heart, and they had transformed the Davao Gulf country into a prosperous miniature Japan. They had established huge *abaca* plantations, fisheries and lumbering industries. They controlled the commerce of Davao City, the schools, newspapers and banks.

In the Divisions battle teams men asked one another, "What about the civilians of Davao? Will they be quiet? Will they fight side by side with the Jap troops? Will they commit mass suicide as on Saipan?" Nobody knew—as yet.

On April 28—after a twelve-hour, two-battalion battle—the men of the spearhead patrols saw the glittering blue of the ocean as they crossed the mountain passes of the eastern range. They were soldiers of the Thirty-Fourth Infantry Regiment, the first to cross Mindanao Island from coast to coast. They secured the Digos beaches and the air field of Padada. The beaches had been intricately fortified. The fortifications were abandoned. The fire lanes of all emplacements faced the sea—Davao Gulf—whence the American invasion was expected. The Japanese command had planned a bitter beach defense and a fighting withdrawal from east to west into mountains. Their intended line of withdrawal had been the line of the Division's advance. Mindanao was now cut in two.

Forty miles to the north lay the city of Davao.

Battle teams of the "Rock of Chickamauga," led by Colonel Clifford, passed through Digos and pounded north along the coastal highway. They seized Toban and Santa Cruz. They captured heavy naval guns mounted in beach positions facing the sea. They smashed three turret-like pillboxes camouflaged with beds of bright red flowers. They captured warehouses crammed with supplies ranging from naval torpedoes to electric fans.

Soldiers speaking:

Sergeant S. T. Dewhirst from Portola, California: I drove along the beach road in a jeep. All of a sudden a Jap sprang out of the bushes and threw a mine under the jeep. Hie mine exploded and the jeep was wrecked. My companion was badly hurt. I was dazed. But I recovered in time to shoot the Nip five times with my pistol. He was still on his feet and he kept running. While running he pulled out a razor and cut his own throat.

Another jeep came along and another Jap darted from the bushes and threw a mine. The driver swerved around the mine and the Jap disappeared.

Private First Class Harold Jones from Ainsworth, Nebraska: I am a machinegunner. We had just broken up a night Banzai attack and all was quiet again. My gun had jammed toward the end of the attack, so I cleaned it and reloaded. Then I dipped the muzzle a little bit to the ground and fired three shots to see if she worked all right. A squeal followed the burst. I had shot a sneaking Nip by accident. Two hours later he woke me up with his moaning. So I gave him another burst to put him out.

Lieutenant Dan Bradley from Detroit, Michigan: My job is to fly a dive bomber. A few miles from Davao my ship caught fire. I was flying at a low altitude. I tried to get my landing wheels down. They wouldn't go down. Then I started for a belly crash, but flames made that impossible. I nosed the burning plane into a climb and bailed out. But I pulled the rip cord too soon. The chute caught in the tail of the plane. I saw the ground rush toward me and I tried to jerk the chute clear of the falling ship. Suddenly the plane rolled over and the chute riffled free. I landed hard in an *abaca* thicket. All I got were scorches and bruises. Later I figured out how my plane caught fire. It was from the blast of a bomb dropped by another plane flying in front.

Captain Julien C. Mason, of Colonial Beach, West Virginia: I'm a civil affairs officer for the Division. Of the many problems that loaded me down when we swept across Mindanao one in particular was a stumper. A Moro chieftain of doubtful loyalty had two sons. One was a provincial governor for the Japanese. The other was a very good guerilla leader. The question was, should we leave their old man in power or not? I solved that problem—I turned it over to higher headquarters to decide.

Sergeant James J. Thompson from Oakland, California: I was leading an advance patrol toward Davao when I spotted a Jap pillbox. I warned my men down. I unloosened a grenade and crawled toward the pillbox. I was just about to toss the grenade into the mouth of the dugout. A thin little wail froze my arm. I listened. The wailing came again. It came from the pillbox. It could have been a trap but it sounded too real. I crept closer and peered into the pillbox. There was a crying baby inside. There were four people in the dugout. An old man and he was shot dead. A young man and he was shot dead too. A young woman stabbed in the belly three times with a bayonet but still weakly alive. A six-months-old baby stabbed once through the belly. The young woman explained: They had tried to flee over to the American side. Japs had caught them. Then they had thrown the whole family into the pillbox.

Captain Paul E. Byrd of West Fargo, North Dakota; Medical Department: At 3 A.M., I was roused by an emergency call from the forward elements. They needed blood plasma in a hurry. So five of us secured the plasma and climbed into a jeep. We dashed over ten miles of pitch-dark road, past jungle, mountain curves and through rugged by-passes around destroyed bridges. We delivered the plasma. But on the way back we were ambushed. Japs fired from roadside thickets with machineguns. Their bullets crashed through the front of the jeep and wounded four of us. The driver had stopped and now he was backing away down the road. Those of us who could still stand jumped out and gave battle. An infantry night patrol came along and chased the Japs into the jungle. There were seventeen bullet holes in the jeep.

Corporal Tony Mulay of Pueblo, Colorado, Corpsman: The yell "Aid man! Aid man!" is the time-honored SOS of the battle-field. On the road to Davao I fixed up some wounded boys. I fixed up wounded boys in battle before this, in New Guinea, Leyte, Luzon, between seventy-five and a hundred of them. They got so used to me that when they need me they don't shout, "Aid man!" They shout, "Tony! oh, Tony, come over here quick." Well, I come. They say sometimes the Japs were shooting at me while I worked. If they did, I didn't notice. You see, I'm pretty busy.

Private First Class Alphonso DeLeon of San Antonio, Texas: I was with a patrol probing into Jap country around Davao. There were some Nips in ambush but we did not see them first. I was the last man in the patrol. The Nips let the patrol pass and then one of them leaped from the bushes and shoved his bayonet into my right side. My own rifle was slung over my shoulder. I whirled and grabbed the Jap's rifle. At the same time my own rifle slipped to the ground. I knocked the Jap back into the bushes. I then tried to shoot him but the Jap's rifle would not work. Disgusted, I slammed the muzzle to the ground and the bayonet broke off clean. That moment a grenade came sailing from the bushes. I dived to the ground but fragments of the grenade bit me in the neck and in the right leg. That was too much. I was mad. I went into the bushes to get at the Japs, but there was no one in sight.

Corporal Floyd W. Gandee of Lorain, Ohio: The night was dark and rainy. I was on perimeter guard in my foxhole. There was about a foot of water in the hole. Nearby was a stream. Suddenly a booby trap we'd set along the stream snapped and exploded. I heaved six grenades in that general direction. Except for the flashes I could see nothing. I followed up the grenades with B.A.R. fire. Then a Jap yelled: "American stop shooting, we've enough, we're leaving." I yelled back, "Stop shooting hell." The rest of the night was peaceful. Next morning I found that I'd killed a Jap lieutenant. He lay about three paces from my foxhole.

April 29 brought slow, hard going on the long road to Davao. Hundreds of buried mines continued to hinder the advance. Logical by-pass routes around burning bridges, too, were heavily mined. The roadside thickets were infested with snipers. Sharp fire fights developed at two Japanese road blocks. The Japanese had felled large trees across the road, mined the trees and emplaced machineguns to cover the block. The Nineteenth Regiment continued to spearhead the drive on Davao. The Thirty-Fourth Regiment weathered a night Banzai attack. Numerous ambushes erupted many miles behind the front. That day a score of Americans were killed or wounded.

"Look, fellows, this one's a dud," said Corporal Roger Manz of Pittsburgh, Pennsylvania. He held up a Jap mortar shell that had landed in his foxhole that morning.

After a careful inspection he tossed the shell out of his hole. There was an instant explosion. Manz was stunned and half buried. Slowly he raised himself to his hands and knees.

"Somebody's got to be wrong once in a while," he muttered.

Private First Class Lawrence Zigler of Lansing, Michigan, accompanied a combat patrol as its radio operator. The patrol came upon a nest of trenches and there was a fight. The enemy was routed in a bayonet assault and finally fled toward a nearby river. The patrol pushed forward and collided with a sudden Japanese counter-attack. In the fight the patrol was pressed against the river. Standing at the edge of the gurgling stream, his forty-five-pound radio on his back, Zigler killed a pursuing Jap with shots from his pistol. Then Zigler tumbled into the river.

The river flowed swiftly and was shoulder deep. Zigler lost his foothold and was swept downstream. He thought of discarding the radio on his back but he held on. It was the patrol's only means of communication.

The current smashed Zigler against a jutting rock. He grasped a ledge and clung. He watched a platoon of Japanese prowl past him along the river's edge. The Japs did not see him. After they had passed, the radio man managed to scale the bank. He found his radio waterlogged and not functioning.

The patrol set up an emergency perimeter. In the center of the perimeter sat Lawrence Zigler, disassembling, drying and cleaning the parts of his radio, then putting them together again. The job completed, he was astonished to hear that the patrol had beaten off Jap skirmishers while he had worked, oblivious of the firing.

A 500-pound airplane bomb was set off by a lurking Japanese as a patrol passed the spot. Six Americans died in the blast. Six others were wounded.

A group of battalion runners surprised twelve Japanese fleeing northward on bicycles. When bullets snarled the Japs abandoned their mounts and scurried into an *abaca* field. The battalion messengers walked no longer. They sped their errands on bicycles made in Nippon.

Firing broke out in the night somewhere between two American battalions commanded by Major Roy W. Marcy of Walla Walla, Washington, and Major Nicolas Sloan of Hoopeston, Illinois. A thousand yards between them, both listened to the firing.

"Marcy's catching it," reasoned Sloan.

"Sloans catching it," reasoned Marcy.

Then they checked by radio.

"No bullets this way," said Major Sloan.

"None here, either," said Major Marcy.

It was a brawl between two Jap raiding parties colliding in the night.

On May 1 the Division's assault teams slugged to the gates of Davao. Mines and wrecked bridges had stopped all motorized advance. From the mountains around Davao Japanese artillery opened in a thunderous bombardment. It was later established that—gun for gun—hostile artillery around Davao outnumbered the Division's field artillery three to one.

Eight hundred riflemen of the Nineteenth Infantry pushed up the slopes of Hill 550, a dominating height overlooking the coastal road and the city of Davao. The hill was desperately defended from scores of pillboxes, caves and tunnels. Seventeen days of murderous cave-and-tunnel fighting went by before the height could be secured.

The Divisions field artillery ground forward. Its guns roared all through the hot afternoon. Cub planes ranged ahead for observation. Mortar, machinegun and rifle fire met the Americans advance along three coastal roads. Japanese detachments attacked a motor park and a bridge repair party along the Divisions 130 mile long route of supply. The Division vanguard captured an enemy bivouac. There were large stores of lumber, engineering equipment, automobiles, bulldozers and tractors and much artillery ammunition.

A lone Japanese crawled into an artillery perimeter and tossed a box full of dynamite into the cannoneers' kitchen. In the hills southwest of Davao "King" Company of the Thirty-Fourth Regiment seized ten Japanese machineguns. Its scouts reported that a maze of hidden emplacements covered all hillsides like spider nests. The unavoidable test was at hand. In number the Japs were stronger.

With nightfall the Division's assault elements stood poised on the banks of the Davao River. Cannon fire grumbled in the hills. Nippon's capital in the Philippines lay dark and silent. Peering across the river that night, Colonel Clifford quietly announced: "Tomorrow we storm Davao."

Chapter Twenty-One
INFANTRY SPEAKING

Sergeant Robert L. Roberts of Newark, New Jersey: Somewhere north of Davao we came to a shack. At least it looked like one. We pumped it full of bullets just to make sure. It turned out to be a fire-spitting pillbox and we hit the ground fast. Two men in my squad were hit. We burned out the Japs. Five or six were running away, flames curling from their backs. They carried American rifles they'd captured in Bataan—years ago.

Private First Class Clyde Burton of Eubank, Kentucky: I was sleeping at night in my foxhole outside of Davao. My buddy stood guard. Suddenly he nudged me. "Slant-eyes a'comin'," he said. I rubbed my eyes and my feet hurt from hundreds of miles of walking and then I realized what was up. Hand grenades were popping all over the place, both Jap and ours. Everybody on the perimeter was blazing away and bullets were flying in on us from all directions. We heard the Japs howl like mad monkeys as they charged us with bayonets. Two of them were coming for me. I let 'em have it. One fell dead, the other plopped into my foxhole still a little bit alive.

Private Joe Stewart of Courtney, Missouri: I was sitting at the edge of the road, cooling my feet in a ditch. I couldn't believe my eyes when I saw eight Japs march single file right down the middle of the road. They were camouflaged and they looked just like a row of bushes moving down the road. It was a beautiful sight. I lined up the sights of my automatic rifle and squeezed the trigger. The first two fell. Then my B.A.R. jammed. I jerked the bolt and fired at the others who were running into the bushes. The B.A.R. jammed again. It was clogged with mud. I was so angry that I wanted to throw my gun at them. Well, I sat there cleaning the thing, when two of the Japs came back to drag the two dead Japs off the road. I got them too.

Private Ralph Cole of Mount Pleasant, Michigan: Night attack. The Japs came in like a laughing pack of hyenas, bayonets in front and tossing grenades. Everything was in an uproar, shrapnel flying, bullets whizzing, tracers zipping like lightning through the jungle. And suddenly a Jap jumped into my foxhole. My machete was sticking in the ground nearby. I grabbed it and hacked away at the Jap. I hacked his arm off with one good swipe. He backed away and I shot him a couple of times. Still he kept coming. He was the hardest dying character I've ever met. Later when I tried to get some sleep he woke me up with his moaning. So I put him out of his misery with two more shots. I noticed then that I was bleeding, too. Shrapnel.

Sergeant Freeman Smith of Norway, Maine: I was moving up a narrow trail about ten yards behind my scouts when I noticed two Japs lying in the bushes about five feet off the trail. At first I thought they were dead. But Japs have a trick of playing dead, letting you pass, then throw dynamite at you from the rear. I hunted around for a pebble to throw at them to make sure. No sense in wasting bullets on dead Japs. But before I could find a pebble I saw one of the Nips reach up and brush a centipede off his forehead. That's all I needed to make up my mind.

Lieutenant Colonel Harold E. Liebe of Tacoma, Washington; Field Artillery: In the fight for an entrance into Davao infantrymen had established a bridgehead at the Davao River. From high in the hills Japs shelled our troops with a six-inch naval gun. Casualties were heavy. My men decided to do something about it. They manhandled a 105 millimeter howitzer across the river and up a hill on nothing but their muscles and guts. From then on it was a point blank duel. It was firing by "bore-sighting"— that is, you look down the barrel of your howitzer until it is on the target. After an hour of dueling we knocked out the competition.

Private Joseph Turner of Warren, Ohio: My job is mine clearing. I was walking along with my mine-clearing crew when suddenly a 250-pound aerial bomb dropped in front of us out of a tree. The Japs had rigged up a block and tackle in a tree along the road, hoisted the bomb to the top, and then waited a safe distance away with the end of the rope that held up the bomb. Lucky for us, that bomb did not explode. Six Japs pulled the rope, bouncing the bomb around the ground until one of our men shot through the rope with his tommygun. At another time we had found a bomb in the road and we had lit a fuse to blow it up. Some Japs in ambush started firing, hoping to keep us pinned down until the bomb exploded on us. They were not successful. We were not always so lucky. On the edge of Davao a bomb disposal squad worked to disarm a mine when the mine exploded. Nothing was left of the squad except a blackish smear on the tree trunks.

On May 2 a Division spearhead commanded by Colonel Clifford punched into Davao. The first problem of the attack was the crossing of the broad Davao River. Clifford solved it by a bold ruse. Division artillery showered a barrage on the logical site for the river crossing. As soon as this barrage lifted, a Japanese counter barrage upon the same area commenced. The enemy commanders were convinced that the major attempt to force the water barrier would be made at this point. But Clifford's riflemen crossed the river over a hastily constructed foot bridge several hundred yards upstream. The attack groups crossed the precarious structure at a fast run. They swarmed into Davao City before the Japanese realized their mistake.

Though the city of Davao was stormed, the rataplan of machineguns, the roar of bombs, the screaming of rockets, the thunder of artillery lashed the countryside around Davao for months. The Japs of Davao fought with arrogance, and with a complete contempt for death. For months to come the men of the Twenty-Fourth Infantry Division were locked in the hardest, bitterest, most exhausting battle of their ten island campaigns. "As bad as Breakneck Ridge," they said. "And bigger."

Possession of Davao City and of Mindanao Island was less a matter of strategic importance than a matter of American prestige. Already with the fall of Leyte, Mindoro and Luzon the Japanese in Mindanao were hopelessly cut off from their homeland. Their planes had been destroyed and their ships had been sunk; and their naval and aviation personnel fought as infantry. But American "face," much damaged by Nippon since 1941, had to be built up anew and stronger by the violent extermination of Jap forces who already had been castrated in a larger military sense. The dogfaces who fought and won this "battle of prestige" fought it without enthusiasm, but with a sullen and melancholy hatred. More than ten thousand Japanese died around Davao at the hands of Twenty-Fourth Division men. Among its own the Division counted two thousand, seven hundred soldiers wounded or missing or killed in the Davao fighting. Since the now distant date of the Divisions thrusts into New Guinea and Leyte, more than 25,000 Japanese fighting men had died in its path. But the blood price our fighting team has paid for its share in guarding Americas life and happiness, measured in terms of maimed and killed comrades, stands very near the six thousand mark—six thousand out of an organization roughly 15,000 strong. In the ever two-sided agony of combat they died, in this last campaign of the island war, in the sweltering *abaca* fields, on the blasted slopes of Hill 550, on brush-covered ridges, in the savage gorges of the Talomo River, in the hostile Mandog mountains and on the fringes of never explored wilderness which surrounds Mount Apo with saturnine and inscrutable green.

To the foot soldiers fighting in Davao Province, the word *abaca* was synonymous with hell. *Abaca* is the plant from which Manila hemp is made. Countless acres around Davao are covered with these thick-stemmed plants, fifteen to twenty feet high; the plants grow as closely together as sugar cane, and their long, lush, green leaves are interwoven in a welter of green so dense that a strong man must fight with the whole weight of his body for each foot of progress through this ocean of verdure. In the *abaca* fields visibility was rarely more than ten feet. No breeze ever reached through the gloomy expanse of green, and more men—American and Japanese—fell prostrate from the overpowering heat than from bullets. The common way for scouts to locate an enemy position in *abaca* fighting was to advance until they received machinegun fire at a range of three to five yards. One rifle platoon lost fourteen scouts in the course of the "*abaca* campaign." The intricate Japanese *abaca* entrenchments were supported and protected by the largest concentration of naval and field artillery ever encountered by the Twenty-Fourth Division. One hundred and ninety pieces of Japanese artillery were captured and destroyed in the battle of Davao.

The assault bridge across the Davao River was the handiwork of a sergeant of combat engineers. There was an old bridge, but a forty-foot gap had been blown out of its middle, and the bridge ends had been mined. Clifford thought that he would have to force the crossing into Davao in assault boats. But forward strode Sergeant Alfred A. Sousa of Honolulu, Hawaii.

"Give me four hours and I'll fix that bridge," he said.

The officers gave the sergeant *carte blanche*. Sousa studied the far end of the bridge. His trained eyes spotted five mines and a bangalore torpedo under a case of blasting powder. Strings for detonating these charges converged on a masked foxhole a hundred feet from the river's edge.

Under the covering muzzles of a rifle squad the engineer plunged into the river. It took him forty-five minutes to buffet his way to the hostile bank. Stealthily he cut the converging strings, aware that at any moment a sniper's bullet or a mine explosion might put his enterprise to an irrevocable end.

The mines were disarmed.

In broad daylight, with only his knife as a weapon, Sousa scouted the enemy side of the river. He was the first American soldier to set foot into Davao since 1942.

His reconnaissance completed, Sousa again bucked the current and summoned his men to the job at hand. Infantry waited, er a few hours and a truckload of sweat a crazy-quilt bridge of ladders, tree trunks, blasted timbers and ropes spanned the Davao River.

A rifle platoon led by Lieutenant Clifton L. Ferguson of Indianapolis, Indiana, was first to storm into the city of Davao. Crossing the river with the spearhead were Colonel Clifford and General Kenneth F. Cramer, the assistant Division commander.

"It looked like a cinch," said burly Cramer. "But after a few minutes it was worse than anything Leyte ever had. Artillery seemed to be firing at us from point blank range and mortar shells were falling all around. Guesses are never good enough. You never know really what's going to happen until you go in there to get shot at. That's the only reliable source of information."

Fanning out from Davao, every battalion of every regiment lay in continuous battle.

Davao was a leveled city. Only a few shells of buildings were standing. Much of the town had been razed by American bombs. But the Japanese had dismantled and carried off into the hills more than one thousand of the best houses. With the vanished buildings went Davao's 19,000 Japanese civilians. The Filipino population, too, had fled. When the Division's Civil Affairs Officer* walked into Davao (with a mimeographed list of ceiling prices in one pocket, 35,000 victory pesos in another) to take over the city's administration, he found that of the town's original 90,000 residents barely one hundred were present to welcome the "liberators." These remnants lived in an agglomeration of rag-tag huts built out of wreckage in an atmosphere of graves, corpses, ruins and a weird congress of skeletons in what once had been Davao Penal Colony. Looking over his domain, the administrator muttered, "Well, there seems to be almost nobody around to be liberated." A frail native woman, Madam Baldomera Sexon, who was the director of Davao's Mission Hospital, told the officer that more than 25,000 Filipino civilians in Davao had died of malaria, typhus and execution at the hands of the Japanese.

* Major William T. Cameron, of Philippine Civil Affairs Unit 29, formerly Master of the High School of Commerce, Boston.

Advance patrols were ordered to look for a secret city which the Japs had built out of the stolen homes of Davao somewhere in unexplored territory. Guerilla scouts filtering through enemy lines reported that the Japanese were training thousands of their women for combat. All Japanese women between twenty and forty were ordered to wear trousers, cut short their hair, and after that they were trained to fight with grenades and bamboo spears. General Eichelberger, the Eighth Army commander, broadcast a warning that "If these Japanese civilians do not surrender, we intend to kill them as we find them."*

American planes dropped thousands of leaflets over Japanese lines. The leaflets asked Japanese civilians to return to Davao: "We do not wish to kill old men, women and children." Safe conduct, food and medical relief were promised.

Not one Jap civilian surrendered.

But Filipinos came in big, terrified hordes. They came in groups of many thousands, guided by steel-helmeted infantry patrols. Their march back to Davao resembled a migration of bedraggled ants. Men were ragged and starved and broken down by forced labor. For months the Japanese had compelled them to dig trenches and tunnel fortifications. Women with babies sucking wilted breasts staggered under the weight of heavy head loads. Children limped on swollen feet. Some had been wounded while crossing artillery impact zones. There were few smiles. And intermingled with the returning civilians came the spies and the people of the underworld.

In the prostrate city two industries flourished: spying and prostitution. Veneral disease was rampant after three years of Japanese occupation. A Jap soldier with syphilis or gonorrhea knew that he would be beaten by his officers; therefore he hid his sickness, and escaped cure. Nearly half of Davao's young women were diseased. Two cigarettes or a piece of soap would buy a girl for a night.

General Woodruff promptly declared Davao "off-limits" for troops not engaged in Jap-killing or municipal administration.

Heavy Japanese artillery pounded Davao for days. A crowded field hospital and a command post suffered direct hits.

During the second night following the capture of Davao the Japanese launched five successive Banzai charges. Japs carrying grenades, rifles, machineguns, and land mines strapped to their bellies raided the center of the town. Many of the mines were exploded by American bullets. The explosions threw Japanese bodies over the

---

* As quoted by Associated Press.

mounds of rubble. A head sailed into the command post of Lieutenant William Paul of Long Beach, California. An arm and two feet dropped into the command post of Captain Victor Bazzinotti of Cadogan, Pennsylvania.

Japanese gunfire destroyed six American tanks.

Japanese fighting men held grimly to their defenses surrounding Davao. Months of ceaseless air bombing and strafing, ceaseless artillery bombardment, ceaseless infantry attacks were required to dislodge them.

Day after day a devouring heat poured from sky and earth. Heat prostrations took a grim daily toll. Some companies counted only seventy men fit for battle. The nights often brought heavy rains and four, five,"six wild-beast counter attacks in the dark. Verbeck's Twenty-First Regimental Combat Team seized Mintal and fought desperately for Libby Drome, the largest of Davao's airfields, then pounded into the wilderness north of 10,000-foot Mount Apo. Clifford's Nineteenth Regiment slugged northward along the shores of Davao Gulf, captured Sasa Airdrome, Samal Island, and the towns of Panacan, Tibunko and Bunawan. The Thirty-Fourth Regiment, meanwhile, struck along the Talomo River Valley toward the bastions of Ula and Tamogan. Thus the Division's battle teams fought simultaneously on three fronts, striking the enemy's main line of resistance in the center and from both flanks.

The Division's field artillery thundered day and night. Fire bombs sown from planes set wide areas of *abaca* afire. The Japanese again resorted to the tragically futile expedient of concentrating masses of Filipinos around their positions as hostages against American bombardments. Ambushes infested all roads between dark and dawn; along the Division's 150-mile supply line no road was safe at any time. Davao City as well as the Division command post came under hostile artillery fire. A Japanese canoe patrol blew up and sank one of the first American supply ships to enter Davao Gulf.

Each night, on each perimeter, Japanese were caught in the attempt to sneak through the foxhole lines with dynamite strapped to their bodies.

In close-quarter night battle Jap soldiers were beaten to death with fists, with rifle butts, with shovels. One officer stood in conference in his battalion command post in a banana grove. His back was resting against one of the bushes. A Japanese materialized from nowhere. He thrust his bayonet through a banana stalk and impaled the officer.

A Japanese raiding party landed in a log canoe near the command post of the Division. They penetrated the command post under cover of darkness, scattering mines.

One weary sergeant commented:

"People visualize pillboxes as little round things that stick up and are visible like the concrete pillboxes in Normandy. But these pillboxes here follow the contour of the ground so that there is absolutely no sign of their presence except the two-inch-wide firing slits. You could walk by one each day for a year and never know it was there unless someone shot at you. The fields and woods are full of Japs. You cut through them with machineguns and flame-throwers and they close in right behind you."

The Division cemetery, well behind the lines, was growing in leaps and bounds. Burial parties were frequently forced to fight their way through to put the dead to rest.

First Lieutenant John A. Schwengels of Beloit, Wisconsin: I am a platoon commander in the Division's Cavalry Reconnaissance Troop. We operate with half-tracks, jeeps and armored cars. Our troop is a spy-slug-and-run outfit, the feelers of the foot-slogging infantry.

My platoon was the first American force to drive into the big Lioanan air strip north of Davao. There were four runways. The roads around them were mined and the Japs had planted innumerable booby traps. My half-track spun around a mine, almost scraping the detonator. For a second my hair stood on end. Then we bounced onto the air field and stopped. Scattered along the strip were some two hundred big aerial bombs. So we dismounted and did some crawling. We crawled on our bellies from bomb to bomb and cut the detonation wires. In between we put a flock of snipers to flight.

After that we reconnoitered the fringes. The tall grass on both sides of the road was quivering with Japs. Every once in a while we stopped and raked the whole business with machineguns. We had two half-tracks and six jeeps, a machinegun on each.

There was one Jap who wouldn't quit tugging on a red cord. We shot the Jap and we cut the cord and then we found that it led to two 500-pound bombs. A little way further, twenty Japs attacked with grenades and mines. Our machineguns sang their song of death.

Next day we were cut off from our infantry by a strong Jap force. We threw some 150 mortar shells in their direction. The shells set off some buried bombs, and when we finally broke through we had to buck through big craters in the road.

The same day we captured a Jap mountain gun. But the Japs forced their way back to the gun and blew it up with dynamite. Then we pulled into an area studded with Jap barracks. The infantry behind us was halted by a hostile barrage and we fell back and hugged the ground and called for our own artillery fire. Our cannoneers dropped a hundred howitzer shells into the Japs while we lay flat and watched. Earth and junk flew all over us. When the barrage stopped, we pushed on again. Next came fire from a pillbox. We knocked it out. Then came fire from a stream bed. We killed thirty Japs and overran the rest.

After that we ran into a dead-end of heavy fire. The lead halftrack tried to back away, but stalled. I jumped out and one of my boys yelled "Look out!" I whirled and faced a Jap who was charging me with a bayonet. I ripped him with my tommygun until his guts spilled on the road.

We fought six days for this one air field, one of seven around Davao, keeping alive by firing first.

Sleepless, sweating, begrimed Captain Sidney B. Luria, a battalion surgeon, patched up 262 battle casualties in five days and five nights of unremitting labor. To his little surgeons tent were carried men with bullet punctures, with smashed arms or legs, with broken skulls, with bodies ripped by shell fragments, with nerves jangled from the constant pounding of high explosive. "Doc" Luria used an average of two bottles of plasma for each man. He worked under artillery barrages, mortar bursts, and during night attacks—by flashlight, crouched under a poncho in foxhole muck. Not one of his patients died.

An exploding bangalore torpedo supplied a thunderous overtone to the singing of Corporal Robert Lussier of Woonsocket, Rhode Island. It also bounced his truck like a rubber ball.

Lussier drove his supply truck along a dark, *abaca*-flanked road. The stars were out and the Frenchman from New England was singing "I'll Walk Alone." He saw a round object, three inches in diameter and about three feet long slide out into the road from the hemp thicket; but busy with his singing he thought nothing about it until the torpedo exploded and bounced his truck.

Lussier roared. He grabbed his carbine and leaped out of the truck. But the Jap had disappeared in the *abaca*.

Lussier peered under his truck. His sensing hands found that fragments from the torpedo had punctured the heavy housing of the differential before tearing through the floor of the vehicle.

He sat beneath his truck and again he sang "I'll Walk Alone," his carbine ready, hoping that the Jap would try again.

He plugged the holes with sticks to keep the oil from running out and then he pulled away from there.

The platoon of Sergeant William Braswell of Jacksonville, Florida, assaulted a barricade of pillboxes north of Davao. A Japanese "woodpecker" (light machinegun) rippled from a hidden foxhole on the right. The burst caught one of the scouts, through the shoulder. Braswell heard the scouts outcry, then saw him fall. The wounded soldier was struggling to roll himself to the cover of a log, but could not make it alone. Braswell sprang to the wounded man's side. Machinegun slugs cut the foliage above their heads and the sergeant saw that his scout's face had suddenly turned into a yellowish gray and that he was frozen with fear. Then Braswell saw what was the matter.

A Japanese grenade had plopped on the scout's back and had lodged between the fallen man's shoulder blades.

The sergeant from Florida had led his platoon through many battles. He had seen death in every conceivable form and at close range. Each time one of his men had died it was as if he, Bill Braswell, had suffered death himself. He lunged forward to toss away the grenade and then it exploded. It killed the wounded scout and blew off Braswell's hand at the wrist.

Field artillery had thoroughly pounded a palm grove where Japanese soldiers had been spotted digging holes. When the shells stopped falling, Private Don Foster, a radioman from Long Beach, California, went forward to scout the impact area. He found the bodies of enemy soldiers in contortions such as only artillery bursts can produce. On the edge of a clearing crossed by a tinkling brook he saw an untouched palm-and-bamboo hut. In a patch of hibiscus in front of the hut lay the still warm body of a woman.

Don Foster cautiously circled the hut and peered inside. In the half-darkness he saw the body of another woman stretched out on the floor slats. In the hollow of her arm she held a tiny infant. A child of about three crouched in a corner of the shack and gazed at the strange soldier out of large black eyes.

Don Foster entered the hut. The second woman, he found, was dead. The infant in her arm was alive, slimy, skeleton-like and acrawl with ants. Foster radioed for help.

A medic said that the mother had died from lack of care after childbirth, and that the infant was about five days old. The older child—a girl—was starved but in good health. Six infantrymen dug a double grave while six others stood guard. They buried the young mother and the older woman. Through an eye dropper they fed the infant canned milk mixed with chlorinated water. They washed the baby and made a diaper out of first aid bandages and saved its life. Their company adopted the infant's three-year-old sister. The 150 foster fathers called her Geraldine Irene—G.I.

During the assault on Maag Hill, Corporal Robert Melin of Visalia, California, saw two of his squad crumple in the path of Japanese machinegun fire. One yelled for help, and the other thrashed about on the steaming earth. Melin crawled forward hard beneath the bullets that were like so many shuttles weaving a pattern of death. He reached the fallen men and dragged them, first one and then the other, into the shelter of a *lauan* tree. He gave them morphine and bandaged their wounds and covered them with their ponchos to alleviate shock. He had finished his job, dimly aware that the fire fight was gradually moving up the sun-baked slope. He gulped a mouthful of water from his canteen when he heard a hoarse pleading from not far away.

"Oh, my leg ... Oh, God ... my leg."

Corporal Melin closed his mouth and thrust his canteen back into the canteen carrier on his belt. He shook himself like a dog that has just escaped from a burning house, and out he crawled again where bullets decapitated blades of green grass. He saw a machinegun spit fire from a grassy mound and he found a soldier whose leg had been broken in three places by a mortar blast.

He gave the crying man morphine, and he gave him sulfa tablets and water. He sprinkled sulfa on the leg wounds and bandaged them. Then he crawled toward a bamboo clump to cut some splints. The wounded soldier had become quiet and his eye followed Melin to the bamboo and they followed him on his return with the freshly-cut splints. Just then the machinegun under the grassy mound again snapped bullets. Melin threw himself flat. He felt something rip through his sleeve and he heard bullets whine past beneath him during the fraction of a second which it took him to hit the ground. He landed with his head between the wounded soldier's feet. The burst of fire had riddled the man he had come to save. With the dogged battle loyalty that does not allow of analytical thinking he dragged his dead comrade to cover of the lauan. He still clutched the bamboo splints as he raised his head and yelled toward the rear for litters.

First Sergeant Woodrow Woods of Whitesboro, Texas, spotted a Jap crouched in a hole at the base of a volcano. The Texan roared, "Get the hell out of that hole!" The Oriental obeyed. "Hands up!" the Topkick roared. The Jap stood still.

His finger on the trigger of his rifle, Woods approached to relieve his captive of some grenades which bulged in the Jap's blouse pockets. The Texan reached, but the bulges were not grenades. The Jap was a sullen, cropped-haired young woman.

Sergeant William Duncan of Roxbury, Massachusetts, asleep in a foxhole, thought he heard some firing.

"What's the matter?" he growled.

His foxhole companion, a boy of nineteen, whispered excitedly, "There was three Japs in the road. I shot one. Gee, Sarge, I got my first Jap."

"Well," he grunted, "Why in hell don't you shoot the other two?"

A mild mannered geologist from Salt Lake City cleaned out a Jap pillbox which had killed two men of his squad. The scientist, Sergeant Rondo Birch, climbed on top of the pillbox. He tossed a grenade through the firing port. A Jap ran out. Birch brought him down with his rifle. Then he tossed a second grenade. Two more Japs popped out and ran some distance, then changed their minds and counter-attacked. Birch fought them from their own pillbox. They exchanged fire, springing forward, shooting, ducking, shouting. After fifteen minutes both were dead—one shot through the head, the other through the heart.

Sergeant Tudor Price of Lake Crystal, Minnesota, heard a noise in the night. He unleashed his machinegun. There were sounds of bodies falling in the brush, then moans, then silence. At dawn he found that he had shot a horse and two dogs.

Soon the dead horse began to smell. Tudor Price was ordered to bury it. All day he dug. Toward evening, his company commander heard him curse and growl maledictions into his foxhole. "What's the matter, Price?" he asked.

"Sir," answered the sergeant, "did you ever bury a horse?"

Between Talomo and the city of Davao there is a wide clearing among the thickets of *abaca*, scrub palm and banana. There are rows upon rows of little wooden crosses, and each cross bears an American name. And there are other rows; rows of open graves as yet unnamed. Still forms swathed in olive-drab blankets lie in the open graves. Others still lie above the ground, sprawled and twisted as they were carried from the battlefield. Bullet victims, artillery victims, grenade victims. Across the humble acre of God artillery shells pass with sibilant howls. The rumble of distant explosions drifts over the crosses and the open graves, and over nearby hills planes are bombing and strafing. A solitary figure stands poised before an open, not empty, grave. It is the figure of a stocky, fearless, unarmed man: the Division Chaplain. Major Paul J. Slavik of St. Paul's Church of New York City is burying the four hundredth American in the Division cemetery near Davao. Except for the crew of Filipino diggers he is alone. His voice is firm and sad, . . .

"We praise and bless Thy glorious Name, O Lord, for the devoted sacrifice of Thy servant who has laid down his life that we might live. Into Thy holy keeping we commend his soul, and humbly pray that we, as did he, may give and never count the cost, fight and never heed the wounds, toil and never seek for rest, labor and ask for no reward save the knowledge that we will do Thy will; through Jesus Christ, our Lord. Amen."

There is a flare-up of rifle fire in the swampy underbrush a few hundred yards off. A patrol of helmeted men with sub-machineguns and rifles crosses the cemetery in swift-moving single file. As they approach the rim of the thickets they fan out into a skirmish line and the crackling of rifles becomes vicious and sustained. A machinegun hammers in the bushes. The Filipino diggers scatter and seek cover. For one short second Paul Slavik is hesitant as to what he should do. But then he is again his old self, calm and strong and duty-bound.

"We commit the body of our comrade to the ground in the Name of the Father, and of the Son, and of the Holy Ghost, looking for the resurrection of the dead and the life of the world to come."

The machinegun in the bushes has fallen silent. The cracking of rifles is moving away into the distance. The diggers emerge from cover and assemble large-eyed under a molave tree and watch. Paul Slavik raises both arms toward the sky. Overhead the eerie wailing of artillery shells continues without interruption. Over the strange, wild countryside his voice becomes a ringing and somber appeal.

"May God the Father, who has created this body;

"May God the Son, who by His blood has redeemed this body together with the soul;

"May God the Holy Ghost, who by baptism has sanctified this body to be His temple—

"Keep these remains unto the day of the resurrection of all flesh."

The chaplain lowers his head in a mute farewell. He addresses the silent man down there under the olive-drab blanket as if the soldier had been his son:

"*The Grace of our Lord Jesus Christ, the love of God, and the Communion of the Holy Ghost he with you forevermore. Amen.*"

He makes the sign of the cross and for a moment he remains in a final, silent prayer. The diggers advance slowly.

At sunset two tough, dirty, sweat-encrusted soldiers moved out among the rows of crosses. Their helmets they carried in their hands. In his helmet each carried a flower he had dug from the edge of the jungle together with its roots and a clump of soil. They halted in front of the fresh mounds and bent low and studied the names on the crosses. Then they found the name.

"That's Robert," one of them muttered. "Christ, last night we had the same foxhole. He was telling me all about what he'd do when he got home again ..."

The voice trailed off.

In silence the two living set aside their rifles and planted their flowers in the fresh mound. Then they stood in upright immobility and stared down at the grave as though they could see their comrade looking up at them through the tropical earth. 'Bye, Bob," said one. The other said nothing. They turned and grasped their rifles firmly and moved away in the twilight.

Staff Sergeant Noah W. Skinner of Richmond, Virginia: I am in charge of an anti-tank squad. Before the war I was a Professor of German at the University of Richmond. Don't ask me why I am in the Philippines—I haven't been able to figure it out either. Anyway, I've learned a few things.

I've often wondered why the Japs are such hardy fighters. They are made that way by their training. Brutality was beaten into them. Jap training was the most brutal in any army. Once a prisoner told me that many Japs committed hara-kiri during training just to get out of it. Jap soldiers must stand at attention while they are being slapped and kicked by their superiors. Any Jap who outranks another had the right to administer punishment at any time. After six months in the field the one-star private became a two-star private, and with promotion he earned the right to beat up the one-star privates, which he did with gusto. Mix the results of this with emperor worship and a deep love of home soil—and you have the Jap soldier.

But remove a Jap soldier from the influence of his superiors and you will often find a very scared and confused man who hates the guts of war and who goes out to get himself killed to get it over with. He is so dangerous as an individual fighter because he expects to be killed. On the other hand, his hara-kiri is less a gesture of "fanaticism" than a last protest of a man at the end of his rope. His hobbies are normal: sleeping, getting drunk, and fornication. . . .

Since the Japanese had only few tanks, we of the anti-tank teams had to find new uses for our guns. We used them to fire "canister." A canister is nothing more than a tin can filled with 120 steel balls. The gun blast spreads the steel balls into a scatter-gun pattern against which no Banzai charge can stand up.

My gun's name was Betsy. Once we were on a perimeter near Mintal, west of Davao. Betsy was in position, loaded and waiting, covering the intersection of two roads. The vicinity was covered with demolished buildings, lumber, concrete and twisted sheets of corrugated iron roofing. It was one of those completely black nights. Along about 0130 I heard a faint rattling among the rubbish. My gunner and I threw grenades toward the spot. Two Jap woodpeckers opened up on us. Grenades flew back and forth. We pointed Betsy first at one woodpecker, then at the other, blasting away with canister. Then we swept the road with more canister. When canister sweeps up a road nothing that's unarmored between the road shoulders has a chance to live.

A few minutes later we heard whispers. It was some Jap giving instructions farther up the road. After that there were three Banzai yells from scores of Japanese throats and on they came. My gun vomited steel. The Banzai collapsed. Through the rest of the night we could hear shuffling and scraping sounds of Japs dragging away their wounded. Then came dawn. With three blasts of canister I had killed eleven enemy soldiers and one officer.

Another night I had my foxhole between the trails of the gun. I was suddenly jolted by a Jap voice muttering almost into my ear. There was a glow of lightning, and there, directly over me, was the silhouette of a Jap bayonet. My carbine spoke. The Nip dropped, his steel clattering against the cannon trail.

From now on I kept alert. I soon spotted another Jap who had crawled up under the barrel of my gun with demolition charges. He was peeping around the tire when I shot him. Before he died he muttered the English words, "Crazy man." More Japs were running in front, so I let go with canister. When I checked over the corpses next morning I found one Jap who must have been standing directly in front of the gun muzzle. He looked as if a 12-inch shell had gone through his middle.

Sergeant Fred Livingston of Boyce, Texas, took a last drag from his cigarette before he spoke to his men.

"This is the place," he said. "You can't see the entrance from here, but I know where it is. Don't fire until you see that I'm there."

With that he crawled away and up the brush-covered slope. It was a routine mission: to blow up a Jap cave. The small, camouflaged entrance of the cave opened just below the crest of a ridge facing the Talomo River.

The men crouched, waiting, their fingers resting on the triggers of their rifles. When they saw their sergeant signal from the top they opened fire.

Livingston was on his feet running. Thirty feet from the cave mouth. Then twenty. He hurled the dynamite bomb, swerved sharply and plunged back down the slope.

There was a big explosion. Then, incredible to the dirt-hugging men, another, more violent, and yet another. The hill bubbled. Flames shot from other concealed tunnels. The whole hilltop disintegrated. The men were stunned and deafened by the blasts which continued to come in split-second intervals. The concussions slammed them into the ground, lifted them into the air, slammed them down again. Smoke and dust covered the summit. Rocks, sprays of earth, smashed corpses and fragments of broken trees rained down the hillside.

The cave had not been a simple cave. It had been one exit of a labyrinth of tunnels packed full of ammunition and gasoline.

Sergeant Gerald Bouffard of Watersville, Maine, led his squad in the attack on a pillbox. The Japanese gunners fired with cool insistence. A stalemate threatened.

Bouffard told his men to cover the strongpoints firing ports with bullets. Under cover of this fusillade the sergeant wriggled around and to the rear of the pillbox. He emptied his Garand into a rear opening. His fifth bullet struck a mine inside the pillbox.

The explosion blew the coconut-log-covered emplacement to shreds. It also blew Bouffard ten yards across the hillside and stripped him naked. Otherwise he was unhurt. Against the scorched slope his nudeness made an excellent target. machineguns from two other strongpoints fired at the naked sergeant.

Bouffard, flat on his belly, shouted with rage. He shouted for flamethrowers. He led the charge like an angry Adam storming the serpent's roost. Both pillboxes were reduced and twenty-three Japs lost their lives in the affray. Bouffard summoned his assistant squad leader.

"Here, Jack," he said. "Take over. Im going back to pull the pants off somebody."

Sergeant Guiseppe Giancarli of Trenton, New Jersey, was the leader of a demolition team. Their job, one day near Davao, was to blow up a number of captured pillboxes to deny their use to enemy night infiltration. As he approached one of the abandoned strongholds he detected a muffled sound of digging. Except for two dead Japanese the pillbox was empty—but the sounds of digging continued.

Giancarli put his ear to the ground. He judged correctly that some Japs were tunneling from another pillbox. He called forward a scout with a sub-machinegun and they all watched the earthen walls of the pillbox with silent fascination. Eventually a gap opened in the wall and there appeared two yellow fists wielding a shovel. The shoveler and two companions behind him died under the tommygun's bursts. Then Giancarli blew up the pillbox with TNT. It was a better grave than most Japs got.

Corporal Charles van Wye of Kansas City, Missouri: I sat behind a machinegun on Hill 550 in the night. It was raining cats and dogs. The Nips were sending over shrapnel rockets, mortar shells and grenades, and we knew that a night attack was brewing.

About fifty yards in front I had stretched a trip wire attached to two booby traps. I heard somebody gallivanting in the bushes but I decided to wait until the trap exploded before I'd open up. They were dragging something through the bushes. Something heavy.

"Bam!"

The booby trap went off and I fired and another gun down the line opened fire too. I poured it into them for a while and then I heard them running downhill. I heard much groaning out in front, so I sprayed the bushes again to put them out of their misery.

Fifteen minutes later they came for more. Our guns pumped about 500 rounds into the bushes before the howling and grenade-play stopped. I was hit in the face, but it wasn't bad enough to stop me. There was some lightning in the sky and in the flashes of lightning I could see Japs dragging away their dead. So we killed a few more.

They charged twice again before dawn. There's nothing in the world to compare with a Banzai attack in the dark. They've been doing this every night now for a solid week. In the daytime we attack, in the night the Nips counter-attack. That morning we found a lot of dead men, rifles, sabers, and a big box full of dynamite in front of our foxholes.

Private Billie McNew of Harriman, Tennessee: We were just digging in for the night when a Jap machinegun opened up out of a hole we hadn't noticed. Some guys cried out with pain. Some were killed and there were two who'd been badly wounded. The medic said they should be evacuated right away.

We needed eight men to carry the litters back about a mile to a jeep which could drive them to a hospital. It was a risky thing to do because being out of a hole after dark in Jap territory is plain asking to be killed.

We started out with the wounded and we had a hell of a time getting them over the mucky slopes and through jungle. We had to fight some snipers op the way. Twice we were fired on from our own perimeters. But we made it to a jeep. The men were put on the jeep and we marched a couple miles more to the hospital to clear out the snipers along the road before the jeep could pass in the dark.

Sergeant Fred Dalessio of Philadelphia: We seldom travel alone through Jap country, and whether we do or not we spray every bush whether we see Nips sitting in the bush or not. But that day on Hill 550 my platoon leader couldn't spare another man and he sent me out alone with a message for the company commander.

So, crawling uphill through the brush I hit a little path and then I looked into the eyes of a Jap two feet away. The Jap was in a pillbox commanding the trail and he was sitting behind a machinegun. I took one big jump and got on top of the position. I thought I'd be pretty safe there until I thought out what I could do.

I couldn't lean over and shoot into the opening and I didn't have any grenades. So I hollered to my buddies to throw me a couple of phosphorus grenades. One of 'em crawled up and tossed me the grenades. The Jap in the pillbox was firing like mad, but he couldn't get out of it. I tossed the grenades and fried him to a crisp.

Private Bennie Butler of Richmond, Virginia: A Jap pillbox suddenly fired. Two men in my squad were hit and we all hugged the ground. My squad leader called me to come up with a couple of grenades. He pointed at the pillbox about ten yards away and said, "See it?—Okay, knock it out." I gulped. I took off my pack and put down my rifle and started inching around the flank, a grenade in each hand. When I got about two yards off I tossed them into the pillbox. The explosion shook the ground under me. Then I looked inside and saw two dead Japs. After that we blew up the pillbox with TNT to make sure no other Japs would sneak back into it after dark.

First Lieutenant Robert H. Bourne of Grand Rapids, Michigan: I was directing fire from Cannon Company by telephone.

"Range two thousand, right twenty degrees," was my order.

A chirping voice interrupted me in perfect English.

"What is the exact location of your guns?" it chirped.

"What the hell's it to you?" I snapped back.

Abruptly the line went dead. Some Jap had made a "party line" out of my field communication.

Davao nights! One night the men along a company perimeter heard the noises of a weird saturnalia. Japs were brawling and singing. There was a wholesale destruction of their own supplies. They blew up seventy-five of their own caves. Debris flew over a radius of five hundred yards. Japs were killed staggering toward the perimeter swinging bottles of sake and chanting. One Japanese sang "The Last Roundup" in English. Next morning riflemen found that Japs had killed some of their own. They had raped and killed Filipino women and children in the village of Tugbok. There, and in five other villages all Filipino civilians had been murdered. There was one Jap officer, dead and mutilated, his hands tied with wire behind his back.

Private Thomas Mechling of Cleveland, Ohio: I had just joined the company and it was my first combat mission.

When the fight with the Japs developed, I was out to the flank of the patrol. I dropped down in jungle grass. Bullets were whizzing around me, but I couldn't see the Japs.

About the time the firing stopped, an artillery shell exploded close to me and I was dazed. When I recovered I looked for the patrol, but it was gone. I didn't know how much time had passed.

I remained where I was the rest of the day and that night, thinking that perhaps our troops would appear. They didn't show up by the next afternoon, so I started through the jungle to the west, where I thought the company was located.

In a few minutes I came to a road. The first thing I saw was a Jap soldier. He was working at a bridge a few hundred feet away, with a group of other Japs. I went back into the brush.

I walked until dark and then I stopped in a deserted native hut near a coconut grove. I stayed there a while and started out again. I never felt so alone in my life.

After walking in circles I returned to the hut for the third time. I decided to spend the night there. After that I didn't try to move at night.

I just slept in the jungle or found a deserted native hut.

I lost track of time after that, just kept wandering through the jungle. There were bananas left behind by the Japs when they retreated from bivouac areas. That is all I ate.

Once I met a Jap face to face and shot him. Another time I threw a grenade at one. I had found the grenade about fifteen minutes before that in the fork of a tree. I didn't wait to see what happened.

Four days before I was found I met two Japs who saw me before I saw them. I had been sleeping. One of them took my tommygun and ran off down the road, leaving the other to take care of me.

The Jap pricked me with his bayonet. Then he motioned me forward. As I started to pass him I hit him in the face with both fists and knocked him down. Then I ran. I was unarmed and half scared to death.

At the time I had been carrying my jacket under my arm, because of the heat rash on my body. I lost it in the scuffle with the Jap, and I surely did miss it when the mosquitoes started biting that night.

Two days later I again met a Jap who saw me first. He raised his rifle and I put up my hands. I said, "Me Filipino," pretending that I could not speak English. I don't know whether he understood or not. I do know that I could not understand what he said or the motions he made.

Finally he made a motion with his rifle. I walked close to him, swung my arms down and knocked the rifle to one side. Then I knocked him down. The rifle fell. I picked it up and shot the Jap through the chest. Then I ran for cover.

A little later as I walked on a trail a Jap stepped from the brush and fired at me. I ran into the jungle and ran into another one. He fired at me, but missed. I grabbed my stomach, pretending I was hit, ran a few yards and dropped down.

The Jap started shouting and in a minute he was joined by a companion. They started toward me and I jumped up and ran.

I staggered away from that vicinity and entered a small village which the Japs had evacuated. There were a lot of machine tools and much equipment around. The village was covered with trenches and machinegun nests. In one of the nests I saw dead Japs who had been mashed by our artillery.

I thought sure I would run into American soldiers around there. But I didn't.

Late in the day I climbed a hill and saw the ocean to the south. That night I could hear the Japs firing mortars about 150 yards above me, to the south, and I felt sure that was where I would find our troops. I tried to sleep but mosquitoes and big ants kept me awake.

Next morning I started southward along a road but ran into a number of Japs who were being shuttled away from a bivouac in trucks. I watched the trucks make several trips, then started out through the brush.

I ran into a burned-over area and through beds of glowing embers. I was half-way across when a Jap, sitting along the road, spotted me. He fired as I turned around and ran back. I felt a sting in my chest, but kept on going.

A bullet had hit me in the back and come out through the chest. Things were sort of faraway and peaceful and I thought I was going to die and nobody would ever find me.

Next thing I knew some Filipinos were carrying me on a board.

The brawny Oregonian balanced the Samurai saber on bandaged hands.

"This isn't a pretty souvenir," said Private William W. Mullen, "but it did its work for me."

He had twisted it from the hands of a Japanese officer and killed him with it.

It was in the sun-beaten hills west of Davao. Mullen's squad was on flank patrol for a spearhead of tanks.

The attack moved forward until a tank trap halted the rolling steel. That meant a pause for the infantrymen. They squatted in the jungle grass to rest. Men were close to each other, but in the dense growth they could not see one another.

"I was sitting with my B.A.R. across my knees," said Mullen. "It seemed peaceful in there, but all of a sudden I heard a rustling in the grass. I looked up and there was a Nip aiming a pistol at me.

"I swung the automatic rifle in his direction and the burst smashed his legs at the hips. Like puppets pulled by a string, five more Jap soldiers popped up, rifles popping toward their shoulders.

"I emptied the magazine.

"The Japs fell in huddles. It had happened so fast that my buddies who were watching had not fired a shot.

"In the silence I began to feel nervous. Where I was the grass was scorched. I felt like a man sitting in a show window. So I moved over where it was thicker and started fumbling in my ammunition pouch to get out a fresh clip.

"Before I could reload my weapon two more Nips leaped up.

"One was an officer with this saber. He was a six-foot Japanese. The other was a little guy with a rifle that had a bayonet on it. The big one with the saber jumped me. I dropped my empty B.A.R. and ducked. The next time he swung with both hands. The saber grazed my hand, but it was tougher luck for him. He had put so much into it that he lost his balance.

"I jumped at him then. I grabbed the blade and twisted it from the guy's grip. The officer was thrown to the ground. That's when I cut my hands.

"I got one stab at him before he started to scramble to his feet. Then I jumped on him, feet first, to break his spine. But I slipped and landed spraddled on his back. Before I could finish him off I heard the second Jap charge me.

"The other soldier had probably been afraid to mix in earlier for fear of killing his own officer, but he was making no bones about it now. I looked over my shoulder and froze. I knew my number was up. He had his rifle stuck out in front of him and the bayonet was coming straight for my back.

"I heard a shot and closed my eyes. Something hit me in the back like a sack of beans and rolled off on the ground. It was the second Jap. One of my buddies had come up and shot him.

'The little Jap wasn't dead, but he was wounded. He still had hold of his rifle. I don't know how I did it, but I took the rifle and bayonet from the one lying beside me and threw it out of his reach while I sat on the officer. They were both pretty weak by that time.

"Then I hacked at both of their necks until I was sure that they were dead."

Corporal James W. Thompson of Coleman, Texas, stared hard at the coconut palm.

Then he dropped flat to the ground. His companion, Sergeant Timothy Mahoney of Gardner, Massachusetts, said:

"There's a sniper in that tree."

Slowly, they raised their rifles.

"Don't shoot—I'm Hernandez."

It was more like a weak croak than a mans voice. But it stopped them.

"I'm an American. I'm Hernandez of "Charlie Company," it came again.

"Shall we fire?" whispered Thompson.

"Better hold it," said Mahoney. He called out: "Who's your regimental commander?"

There was a pause.

"I'm from "Charlie Company," said the voice. "Captain Childs is my commander."

The scouts were from "Mike" Company. They didn't know the "C"

Company commander.

"Let's take a chance," said Mahoney. He shouted, "Climb out of that tree."

A dirty, bewhiskered form more fell than climbed from the tree and staggered toward them. They halted him once for a brief examination, then let him fall forward into their arms.

"Thank God," the rescued man sobbed.

He was Private Manuel C. Hernandez of Oxnard, California. He had spent eleven days inside the Japanese defense lines, hungry, thirsty, shocked by American artillery fire and air strikes.

His company had established a road block near Mintal, on the outskirts of Davao. The Japanese had attacked this block with overwhelming force. "Charlie" Company was cut off from its battalion through twenty-six hellish hours.

Another company had finally broken through and they had drawn back together into Mintal where they held.

"I didn't know a relief was fighting through to us," said Hernandez. "I crawled down to a little creek for water. It was kept under fire by the Japs, but I was so thirsty I didn't care.

"I never reached that stream. I must have fainted. I came to with an empty feeling in my stomach. The firing had stopped and I didn't know what to make of it. But it didn't take me long to find out. I raised up a little and there were Japs all around. My company had gone.

"I crawled on to the water and drank from the muddy brook.

I filled my canteen and pulled myself back into the *kunai*. It was quiet for a long time. Dive bombers woke me up next morning. Plane after plane dove into the Nip positions. They dropped Napalm and high explosive bombs all around me. I was covered with dirt and leaves by the explosions, and I guess that helped hide me. The Japs were excited and afraid and they ran all around my position. Maybe they thought I was dead. Maybe they were too busy getting out of there to care. Most of them were killed by the bombs or by the bullets when the planes came back and strafed.

"I was knocked deaf for a while, but I knew I had to change my position. I crawled to a big tree. The Japs didn't scare me any more, but those planes did. I thought the air strike was in advance of an American push, so I went up into the tree so I could see.

"I saw an advance all right, but it wasn't Americans. They were Nips.

"That movement brought our artillery down on the area again. They weren't shooting at a point. They were just shooting over the whole place. It seemed like it lasted for hours. Trees fell all around me and shrapnel whanged into my tree. I hung tight. I was afraid to move.

Down below the Japs fell like flies.

"I had decided to go after water again that night, but it started to rain and I caught enough in my helmet to fill my canteen and myself. I spent that night and the next in the tree. I couldn't see any Japs, but I knew that they were around, and I was so weak I was afraid to climb down. Then I stayed there another day and night and another. Every time I thought of coming down I would see some Japs and would hang on a little longer.

"The fifth day I was so hungry something had to happen. I was seeing things, steaks, and such, and I thought I heard girls laugh at me. I managed to fall out of the tree without hurting myself and found a papaya tree the artillery had knocked down. I had one ripe papaya. I ate half of it and put the rest in my pack. Then I took a nap and got some water. That gave me strength and courage.

"I hunted around in the packs of the dead Japs for food. There wasn't any. But across the little river I saw a shack with smoke coming from the roof. I crawled toward it.

"When I got pretty close a Jap soldier looked out of the window and saw me. Before I could aim my rifle he ran into the jungle. I lay by a tree until evening and watched and he didn't come back, so I went on up. I made two circles around the house before going in. But it was all in vain. The rice he had been cooking was burned black. I went back to my pack and ate the rest of the papaya.

"I heard American rifle fire that night, but I was too weak to go toward it.

"The next morning I climbed my tree again.

"Things got pretty blurred after that. I saw and heard the strangest things but they weren't real. One minute I thought I was at a school dance, and the next I was chased by a crocodile. Days and nights came and went. There were more bombings and shellings and strafing. I strapped myself with my belt so I wouldn't fall out of the tree and I guess I was unconscious most of the time.

"Then I saw that two-man patrol. I just happened to wake up and see it, and I thought that wasn't real either. But when I looked into those muzzles I woke up. I cried, I was so glad. I started calling to them, but I couldn't make them hear me and I was afraid they were not real. Then they saw me and almost shot me. That moment I was more afraid than I ever had been before."

Private First Class Raymond Skrobuton of Chicago, Illinois: Twelve of us—six to a foxhole—were guarding a bridge. Each foxhole had a .30-caliber machinegun. But the rain came down in sheets all night and our guns became useless. We couldn't hear a thing but the drumming of the rain and occasionally one of our booby traps going off.

Around one o'clock when Harry Pope (of Blackfoot, Idaho) and I were looking out toward the stream, three Japs jumped into our foxhole from the rear. I looked around and it seemed all of our men were gone. So I took off into the darkness. About twenty feet away in the stream I lay down in water with my head on a log.

Two Japs came wading up the stream. They stopped and felt my head and then my body. Then they went toward the foxhole, apparently thinking I was dead.

Pretty soon another Jap came along and I held my head under water. But he stood there so long I was forced to come up for air. I jumped up, knocked the rifle out of his hands, and grabbed it to bayonet him with. I lunged, but the Jap grabbed the rifle and pushed it aside. I pulled back sharply, but in the meantime he released the bayonet and charged me with it. I jumped in close and grabbed him. We fought for that bayonet. Finally I took it away from him, but he bit my finger.

I was slashing away at him when I heard a grenade thrown at us from a foxhole. We both fell in the water, but were blown out by the concussion of the grenade. I slashed him a couple more times and he bit my hand again and hung on. I kicked him in the stomach until he let go.

Another grenade went off and we went into the water again. We fought our way out. I felt weak and he was bleeding all over me. He had my shoulders pinned down and he was hitting me. Then I remembered the penknife I had in my pocket. With my free hand I took my knife out of my pocket and opened it with my teeth. I slashed his face. He weakened and I slit at his throat. Then I pushed his head under water with my foot and drowned him.

After that I crawled under a banana tree and lay there. Flashes of lightning showed a Jap lying beside me. I was too weak to move or try to get him. When daylight came I saw that he was dead.*

Sergeant Joseph Helwig of Ashland, Pennsylvania: I went forward with a twenty-five-man patrol to reconnoiter a nest full of Japs. As we reached a cliff-like river bank we were attacked from both flanks and from the rear. The Japanese were yelling and shooting and tossing grenades. We hit the ground in a circle and fought back.

I killed two Japs with my carbine. Sometimes a carbine isn't enough

---

* As told to Walter Simmons, Chicago *Tribune* front line correspondent.

to stop a Jap. There were Japs who kept coming like all wrath even after youve put three or four carbine slugs into them. But those two made gurgling noises and fell. Others jumped over them and came on hooting. They were almost on top of us and our backs were to a precipice of the Talomo River.

Well, we had a machinegun. A machinegun is the most important tool in battle. I grabbed it and fired until the metal burned my hands. Meanwhile my comrades were able to scramble down the cliff.

I was the last man and I didn't want to leave my gun to the Japs. The gun was sizzling hot—as hot as a red-hot stove in February back home. My hands were seared and I could smell it. I wrapped my jacket around the gun and pressed the whole thing against my chest and tumbled down the steep bank and started to cross the river.

I got out to the middle of the river all right, but then came trouble. The current knocked me off balance. I started to drift downstream. I hung on to my gun with one hand and paddled with the other. I paddled like never anybody in all time has paddled before. Frantic, that's the word. One of my buddies on the other bank saw my predicament and he waded out some distance downstream and held out a bamboo pole for me to grasp. All this time the Japs followed us down the river.

I clutched the end of the bamboo pole with one hand and held on. The current swung me in an arc and then into a mud bank.

The fellows in my platoon—those that weren't hit too bad—had climbed up the bank of the river and there they were pinned down by the same hooting bunch of Japs. The Japs were firing across the river. I scrambled up the bank. On the way I lost my machinegun and it fell back down into the river. I dived after it and retrieved it and scrambled up the bank again. There I set up the gun and swung it into action. A guy came running with a box of ammunition. He was feeding the gun. I fired. A third man behind a tree higher up acted as our observer.

I sprayed the area from right to left and then back again from left to right. The gun was smoking and red. The heat burned my eyebrows and melted the front sight and I smelled oil burning inside the mechanism. I fired up four boxes—an even thousand rounds. There was a mess of dead and dying Nips along the river, but there were others still brimming with fight Some of my buddies were stung by Jap slugs and one guy was crying for his mother. The rest had pulled back to better positions.

I told my observer to get the hell out of here while he could. My assistant and I dismounted the gun and started to crawl back too.

Then my buddy got hit in the leg. A bone was snapped and he

couldn't walk. It was getting dark and the rest of the patrol had gone. I heard a radio operator in the bushes trying to get in touch with friendly troops. I had to act fast. I thought I'd rather be cursed and damned then let the Japs get my gun. So I crawled into a thicket and dug a hole with my hands where the earth was soft. I buried the gun and covered it up with leaves and then I went back to get my wounded buddy.

My buddy groaned. He was trying to tell me something. Finally I could hear him. "Japs are coming up the trail," he said.

I saw the Japs and I grabbed my carbine and pumped fifteen shots in their direction. It was too dark to see much, but one of them fell on his face and the rest faded into the bushes.

It wasn't safe to sit up. I told my buddy to grab hold of my leg and hang on. That's what he did. I kept creeping along on my belly with my buddy trailing behind. Pretty soon I was too tired to move. I just felt too tired to pull myself forward another inch. So I stopped. There was a track of blood where I'd dragged my buddy through the undergrowth. Mosquitoes were buzzing around us. My buddy was faint. I leaned over him and cut away his pants to bandage his wound, but his bone was sticking out. I cut a couple of sticks to use as splints and started to work. All of a sudden he sighed and went limp. A burst of machinegun bullets had gone through him.

I almost cracked. Theres just so much a man can stand before he cracks. I'd gone through four campaigns and I've been hit twice in this Jap-war, and I never felt so near cracking as I did that night. Then I noticed that my dead buddy still had his tommygun strapped over his shoulder. I rolled him into the bushes and spoke the beginning of the Lord's Prayer. Then I buried his tommygun and started to look for my patrol.

They must have left me for dead. I crawled around for a while and all I could find were Japs slithering through the bushes. It was very dark by now. Better lie still, I thought. If you move around your buddies will shoot you for sure if the Japs miss you.

I saw the tracers whizzing and here and there one of them plunked into a tree trunk and burned for a second like a blue-and-yellow butterfly. Japs were shouting to each other in the dark. Some grenades exploded somewhere. A storm came up and the rain came down like a solid waterfall. Then mortar shells started dropping. They hit the treetops and burst right there and the fragments whined down into the jungle.

They were our own mortar shells. No duds. Not one. Our mortars were shelling the Japs. But mortar shells don't know the difference between an American and a Jap. I dived between two rocks and gashed my knee. An explosion threw a barrel of mud into my face. I kept creeping and crawling in and out of foxholes that the Japs had dug. Jap holes are deep, much deeper than we dig 'em. Most of them were half full of water but I was soaked through anyway. Finally I got out of range.

I crawled into the bushes and rested. I got rid of everything metal that might clink or reflect the lightning. Lightning was coming down into the woods. The rain and the lightning went on all night. My carbine was full of mud but I washed it in the rain and kept it under my jacket. The Japs were scouting. They passed in groups four to five men strong, as silent as wraiths. I saw my whole past glide by me as I waited. I shook hands with myself and said goodbye to everyone I knew.

The night was as long as hell. Dawn was slow in coming. I shivered with fever. I crawled out on the trail and looked for footprints. The rain had wiped them away. I lurched through the woods until I came to a wire. That was U. S. wire. I followed the wire to an outpost. They gave me coffee and I fainted.

When I woke up I was in an ambulance. There were some soldiers in the ambulance and a corpsman worked over them and the door was open. Out there stood some guys talking. Just then a blond kid came running up from the command post. He had mud on his face and he was very excited.

"The Old Man got it on the radio," he said. "Germany has surrendered."

Everybody stopped talking. Nobody asked a question. Nobody said a word. Nobody smiled. Only one of the wounded fellows tossed around and moaned a little bit. Jap artillery and our artillery were busy over Davao, and the sound of machinegun fire was over the hills like an evil cloud.

Private First Class Abel Souza of Oakland, California: I don't want to tell you about myself. I want to tell you about my buddy, James Diamond, whose home is in Gulfport, Mississippi. He can't talk for himself because he is dead. A sniper killed him by the Talomo River.

James Diamond became my buddy when the Division was rooting Japs from the woods in New Guinea. We fought on Breakneck Ridge together, out there in the rain of Leyte, and after that we killed Japs in Lubang and then we hit Mindanao and hiked a hundred miles over the mountains, and when we came to Davao we were still buddies.

Both of us were fighting in bloody Mintal, in the hemp hell around Libby Drome, and along the Talomo River where the Japs had machineguns and artillery dug in above the steep banks. One day we crossed that river under fire and struggled up the opposite side and suddenly three pillboxes and a lot of snipers gave us hell. Some guys were hit and lay on the ground, screaming, and there were some who were dead, and some who lost their footing in the river and rolled downstream with the current. Everybody lay low. Nobody dared to move except the wounded who had to kill their agony. The snipers and machineguns were playing lead our way and more guys were hit. Then James Diamond got up without a word.

Let me tell you about Jim Diamond. He was a friendly sort of guy. He liked to talk, and he liked girls, and he was doing things all the time. He was a ball player, too. He was tall and blond and husky, and maybe twenty-six years old. He had a good brain, and he figured he'd be going home to Mississippi before the year was over. Well, Jim got up when the sniper nearest to us started tossing grenades. The grenades exploded and we could hear the slivers whizzing past us. Jim went out to get that sniper. The sniper threw another grenade and Jim called to us to keep low. Then he pounced on the sniper and killed him.

By that time some howitzers were sweating across the river and Jim stood up again and directed the fire from their guns and cannon on the pillboxes and the other snipers. He just stood there in the open and pointed his arm at the spots he wanted the armor to hit. This gave us others a chance to put one of our machineguns into action and Jim came back to us and grinned.

But a little later a burst from one of the Jap pillboxes knocked away one of the legs of our machinegun tripod and the gun toppled over and stopped firing. The Nips saw their chance and rushed forward. Jim Diamond was on his feet again faster than I can say it. He sprayed the Japs with his sub-machinegun and forced them down until we were set up again for action. After that he called for the tank destroyers to come forward but they wouldn't come. So Jim went back and climbed on the turret of one and showed them where the Japs were dug in, and pretty soon some more pillboxes were knocked out.

That night we spent on the perimeter, in foxholes, one man watching, the other trying to sleep under his poncho. There was a little bit of trouble when Japs tried to sneak in, but nothing much came of it except that it kept us all awake and we were mad. The mosquitoes were vicious up there and we were bothered by ants and centipedes. Jim let me use the last of his insect repellent to rub on my ears, hands, knees and elbows.

Next morning we ate cold rations and attacked again. A number of guys were wounded and things were so hot that the aid men had trouble coming through. Jap bullets and mortar shells boiled the water of the river and it looked as if nobody could go across. Jim Diamond stood up and jammed his helmet on hard and said he'd carry the wounded guys back across the river. That river ran fast and it was five feet deep. Jap artillery had smashed a bridge our engineers had put up the day before. We all thought that it couldn't be done, that nobody could get across and live. But Jim did it. And seeing him, we pitched in and helped.

In the afternoon Jim was hit by fragments from a bursting Jap shell. He was bleeding and you could see by his face that he was in pain. But he was so intent on helping the other wounded across the river that he would not lay low and have himself fixed up. Nobody would have blamed him if he'd grasped that chance to get himself sent to the rear. Four campaigns, that's a hell of a lot of shooting and hardship most people will never know of. A fellow's luck can't hold out all the time. The longer you're in this the more you have the feeling that soon there's a bullet coming your way. Jim must have had that feeling.

He worked across the river and went to a jeep somebody had left there for dead. He tried the jeep and it ran. He loaded two of the wounded guys in the jeep and drove off through the mortar and artillery barrage the Japs were putting down on the road to cut us off. Jim Diamond got through and came back and loaded two more wounded in his jeep. He made that trip four times and carried out eight hurt soldiers, and that means that he drove eight times through the shell bursts. All four tires of his jeep were mangled by shrapnel before he was finished. I felt so proud of my buddy that I could have wept.

Next day we got orders to fall back and give up the bridge-head across the Talomo River. They needed our battalion for a flank attack, they said. One squad was sent to the river bank to try to repair the shot-out bridge. But fire was so heavy that the squad could not work there. It looked as if we were trapped for good.

Jim Diamond stood up and said that he'd go and repair that bridge so that the battalion could carry out its orders.

"Jim," I said, "Im goin' with you."

Together we ducked to the river bank. There were a lot of broken timbers around and some rope the engineers had left behind, and there was also a roll of telephone wire. Just then the mortar barrage opened up again and we both thought we couldn't make it.

"We'll do it anyway," said Jim.

We repaired that bridge with frayed timbers and rope. It wasn't much of a bridge, but enough for a man in trouble to run over if he's learned how to keep his balance.

The battalion got across all right in small groups, and on the rush. It was pitch dark nighttime. The Japs sensed our retreat and followed it up, thinking they could wipe us out. Fifty-nine Japs were killed in that counter attack. Then Jim worked most of the night bringing the wounded out of the danger line. Everybody in the company kidded him by calling him the "incredible Diamond."

A few days later our battalion was cut off in another sector, and we had no food and water, and we were running low on ammunition. Jim stood up and volunteered to lead a patrol through five hundred yards of thickets full of Japs to bring out our wounded and to bring in water and supplies. After they'd gone about half way, a Jap machinegunner spotted them and raked them with lead. One man in the patrol was wounded. All others hugged the ground and wondered what to do next. There wasn't the tiniest hope to get away unless we could bring strong offensive fire to bear on the Japs.

Suddenly Jim shouted. He had spotted an abandoned machinegun some fifty yards away. An ammunition belt ran through that gun and there was an ammunition box standing next to it Jim dropped his tommygun and made a fast rush toward that machinegun. He would turn that gun on the Japs and force them to duck and that'd make it possible for us to back out of the trap. He almost reached that gun. Somewhere some sniper fired a single shot and Jim pitched to the ground.

He was still alive when we dragged him with us as we fought our way back to our battalion. He tried to be helpful and he was quiet and said nothing. We put him on his way to a hospital. The next we heard was that he'd died before he got there.

He was buried and we wept. We all felt that Jim Diamond should never have died. He'd been due to go home. But our rifles kept roaring, and what they said was—cursed be anybody among us or back home who thinks that Jim Diamond did not sacrifice his life *for him.*

Chapter Twenty-Two

SURRENDER

On the day on which Lieutenant General R. L. Eichelberger, Commanding General of the Eighth Army, officially pronounced the end of organized enemy resistance on Mindanao, we buried Colonel Thomas E. Clifford in the Division cemetery outside of Davao. The dauntless and beloved commander of the "Rock of Chickamauga," indestructible in the ordeal on Kilay Ridge, cockily in the vanguard when we stormed Davao, never second to any man in danger, was blasted to death by a Japanese mortar shell near Tamogan. It happened days after that mountain town had been deemed secured. Die-hard Japanese survivors had fired the shell from an *abaca* hideout. Clifford had fallen wounded in the burst. One of the colonels aides had rushed to the side of his fallen commander. There is a saying among soldiers that two shells never explode on the same spot. But a second Japanese shell plummeted out of the sky and burst on the spot of the first. It killed Clifford and critically wounded his aide.

Ten of us stood at Clifford's grave in silence under the harsh sun. The chaplain's voice was quiet and sad, and flies crawled over the olive drab blanket which was the dead leader's casket. To his right was the grave of a sergeant from Massachusetts, to his left the grave of a private from Utah. In a husky voice, Colonel William Verbeck commanded, "Attention!" We stood like ramrods and saluted. A few days later the people of Davao celebrated the end of the war by naming their rubble-framed town plaza Clifford Square.

On that day, a soldier who was the father of five children, with enough "points" to his credit to sail for home on the next ship, was blown to pieces by a Japanese mine. And three hours before the "Cease Firing" order was beamed to all the corners of the Far East, seven American infantrymen were killed north of Davao by bursts of machinegun fire from ambush.

Under the palms of Talomo Beach we sat huddled under ponchos, watching a motion picture in a drizzling rain, when the performance suddenly was interrupted. An officer holding a flashlight climbed on a platform and said curtly, "We just received a radio message that the Japanese are surrendering."

A tremendous cheer went up in the darkness of jungle and plantation. The thing that in the feeling of most of us had become malevolent eternity had abruptly come to an end. Carbines and Garands crackled in great clouds of sound. Along the outer perimeters machineguns chattered toward the sky. Men howled like dogs and crowed like cocks. Parachute flares floated beneath the clouds, whistles shrilled in the swamps, and from the *abaca* expanses showers of tracer bullets swished through the rain. The Japs of Mindanao, oblivious of their empire's downfall, thought a night attack was under way and sent squalls of lead into the dripping darkness. In a palm grove south of Talomo, other Japanese soldiers clandestinely watching a Twenty-First Regiment motion picture show, suddenly decided to heave grenades into the crowd. Two Americans were killed and several wounded.

Obedience to the order to cease firing was as difficult as the reversal of an old habit. Killing Japanese on sight had become a matter of reflex and instinct. The unexpected brake applied upon the urge to kill caused slight confusion. One American soldier was murdered in a brawl with his fellows. Another was found knifed to death, apparently by a Filipino, in a fray involving a native girl. But on the morning of August 15 the situation reverted to "normal." A company of infantry encamped near the *barrio* of Bunawan radioed that it was being machinegunned by a force of Japanese. A battery of field artillery went into action to disperse the attackers. Brigadier General Kenneth Cramer watched the shells whine over the *abaca* at two-second intervals. And before the rumble of the forty-eighth shell explosion had died away, a radio operator jumped into the air and called out: "Message! Message! End of mission. End of war."

Cramer turned to his men and smiled. The chunky soldier-senator from Connecticut who for years had shared his riflemen's hardships in the agonized advances and the killing, shoved his helmet back from his leathery forehead and laughed happily. "Make a note of this," he said. "We may have heard the last shell that was fired in this war." Thoughtfully he added: "The question is—will the Japs believe us?"

The "cease fire" order was official. Patrols were cancelled near Biao, Baguio and Tamogan. The Division's advances among the wild foothills of Mount Apo and Mount Monoy were halted. Riflemen were ordered to capture stragglers on the dim Kibawe Trail instead of slaying them.

At the road junctions detachments of military police were alerted to guide captives to the rear. But the next morning found the combat patrols again in full swing.

A "Fox" Company, Nineteenth Regiment, truck convoy was ambushed out of *abaca* thickets and twelve Americans were hit. "Able" Company riflemen surprised and killed twenty Japanese on the precipices of the Tamogan River. Anti-Tank Company patrols killed five. "George" Company lost nine men in a skirmish and killed eighteen Japs. Near Baguio a combat patrol surprised thirty-seven Japanese naval troops cultivating camotes and rice in a jungle clearing. There was no chance to explain that hostilities were over. All the Japs were killed. On the upper reaches of the Libuganon River a force of Japanese traveling downstream on palm-log rafts attempted to break an American river block; machineguns raked the rafts, which drifted on toward Davao Gulf, unmanned, and fifty-five dead were counted along the muddy banks. There were patrol clashes near Licanan Airdrome and along the shores of Sarangani Bay. Near Budbud and Dalliao small enemy detachments launched suicide charges in the night. There were thousands of armed Japanese roaming the mountains of Davao Province in scattered bands; they were without contact with one another, without radios, without a uniform command. There were also thousands of armed Moros and Filipino irregulars roaming the forests who blithely disregarded any order to cease firing; they went on killing any Jap for his rifle, wrist watch or boots, or if the Jap owned none of those— they killed him for revenge.

A Filipino woman, the wife of a captured Japanese officer, reported that the Japanese commander, General Harada, lay ill with malaria in an almost inaccessible canyon, tended by half-breed comfort girls and kept alive on a daily food allotment of one half handful of rice. His chief of staff, the lady reported, subsisted on boiled jungle vegetation. Meanwhile, a Davao shoemaker, Alfonso Daiparine, hung out a sign which read: "Hail to America—Hell to Japan. May the Japanese tribes decrease." The Japanese colonists would never return to Davao; their goods and plantations would be sold to the highest bidder. In the overcrowded and bomb-battered St. Peters Church of Davao, Father Clovis Thibault who had just returned from years of hiding in caves read a thanksgiving mass and four thousand brown people bowed their heads and wept.

The Division's command worked hard to convince the Japanese that the war was over. Thousands of "surrender leaflets" were dropped over the jungles by planes. Sound trucks toured the front, blaring surrender messages in Japanese. Japanese prisoners of war were released to urge their compatriots to cease resistance and emerge. The regiments established prisoner reception points at all road and trail junctions. Red arrows pointed the way. Signs in Japanese were posted along the fringes of unexplored wilderness. "Welcome Japs," they read. "Kill and Be Killed No More." . . . "Surrender Here—Fine Food, Free Transportation, No Walking." . . . "Surrender Now, Safety Guaranteed." . . . "Register Here for Free Trip to Nippon." But for days no Japs surrendered. The sound trucks met sniper fire. Released prisoners of war were killed by their uncaptured fellows. Over the Division's Special Services radio came news of an unbridled "Victory" celebration on New York's '"Hines Square. Infantrymen grumbled their contempt for the distant revelers as the feeling grew along the perimeters that the Japanese would not come in. It's over. It's great. But rifles were still oiled and loaded on Mindanao. New graves were dug for Americans to be buried with combat boots protruding from under olive drab blankets. The killing continued sporadically for weeks after the official surrender.

Sixteen days after the capitulation of Japan, the Division commander succeeded in establishing contact with General Harada. An infantry patrol had captured a Japanese major, the former chief of the *Kempai* (Military Police) of Davao, who knew where the Japanese commander was hiding. Guerillas clamored for the major's life. But General Woodruff equipped the Jap with American rations and an American radio and told him to go out and inform General Harada of the termination of hostilities. A jeep carried the messenger to the end of all roads along the upper Talomo River, but the emissary refused to plunge into the jungle alone. The major, who in his time had ordered the execution of hundreds of Filipino patriots, was afraid of crossing forests teeming with armed natives. A patrol then escorted the Jap through the guerilla zone, and after a three day trek he radioed that he had found General Harada.

Harada declared himself willing to surrender. But he asked American cooperation in informing the hundreds of lost detachments of his dispersed command. He also asked General Woodruff to build a bridge across a difficult stream west of Tamogan, for most of his men were too ill from malaria, hunger and untended wounds to ford the river. Division engineers built the bridge. Surrender orders over the Jap general's signature were distributed by Americans. Japanese began to trickle into captivity.

It was a grim and wretched procession. Many of the enemy warriors who had fought so long and so well resembled meandering skeletons in rags. Only few had shoes. Many came in crawling on hands and knees, near death but grinning with politeness. Almost all were famished, malarious, and suffering from scrub typhus, dysentery and jungle rot. Japanese mothers surrendered, carrying dying infants. Of Davao's estimated 19,000 Japanese civilians less than 5,000 remained alive. The jungles north of Mandog, Tamogan, and around the volcanic fastness of Mount Apo were strewn with the corpses of men, women and children who had died of hunger, disease, or under the bayonets of their own military. In a secret jungle town not far from the village of Sirib which the Japs had built with the stolen houses of Davao, one of the Divisions combat reporters found a mass of Japanese women and children whose throats had been cut from ear to ear. Natives reported that this mass murder—one of many—was performed by Japanese soldiers upon their own kin when food gave out and retreat became an agony without hope.

General Harada surrendered, together with the surviving members of his staff, including an admiral. All of them were more dead than alive, but strangely unbroken in their soldierly dignity. Yet, many of their soldiers refused to give up. Gathered in desperate little bands they marched deeper into the mountains, looting *barrio*s on their way, killing native civilians and carrying off young women.

Toward the end of September, 1945, the Division was ordered to move into Japan. The sky over Davao Gulf was a virgin blue and the peak of Mount Apo towered purple against the azure. A hard sun flamed on the cobalt sea. The black sands of Talomo Beach teemed with bathing men. A convoy of gray transports stood in from the Pacific. Soldiers crowded the decks of the ships—young, crisp, clean soldiers, battle virgins fresh from the training camps.

The gaunt and yellowed bathers on Talomo Beach watched the newcomers land.

Someone chanted with sardonic glee: "You will be sorreee . . . and we are going home."

The newcomers grinned bravely, devouring sunlight on their unrusted helmets. A veteran sergeant paddled among the anchored transports in a canoe fashioned from an airplane gasoline tank shouting, "Welcome, welcome."

Men of the Twenty-Fourth were glad. "Christ," was the feeling of every one of us, "I never thought I'd leave these goddamned islands alive and so soon. Im glad; hell, Im so glad. Back home the homes will be more drab than we pictured them in our dreams, and the women won't be as glamorous maybe as our pinups made us like to believe, but they'll be wonderful and sweet all the same, and an honest to goodness elm or oak is worth more in our hearts than a hundred million coconut palms, and people will wear shoes and have soap to make them smell clean and everything will be whole instead of wrecked and ruined as we had to wreck and ruin these islands against our own will. Look at Mount Apo: the ugliest mountain in the world. Hell, they'll be killing Jap stragglers in these islands ten years from now. Only hope that none of the Moros will dig up our buried buddies to steal their blankets and boots."

On the beach road, convoys of bullet-scarred trucks loaded replacements and then rumbled away toward the regimental bivouacs in the ocean of *abaca*. The newcomers who crowded the trucks wiped sweat out of their eyes and peered curiously at the hot, savage countryside. They stared at the burned houses, the graves, the decapitated palms, the wrecks of trucks and airplanes littering the roadsides, the listless and emaciated natives, and they leaned forward to decipher signs at junctions along their dusty course. "There's Malaria in the Area," said one sign. 'Take Atabrine or IT Will GET YOU." Another read: "Polluted Water, Don't Drink from This Stream." And another: "Keep Weapons Ready. Beware of Snipers and Explosives." And there was a gay, freshly painted poster, red on white:

TO WHOM IT MAY CONCERN
GO SLOW
CAUTION
PLEASE DONT KILL OUR REPLACEMENTS

THE END

www.ingramcontent.com/pod-product-compliance
Lightning Source LLC
Chambersburg PA
CBHW071954110526
44592CB00012B/1083